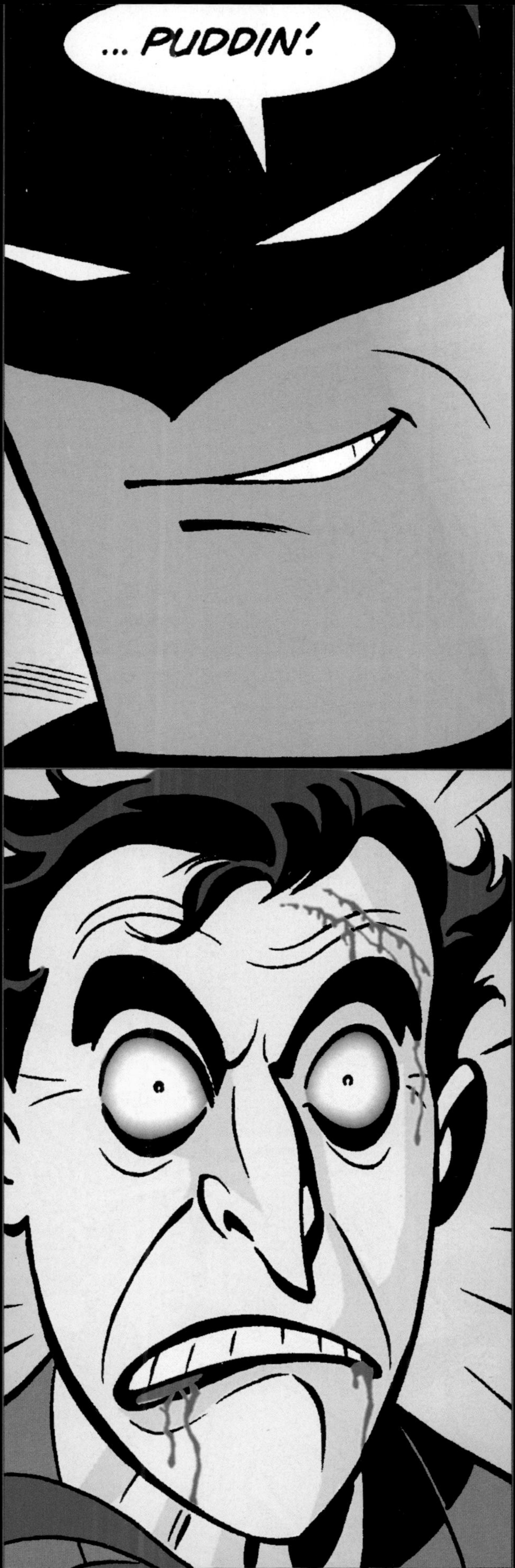
...PUDDIN!

BATMAN MAD LOVE AND OTHER STORIES

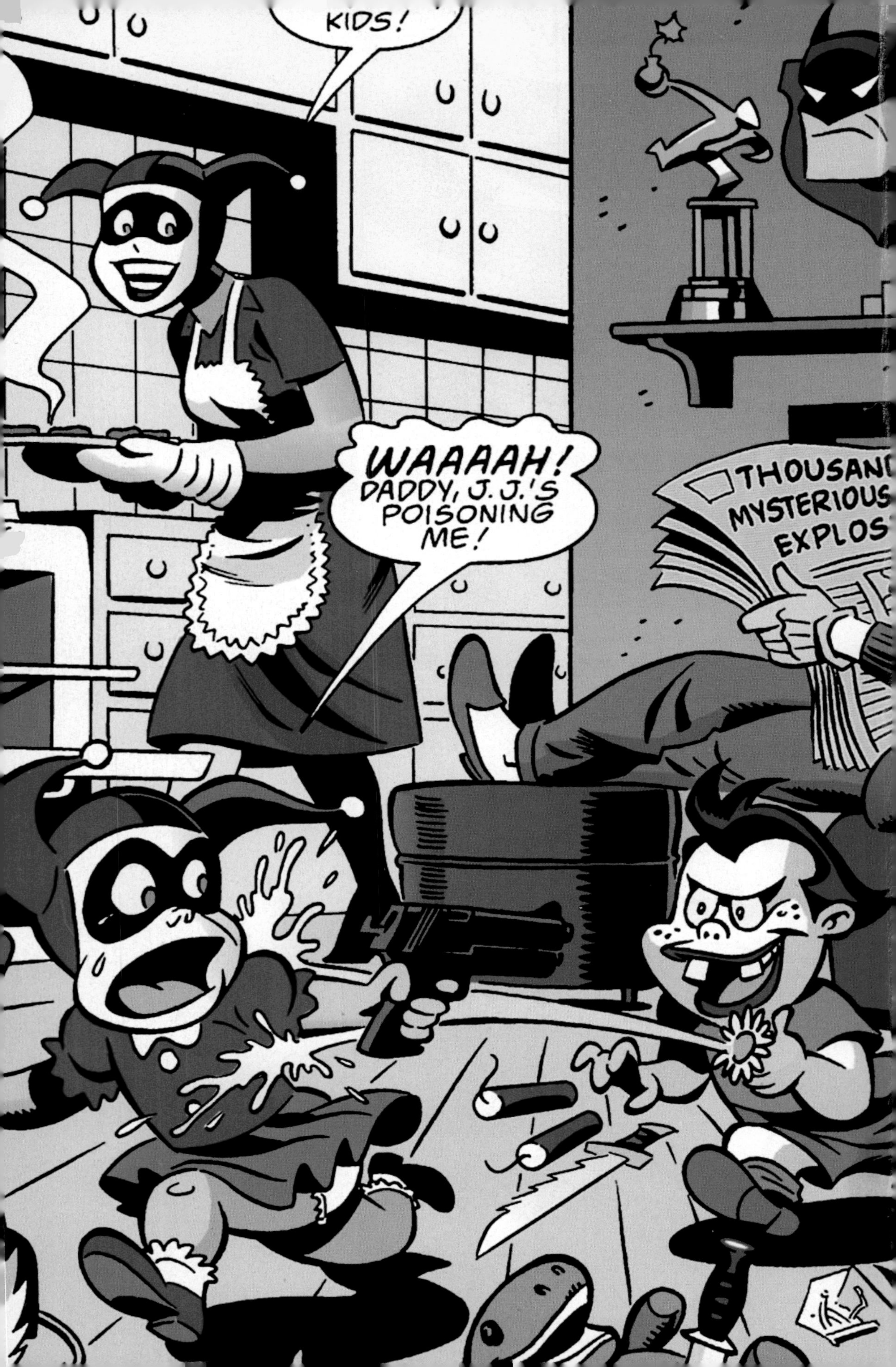
KIDS!
WAAAAH! DADDY, J.J.'S POISONING ME!
THOUSAN
MYSTERIOUS
EXPLOS

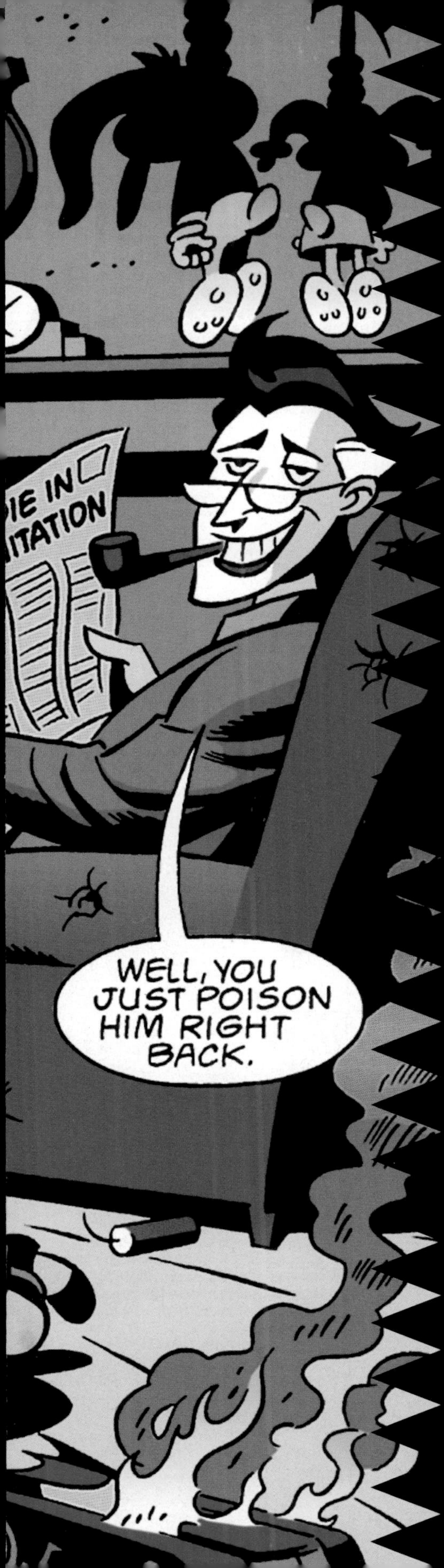
WELL, YOU JUST POISON HIM RIGHT BACK.

BATMAN MAD LOVE AND OTHER STORIES

Paul Dini
Bruce Timm
Writers

Bruce Timm
Rich Burchett
John Byrne
Dan DeCarlo
Klaus Janson
Glenn Murakami
Mike Parobeck
Matt Wagner
Artists

Mark Chiarello
Glen Murakami
Rick Taylor
Bruce Timm
Colorists

Comicraft
Tim Harkins
Todd Klein
Letterers

BATMAN created by Bob Kane

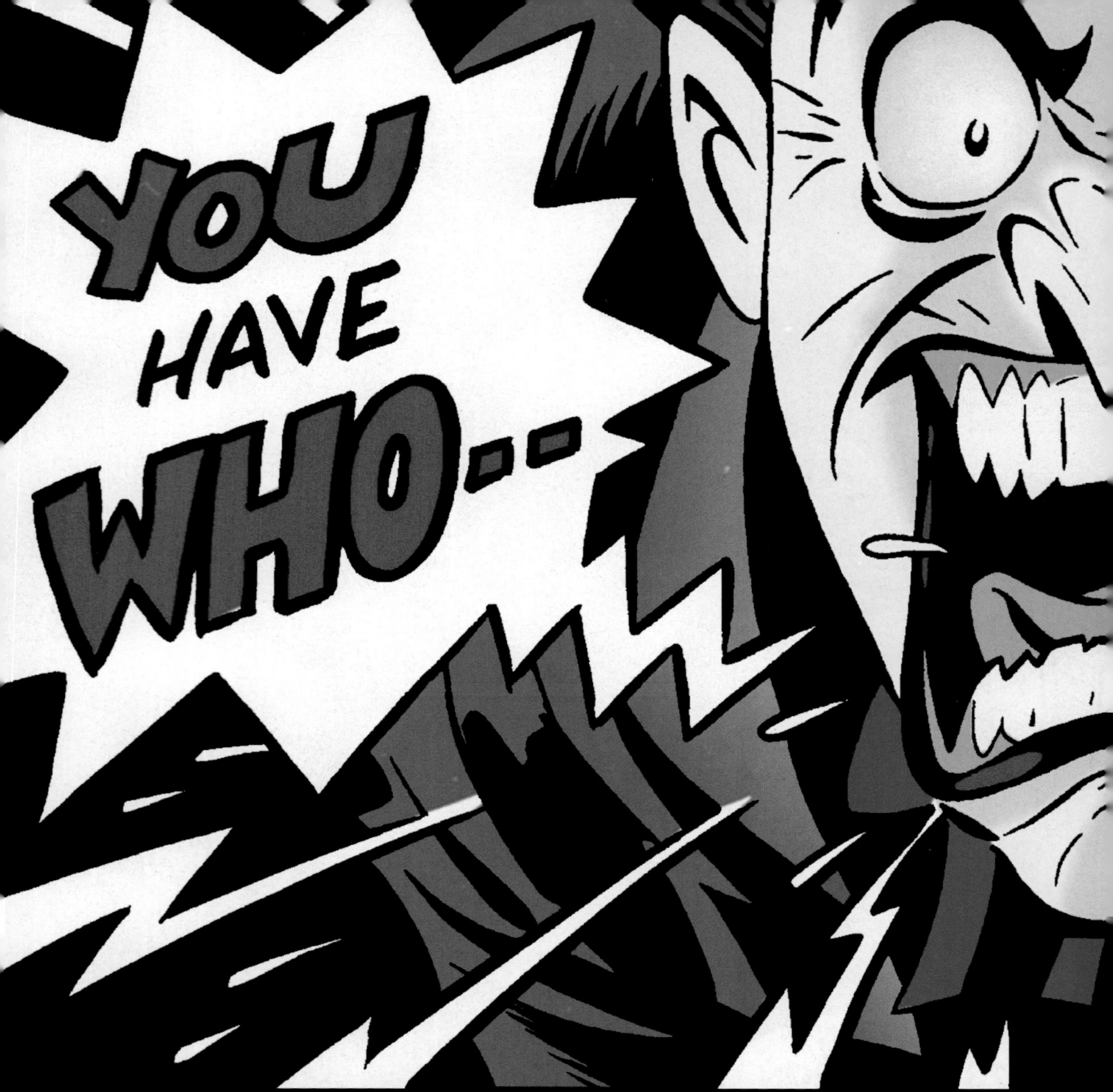
YOU HAVE WHO--

Scott Peterson
Charles Kochman Editors – Original Series
Darren Vincenzo Associate Editor – Original Series
Sean Mackiewicz Editor
Robbin Brosterman Design Director – Books
Louis Prandi Publication Design

Bob Harras Senior VP – Editor-in-Chief, DC Comics

Diane Nelson President
Dan DiDio and Jim Lee Co-Publishers
Geoff Johns Chief Creative Officer
John Rood Executive VP – Sales, Marketing & Business Development
Amy Genkins Senior VP – Business &Legal Affairs
Nairi Gardiner Senior VP – Finance
Jeff Boison VP – Publishing Planning
Mark Chiarello VP – Art Direction & Design
John Cunningham VP – Marketing
Terri Cunningham VP – Editorial Administration
Alison Gill Senior VP – Manufacturing & Operations
Hank Kanalz Senior VP – Vertigo & Integrated Publishing
Jay Kogan VP – Business & Legal Affairs, Publishing
Jack Mahan VP – Business Affairs, Talent
Nick Napolitano VP – Manufacturing Administration
Sue Pohja VP – Book Sales
Courtney Simmons Senior VP – Publicity
Bob Wayne Senior VP – Sales

SUSTAINABLE FORESTRY INITIATIVE
Certified Chain of Custody
At Least 20% Certified Forest Content
www.sfiprogram.org
SFI-01042
APPLIES TO TEXT STOCK ONLY

Cover by Bruce Timm
BATMAN: MAD LOVE AND OTHER STORIES
Published by DC Comics.
Originally published in single magazine form in THE BATMAN ADVENTURES: MAD LOVE, THE BATMAN ADVENTURES ANNUAL 1-2, THE BATMAN ADVENTURES: HOLIDAY SPECIAL 1, ADVENTURES IN THE DC UNIVERSE 3, BATMAN BLACK AND WHITE 1, THE BATMAN ADVENTURES: DANGEROUS DAMES & DEMONS, BATGIRL ADVENTURES 1, BATMAN GOTHAM ADVENTURES 10, BATMAN ADVENTURES 3.

DC Comics, 1700 Broadway, New York, NY 10019
A Warner Bros. Entertainment Company
Printed by RR Donnelley, Salem, VA, USA. 5/10/13.
Third Printing.
ISBN: 978-1-4012-3115-6

Library of Congress Cataloging-in-Publication Data

Dini, Paul.
Batman : mad love and other stories / Paul Dini, Bruce Timm.
p. cm.
"Originally published in single magazine form in The Batman Adventures: Mad Love, The Batman Adventures Annual 1-2, The Batman Adventures: Holiday Special 1, Adventures in the DC Universe 3, Batman Black and White 1, The Batman Adventures: Dangerous Dames & Demons, The Batman Chronicles Gallery 1, Batgirl Adventures 1, Batman Gotham Adventures 10."
ISBN 978-1-4012-3115-6
1. Graphic novels. I. Timm, Bruce. II. Title. III. Title: Mad love and other stories.
PN6728.B36D564 2012
741.5'973–dc23

2012032623

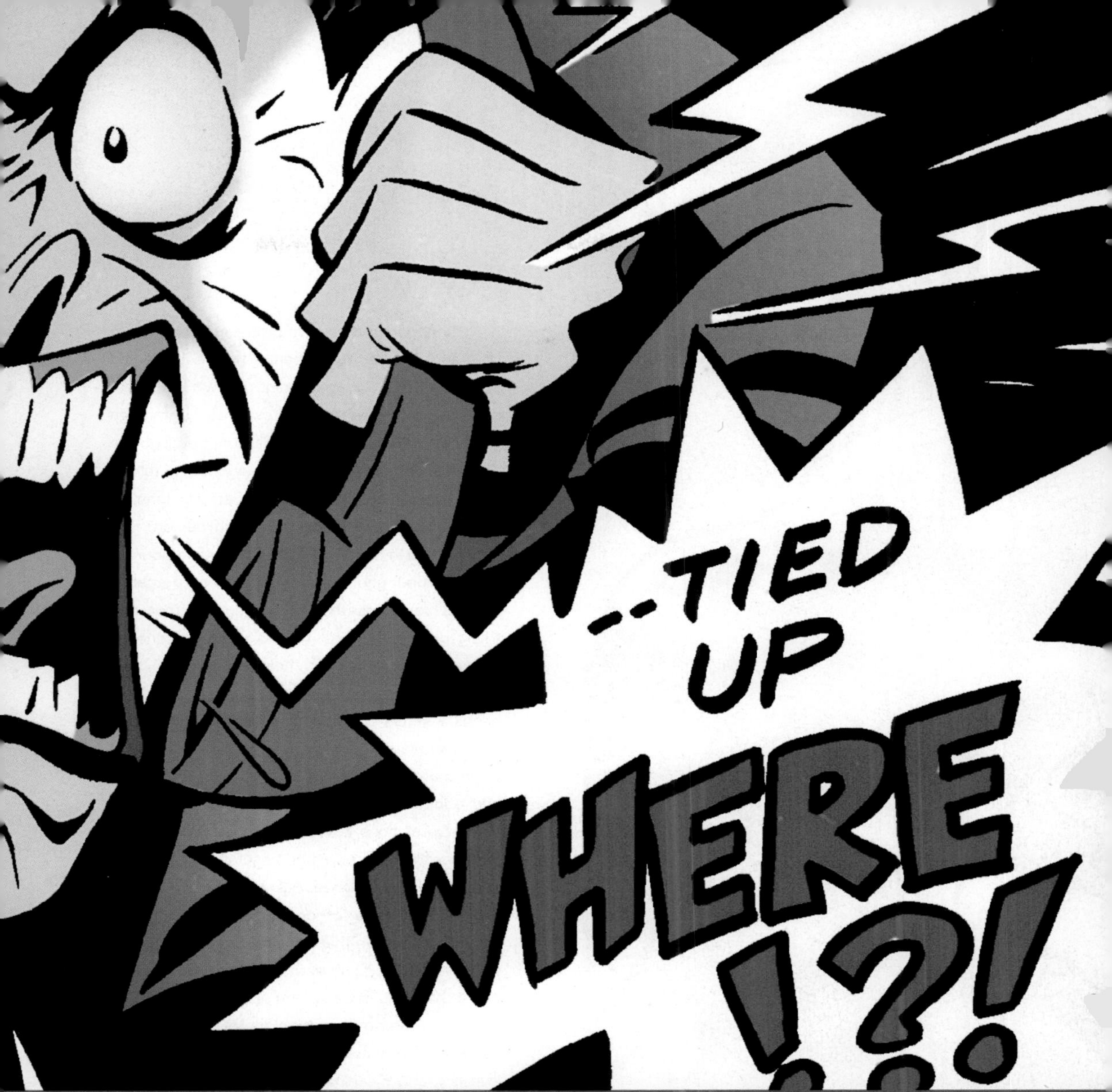

--TIED UP
WHERE !?!

FOREWORD
By Paul Dini

It's happened to me, it's probably happened to you, and if it hasn't happened yet, rest assured someday it will. At some point you will meet that one special person who will put their fist through your heart. Forgive the gory allusion, but if you've ever been in mad love, you know what I'm talking about. Mad love is when you fall so passionately for a person (particularly the *wrong* person) that nothing else in the world matters. You find yourself thinking about your heartthrob constantly, creating fantasy scenarios that bring you together and trying your damnedest to make those scenarios happen in real life. You believe that you have finally found that one magical being who suddenly brings a sense of meaning to your existence and you will pursue them with all the fervor of Wile E. Coyote after a Roadrunner dinner — with, I might add, about as much success.

We've all done it. We've all selected the wrong partners, all gotten hurt, and hopefully all moved on wiser for the experience. But there are those who, even in the face of constant disappointment, continue to believe that the intensity of their desire will be rewarded by an eventual jackpot of affection. And if that's the slot machine you're playing, friend, you'd better leave the casino 'cause that one don't pay out. Advice to someone in the throes of mad love is pretty meaningless, because any capacity they once had for rational thought has long since split for Aruba. Despite the setbacks and heartaches, the pursuer tunes out their inner voice of sanity and is more than willing to swallow the tears, paint on a smile, and once again resume the chase.

Welcome to the world of Harley Quinn. Or the version of Harley I was writing in 1993. I originally created Harley as a sideline character in the *Batman: The Animated Series* episode "Joker's Favor." Later I saw in her the chance to tell a story about her past that would lift her up from being just another goon in a funny suit. The fact that Harley felt affection for the Joker was bizarre; adding the idea that she had once been his therapist made it tragic. *Batman* producer/director/pal Bruce Timm and I had been invited to do a special issue of DC's BATMAN ADVENTURES, and we had been toying with a Harley origin story.

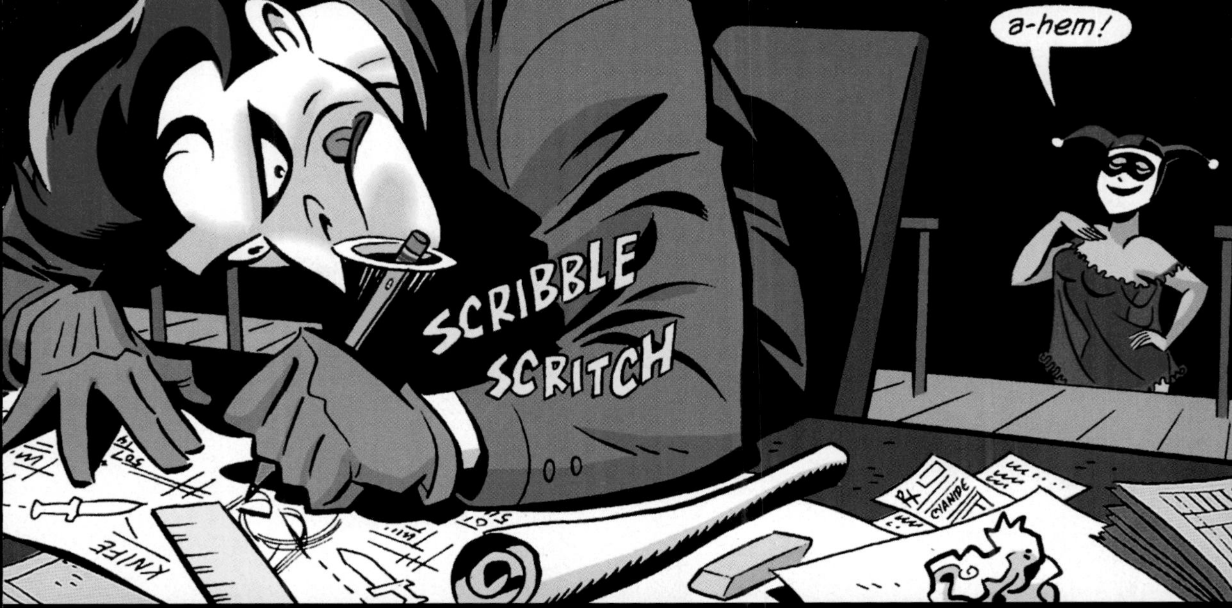
a-hem!
SCRIBBLE
SCRITCH
KNIFE
CYANIDE

When I told Bruce of this weird twist I wanted to bring to Harley's history, he enthusiastically went for it. Like two kids working out a jigsaw puzzle, we fit the rest of the story — now appropriately titled MAD LOVE — into place over bad hamburgers at a crummy tropical restaurant.

Two years before, Bruce and I (among many others) started production on *Batman: The Animated Series* with a feeling of elation, high expectations, and the nagging fear that we would probably fall on our butts. And now that he and I were taking the plunge into comics, we found ourselves feeling the same way again. Though we knew failure might be in the offing, we soon began having too much fun with the story to care. We'd be constantly running into each other's office — Bruce to show me cool page layouts and sexy Harley poses, me to deliver rewritten script pages that Bruce had already cut for length. Mind you, I'm not complaining. As a director and gifted storyboard artist, Bruce knew where to focus on the story for maximum impact and move it with a cinematic drive. Seeing him work that way was a learning experience for me, and it definitely helped my later comics writing (to say nothing of showing me how to keep the page count down on my animation scripts, a rule I still manage to blow fairly often — sorry, Bruce). One more thing about Bruce Timm: he draws great animals. He claims he doesn't, but I think he gave the Joker's hyenas a lot of appeal while still keeping them menacing. Besides, look at that big seaweed serpent in the Poison Ivy story. That's practically an animal and it rules.

After MAD LOVE, Bruce and I worked together on many other comic stories, all of which are contained here. Some, like the Batgirl and Ivy stories, were fun romps. Others, like the Demon tale, were epics. Bruce's afterword to this volume goes into the creation of those stories with more detail and accuracy than I can muster here, so I'll leave that to him. I'll just say they were all a blast to work on, and I welcomed every opportunity to work with Bruce whenever our insane schedules would allow it, and still do.

It's been a while since we created these stories, but I always look back on them with a lot of pride and affection. I don't think of MAD LOVE as a victim's tale, but a cautionary one about what happens when someone loves recklessly, obsessively, and for too long. Through Harley's tragicomic experiences, we catch a glimpse of ourselves in a funhouse mirror, distorted and all too willing to play the fool for someone we'd be much better off without. But through that awareness can come change, and that's a good thing indeed.

And even Harley has changed a little in the interim. No longer content to follow after the Joker, she's off on new adventures, both on screen and in the comics. Sometimes she's paired up with her gal pal Poison Ivy, sometimes she's out causing mischief on her own. In a way that's gratifying, as no one should stay pining for someone (particularly *that* someone) too long. And even when she slips and links up with her old beau again, Harley's his equal partner in crime, and not the eager-to-please hench-wench of old.

That's not a reformation by a long shot, but it's a tentatively hopeful step in a debatably right direction. And if there's hope for Harley Quinn, then there's hope for the mad lovers in us all.

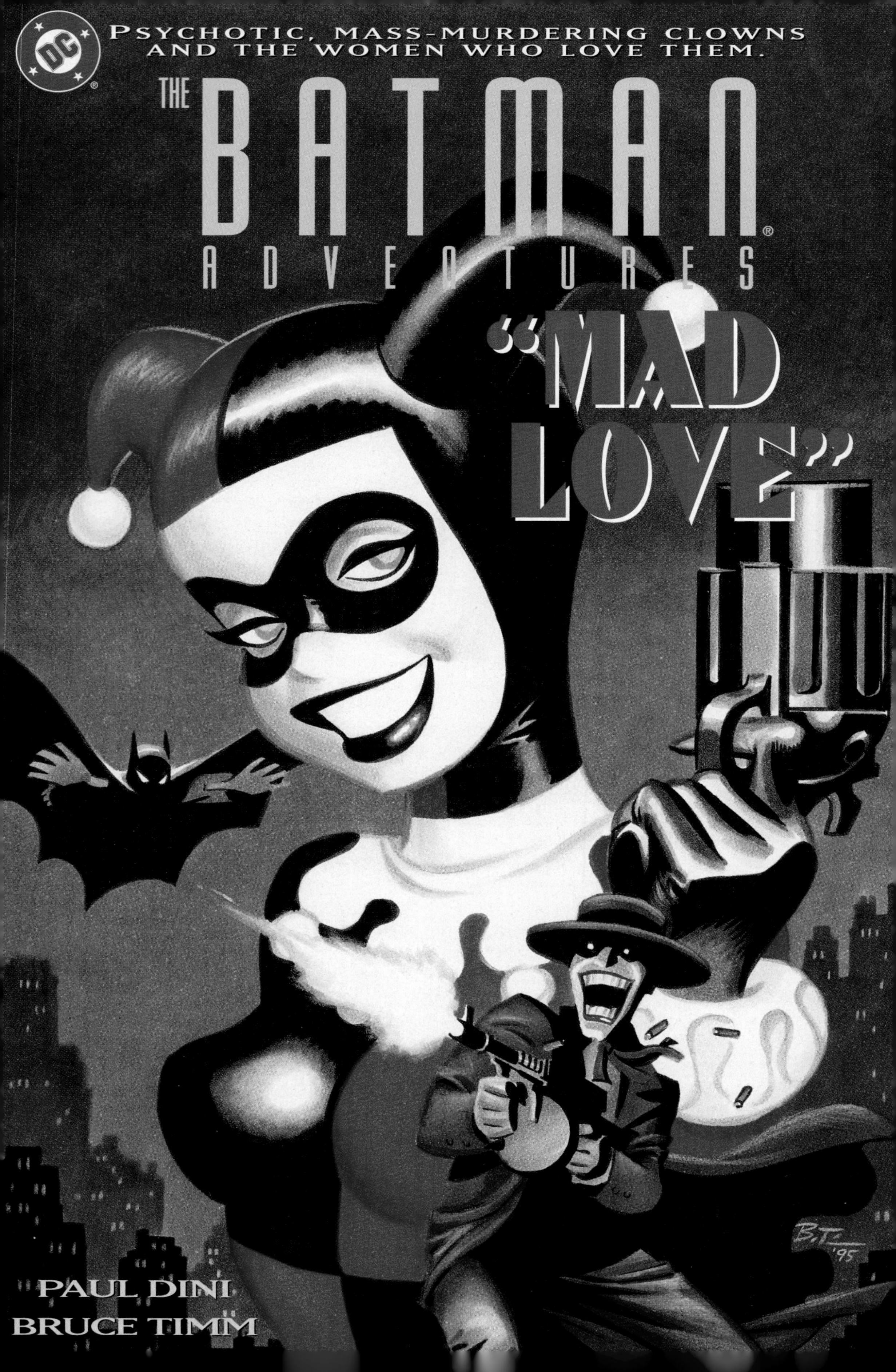
PSYCHOTIC, MASS-MURDERING CLOWNS
AND THE WOMEN WHO LOVE THEM.
THE BATMAN ADVENTURES
"MAD LOVE"
B.T. '95
PAUL DINI
BRUCE TIMM

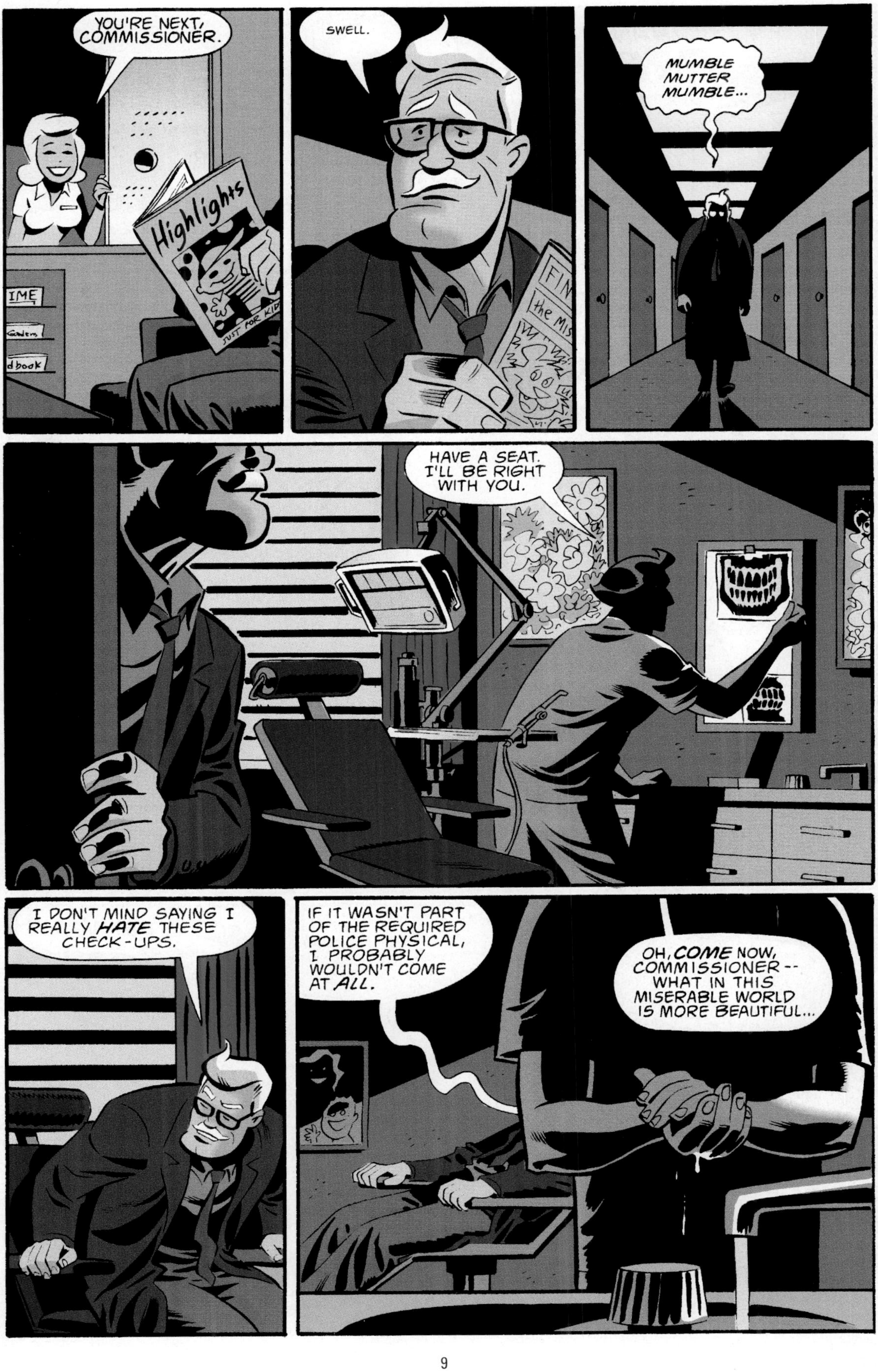
YOU'RE NEXT, COMMISSIONER.
Highlights
JUST FOR KIDS
SWELL.
MUMBLE MUTTER MUMBLE...
HAVE A SEAT. I'LL BE RIGHT WITH YOU.
I DON'T MIND SAYING I REALLY HATE THESE CHECK-UPS.
IF IT WASN'T PART OF THE REQUIRED POLICE PHYSICAL, I PROBABLY WOULDN'T COME AT ALL.
OH, COME NOW, COMMISSIONER -- WHAT IN THIS MISERABLE WORLD IS MORE BEAUTIFUL...

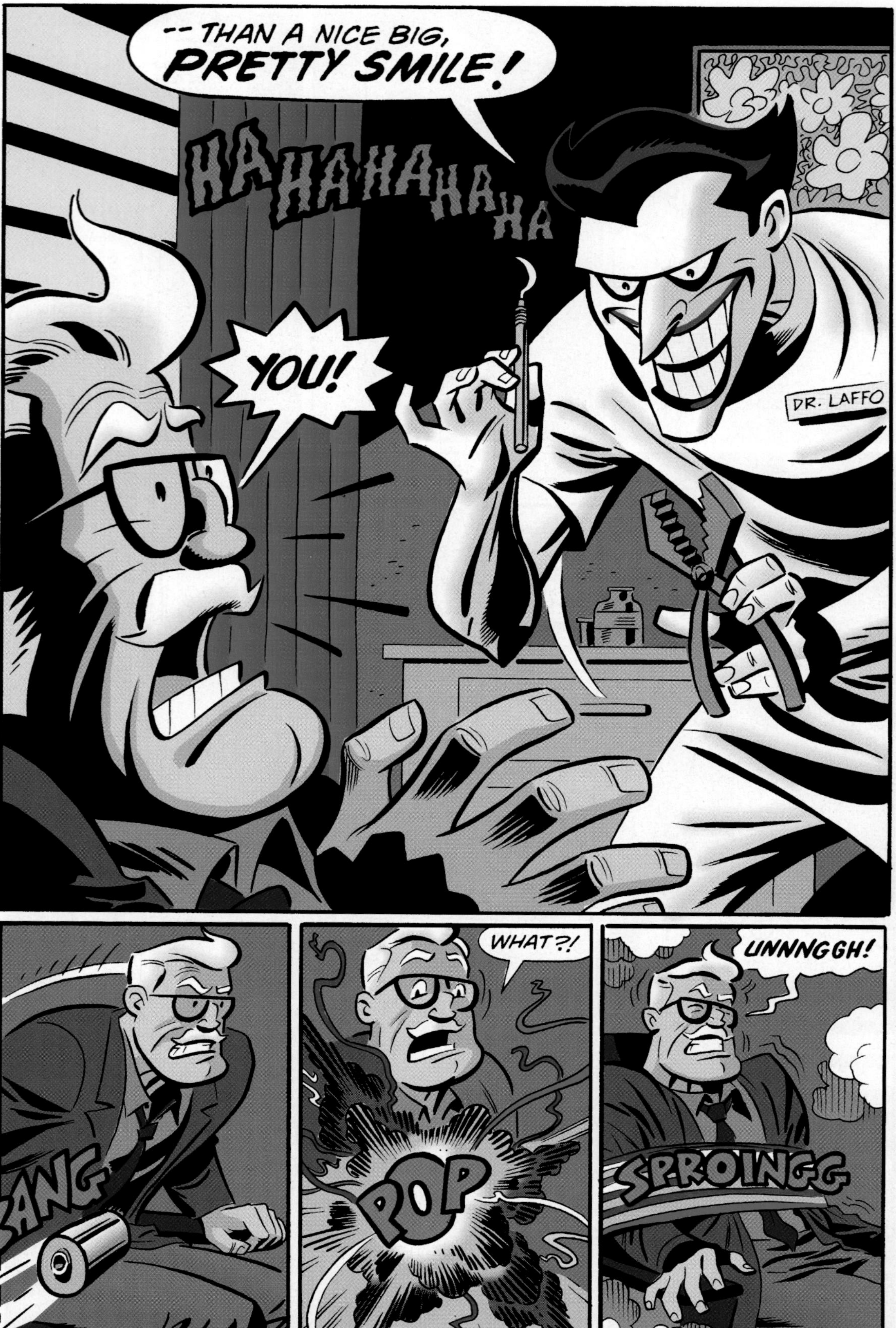
-- THAN A NICE BIG, PRETTY SMILE!
HAHAHAHAHAHA
YOU!
DR. LAFFO
BANG
WHAT?!
POP
UNNNGGH!
SPROINGG

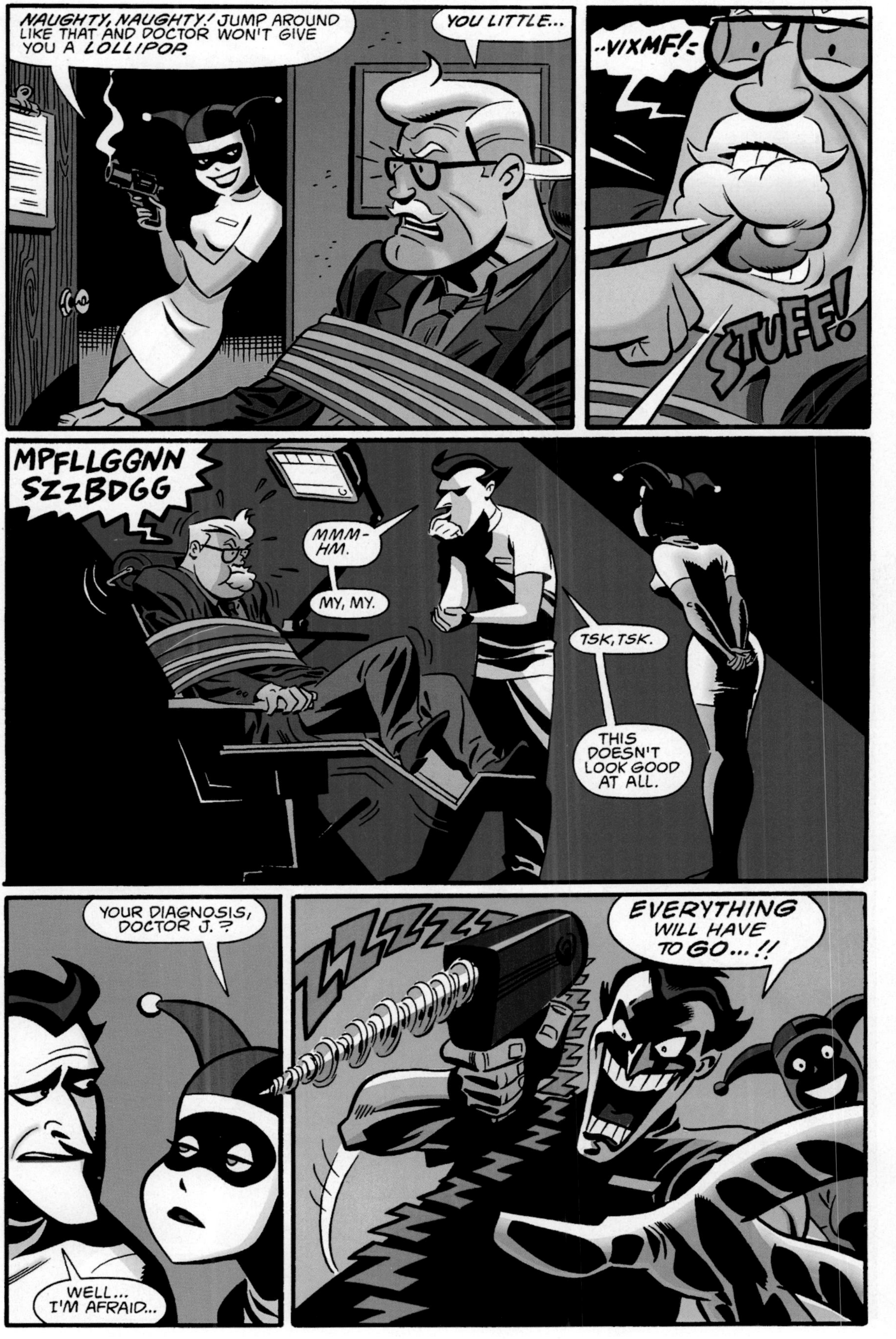
NAUGHTY, NAUGHTY! JUMP AROUND LIKE THAT AND DOCTOR WON'T GIVE YOU A LOLLIPOP.
YOU LITTLE...
..VIXMF!:-
STUFF!
MPFLLGGNN SZzBDGG
MMM-HM.
MY, MY.
TSK, TSK.
THIS DOESN'T LOOK GOOD AT ALL.
YOUR DIAGNOSIS, DOCTOR J.?
WELL... I'M AFRAID...
EVERYTHING WILL HAVE TO GO...!!

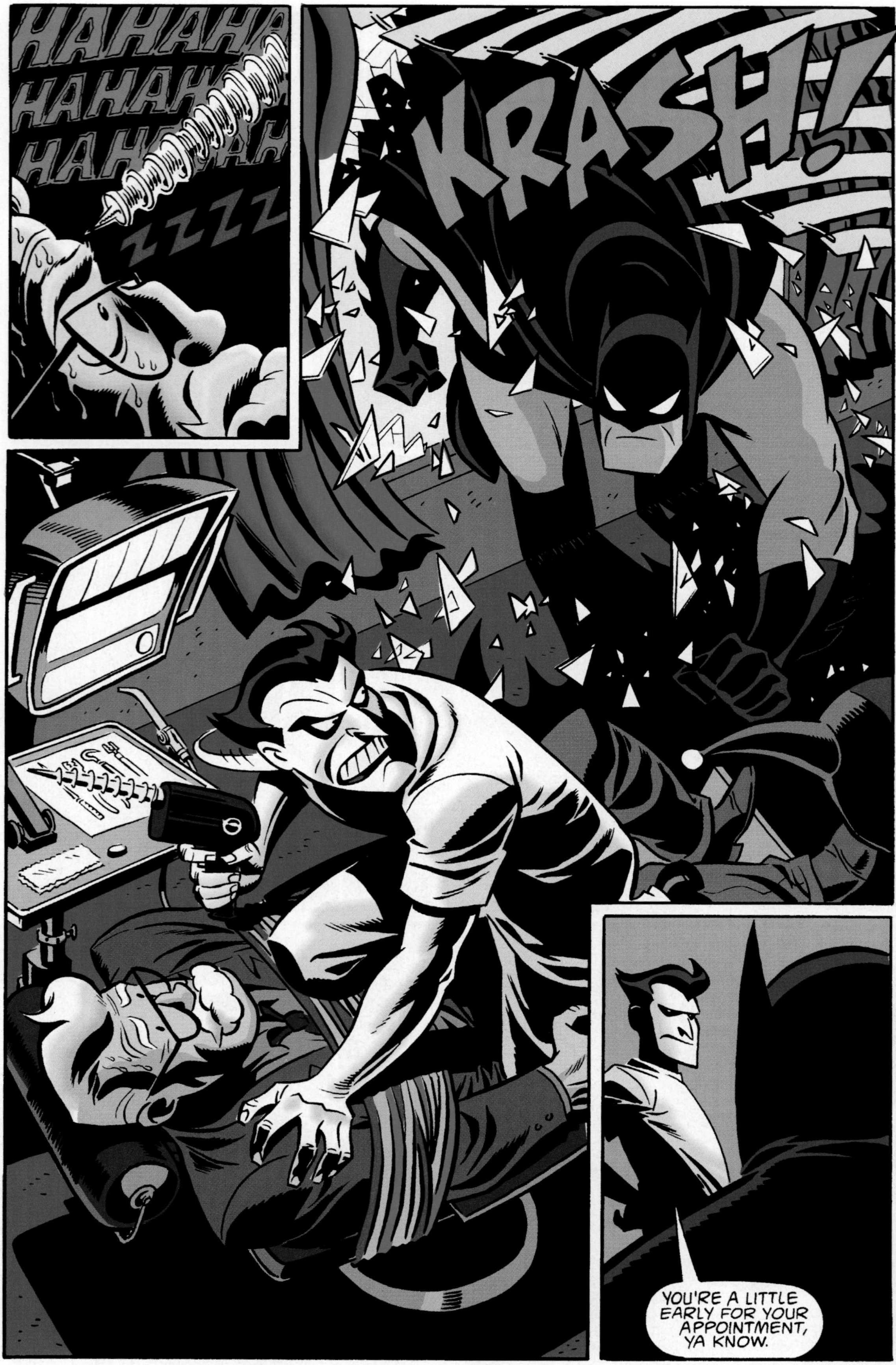
HAHAHA
HAHAHA
HAHAHA
ZZZZ
KRASH!!
YOU'RE A LITTLE EARLY FOR YOUR APPOINTMENT, YA KNOW.

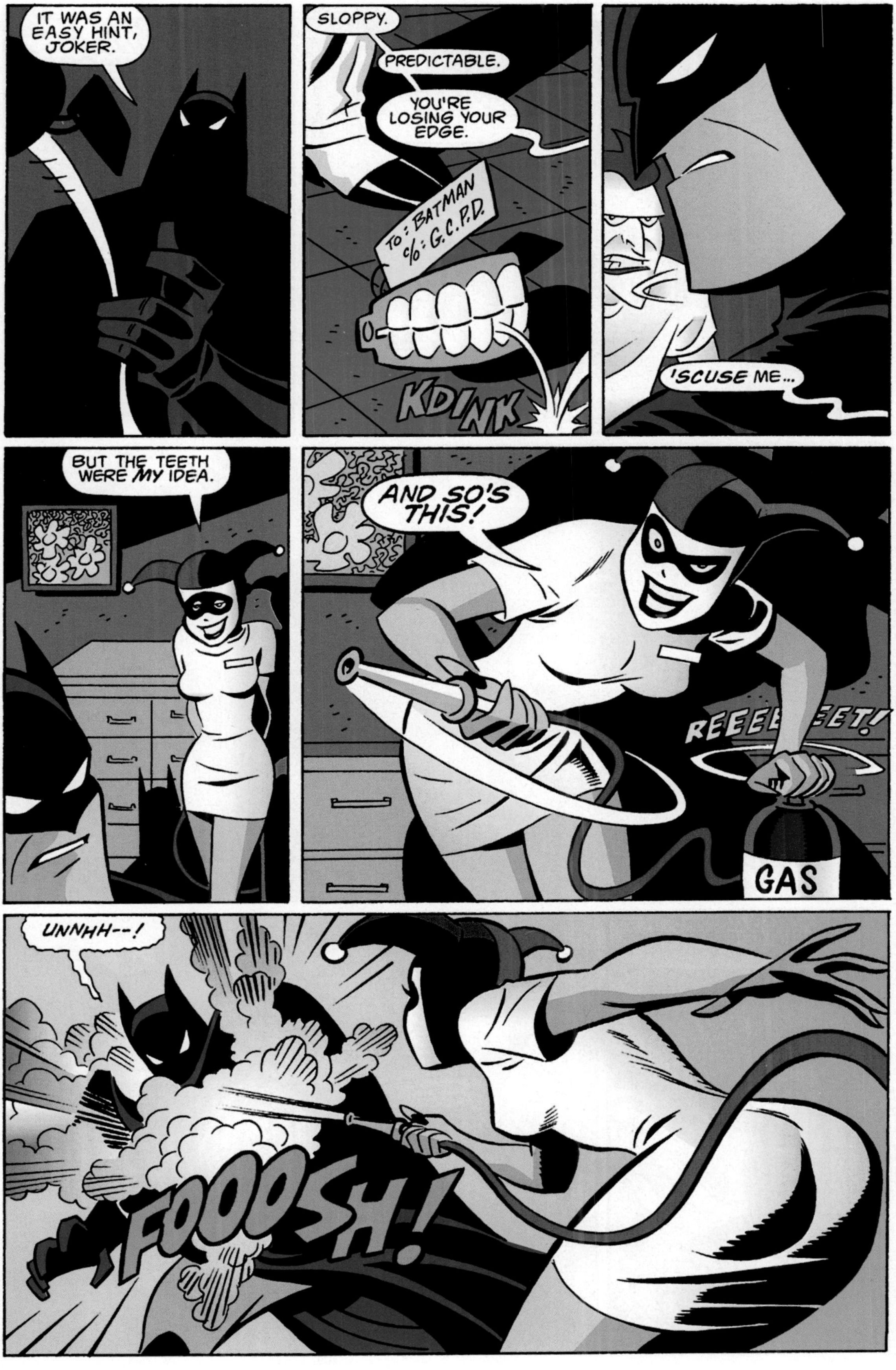
IT WAS AN EASY HINT, JOKER.
SLOPPY.
PREDICTABLE.
YOU'RE LOSING YOUR EDGE.
TO: BATMAN c/o: G.C.P.D.
KDINK
'SCUSE ME...
BUT THE TEETH WERE MY IDEA.
AND SO'S THIS!
REEEEEEET!
GAS
UNNHH--!
FOOOSH!

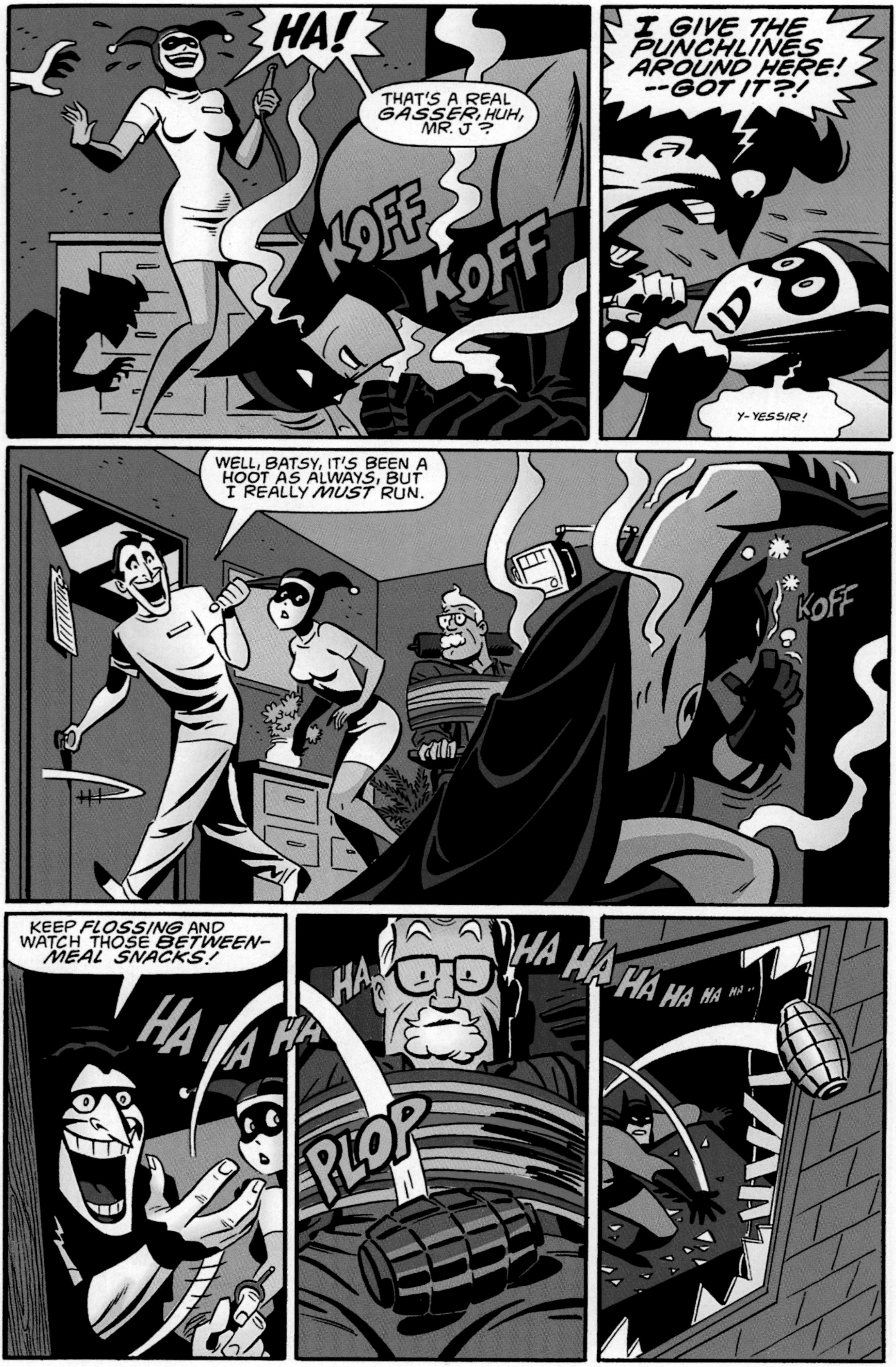
HA!
THAT'S A REAL GASSER, HUH, MR. J?
KOFF
KOFF
I GIVE THE PUNCHLINES AROUND HERE! --GOT IT?!
Y-YESSIR!
WELL, BATSY, IT'S BEEN A HOOT AS ALWAYS, BUT I REALLY MUST RUN.
KOFF
KEEP FLOSSING AND WATCH THOSE BETWEEN-MEAL SNACKS!
HA HA HA
HA
PLOP
HA HA HA HA HA HA HA..

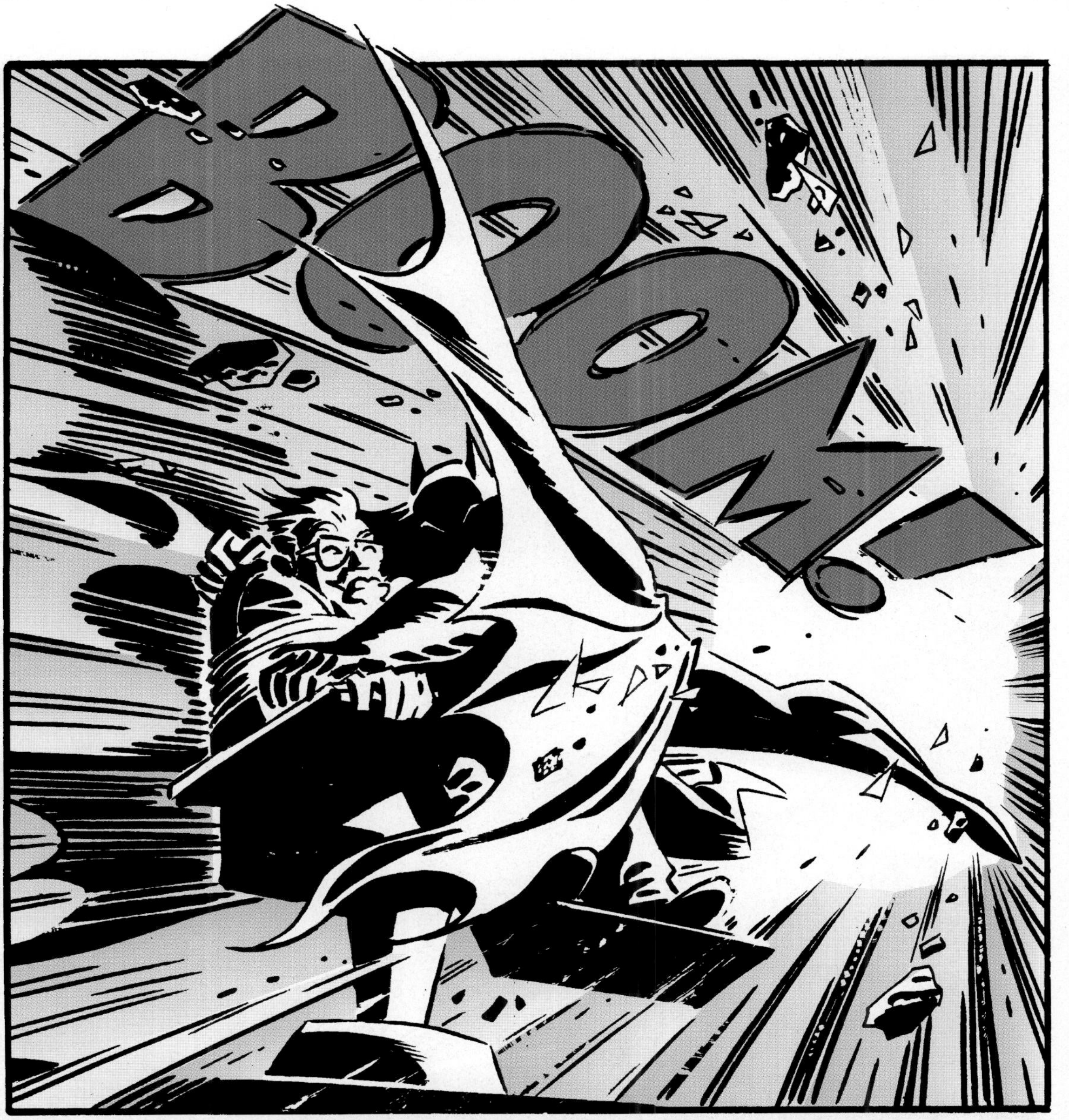
BOOOM!

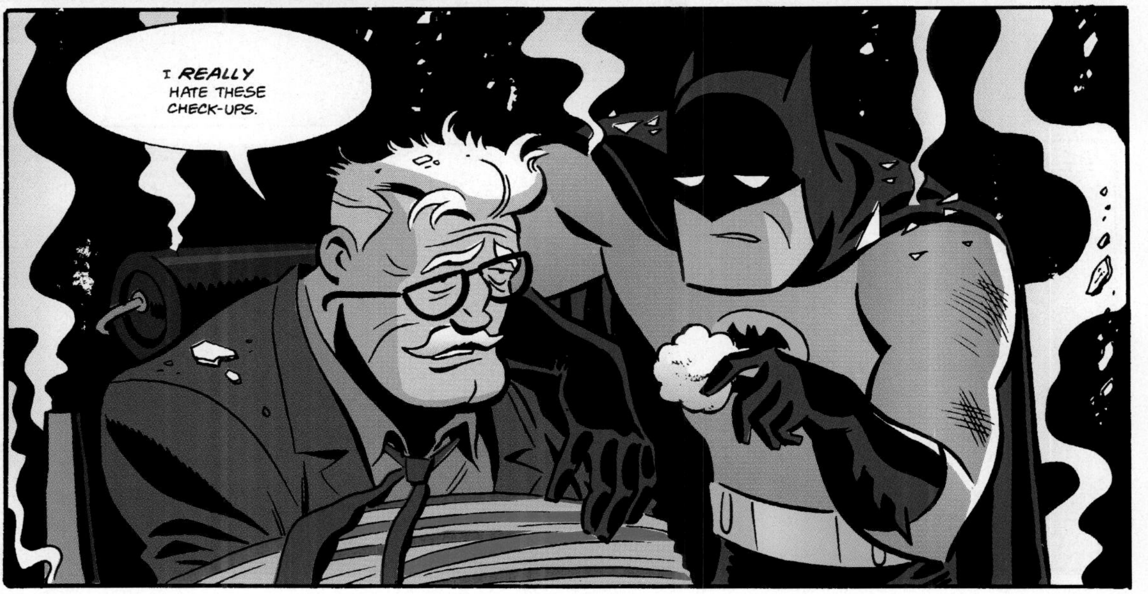
I REALLY HATE THESE CHECK-UPS.

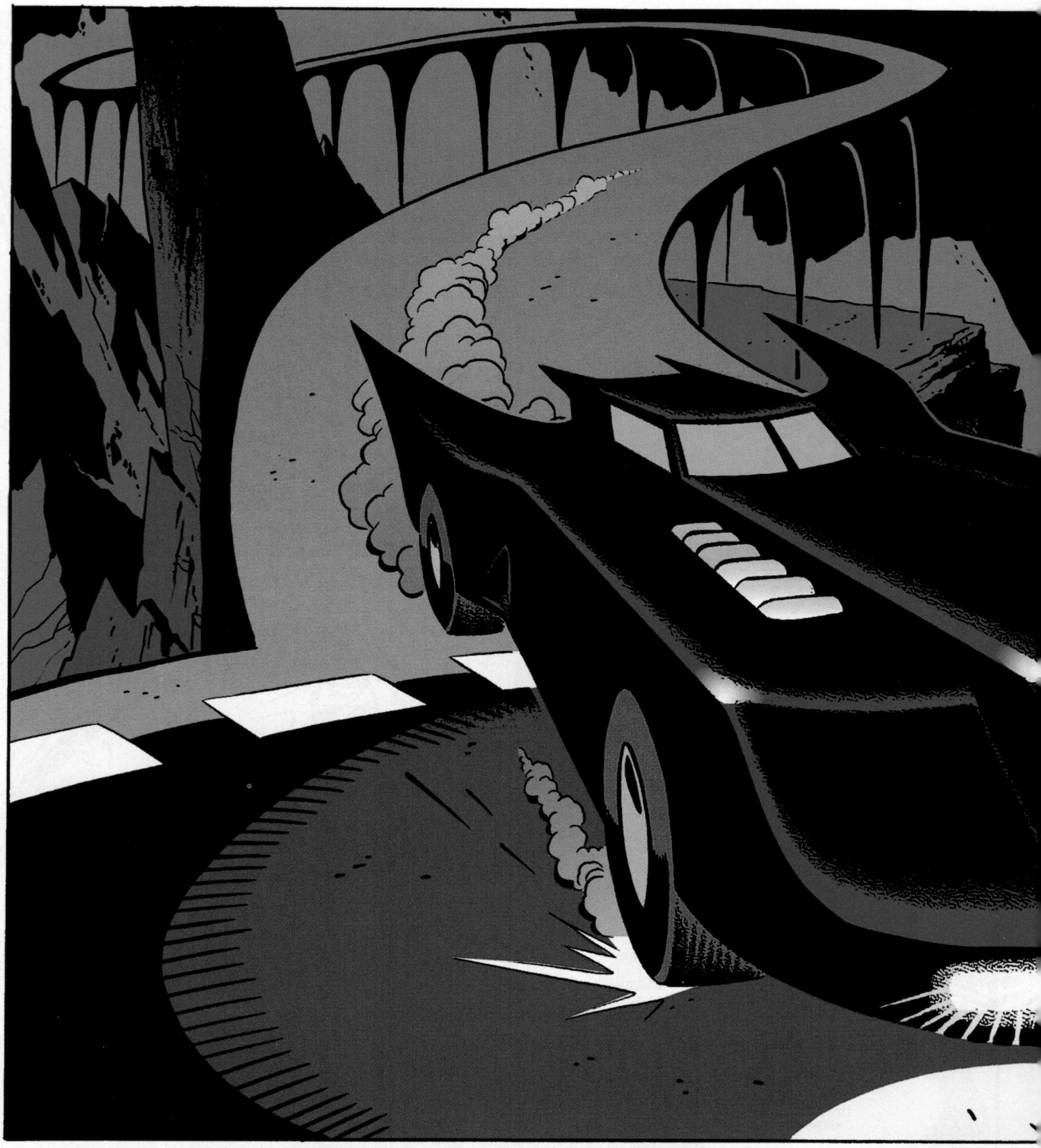

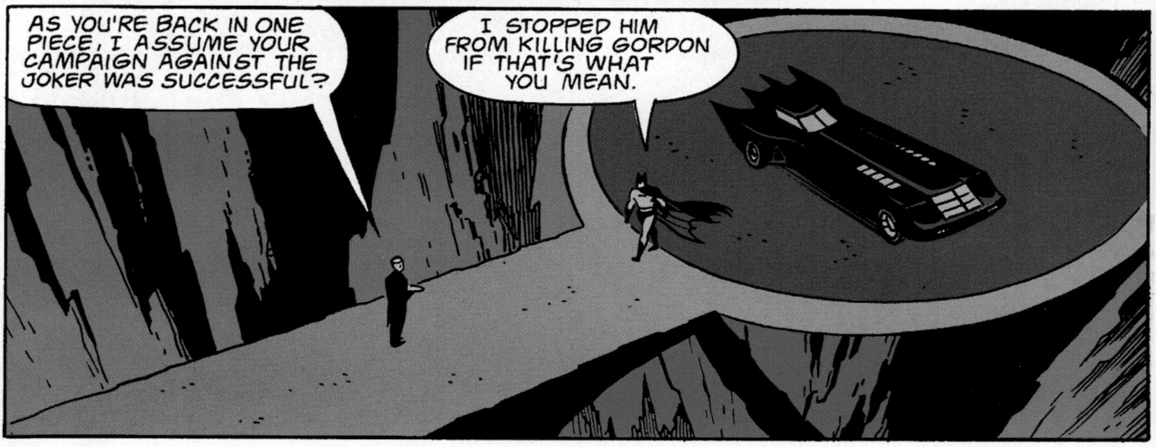
AS YOU'RE BACK IN ONE PIECE, I ASSUME YOUR CAMPAIGN AGAINST THE JOKER WAS SUCCESSFUL?
I STOPPED HIM FROM KILLING GORDON IF THAT'S WHAT YOU MEAN.

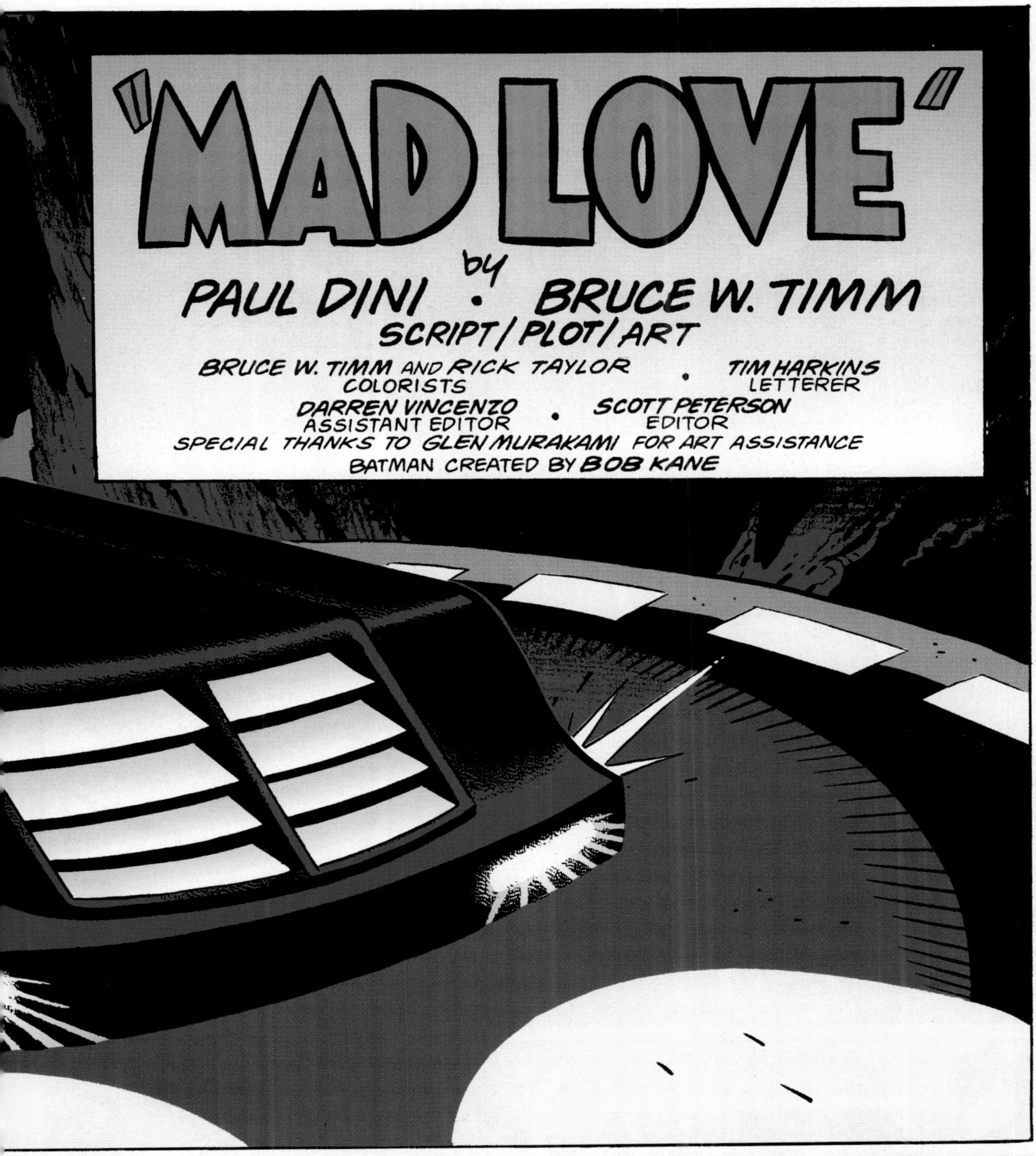
"MAD LOVE"
by
PAUL DINI • BRUCE W. TIMM
SCRIPT/PLOT/ART
BRUCE W. TIMM AND RICK TAYLOR COLORISTS • TIM HARKINS LETTERER
DARREN VINCENZO ASSISTANT EDITOR • SCOTT PETERSON EDITOR
SPECIAL THANKS TO GLEN MURAKAMI FOR ART ASSISTANCE
BATMAN CREATED BY BOB KANE

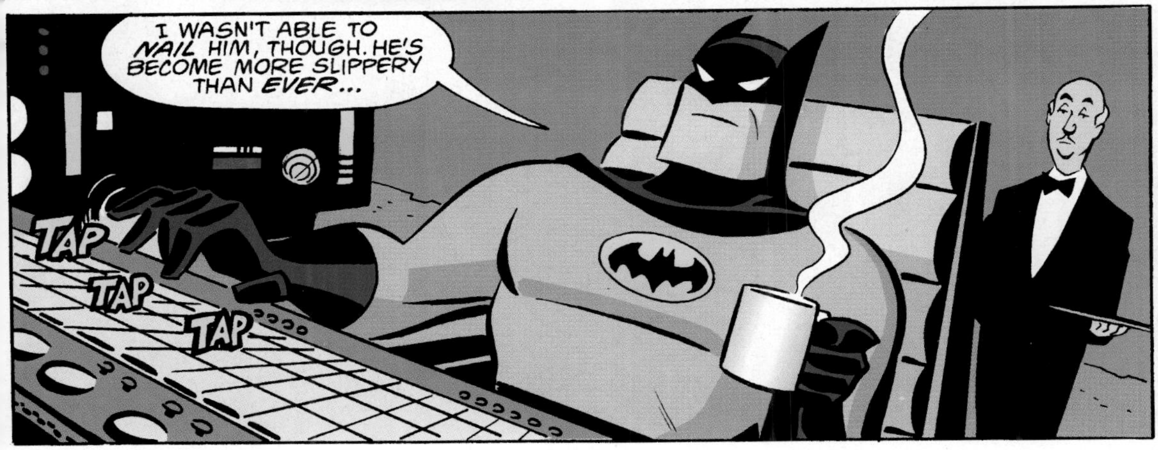
I WASN'T ABLE TO NAIL HIM, THOUGH. HE'S BECOME MORE SLIPPERY THAN EVER...
TAP
TAP
TAP

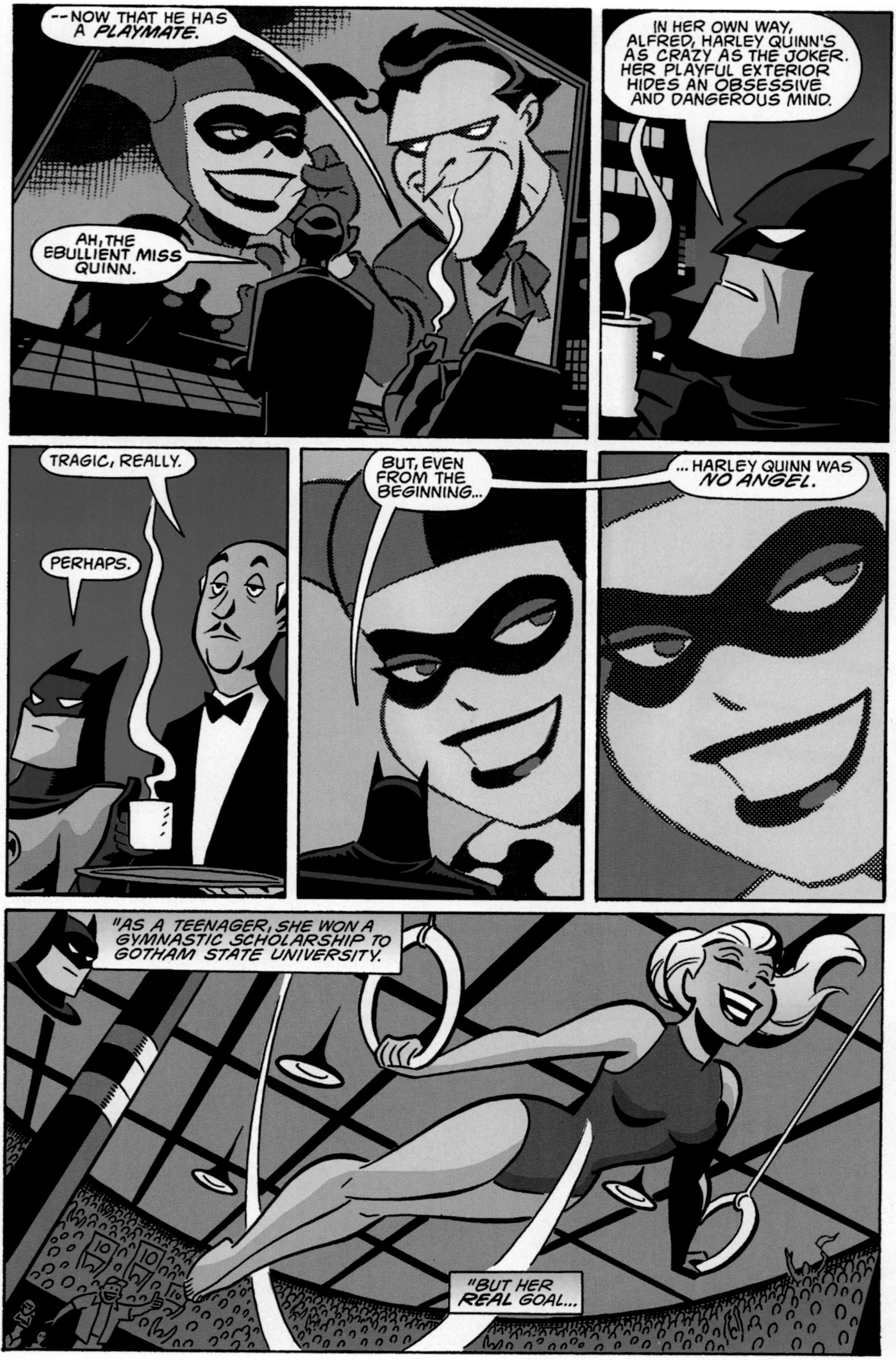
--NOW THAT HE HAS A PLAYMATE.
AH, THE EBULLIENT MISS QUINN.
IN HER OWN WAY, ALFRED, HARLEY QUINN'S AS CRAZY AS THE JOKER. HER PLAYFUL EXTERIOR HIDES AN OBSESSIVE AND DANGEROUS MIND.
TRAGIC, REALLY.
PERHAPS.
BUT, EVEN FROM THE BEGINNING...
...HARLEY QUINN WAS NO ANGEL.
"AS A TEENAGER, SHE WON A GYMNASTIC SCHOLARSHIP TO GOTHAM STATE UNIVERSITY.
10
10
"BUT HER REAL GOAL...

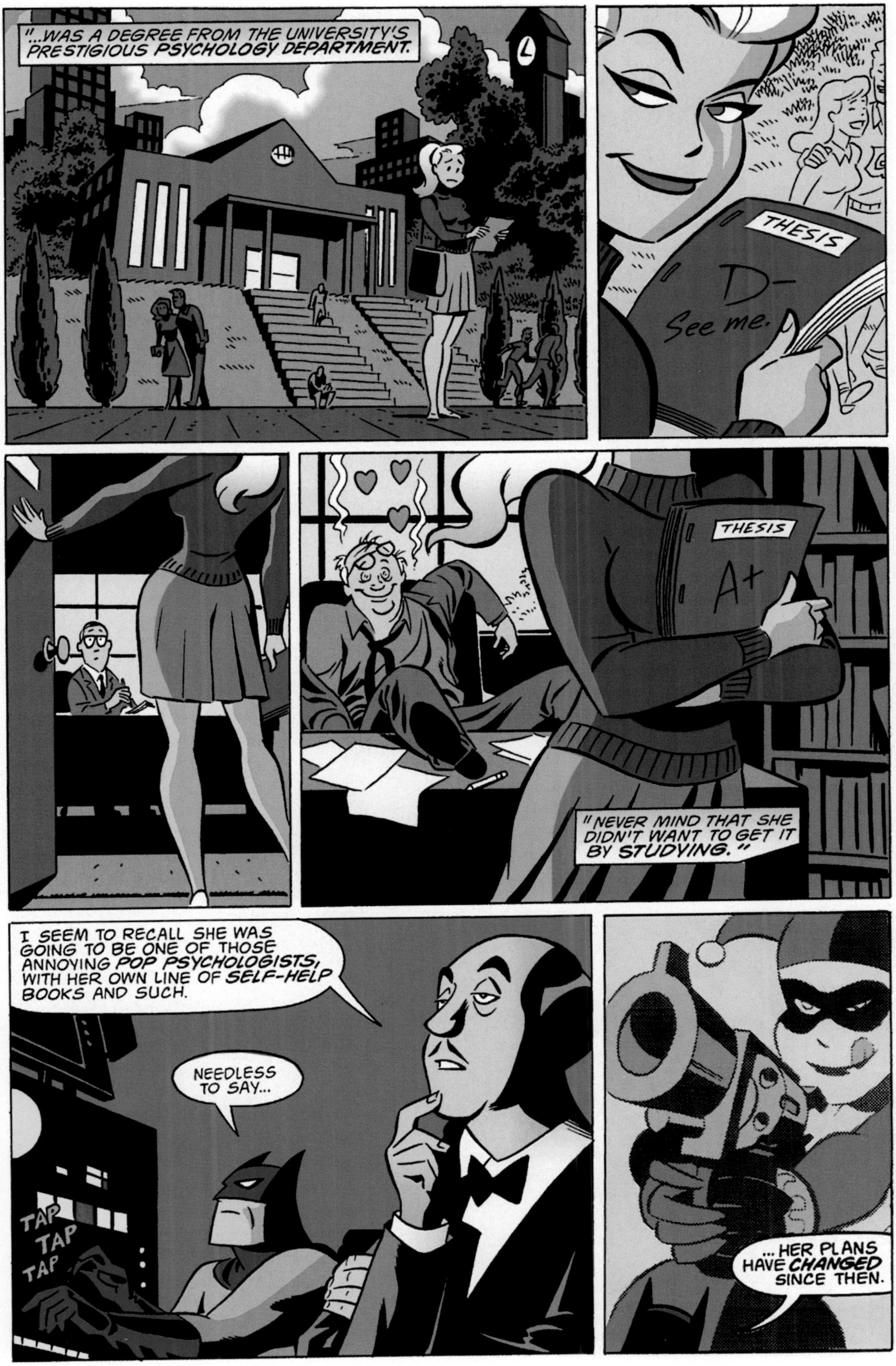
"...WAS A DEGREE FROM THE UNIVERSITY'S PRESTIGIOUS PSYCHOLOGY DEPARTMENT.
THESIS
D-
See me.
THESIS
A+
"NEVER MIND THAT SHE DIDN'T WANT TO GET IT BY STUDYING."
I SEEM TO RECALL SHE WAS GOING TO BE ONE OF THOSE ANNOYING POP PSYCHOLOGISTS, WITH HER OWN LINE OF SELF-HELP BOOKS AND SUCH.
NEEDLESS TO SAY...
TAP TAP TAP
...HER PLANS HAVE CHANGED SINCE THEN.

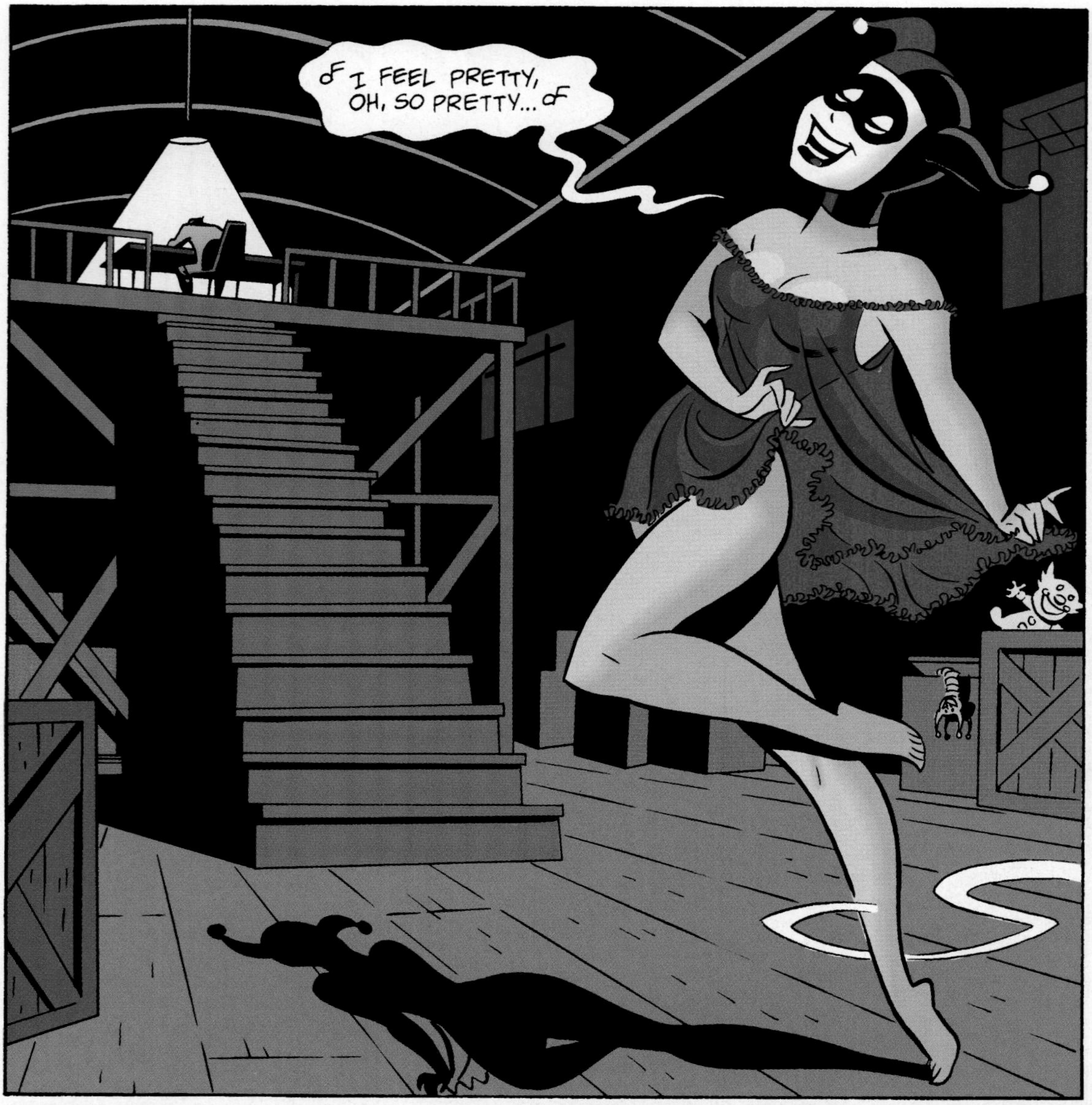
♪ I FEEL PRETTY, OH, SO PRETTY... ♪

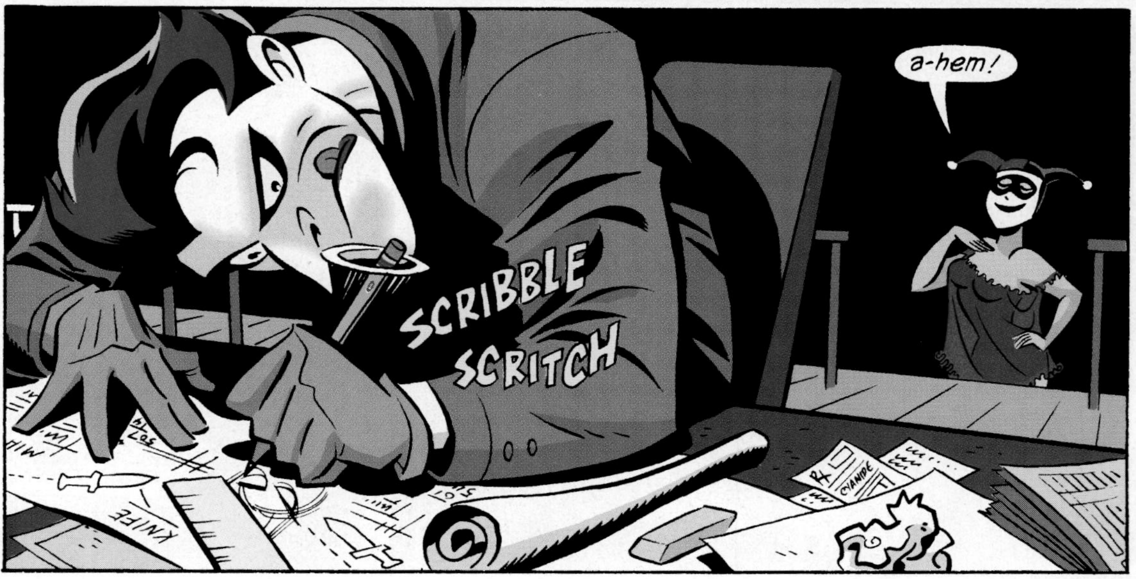
a-hem!
SCRIBBLE
SCRITCH
KNIFE
CYANIDE

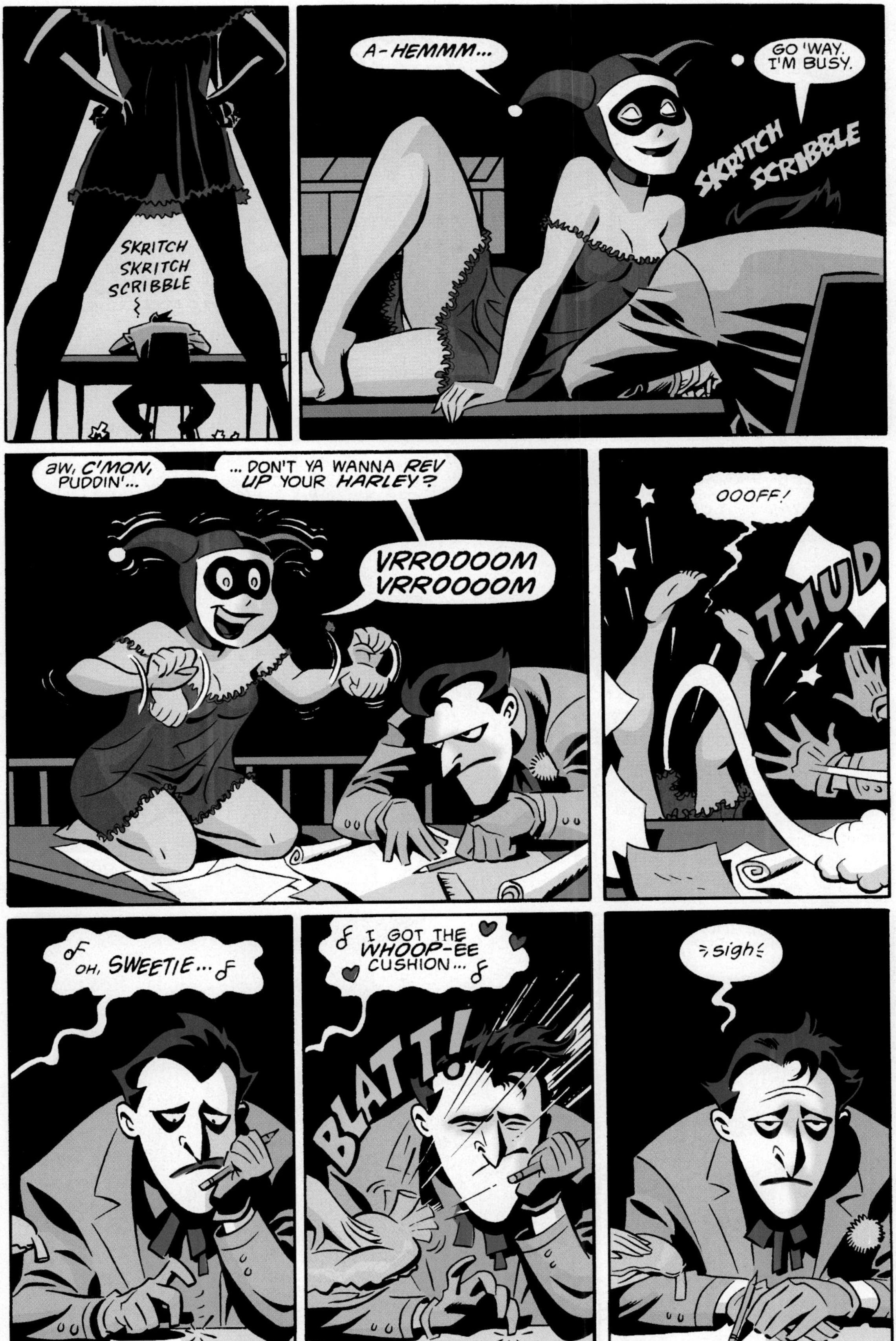
SKRITCH
SKRITCH
SCRIBBLE
A-HEMMM...
GO 'WAY. I'M BUSY.
SKRITCH
SCRIBBLE
AW, C'MON, PUDDIN'...
...DON'T YA WANNA REV UP YOUR HARLEY?
VRROOOOM
VRROOOOM
OOOFF!
THUD
OH, SWEETIE...
I GOT THE WHOOP-EE CUSHION...
BLATT!
sigh

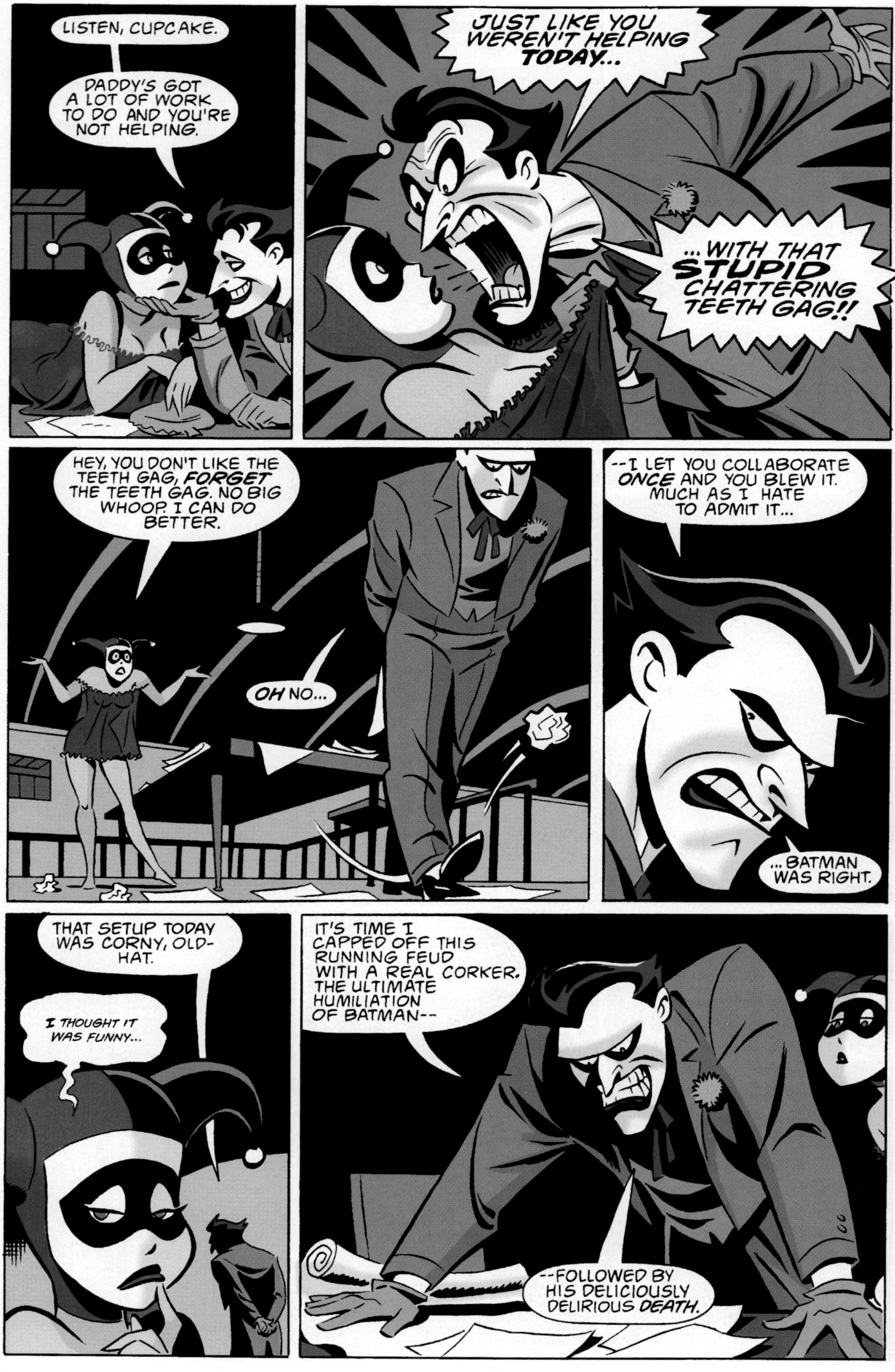
LISTEN, CUPCAKE.
DADDY'S GOT A LOT OF WORK TO DO AND YOU'RE NOT HELPING.
JUST LIKE YOU WEREN'T HELPING TODAY...
...WITH THAT STUPID CHATTERING TEETH GAG!!
HEY, YOU DON'T LIKE THE TEETH GAG, FORGET THE TEETH GAG. NO BIG WHOOP. I CAN DO BETTER.
OH NO...
--I LET YOU COLLABORATE ONCE AND YOU BLEW IT. MUCH AS I HATE TO ADMIT IT...
...BATMAN WAS RIGHT.
THAT SETUP TODAY WAS CORNY, OLD-HAT.
I THOUGHT IT WAS FUNNY...
IT'S TIME I CAPPED OFF THIS RUNNING FEUD WITH A REAL CORKER. THE ULTIMATE HUMILIATION OF BATMAN--
--FOLLOWED BY HIS DELICIOUSLY DELIRIOUS DEATH.

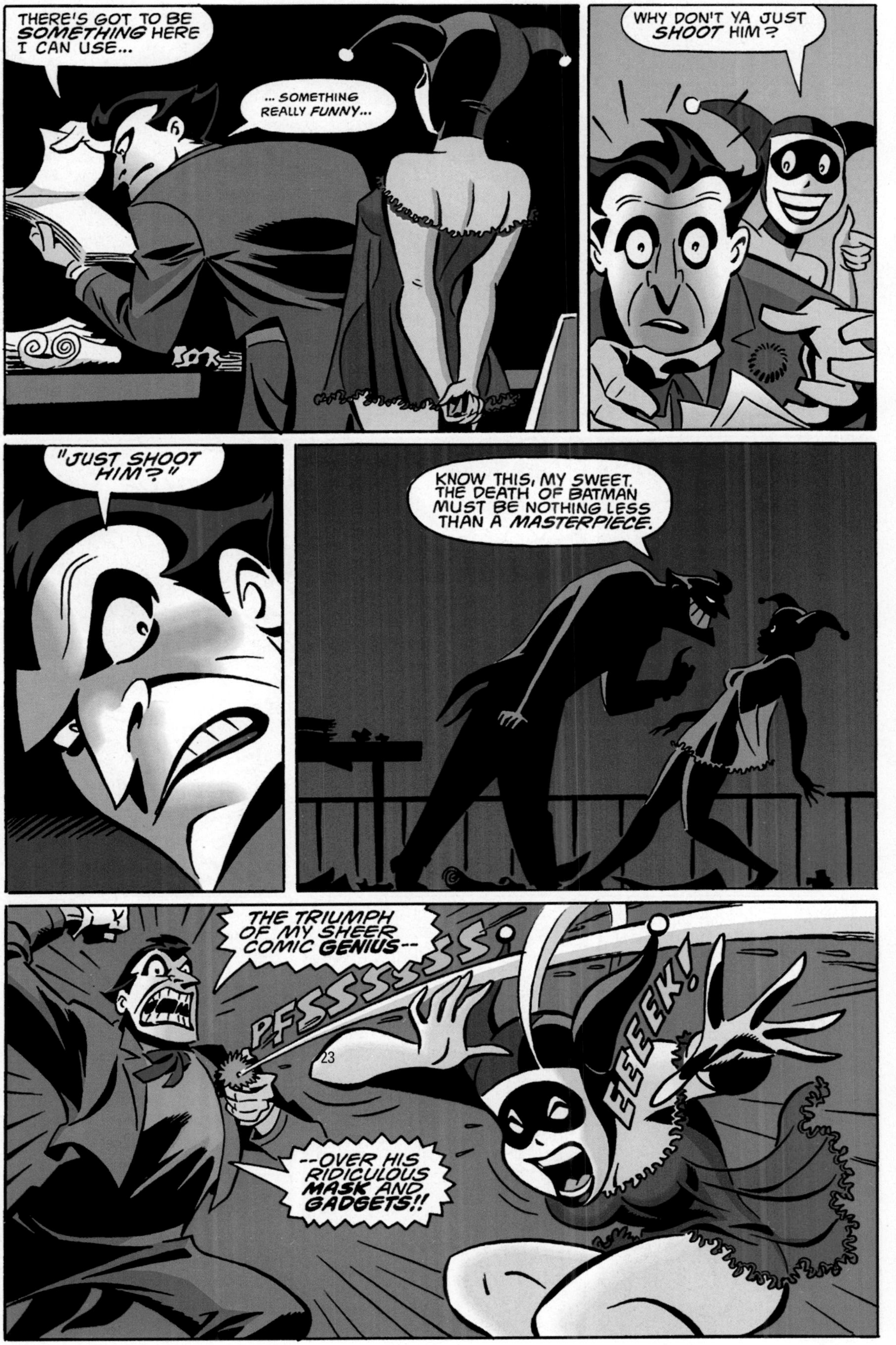

THERE'S GOT TO BE SOMETHING HERE I CAN USE...
... SOMETHING REALLY FUNNY...
WHY DON'T YA JUST SHOOT HIM?
"JUST SHOOT HIM?"
KNOW THIS, MY SWEET. THE DEATH OF BATMAN MUST BE NOTHING LESS THAN A MASTERPIECE.
THE TRIUMPH OF MY SHEER COMIC GENIUS--
PFSSSSSSSS
EEEEK!
--OVER HIS RIDICULOUS MASK AND GADGETS!!

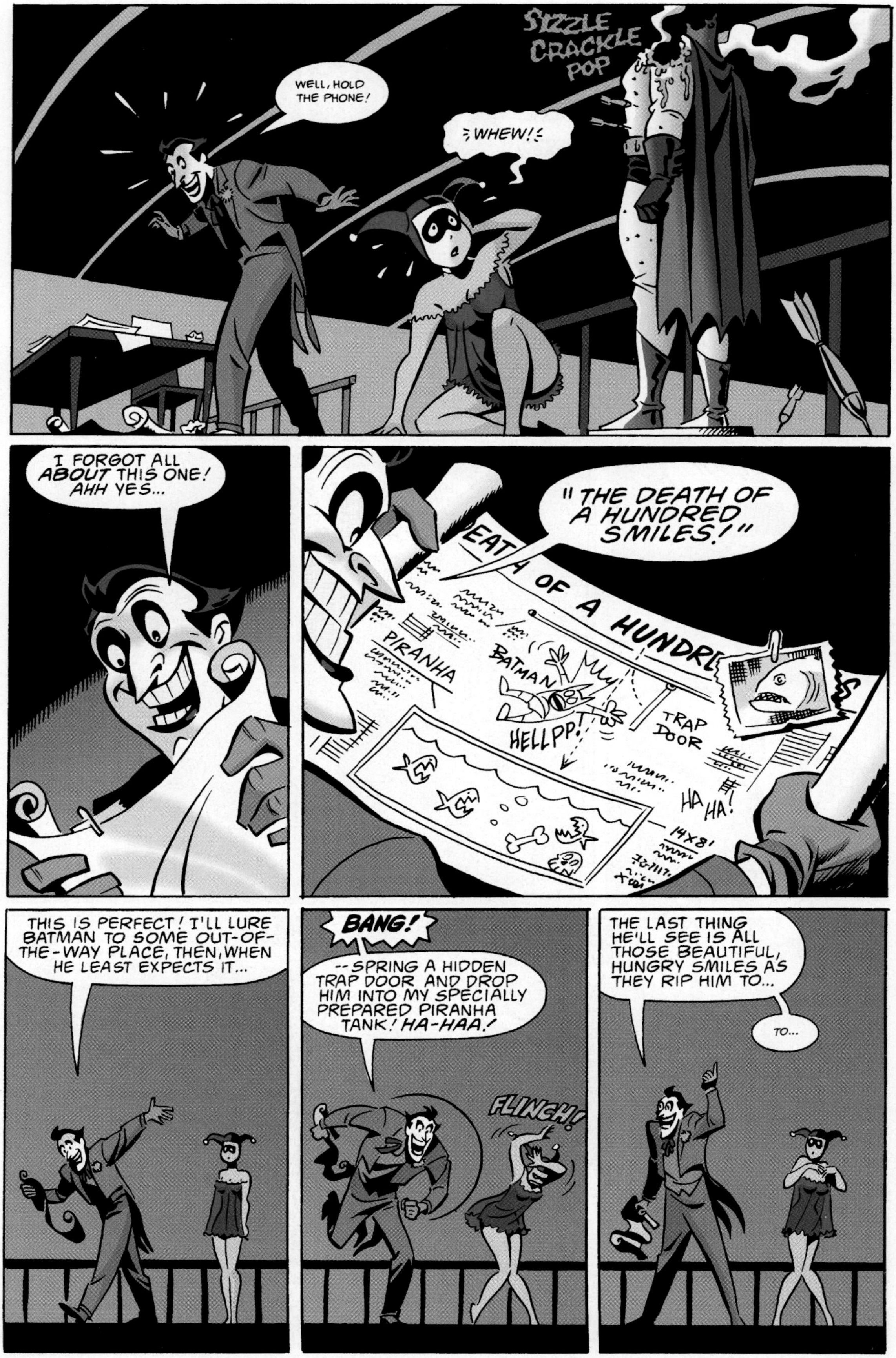
SIZZLE CRACKLE POP
WELL, HOLD THE PHONE!
WHEW!
I FORGOT ALL ABOUT THIS ONE! AHH YES...
"THE DEATH OF A HUNDRED SMILES!"
EATH OF A HUNDR
PIRANHA
BATMAN
HELLPP!
TRAP DOOR
HA HA!
14X8'
THIS IS PERFECT! I'LL LURE BATMAN TO SOME OUT-OF-THE-WAY PLACE, THEN, WHEN HE LEAST EXPECTS IT...
BANG!
--SPRING A HIDDEN TRAP DOOR AND DROP HIM INTO MY SPECIALLY PREPARED PIRANHA TANK! HA-HAA!
FLINCH!
THE LAST THING HE'LL SEE IS ALL THOSE BEAUTIFUL, HUNGRY SMILES AS THEY RIP HIM TO...
TO...

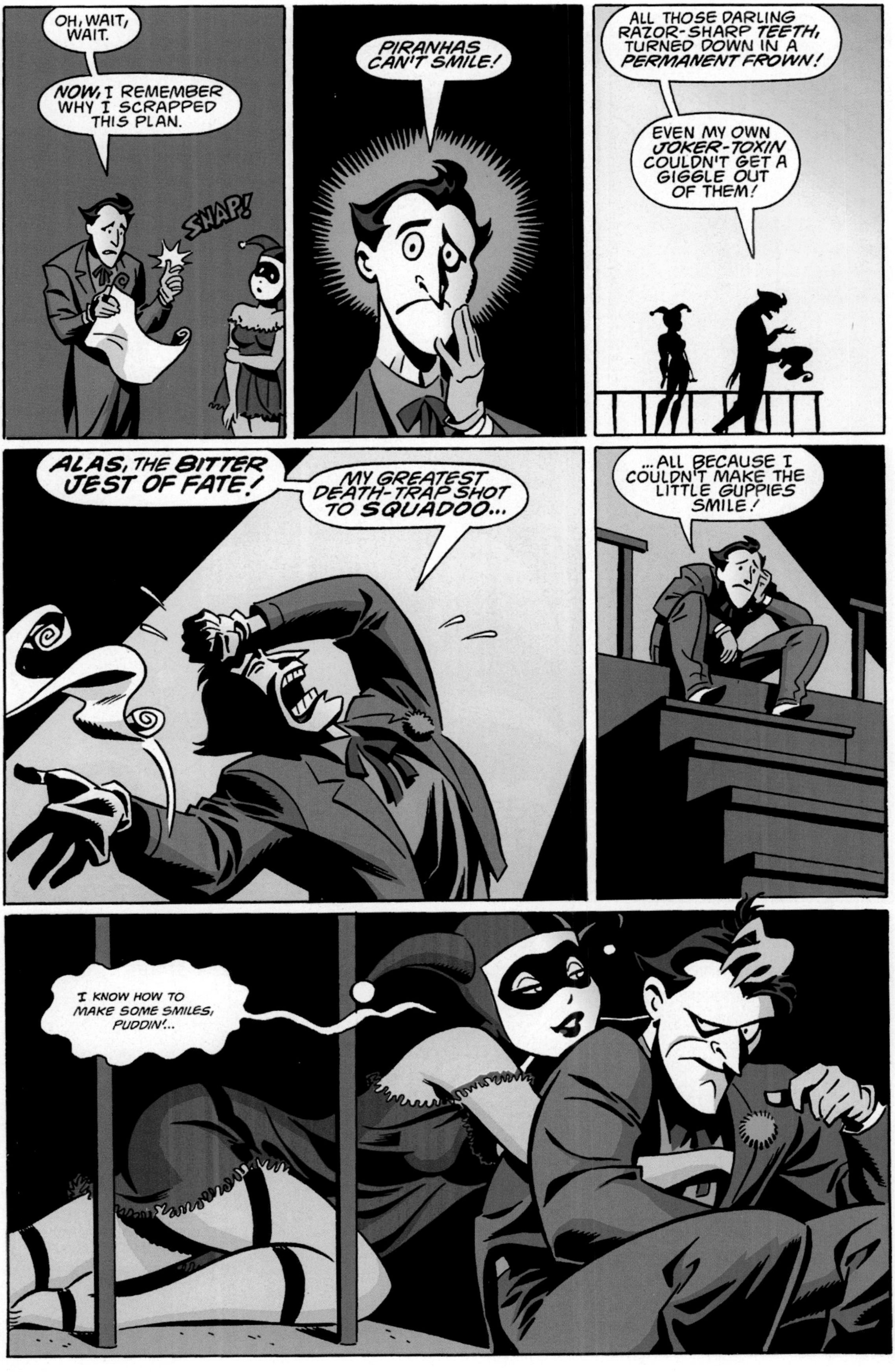
OH, WAIT, WAIT.
NOW, I REMEMBER WHY I SCRAPPED THIS PLAN.
SNAP!
PIRANHAS CAN'T SMILE!
ALL THOSE DARLING RAZOR-SHARP TEETH, TURNED DOWN IN A PERMANENT FROWN!
EVEN MY OWN JOKER-TOXIN COULDN'T GET A GIGGLE OUT OF THEM!
ALAS, THE BITTER JEST OF FATE!
MY GREATEST DEATH-TRAP SHOT TO SQUADOO...
...ALL BECAUSE I COULDN'T MAKE THE LITTLE GUPPIES SMILE!
I KNOW HOW TO MAKE SOME SMILES, PUDDIN'...

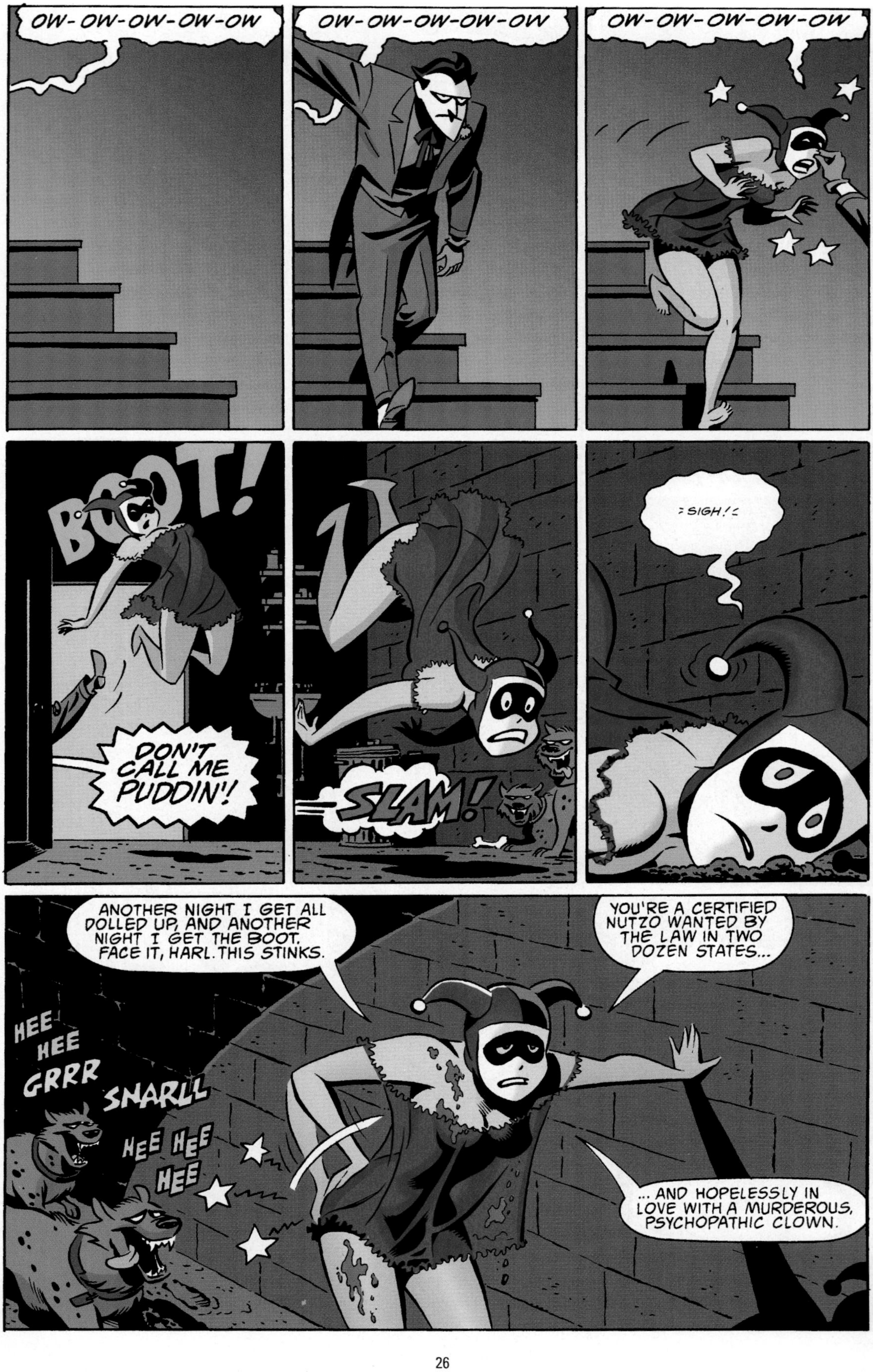
OW-OW-OW-OW-OW
OW-OW-OW-OW-OW
OW-OW-OW-OW-OW
BOOT!
DON'T CALL ME PUDDIN'!
SLAM!
SIGH!
ANOTHER NIGHT I GET ALL DOLLED UP, AND ANOTHER NIGHT I GET THE BOOT. FACE IT, HARL. THIS STINKS.
YOU'RE A CERTIFIED NUTZO WANTED BY THE LAW IN TWO DOZEN STATES...
HEE HEE
GRRR
SNARLL
HEE HEE HEE
... AND HOPELESSLY IN LOVE WITH A MURDEROUS, PSYCHOPATHIC CLOWN.

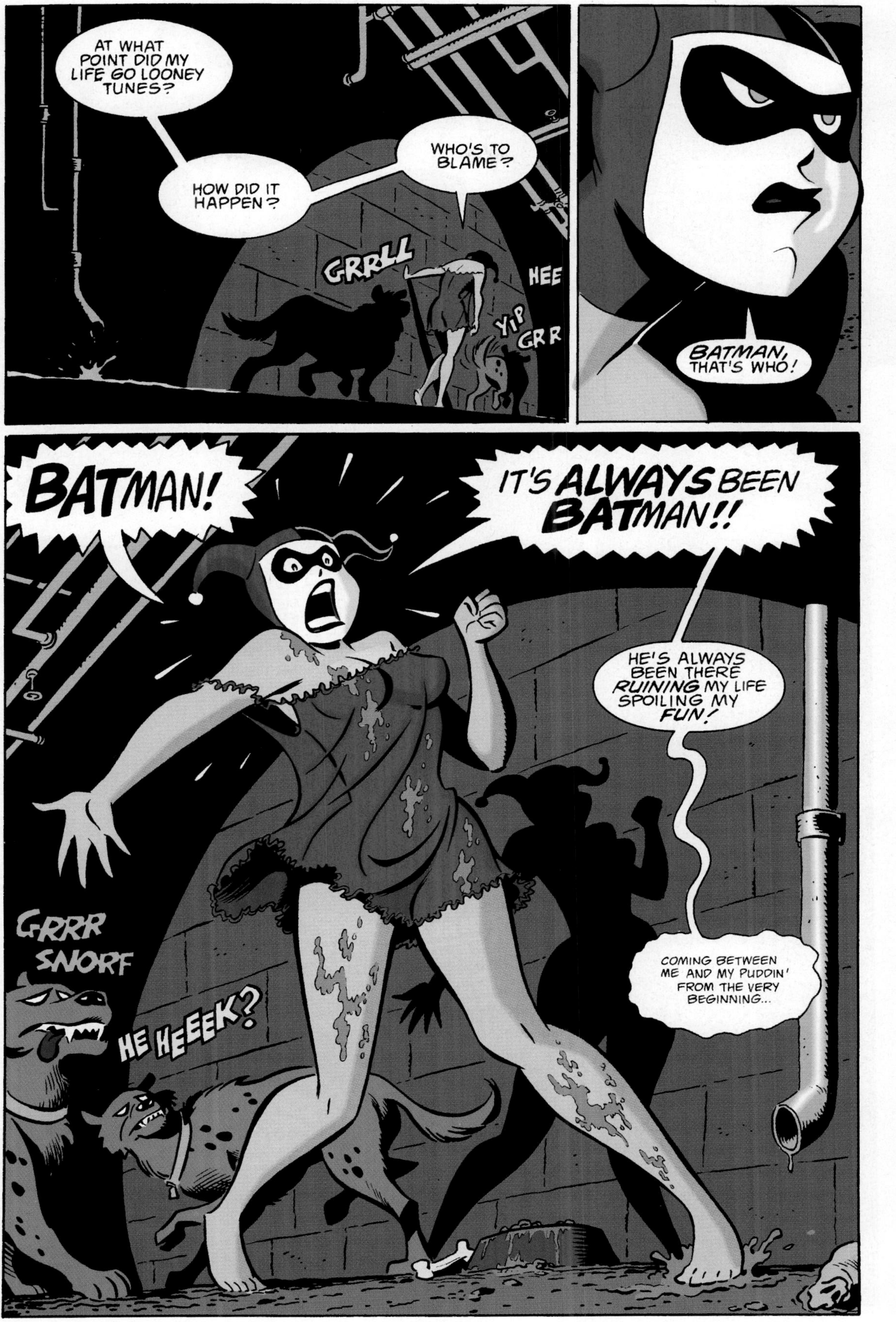
AT WHAT POINT DID MY LIFE GO LOONEY TUNES?
HOW DID IT HAPPEN?
WHO'S TO BLAME?
GRRLL
HEE
YIP
GRR
BATMAN, THAT'S WHO!
BATMAN!
IT'S ALWAYS BEEN BATMAN!!
HE'S ALWAYS BEEN THERE RUINING MY LIFE SPOILING MY FUN!
COMING BETWEEN ME AND MY PUDDIN' FROM THE VERY BEGINNING...
GRRR
SNORF
HE HEEEK?

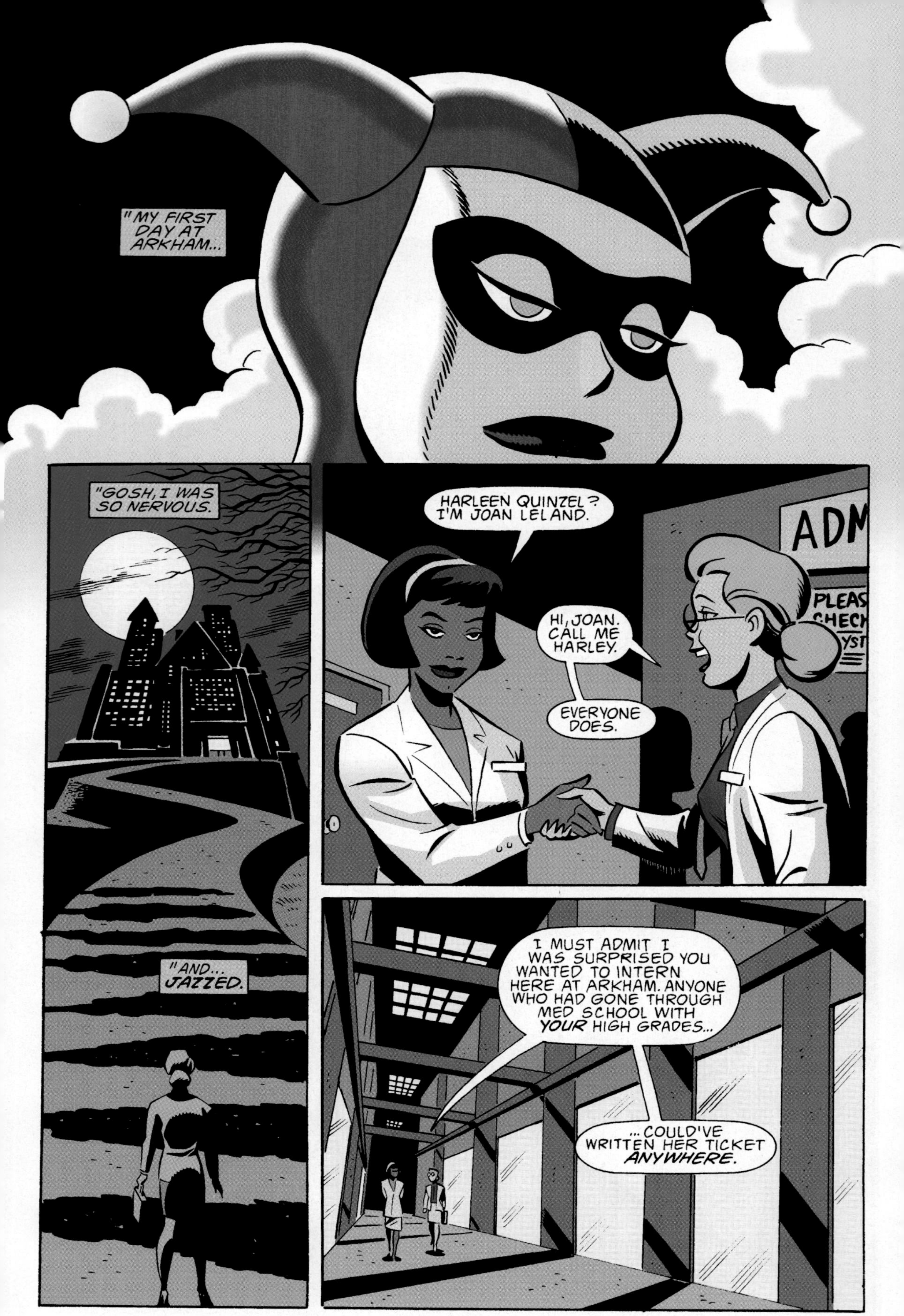
"MY FIRST DAY AT ARKHAM...
"GOSH, I WAS SO NERVOUS.
"AND... JAZZED.
HARLEEN QUINZEL? I'M JOAN LELAND.
HI, JOAN. CALL ME HARLEY.
EVERYONE DOES.
ADM
PLEAS
CHECK
I MUST ADMIT I WAS SURPRISED YOU WANTED TO INTERN HERE AT ARKHAM. ANYONE WHO HAD GONE THROUGH MED SCHOOL WITH *YOUR* HIGH GRADES...
...COULD'VE WRITTEN HER TICKET *ANYWHERE*.

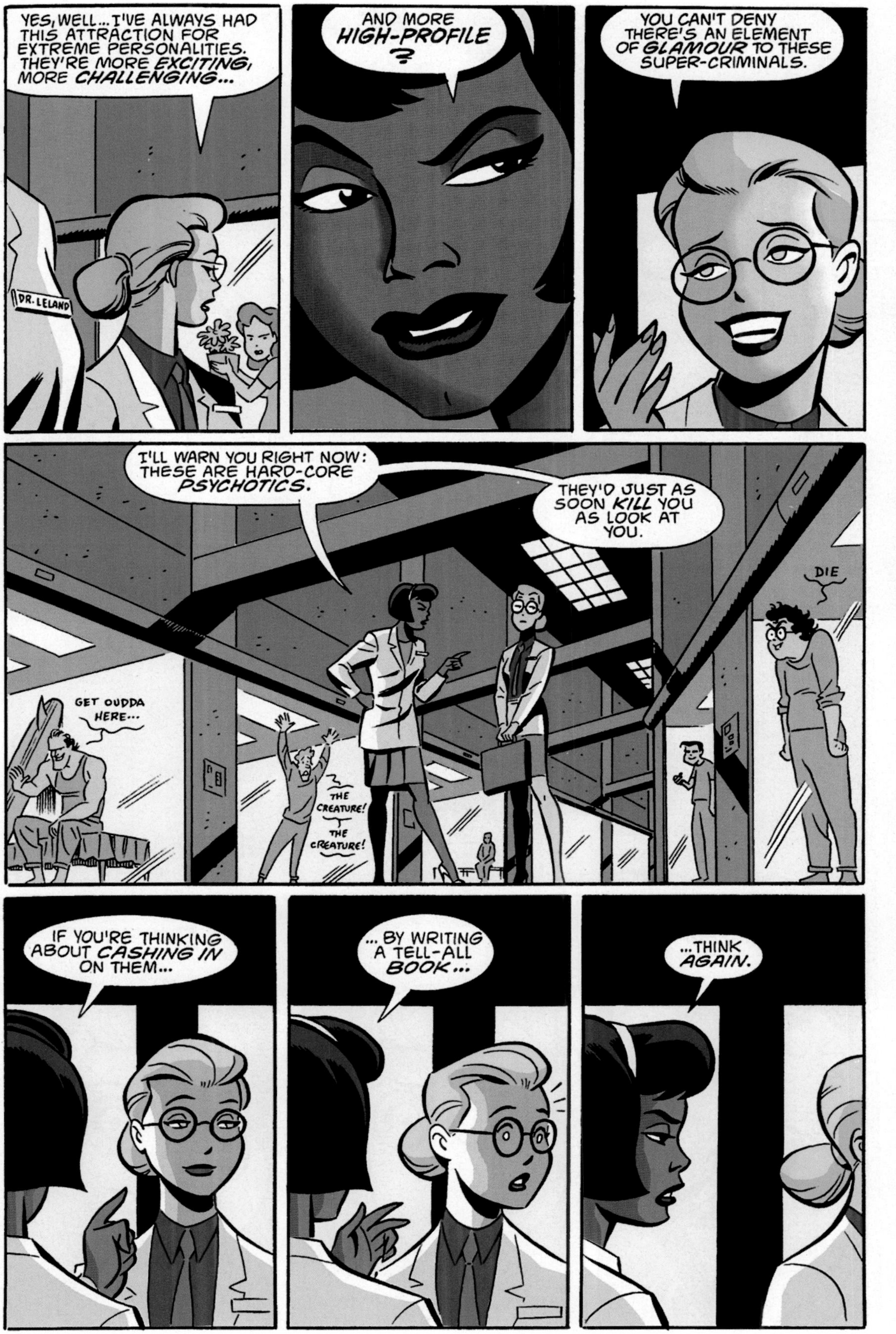

YES, WELL... I'VE ALWAYS HAD THIS ATTRACTION FOR EXTREME PERSONALITIES. THEY'RE MORE EXCITING, MORE CHALLENGING...
DR. LELAND
AND MORE HIGH-PROFILE?
YOU CAN'T DENY THERE'S AN ELEMENT OF GLAMOUR TO THESE SUPER-CRIMINALS.
I'LL WARN YOU RIGHT NOW: THESE ARE HARD-CORE PSYCHOTICS.
THEY'D JUST AS SOON KILL YOU AS LOOK AT YOU.
DIE
GET OUDDA HERE...
THE CREATURE! THE CREATURE!
IF YOU'RE THINKING ABOUT CASHING IN ON THEM...
...BY WRITING A TELL-ALL BOOK...
...THINK AGAIN.

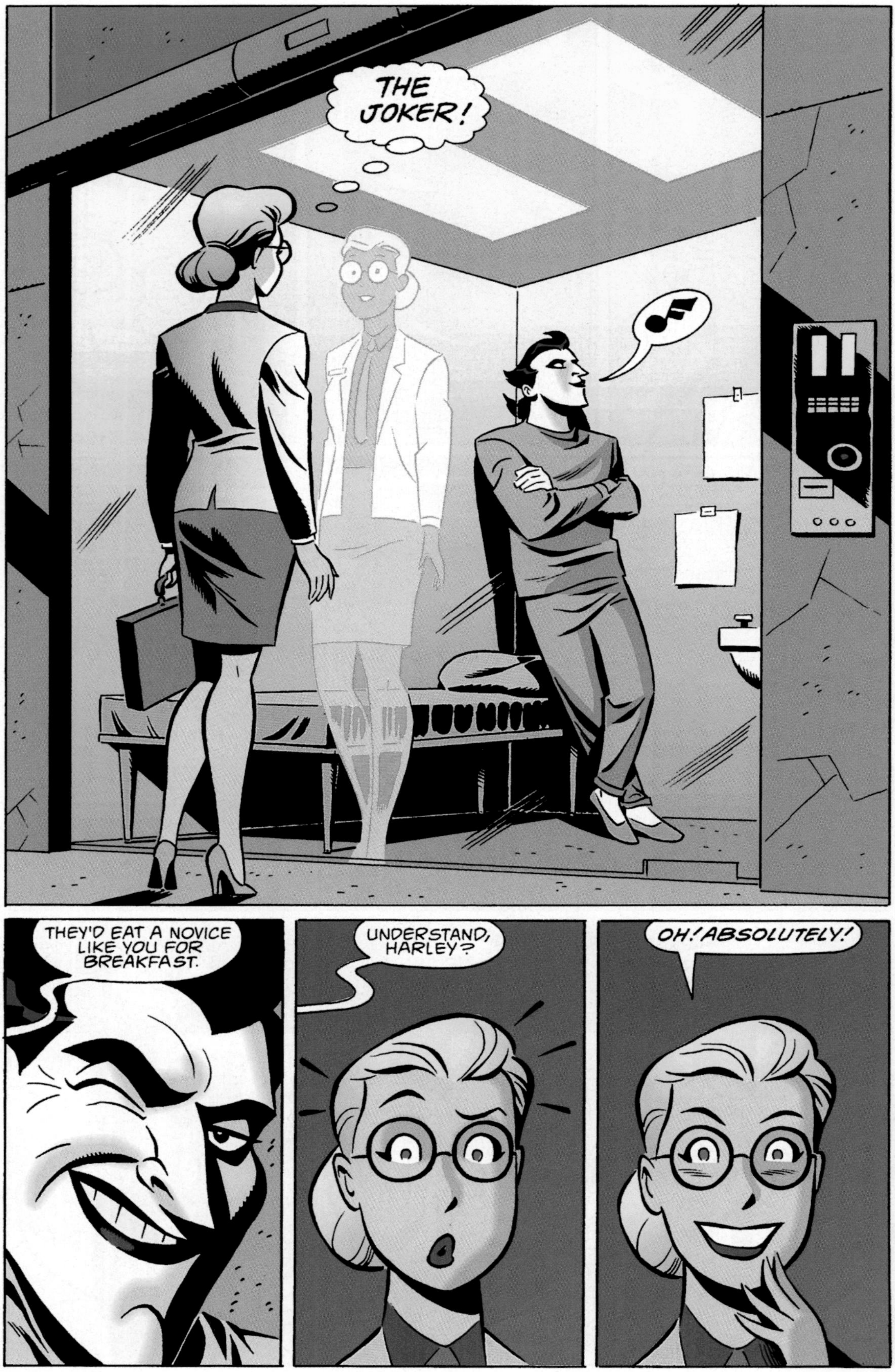
THE JOKER!
THEY'D EAT A NOVICE LIKE YOU FOR BREAKFAST.
UNDERSTAND, HARLEY?
OH! ABSOLUTELY!

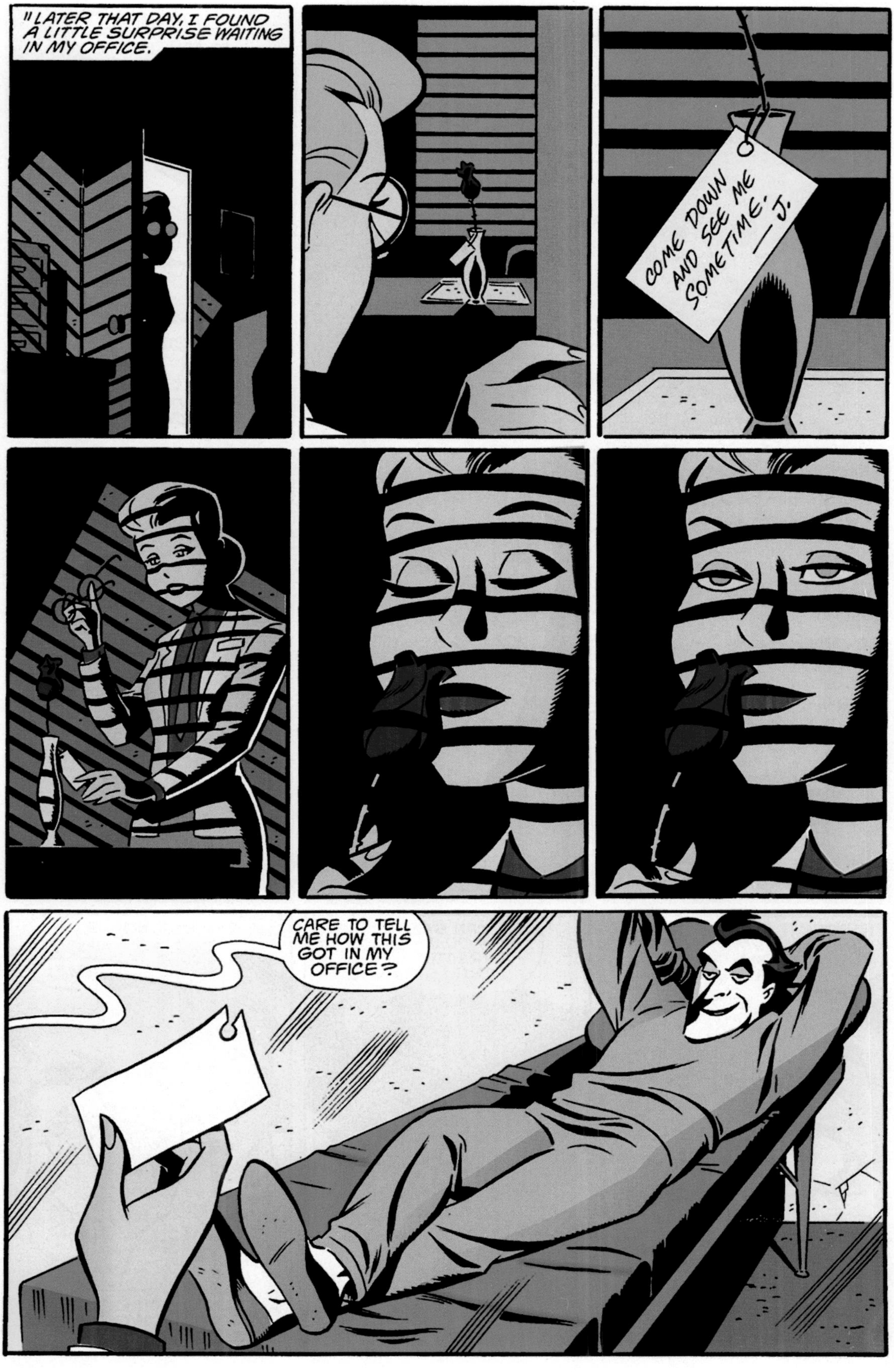
"LATER THAT DAY, I FOUND A LITTLE SURPRISE WAITING IN MY OFFICE.
COME DOWN AND SEE ME SOMETIME. —J.
CARE TO TELL ME HOW THIS GOT IN MY OFFICE?

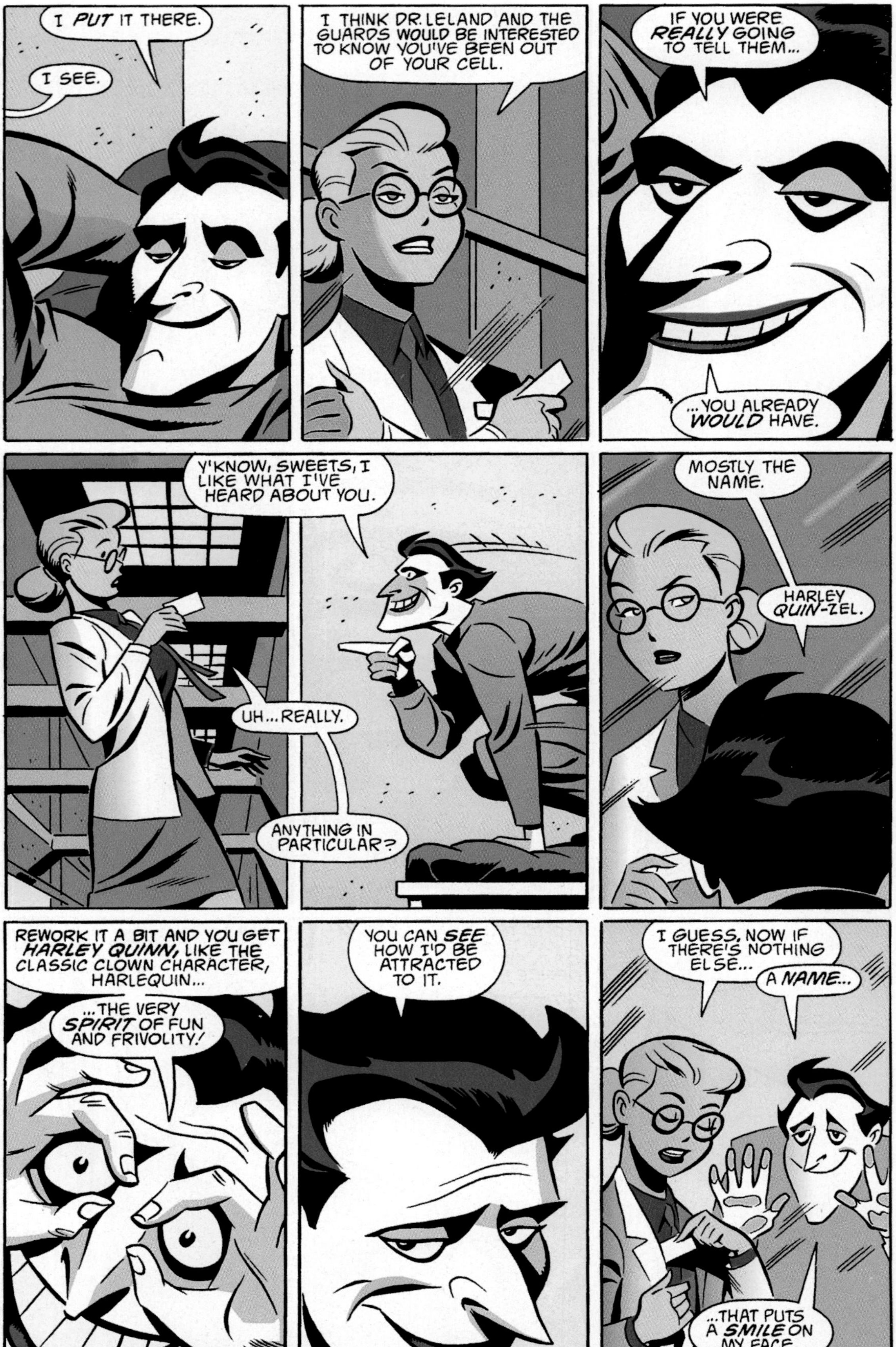
I PUT IT THERE.
I SEE.
I THINK DR. LELAND AND THE GUARDS WOULD BE INTERESTED TO KNOW YOU'VE BEEN OUT OF YOUR CELL.
IF YOU WERE REALLY GOING TO TELL THEM...
...YOU ALREADY WOULD HAVE.
Y'KNOW, SWEETS, I LIKE WHAT I'VE HEARD ABOUT YOU.
UH... REALLY.
ANYTHING IN PARTICULAR?
MOSTLY THE NAME.
HARLEY QUIN-ZEL.
REWORK IT A BIT AND YOU GET HARLEY QUINN, LIKE THE CLASSIC CLOWN CHARACTER, HARLEQUIN...
...THE VERY SPIRIT OF FUN AND FRIVOLITY!
YOU CAN SEE HOW I'D BE ATTRACTED TO IT.
I GUESS. NOW IF THERE'S NOTHING ELSE...
A NAME...
...THAT PUTS A SMILE ON MY FACE.

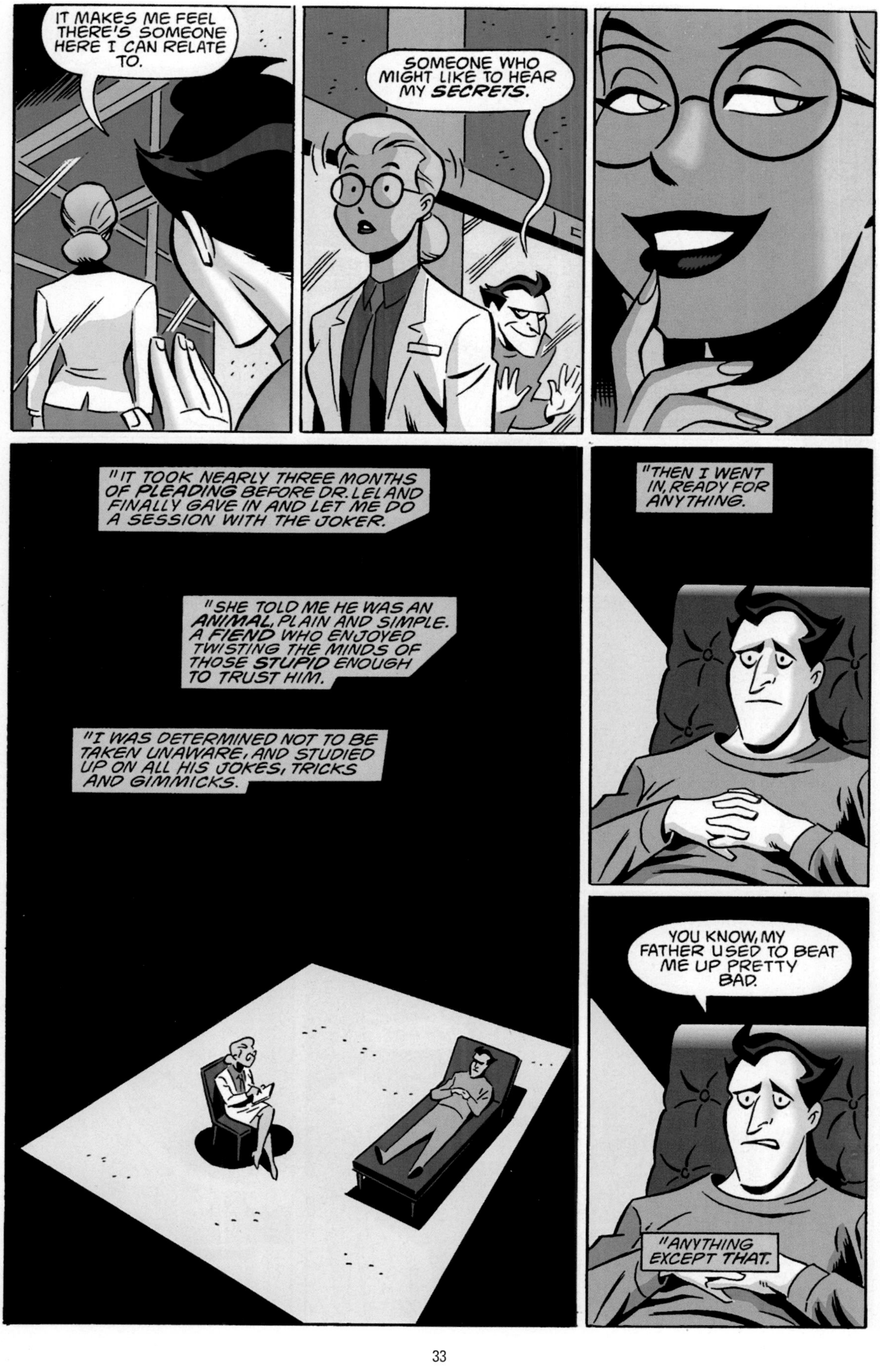

IT MAKES ME FEEL THERE'S SOMEONE HERE I CAN RELATE TO.
SOMEONE WHO MIGHT LIKE TO HEAR MY SECRETS.
"IT TOOK NEARLY THREE MONTHS OF PLEADING BEFORE DR. LELAND FINALLY GAVE IN AND LET ME DO A SESSION WITH THE JOKER.
"SHE TOLD ME HE WAS AN ANIMAL, PLAIN AND SIMPLE. A FIEND WHO ENJOYED TWISTING THE MINDS OF THOSE STUPID ENOUGH TO TRUST HIM.
"I WAS DETERMINED NOT TO BE TAKEN UNAWARE, AND STUDIED UP ON ALL HIS JOKES, TRICKS AND GIMMICKS.
"THEN I WENT IN, READY FOR ANYTHING.
YOU KNOW, MY FATHER USED TO BEAT ME UP PRETTY BAD.
"ANYTHING EXCEPT THAT.

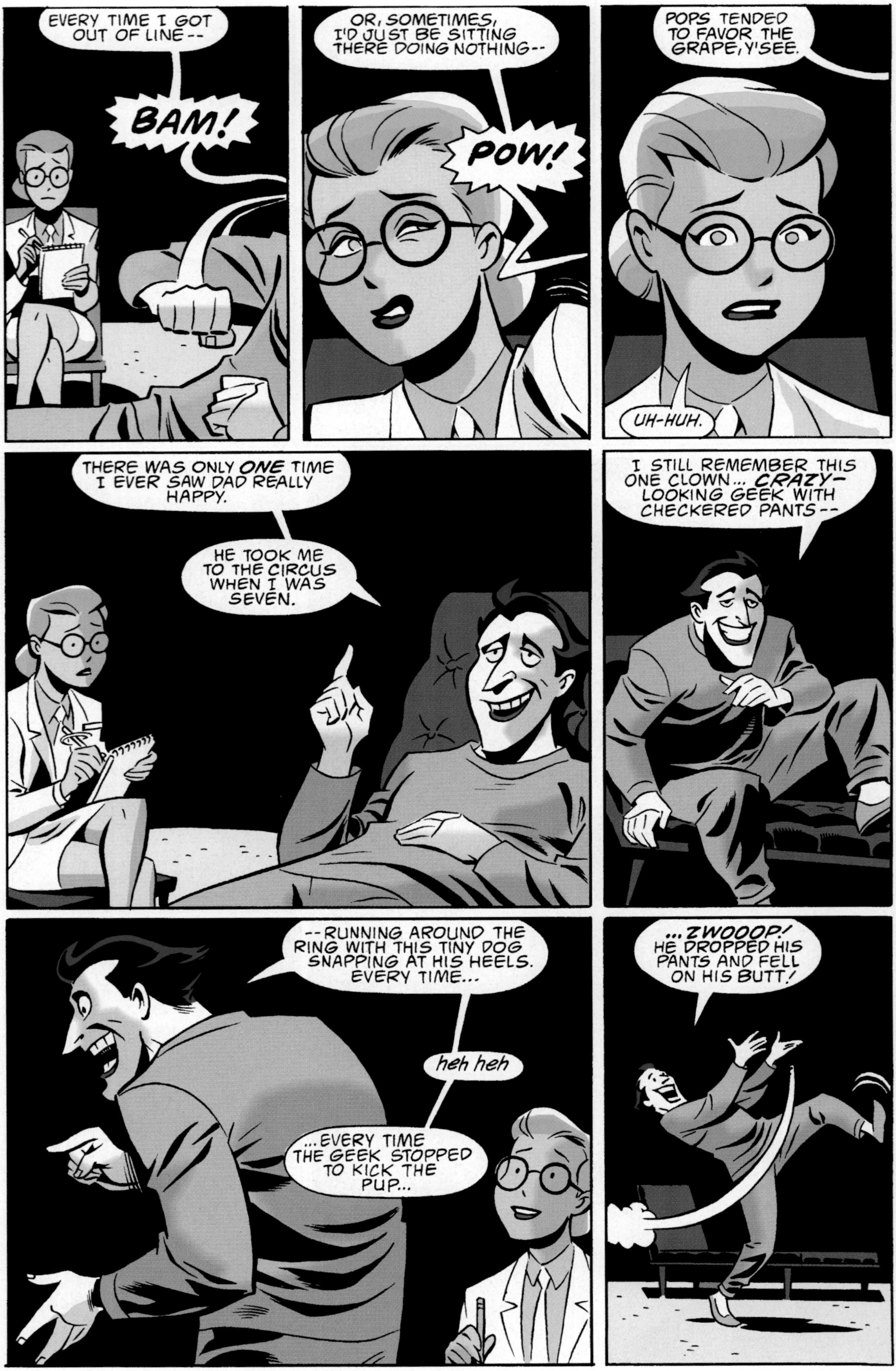
EVERY TIME I GOT OUT OF LINE--
BAM!
OR, SOMETIMES, I'D JUST BE SITTING THERE DOING NOTHING--
POW!
POPS TENDED TO FAVOR THE GRAPE, Y'SEE.
UH-HUH.
THERE WAS ONLY ONE TIME I EVER SAW DAD REALLY HAPPY.
HE TOOK ME TO THE CIRCUS WHEN I WAS SEVEN.
I STILL REMEMBER THIS ONE CLOWN... CRAZY-LOOKING GEEK WITH CHECKERED PANTS--
--RUNNING AROUND THE RING WITH THIS TINY DOG SNAPPING AT HIS HEELS. EVERY TIME...
heh heh
...EVERY TIME THE GEEK STOPPED TO KICK THE PUP...
...ZWOOOP! HE DROPPED HIS PANTS AND FELL ON HIS BUTT!

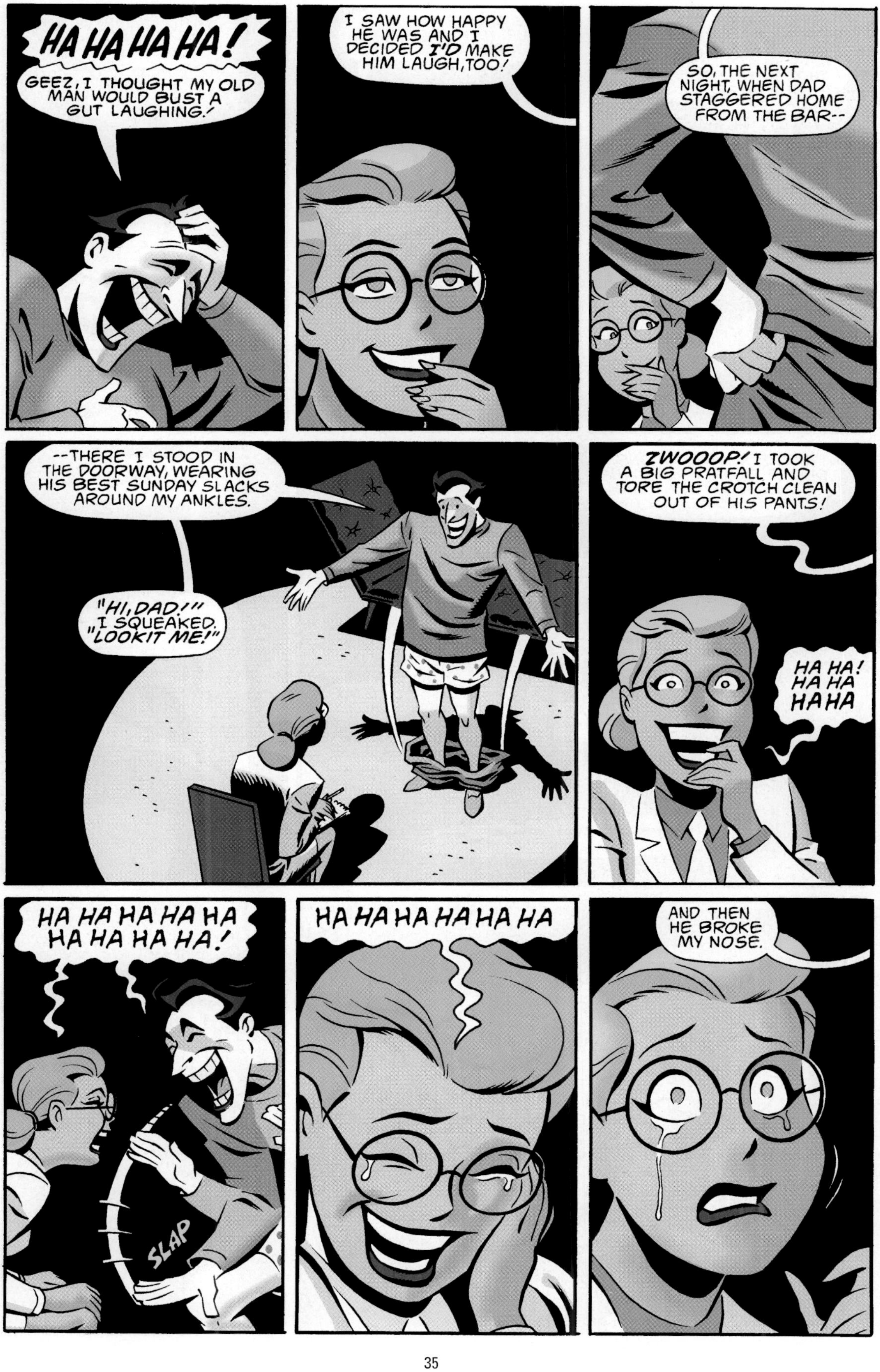
HA HA HA HA HA!
GEEZ, I THOUGHT MY OLD MAN WOULD BUST A GUT LAUGHING!
I SAW HOW HAPPY HE WAS AND I DECIDED I'D MAKE HIM LAUGH, TOO!
SO, THE NEXT NIGHT, WHEN DAD STAGGERED HOME FROM THE BAR--
--THERE I STOOD IN THE DOORWAY, WEARING HIS BEST SUNDAY SLACKS AROUND MY ANKLES.
"HI, DAD!" I SQUEAKED. "LOOKIT ME!"
ZWOOOP! I TOOK A BIG PRATFALL AND TORE THE CROTCH CLEAN OUT OF HIS PANTS!
HA HA! HA HA HA HA
HA HA HA HA HA HA HA HA HA HA!
SLAP
HA HA HA HA HA HA HA HA
AND THEN HE BROKE MY NOSE.

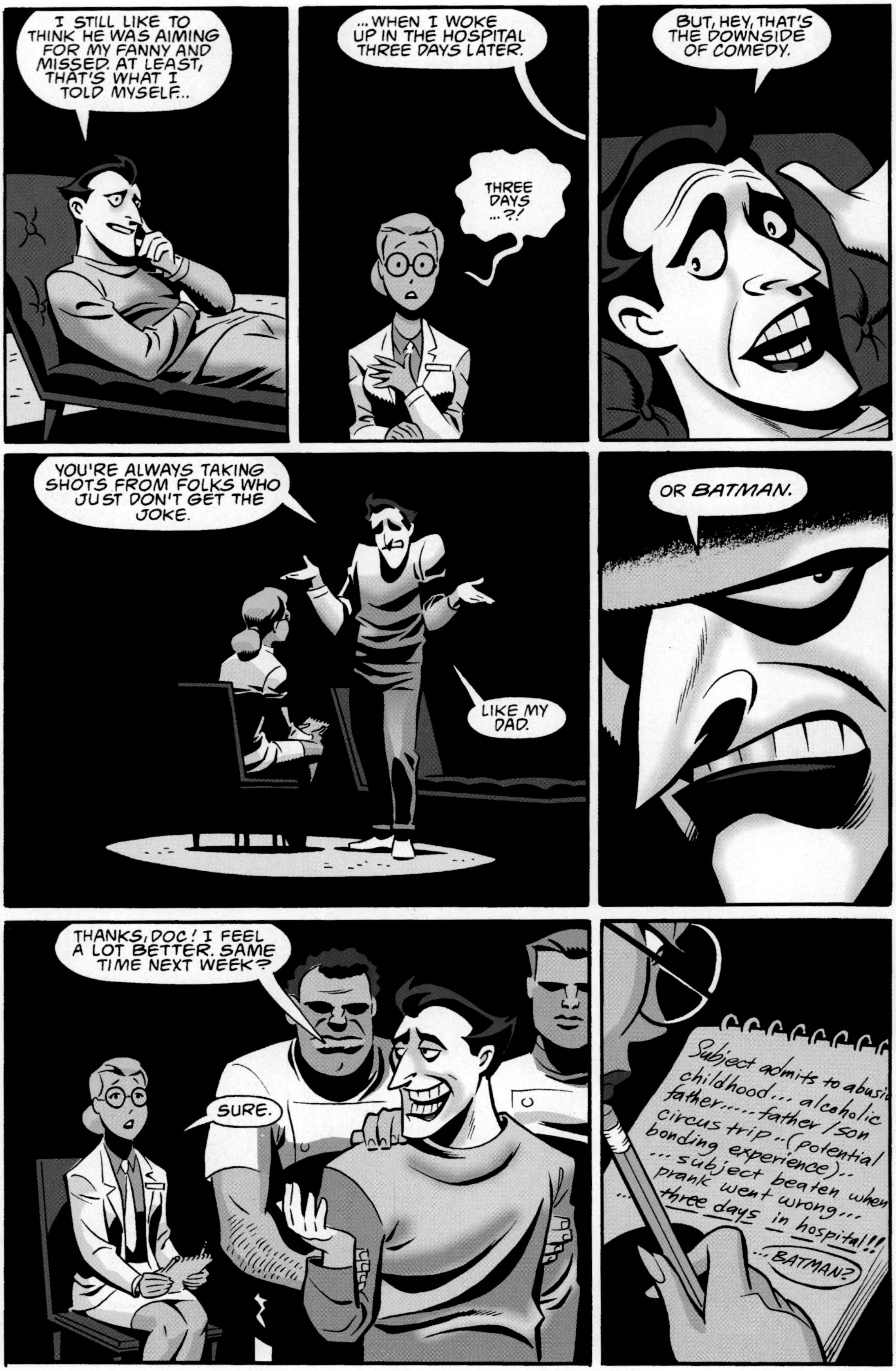
I STILL LIKE TO THINK HE WAS AIMING FOR MY FANNY AND MISSED. AT LEAST, THAT'S WHAT I TOLD MYSELF...
...WHEN I WOKE UP IN THE HOSPITAL THREE DAYS LATER.
THREE DAYS ...?!
BUT, HEY, THAT'S THE DOWNSIDE OF COMEDY.
YOU'RE ALWAYS TAKING SHOTS FROM FOLKS WHO JUST DON'T GET THE JOKE.
LIKE MY DAD.
OR BATMAN.
THANKS, DOC! I FEEL A LOT BETTER. SAME TIME NEXT WEEK?
SURE.
Subject admits to abusi childhood... alcoholic father.....father/son circus trip..(potential bonding experience).. ...subject beaten when prank went wrong... ...three days in hospital!!
...BATMAN?

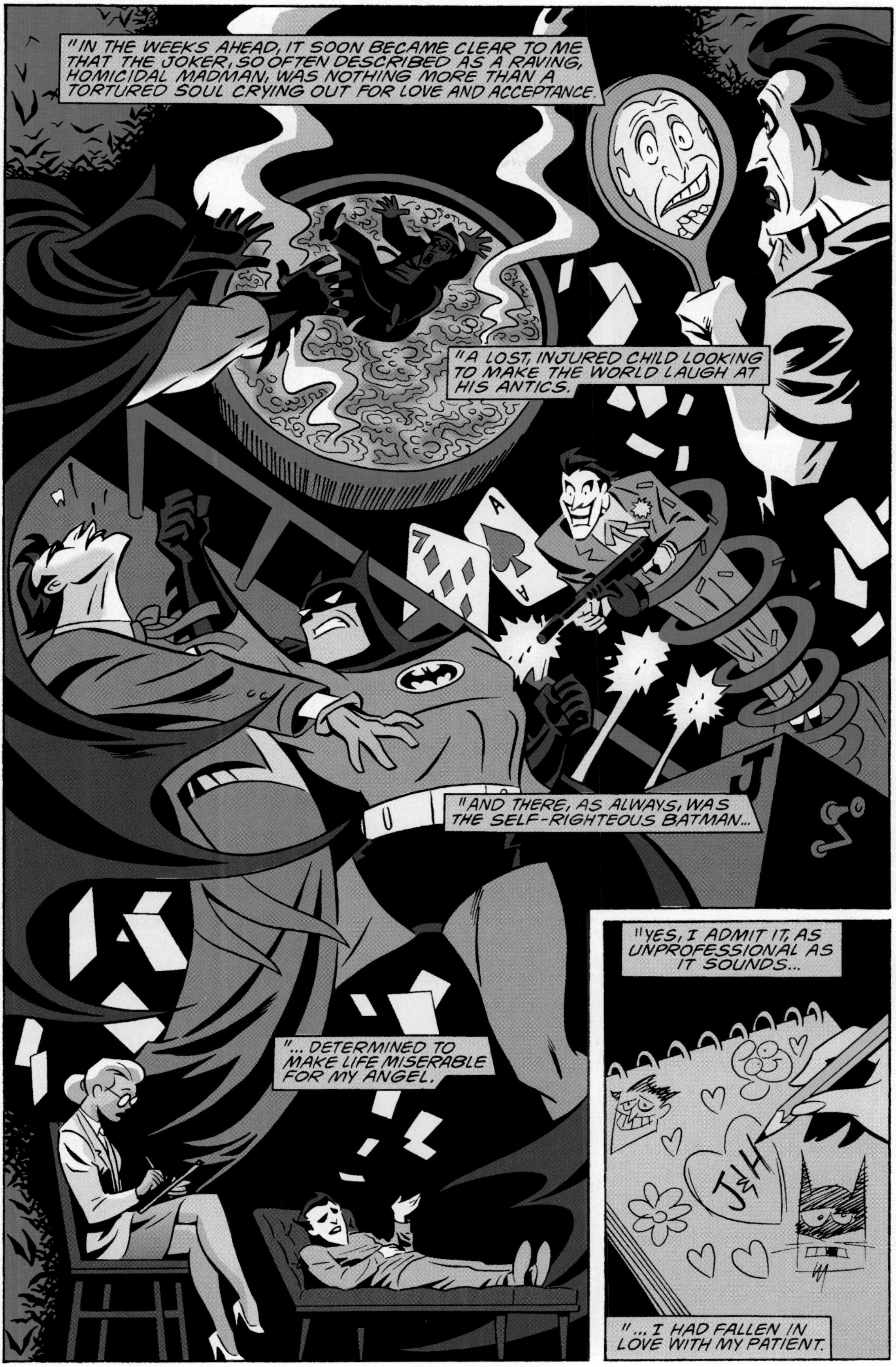
"IN THE WEEKS AHEAD, IT SOON BECAME CLEAR TO ME THAT THE JOKER, SO OFTEN DESCRIBED AS A RAVING, HOMICIDAL MADMAN, WAS NOTHING MORE THAN A TORTURED SOUL CRYING OUT FOR LOVE AND ACCEPTANCE.
"A LOST, INJURED CHILD LOOKING TO MAKE THE WORLD LAUGH AT HIS ANTICS.
"AND THERE, AS ALWAYS, WAS THE SELF-RIGHTEOUS BATMAN...
"... DETERMINED TO MAKE LIFE MISERABLE FOR MY ANGEL.
"YES, I ADMIT IT, AS UNPROFESSIONAL AS IT SOUNDS...
J♥H
"... I HAD FALLEN IN LOVE WITH MY PATIENT.

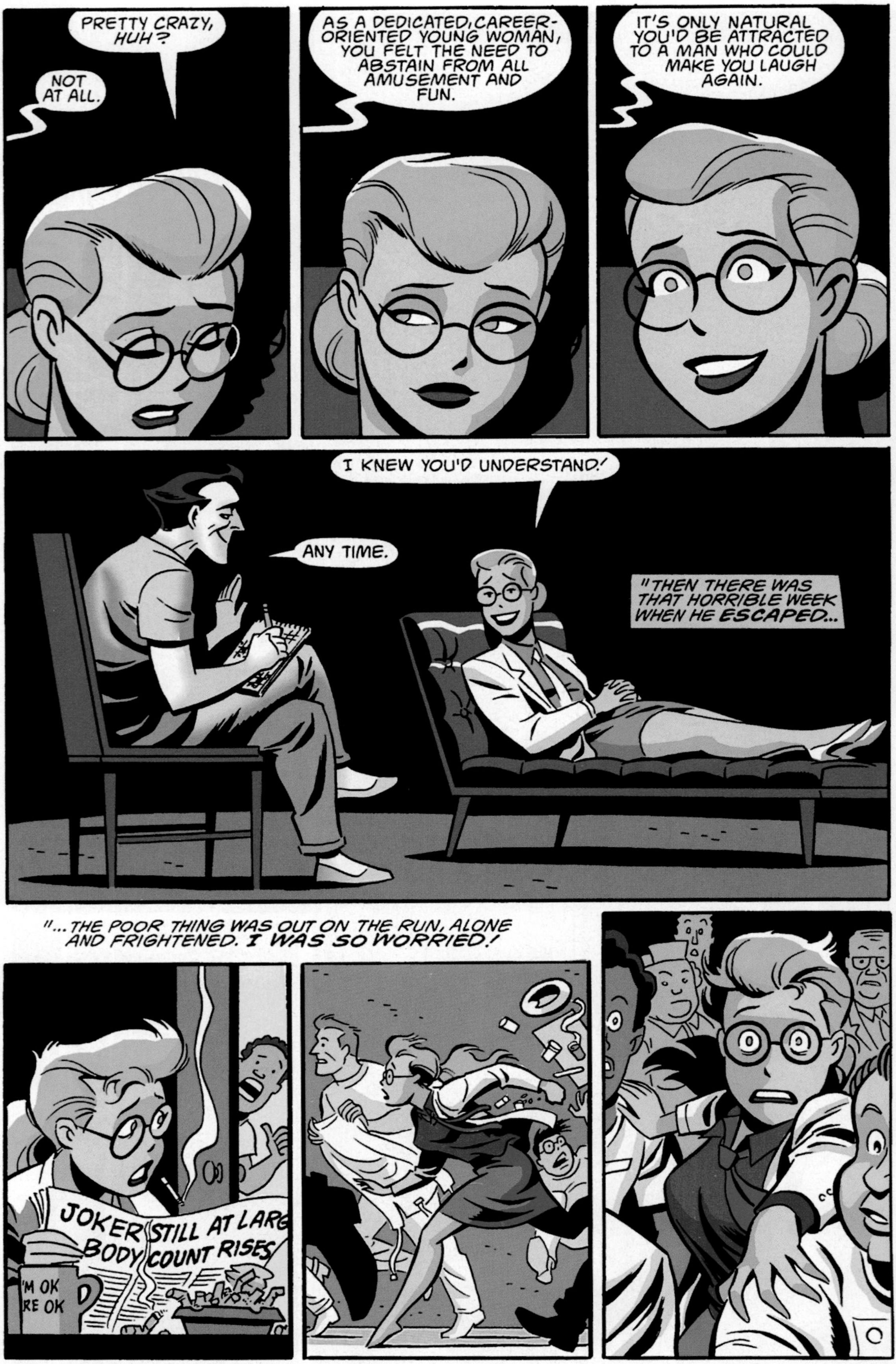

PRETTY CRAZY, HUH?
NOT AT ALL.
AS A DEDICATED, CAREER-ORIENTED YOUNG WOMAN, YOU FELT THE NEED TO ABSTAIN FROM ALL AMUSEMENT AND FUN.
IT'S ONLY NATURAL YOU'D BE ATTRACTED TO A MAN WHO COULD MAKE YOU LAUGH AGAIN.
I KNEW YOU'D UNDERSTAND!
ANY TIME.
"THEN THERE WAS THAT HORRIBLE WEEK WHEN HE ESCAPED...
"...THE POOR THING WAS OUT ON THE RUN, ALONE AND FRIGHTENED. I WAS SO WORRIED!
JOKER STILL AT LAR
BODY COUNT RISES
'M OK
RE OK

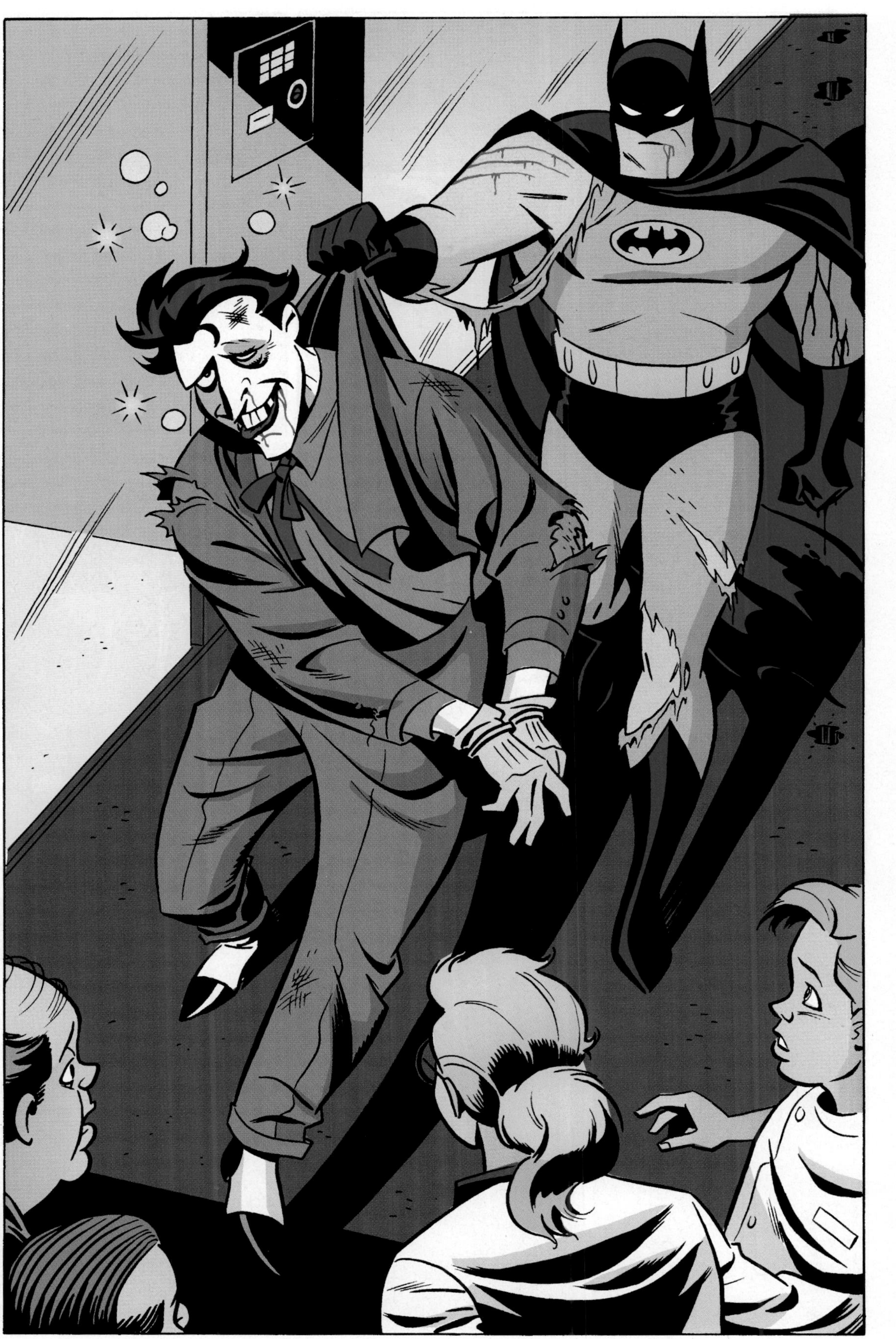

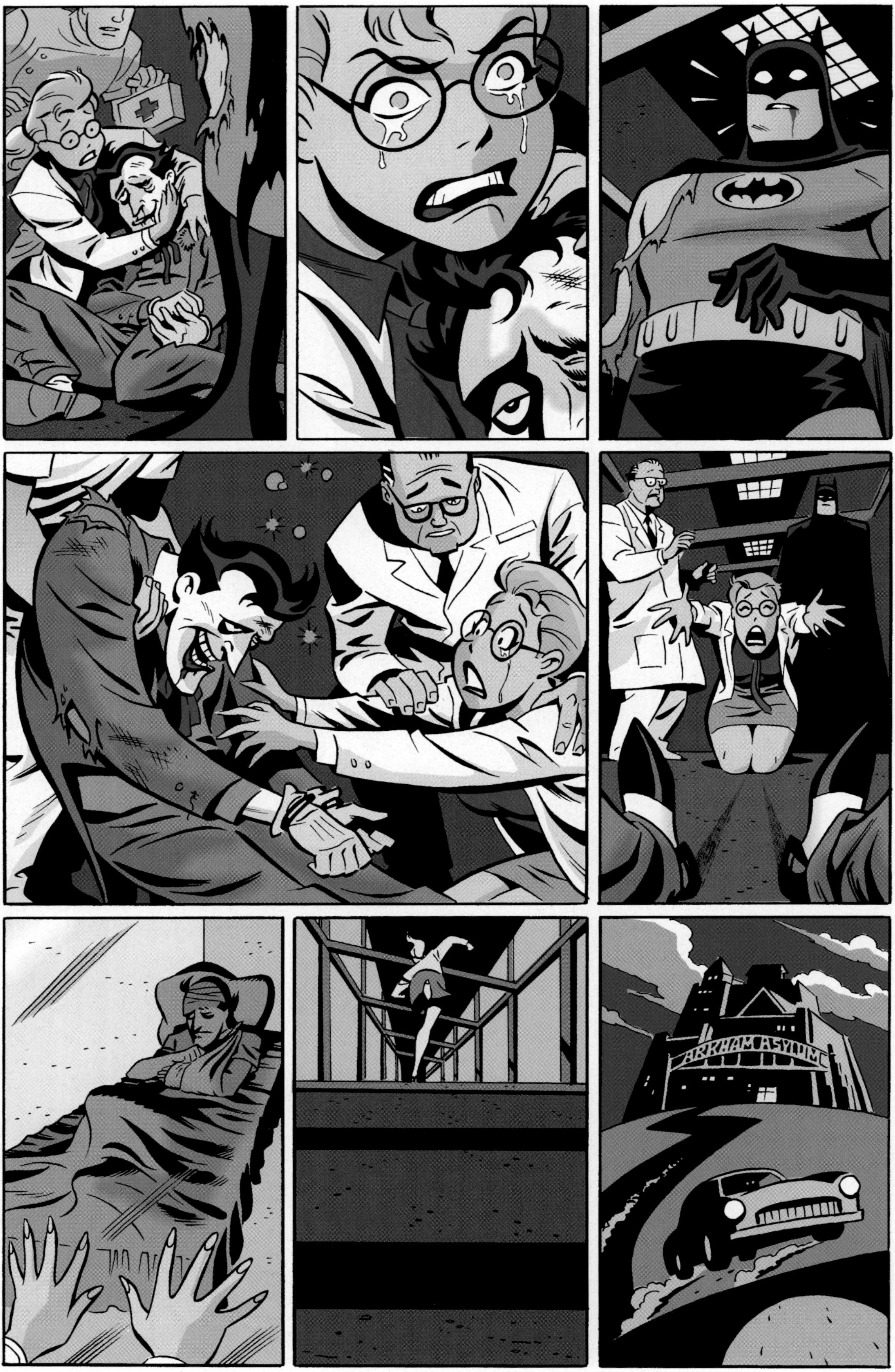
ARKHAM ASYLUM

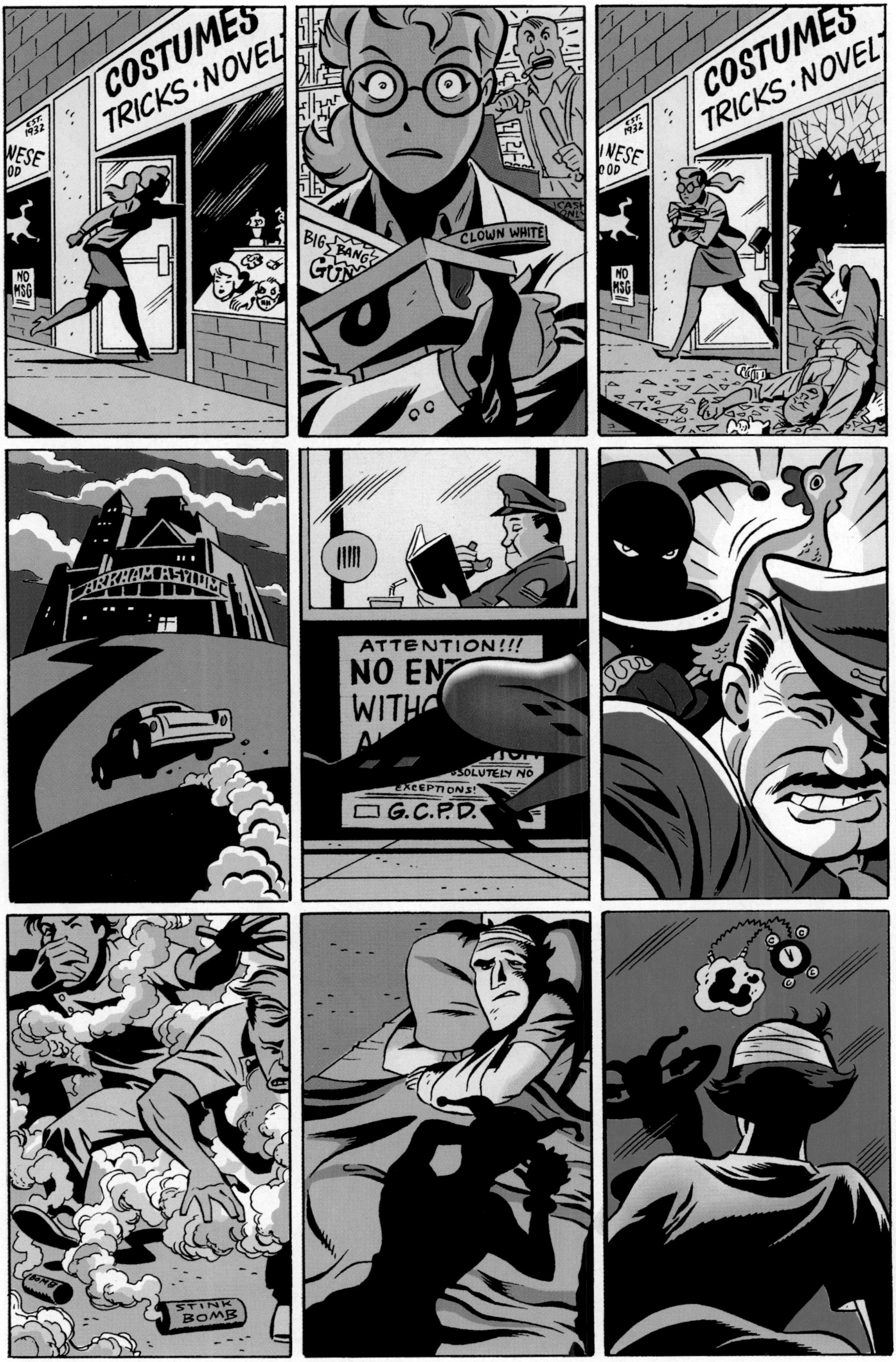
COSTUMES
TRICKS · NOVEL
EST. 1932
NESE
OD
NO MSG
BIG BANG GUN
CLOWN WHITE
CASH ONLY
COSTUMES
TRICKS · NOVEL
EST. 1932
NESE
OD
NO MSG
ARKHAM ASYLUM
ATTENTION!!!
NO ENT
WITHO
EXCEPTIONS!
G.C.P.D.
BOMB
STINK BOMB

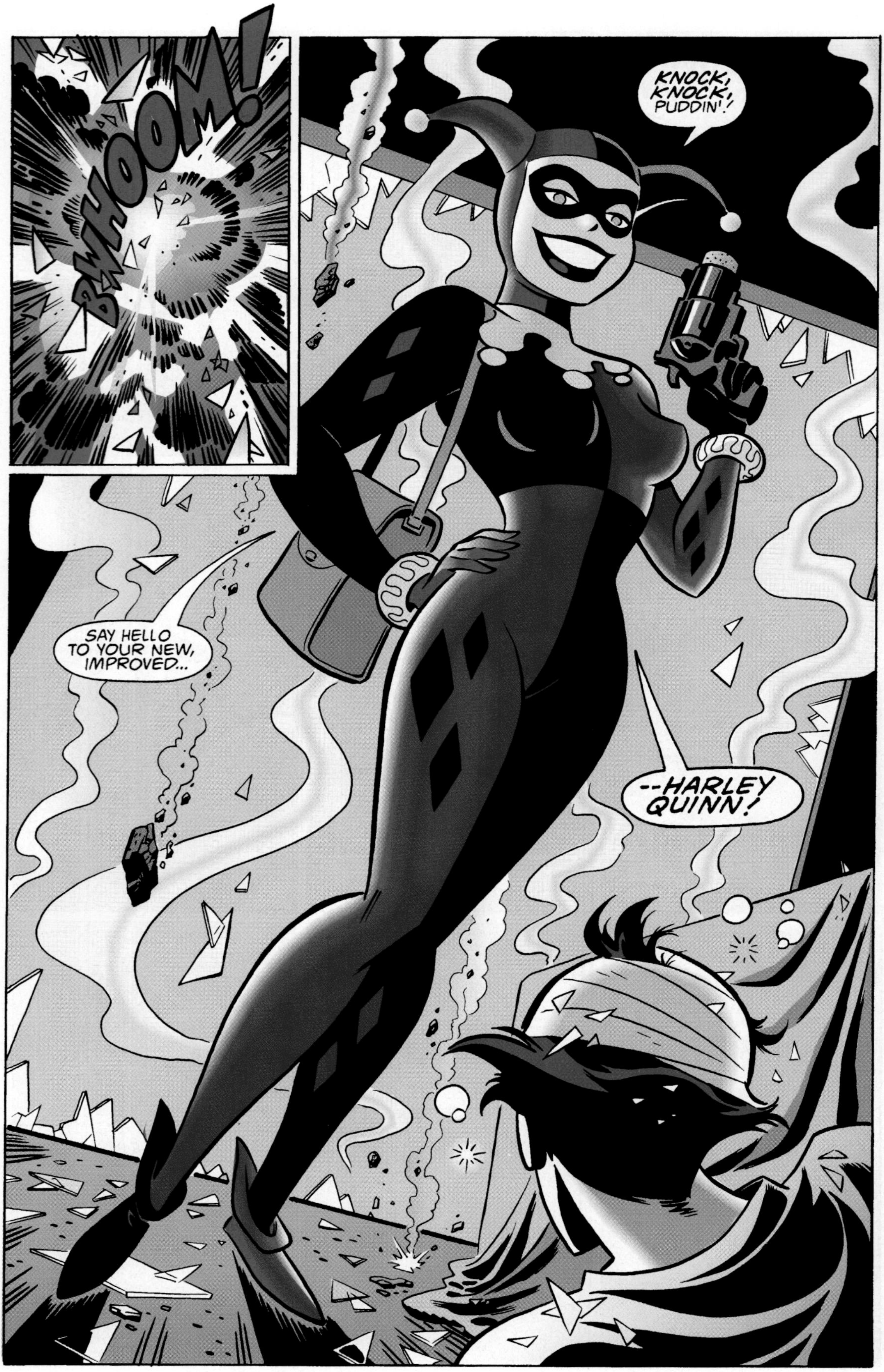
BWHOOM!
KNOCK, KNOCK, PUDDIN'!
SAY HELLO TO YOUR NEW, IMPROVED...
--HARLEY QUINN!

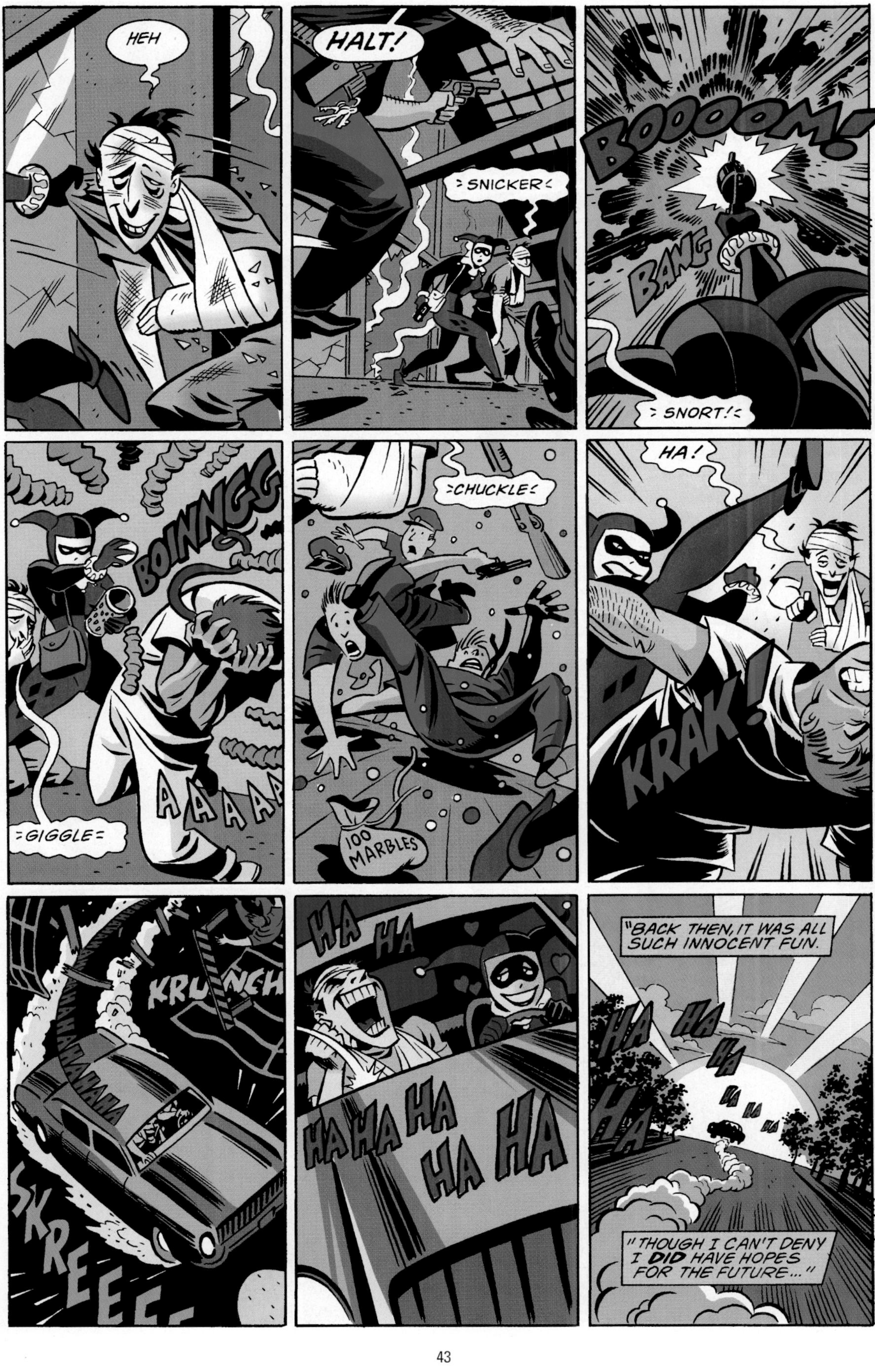
HEH
HALT!
SNICKER
BOOOOOM!
BANG
SNORT!
BOINNGG
GIGGLE
AAAAA
CHUCKLE
100 MARBLES
HA!
KRAK!
KRUNCH
HAHAHAHAHAHAHA
SKREEEE
HA HA
HA HA HA HA HA HA
"BACK THEN, IT WAS ALL SUCH INNOCENT FUN.
HA HA HA HA HA HA HA HA HA HA
"THOUGH I CAN'T DENY I **DID** HAVE HOPES FOR THE FUTURE..."

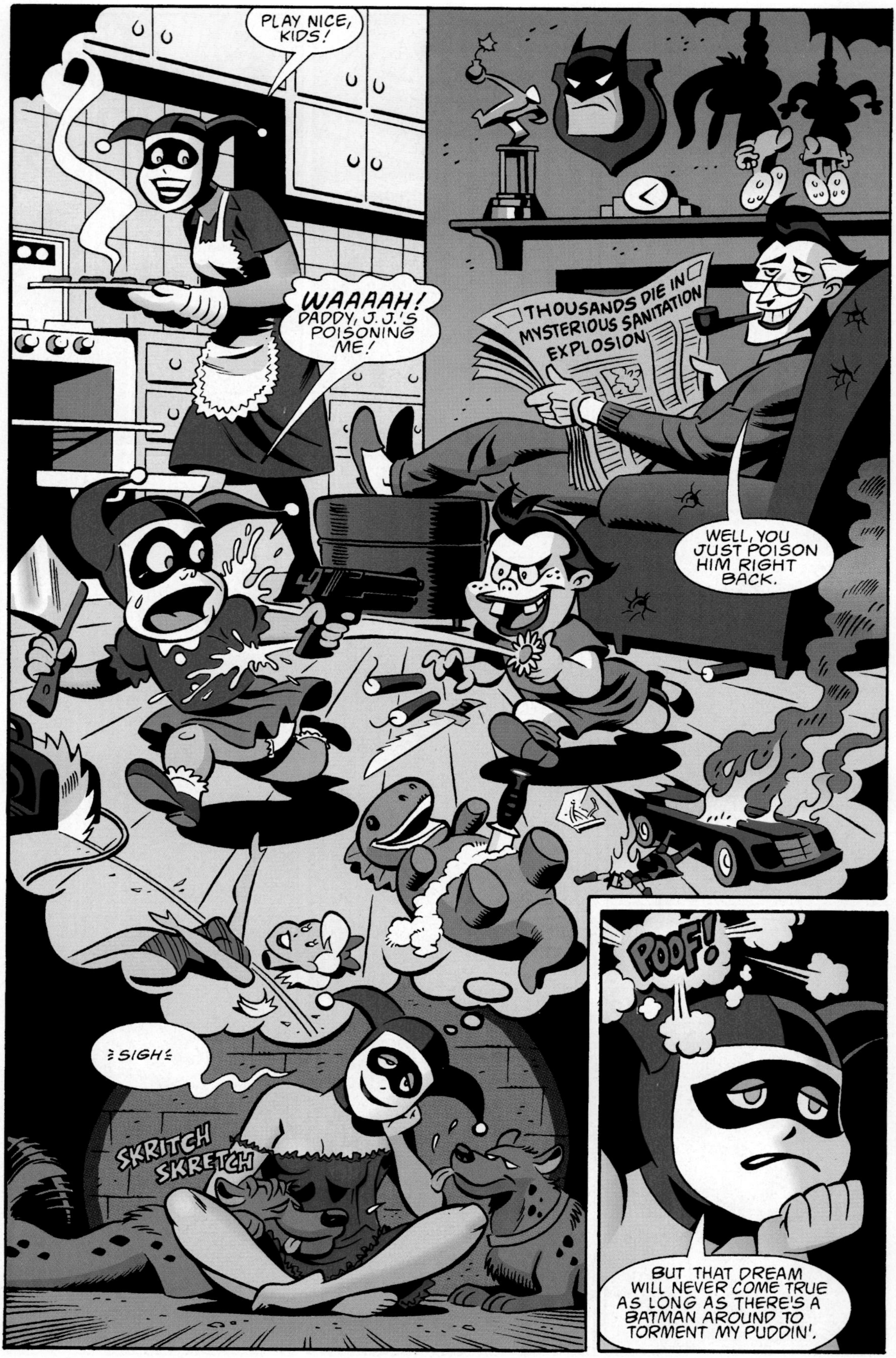
PLAY NICE, KIDS!
WAAAAH! DADDY, J.J.'S POISONING ME!
THOUSANDS DIE IN MYSTERIOUS SANITATION EXPLOSION
WELL, YOU JUST POISON HIM RIGHT BACK.
POOF!
≷SIGH≶
SKRITCH SKRETCH
BUT THAT DREAM WILL NEVER COME TRUE AS LONG AS THERE'S A BATMAN AROUND TO TORMENT MY PUDDIN'.

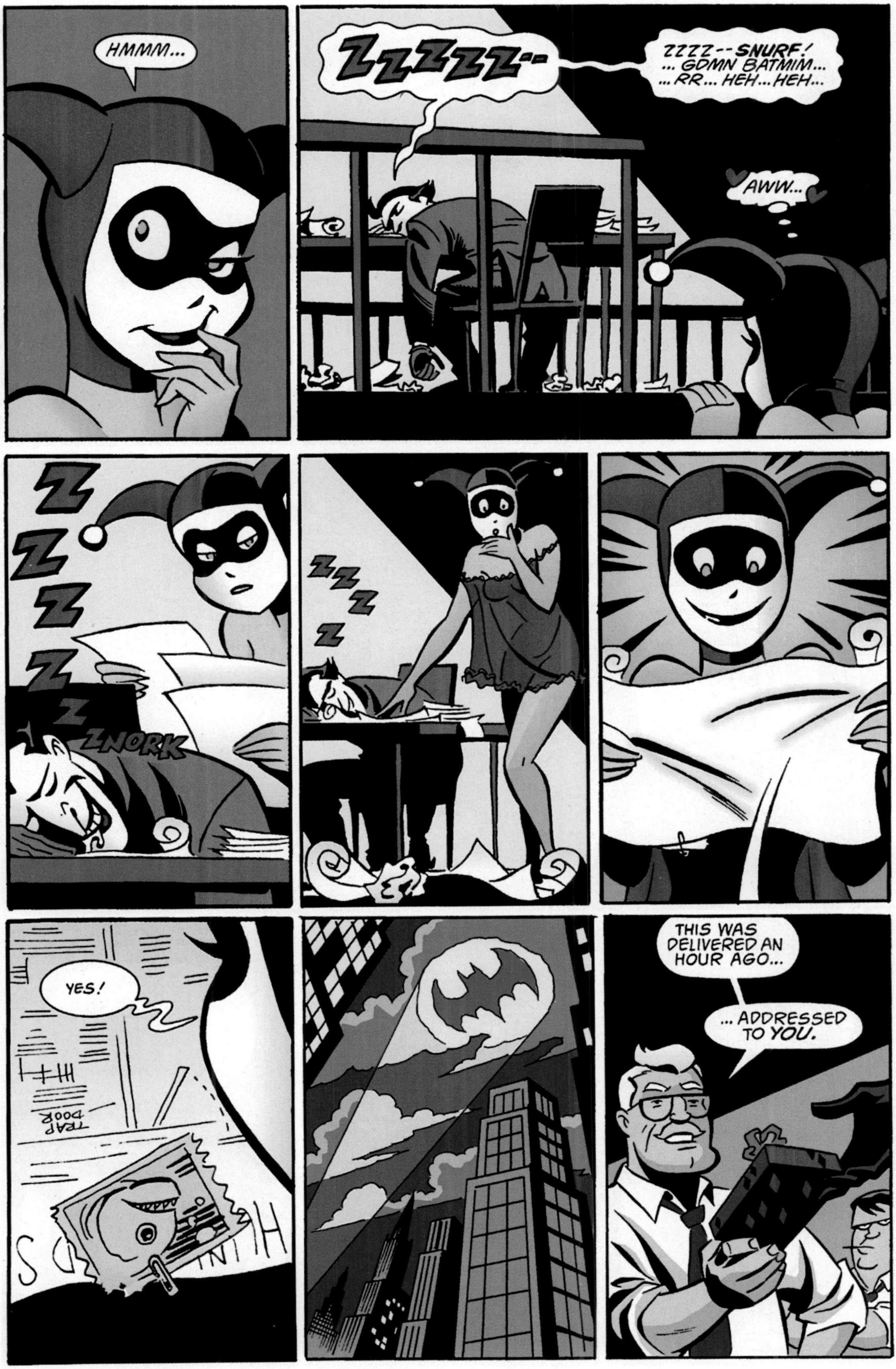
HMMM...
ZZZZZZ--
ZZZZ--SNURF! ...GDMN BATMIM... ...RR... HEH...HEH...
AWW...
ZZZZZ
ZNORK
ZZZZ
YES!
TRAP DOOR
THIS WAS DELIVERED AN HOUR AGO...
...ADDRESSED TO YOU.

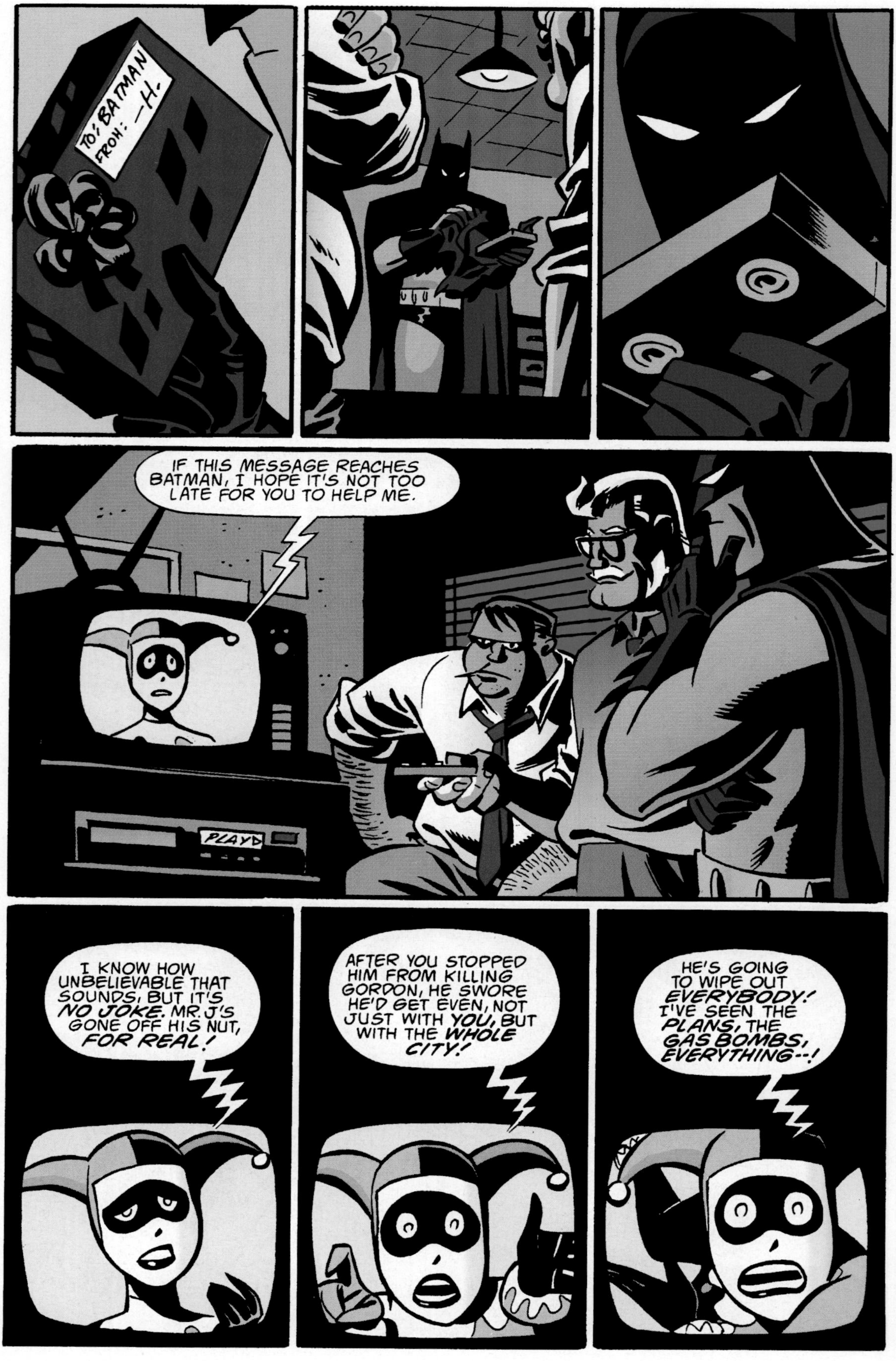
TO: BATMAN
FROM: —H.
IF THIS MESSAGE REACHES BATMAN, I HOPE IT'S NOT TOO LATE FOR YOU TO HELP ME.
PLAY
I KNOW HOW UNBELIEVABLE THAT SOUNDS, BUT IT'S NO JOKE. MR. J'S GONE OFF HIS NUT, FOR REAL!
AFTER YOU STOPPED HIM FROM KILLING GORDON, HE SWORE HE'D GET EVEN, NOT JUST WITH YOU, BUT WITH THE WHOLE CITY!
HE'S GOING TO WIPE OUT EVERYBODY! I'VE SEEN THE PLANS, THE GAS BOMBS, EVERYTHING--!

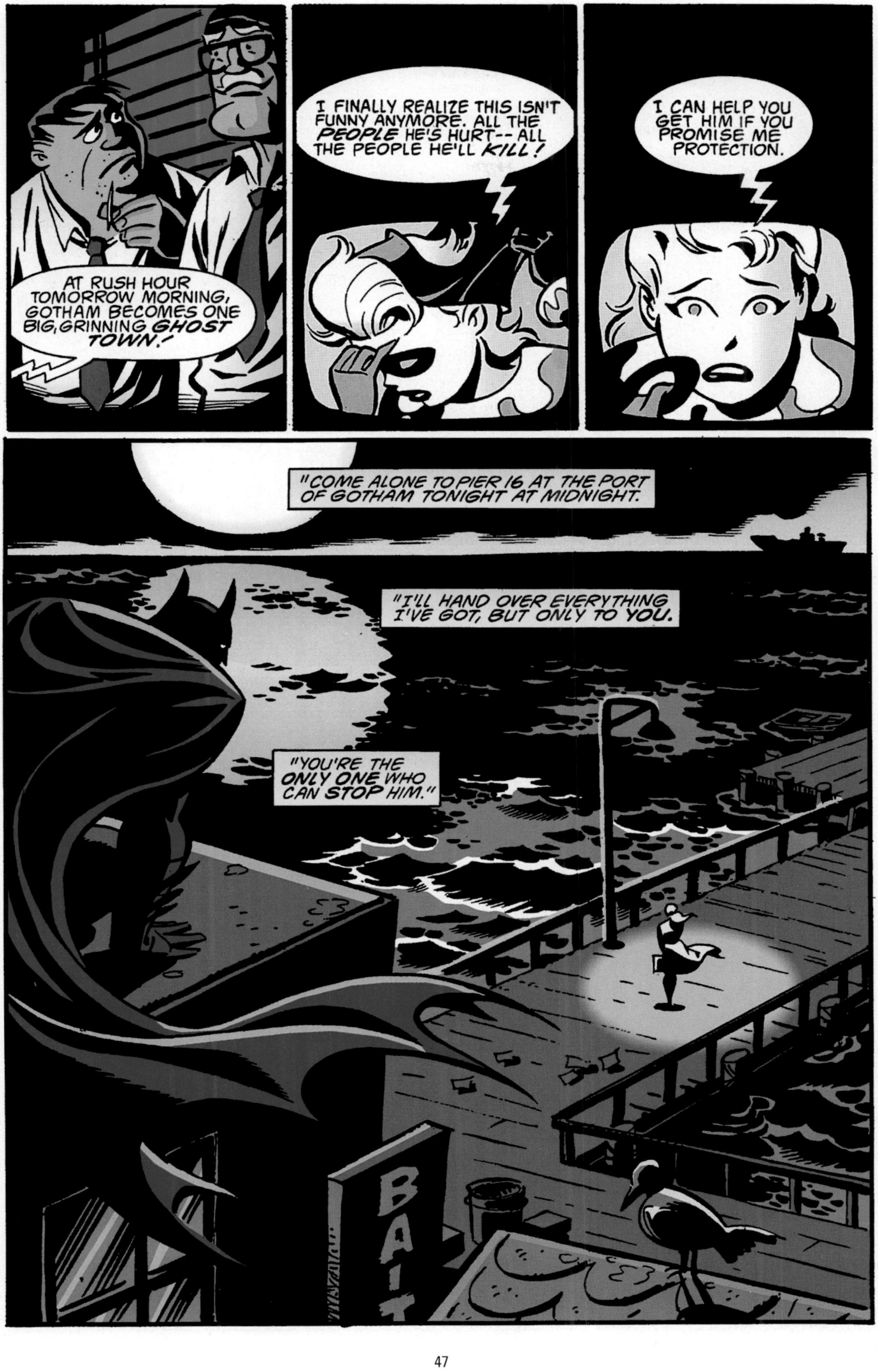
AT RUSH HOUR TOMORROW MORNING, GOTHAM BECOMES ONE BIG, GRINNING GHOST TOWN!
I FINALLY REALIZE THIS ISN'T FUNNY ANYMORE. ALL THE PEOPLE HE'S HURT-- ALL THE PEOPLE HE'LL KILL!
I CAN HELP YOU GET HIM IF YOU PROMISE ME PROTECTION.
"COME ALONE TO PIER 16 AT THE PORT OF GOTHAM TONIGHT AT MIDNIGHT.
"I'LL HAND OVER EVERYTHING I'VE GOT, BUT ONLY TO YOU.
"YOU'RE THE ONLY ONE WHO CAN STOP HIM."
BAIT

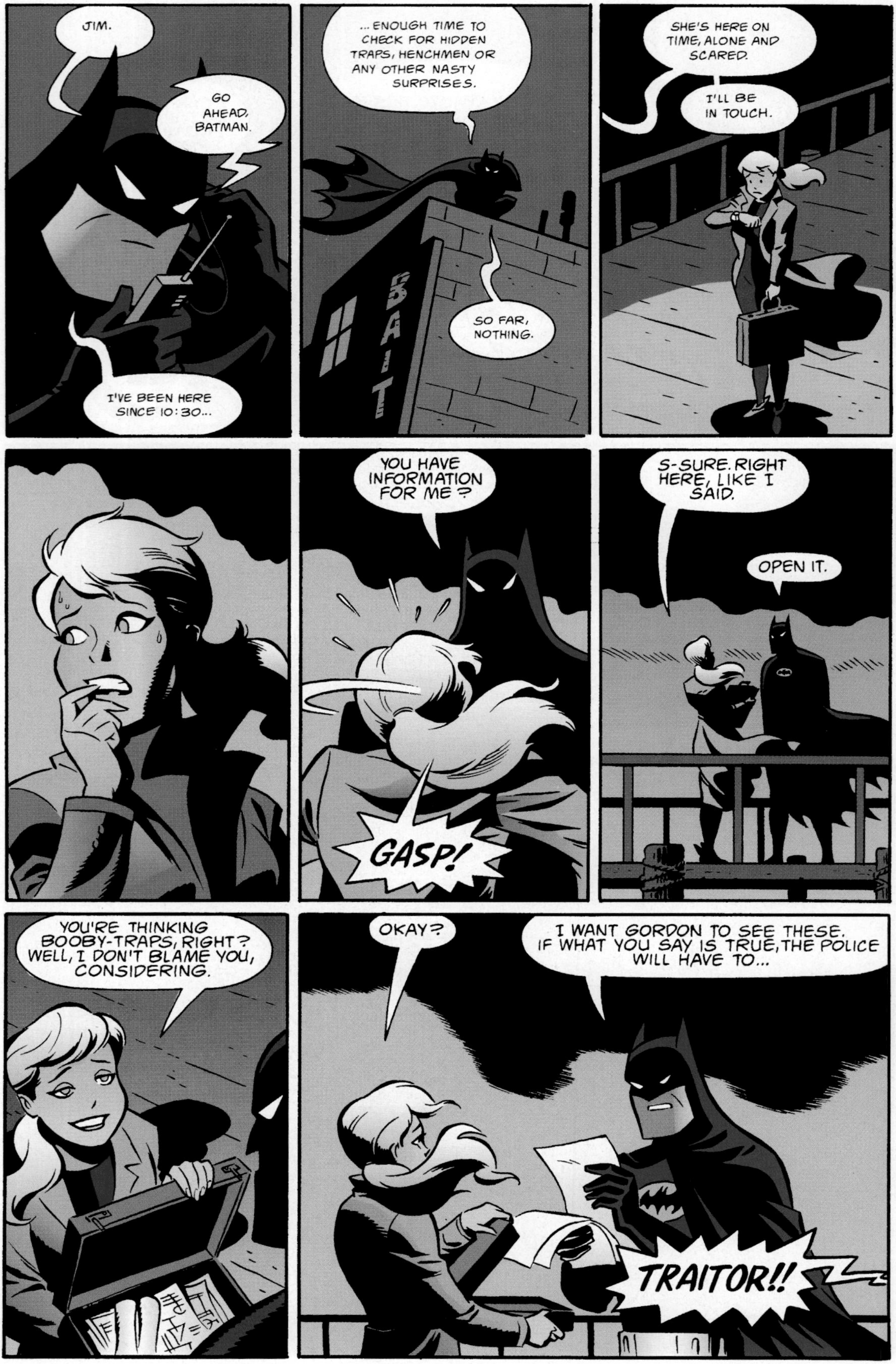
JIM.
GO AHEAD, BATMAN.
I'VE BEEN HERE SINCE 10:30...
...ENOUGH TIME TO CHECK FOR HIDDEN TRAPS, HENCHMEN OR ANY OTHER NASTY SURPRISES.
BAIT
SO FAR, NOTHING.
SHE'S HERE ON TIME, ALONE AND SCARED.
I'LL BE IN TOUCH.
YOU HAVE INFORMATION FOR ME?
GASP!
S-SURE. RIGHT HERE, LIKE I SAID.
OPEN IT.
YOU'RE THINKING BOOBY-TRAPS, RIGHT? WELL, I DON'T BLAME YOU, CONSIDERING.
OKAY?
I WANT GORDON TO SEE THESE. IF WHAT YOU SAY IS TRUE, THE POLICE WILL HAVE TO...
TRAITOR!!

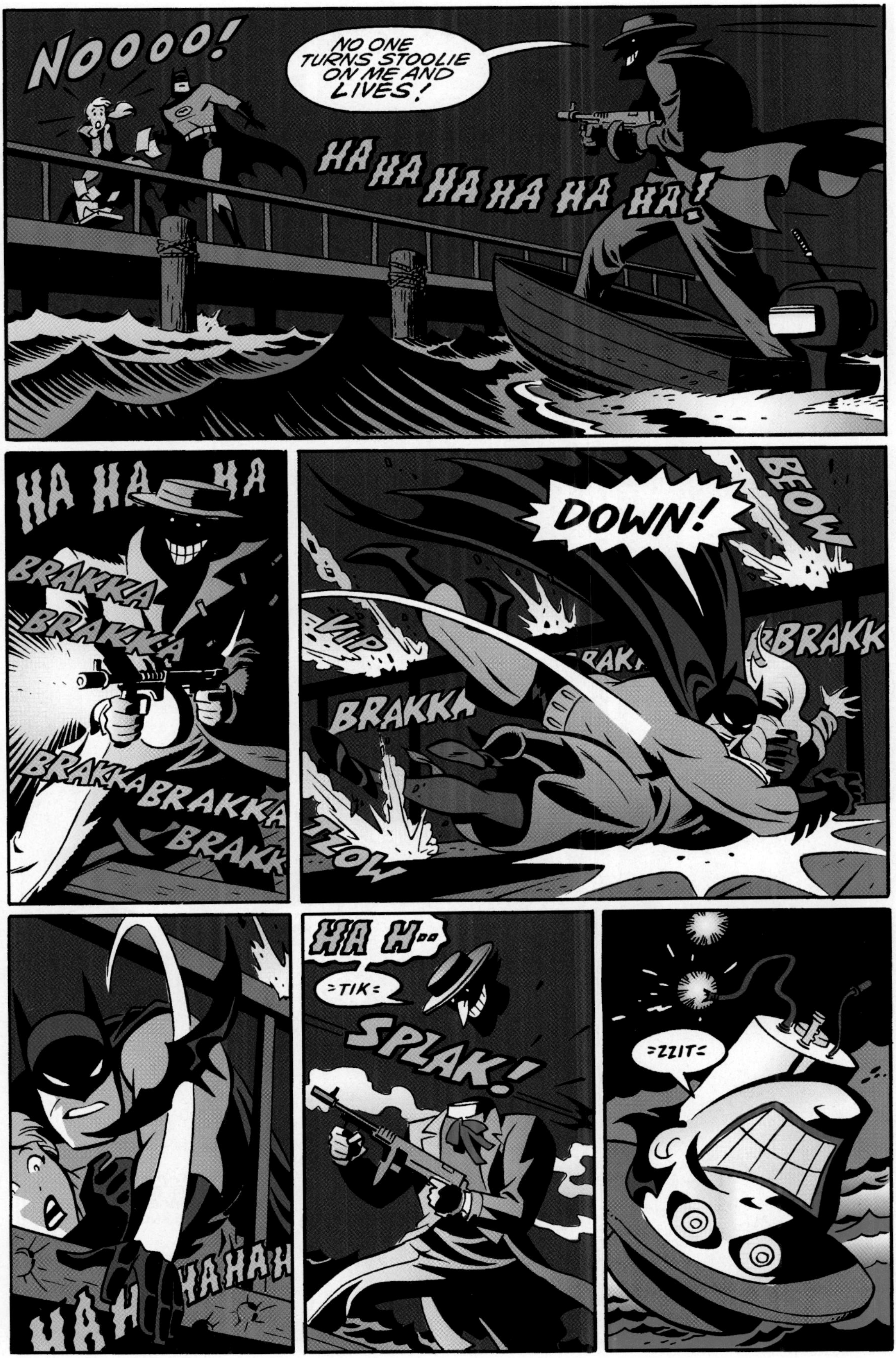
NOOOO!
NO ONE TURNS STOOLIE ON ME AND LIVES!
HA HA HA HA HA HA HA!
HA HA HA
BRAKKA
BRAKKA
BRAKKABRAKKA
BRAKK
DOWN!
BEOW
VIP
BRAKK
BRAKKA
TZOW
HAHAHAH
HA H..
=TIK=
SPLAK!
=ZZIT=

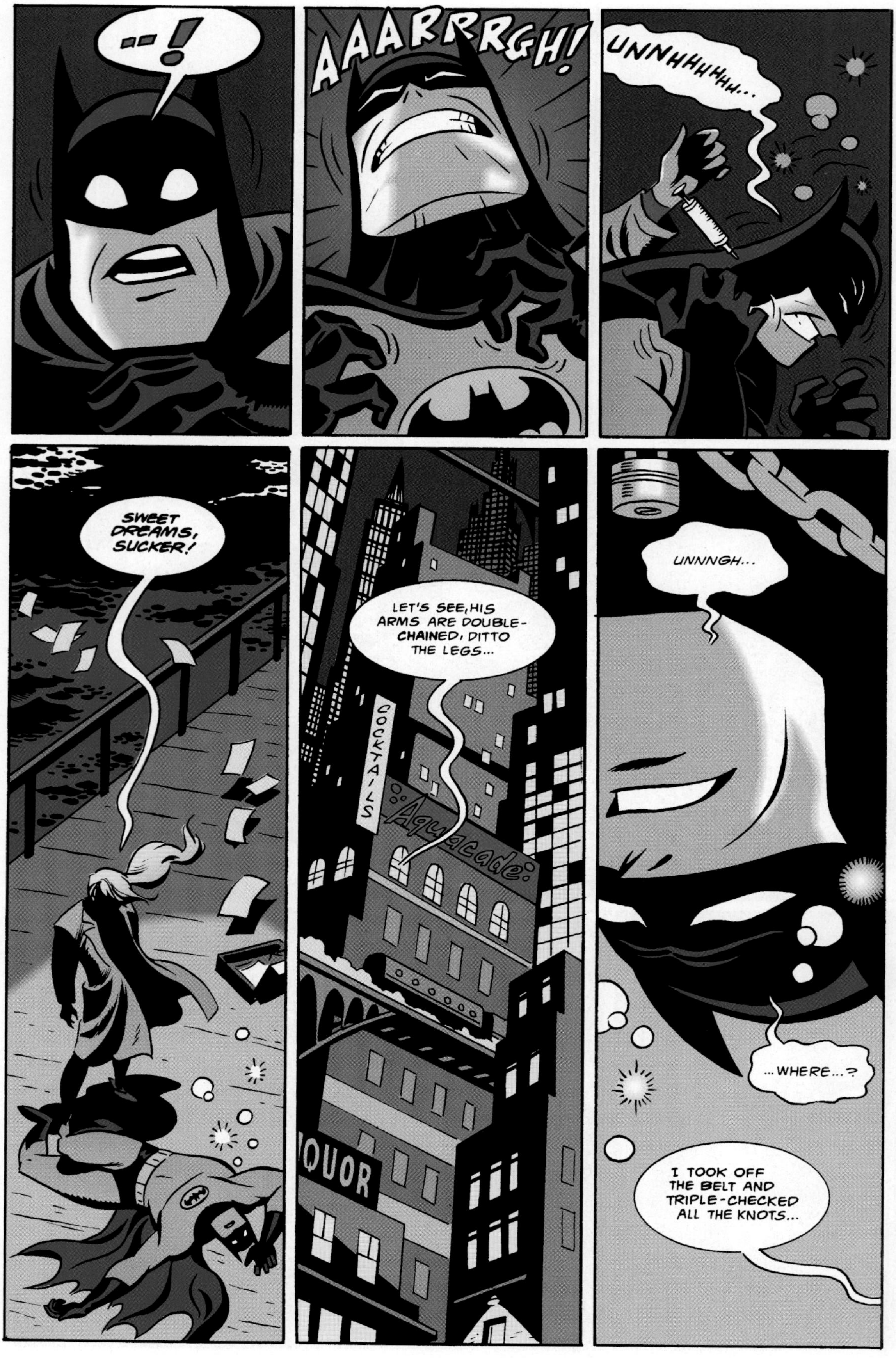
--!
AAARRRGH!
UNNHHHHH...
SWEET DREAMS, SUCKER!
LET'S SEE, HIS ARMS ARE DOUBLE-CHAINED, DITTO THE LEGS...
COCKTAILS
Aquacade
QUOR
UNNNGH...
...WHERE...?
I TOOK OFF THE BELT AND TRIPLE-CHECKED ALL THE KNOTS...

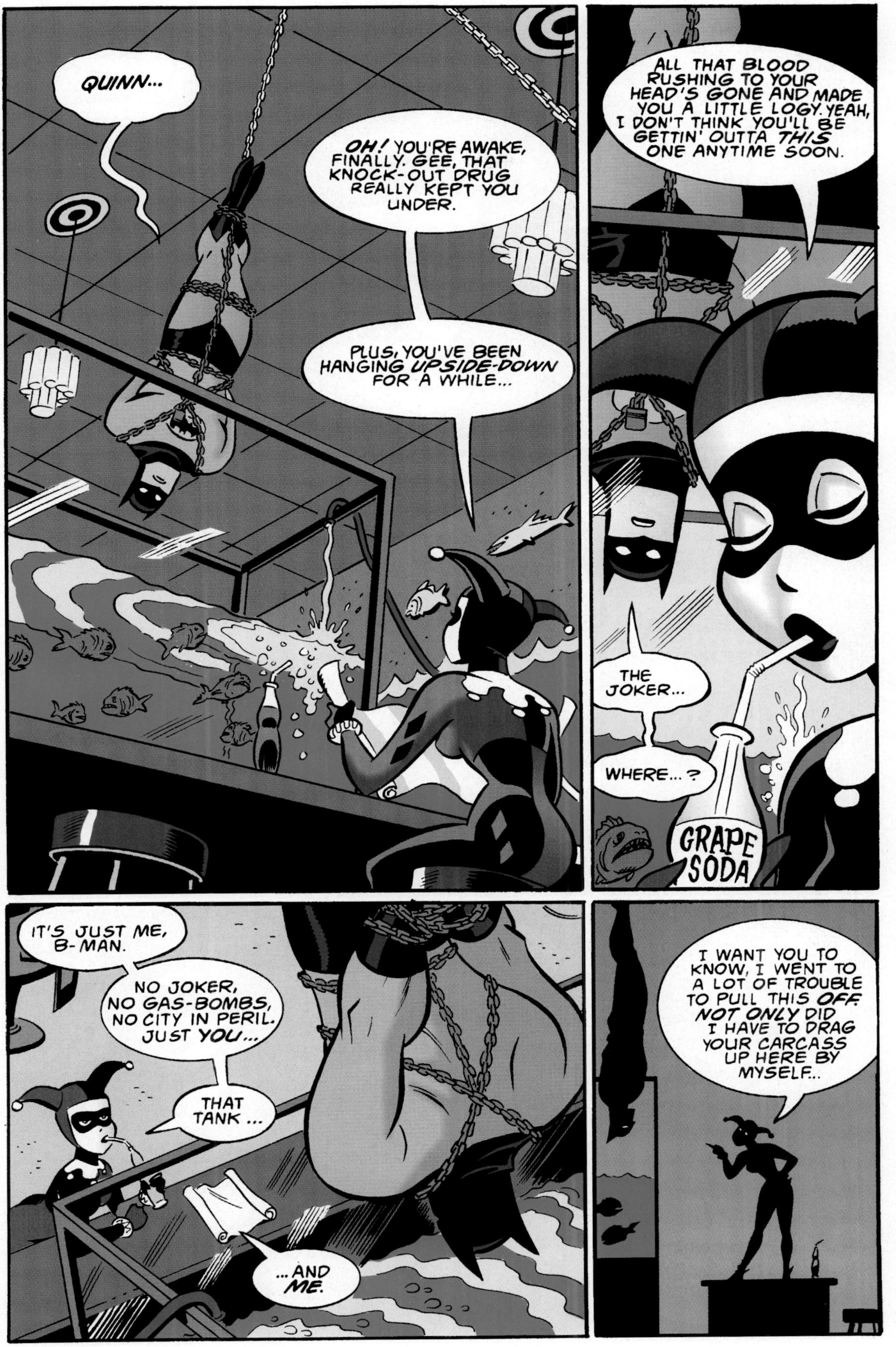
QUINN...
OH! YOU'RE AWAKE, FINALLY. GEE, THAT KNOCK-OUT DRUG REALLY KEPT YOU UNDER.
PLUS, YOU'VE BEEN HANGING UPSIDE-DOWN FOR A WHILE...
ALL THAT BLOOD RUSHING TO YOUR HEAD'S GONE AND MADE YOU A LITTLE LOGY. YEAH, I DON'T THINK YOU'LL BE GETTIN' OUTTA THIS ONE ANYTIME SOON.
THE JOKER...
WHERE...?
GRAPE SODA
IT'S JUST ME, B-MAN.
NO JOKER, NO GAS-BOMBS, NO CITY IN PERIL. JUST YOU...
THAT TANK ...
...AND ME.
I WANT YOU TO KNOW, I WENT TO A LOT OF TROUBLE TO PULL THIS OFF. NOT ONLY DID I HAVE TO DRAG YOUR CARCASS UP HERE BY MYSELF...

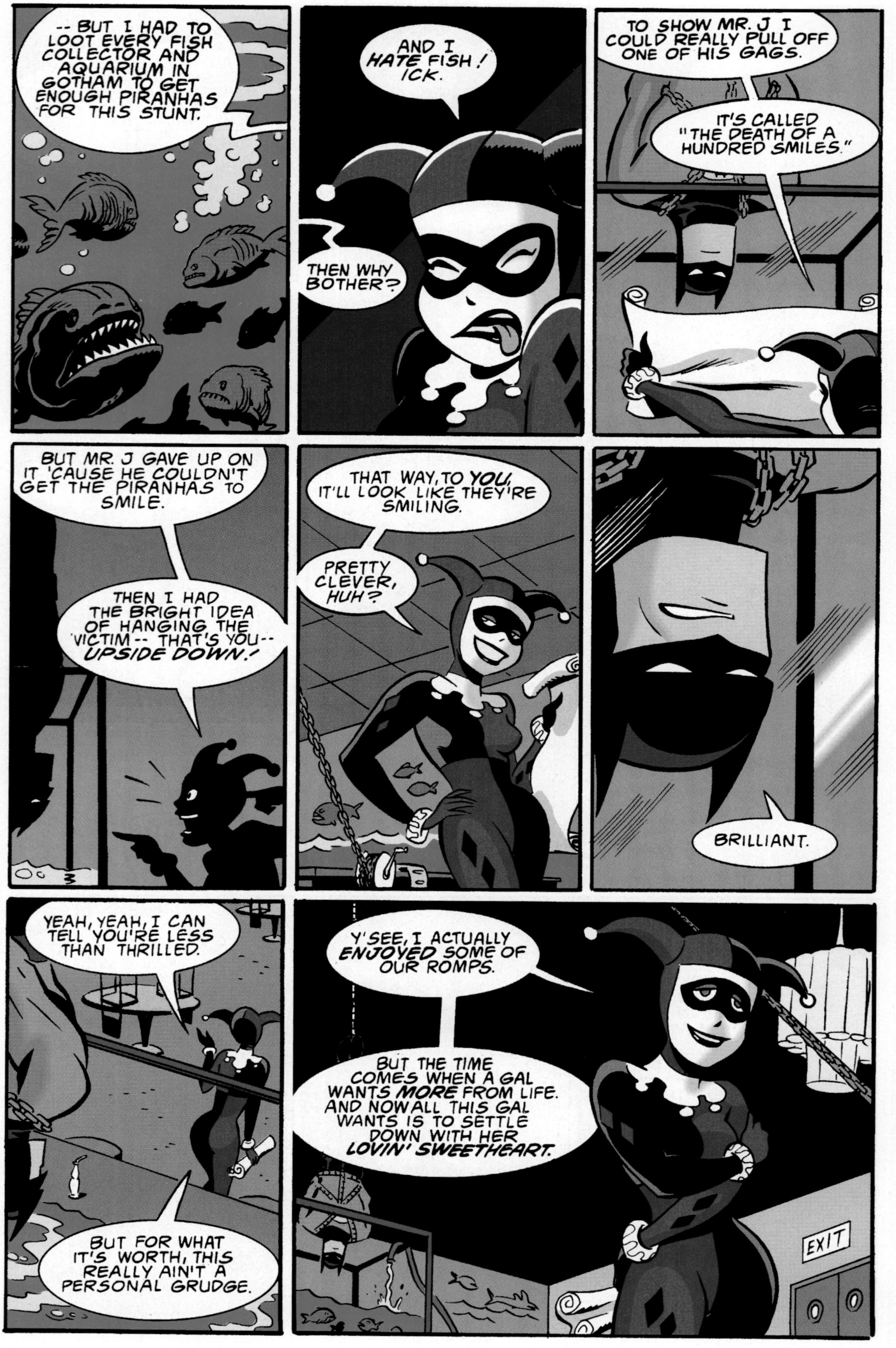
-- BUT I HAD TO LOOT EVERY FISH COLLECTOR AND AQUARIUM IN GOTHAM TO GET ENOUGH PIRANHAS FOR THIS STUNT.
AND I HATE FISH! ICK.
THEN WHY BOTHER?
TO SHOW MR. J I COULD REALLY PULL OFF ONE OF HIS GAGS.
IT'S CALLED "THE DEATH OF A HUNDRED SMILES."
BUT MR. J GAVE UP ON IT 'CAUSE HE COULDN'T GET THE PIRANHAS TO SMILE.
THEN I HAD THE BRIGHT IDEA OF HANGING THE VICTIM -- THAT'S YOU -- UPSIDE DOWN.!
THAT WAY, TO YOU, IT'LL LOOK LIKE THEY'RE SMILING.
PRETTY CLEVER, HUH?
BRILLIANT.
YEAH, YEAH, I CAN TELL YOU'RE LESS THAN THRILLED.
BUT FOR WHAT IT'S WORTH, THIS REALLY AIN'T A PERSONAL GRUDGE.
Y'SEE, I ACTUALLY ENJOYED SOME OF OUR ROMPS.
BUT THE TIME COMES WHEN A GAL WANTS MORE FROM LIFE. AND NOW ALL THIS GAL WANTS IS TO SETTLE DOWN WITH HER LOVIN' SWEETHEART.
EXIT

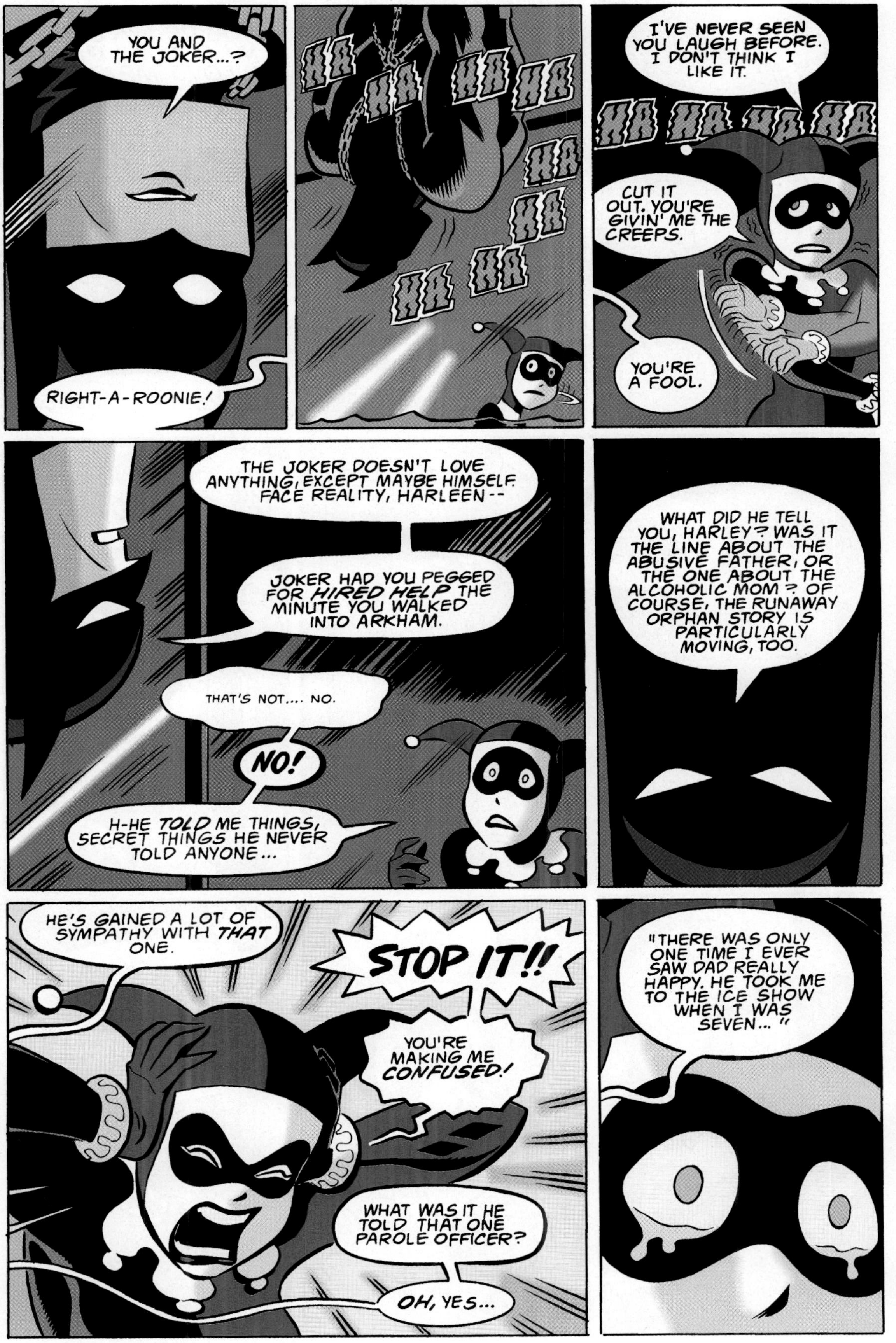
YOU AND THE JOKER...?
RIGHT-A-ROONIE!
HA HA HA HA HA HA HA HA HA
I'VE NEVER SEEN YOU LAUGH BEFORE. I DON'T THINK I LIKE IT.
HA HA HA HA
CUT IT OUT. YOU'RE GIVIN' ME THE CREEPS.
YOU'RE A FOOL.
THE JOKER DOESN'T LOVE ANYTHING, EXCEPT MAYBE HIMSELF. FACE REALITY, HARLEEN--
JOKER HAD YOU PEGGED FOR HIRED HELP THE MINUTE YOU WALKED INTO ARKHAM.
THAT'S NOT.... NO.
NO!
H-HE TOLD ME THINGS, SECRET THINGS HE NEVER TOLD ANYONE...
WHAT DID HE TELL YOU, HARLEY? WAS IT THE LINE ABOUT THE ABUSIVE FATHER, OR THE ONE ABOUT THE ALCOHOLIC MOM? OF COURSE, THE RUNAWAY ORPHAN STORY IS PARTICULARLY MOVING, TOO.
HE'S GAINED A LOT OF SYMPATHY WITH THAT ONE.
STOP IT!!
YOU'RE MAKING ME CONFUSED!
WHAT WAS IT HE TOLD THAT ONE PAROLE OFFICER?
OH, YES...
"THERE WAS ONLY ONE TIME I EVER SAW DAD REALLY HAPPY. HE TOOK ME TO THE ICE SHOW WHEN I WAS SEVEN..."

CIRCUS.

HE SAID IT WAS THE CIRCUS.

HE'S GOT A MILLION OF THEM, HARLEY.

LIKE ANY OTHER COMEDIAN, HE USES WHATEVER MATERIAL WILL WORK.

YOU'RE *WRONG!* MY PUDDIN' *DOES* LOVE ME! HE *DOES!*

YOU'RE THE PROBLEM!

ALWAYS IN THE WAY!

ALWAYS COMING BETWEEN *US!*

WE'D BE *HAPPY* IF IT WEREN'T FOR YOU!

NOW YOU'RE GONNA *DIE* AND MAKE EVERYTHING *RIGHT!*

EXCEPT HE'LL NEVER BELIEVE YOU DID IT.

WHAT?

S-SURE HE WILL...

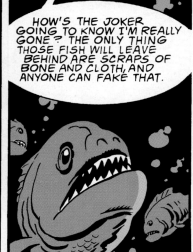

HOW'S THE JOKER GOING TO KNOW I'M REALLY GONE? THE ONLY THING THOSE FISH WILL LEAVE BEHIND ARE SCRAPS OF BONE AND CLOTH, AND ANYONE CAN FAKE THAT.

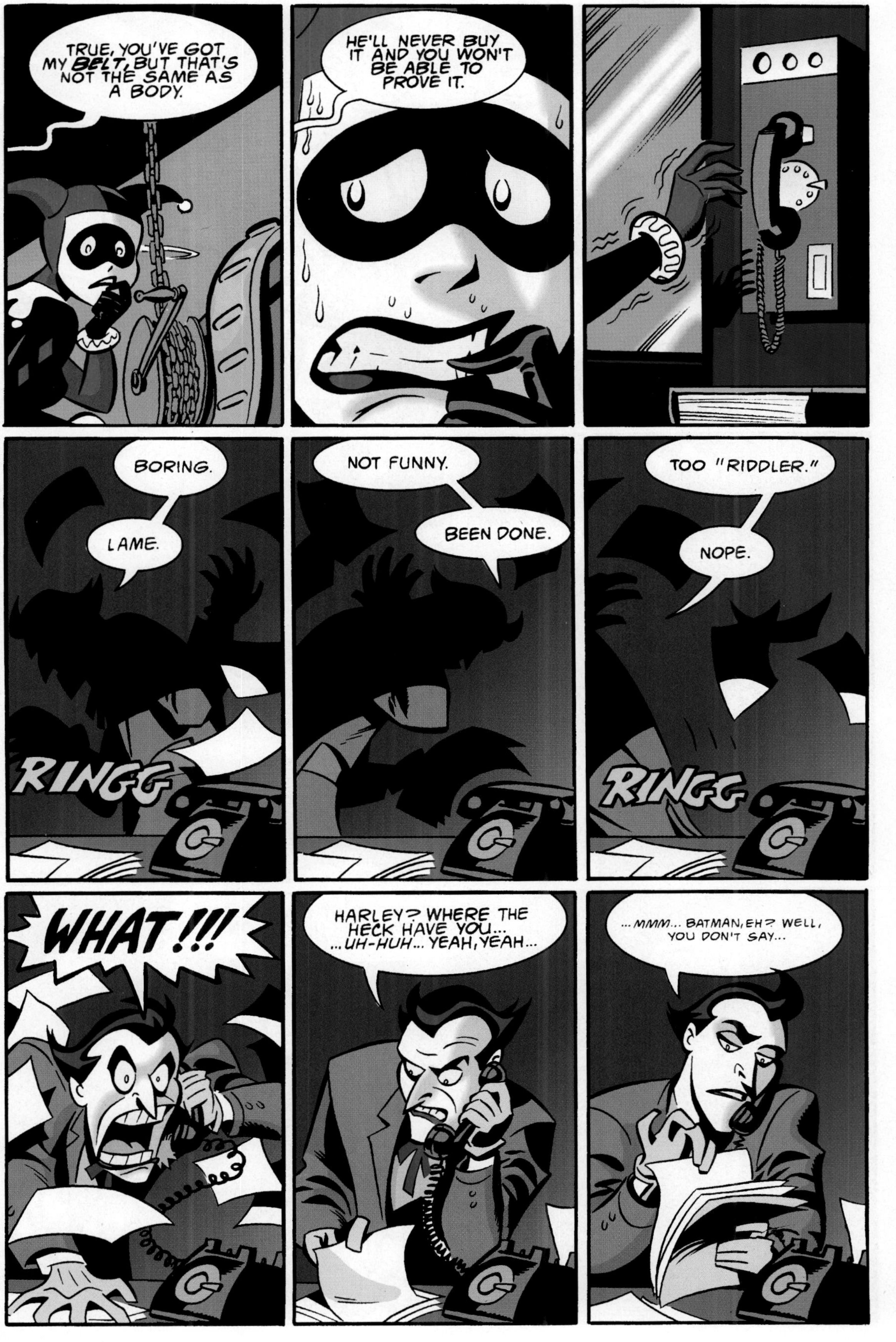
TRUE, YOU'VE GOT MY BELT, BUT THAT'S NOT THE SAME AS A BODY.
HE'LL NEVER BUY IT AND YOU WON'T BE ABLE TO PROVE IT.
BORING.
LAME.
RINGG
NOT FUNNY.
BEEN DONE.
TOO "RIDDLER."
NOPE.
RINGG
WHAT!!!
HARLEY? WHERE THE HECK HAVE YOU... ...UH-HUH... YEAH, YEAH...
...MMM... BATMAN, EH? WELL, YOU DON'T SAY...

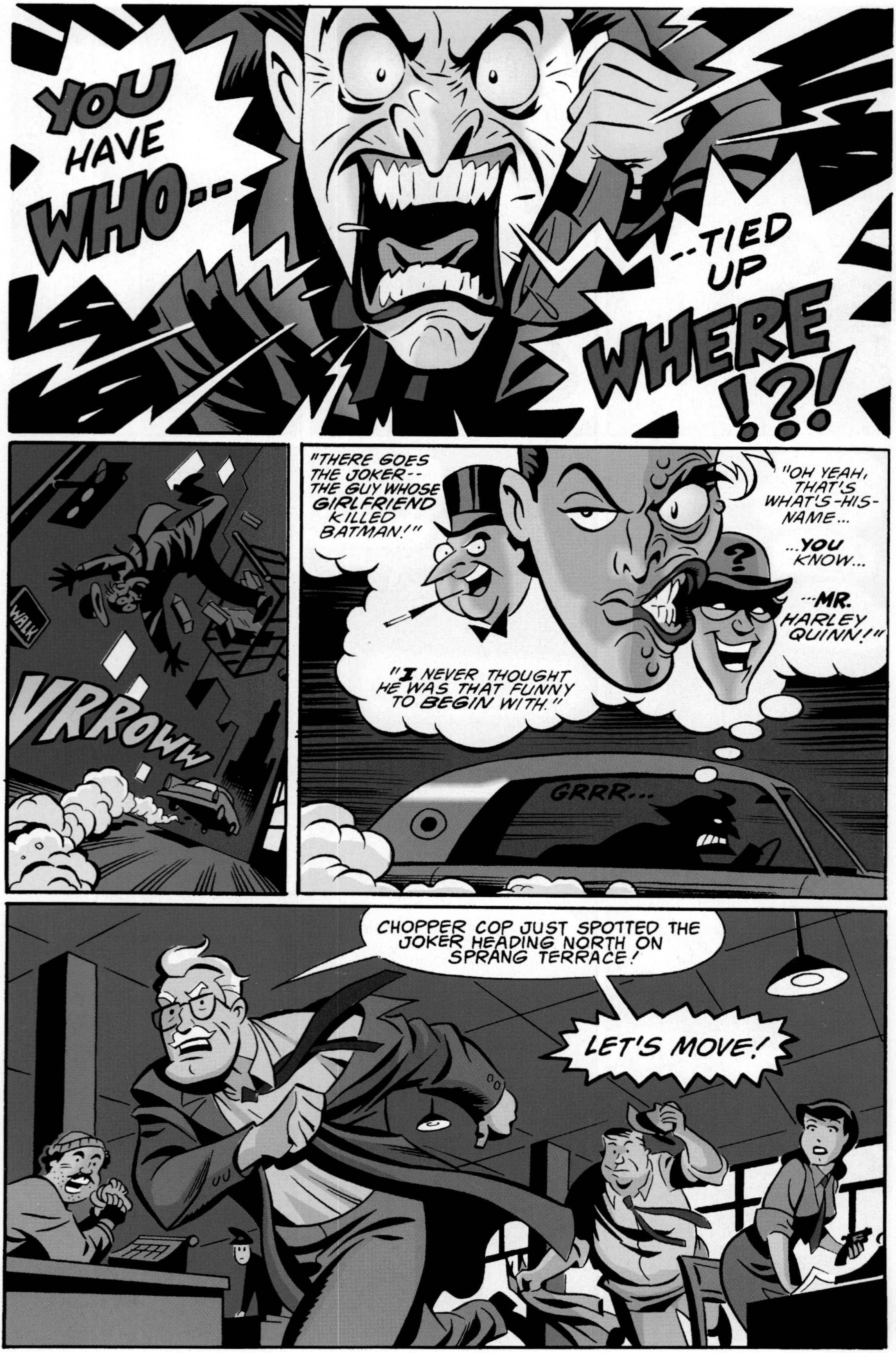
YOU HAVE WHO--
--TIED UP WHERE !?!
VRROWW
"THERE GOES THE JOKER-- THE GUY WHOSE GIRLFRIEND KILLED BATMAN!"
"OH YEAH, THAT'S WHAT'S-HIS-NAME... ...YOU KNOW... ...MR. HARLEY QUINN!"
"I NEVER THOUGHT HE WAS THAT FUNNY TO BEGIN WITH."
GRRR...
CHOPPER COP JUST SPOTTED THE JOKER HEADING NORTH ON SPRANG TERRACE!
LET'S MOVE!

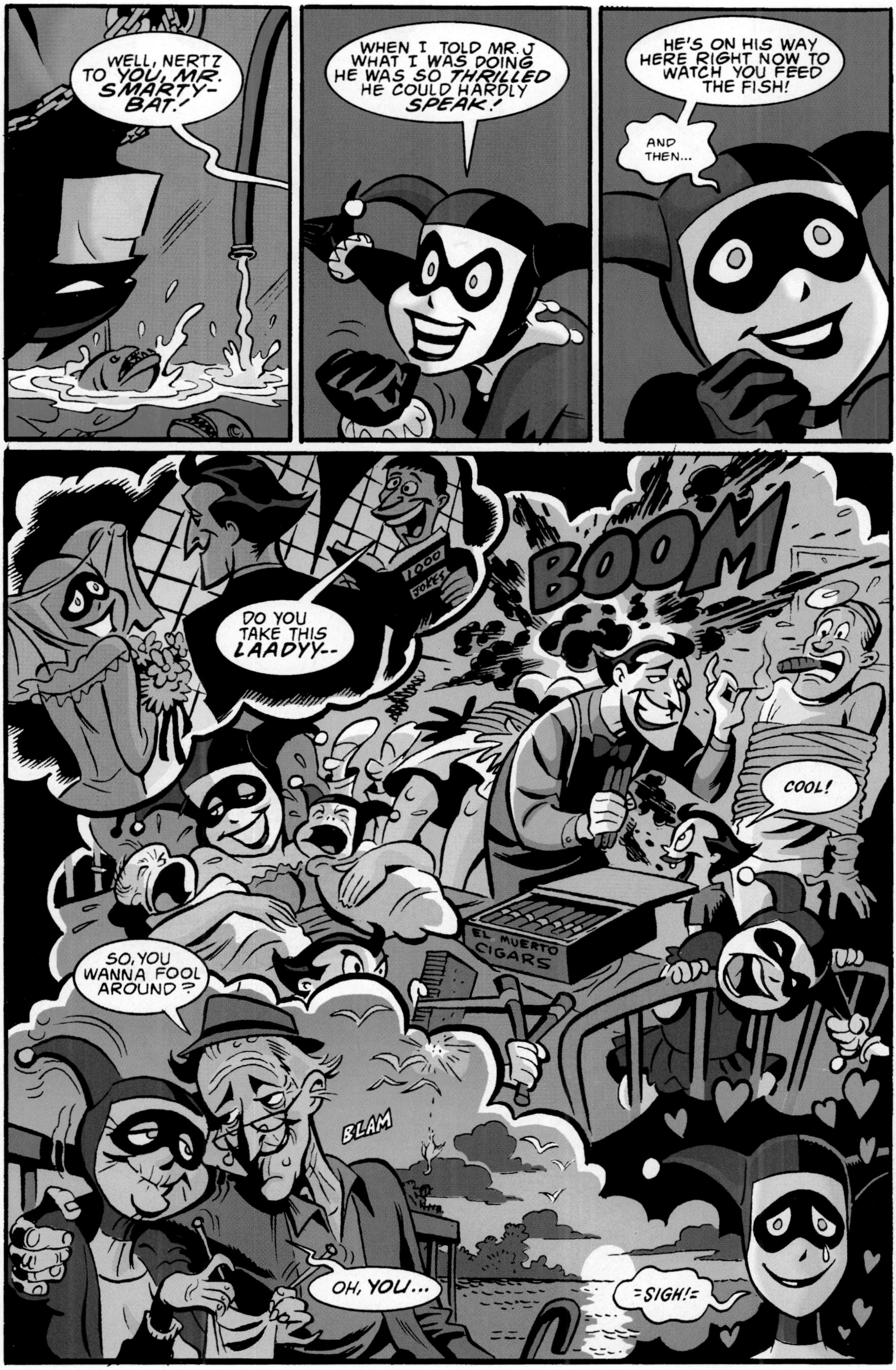
WELL, NERTZ TO YOU, MR. SMARTY-BAT!
WHEN I TOLD MR. J WHAT I WAS DOING HE WAS SO THRILLED HE COULD HARDLY SPEAK!
HE'S ON HIS WAY HERE RIGHT NOW TO WATCH YOU FEED THE FISH!
AND THEN...
DO YOU TAKE THIS LAADYY--
1000 JOKES
BOOM
COOL!
EL MUERTO CIGARS
SO, YOU WANNA FOOL AROUND?
BLAM
OH, YOU...
=SIGH!=

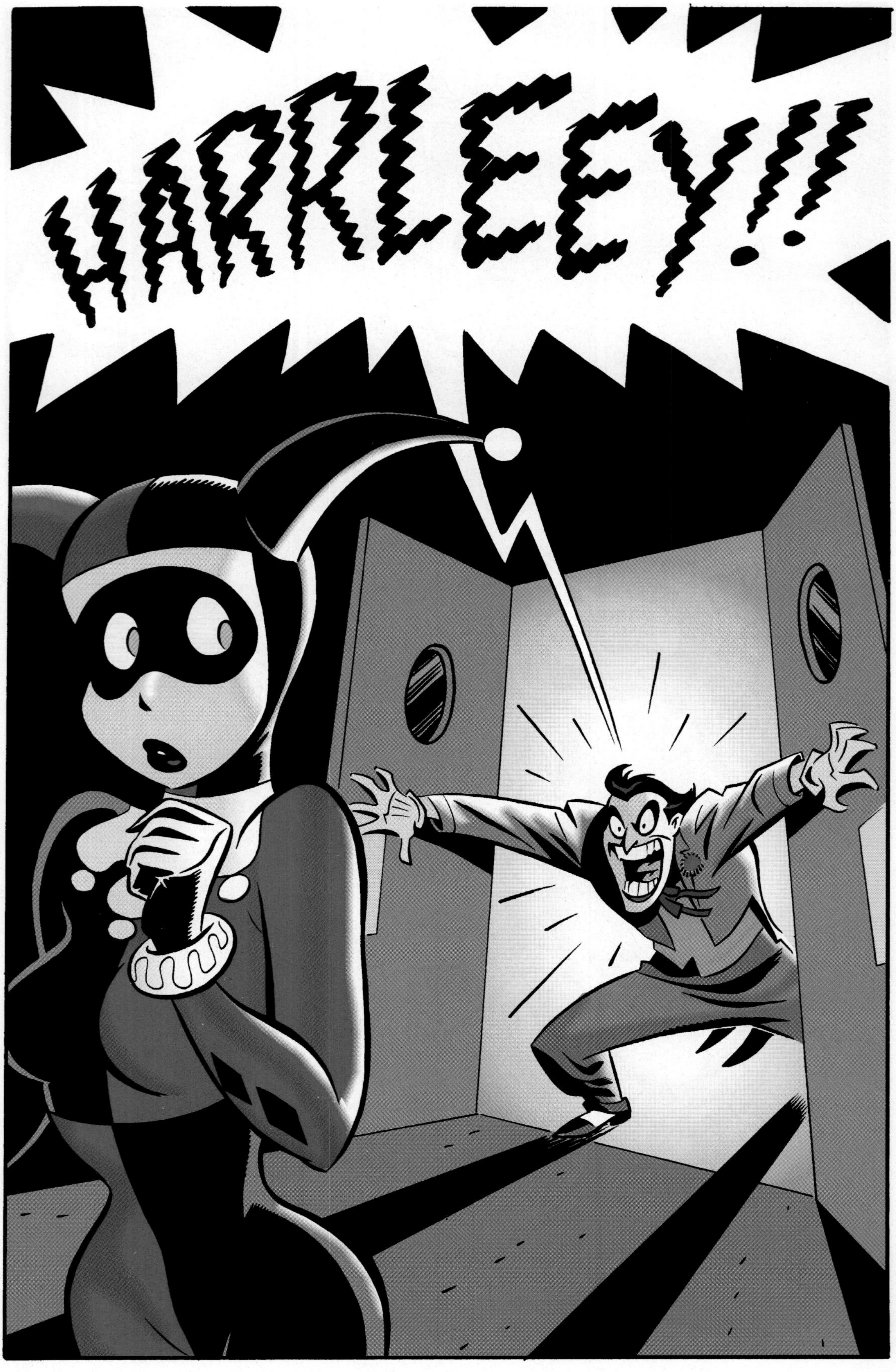
HARRLEEY!!

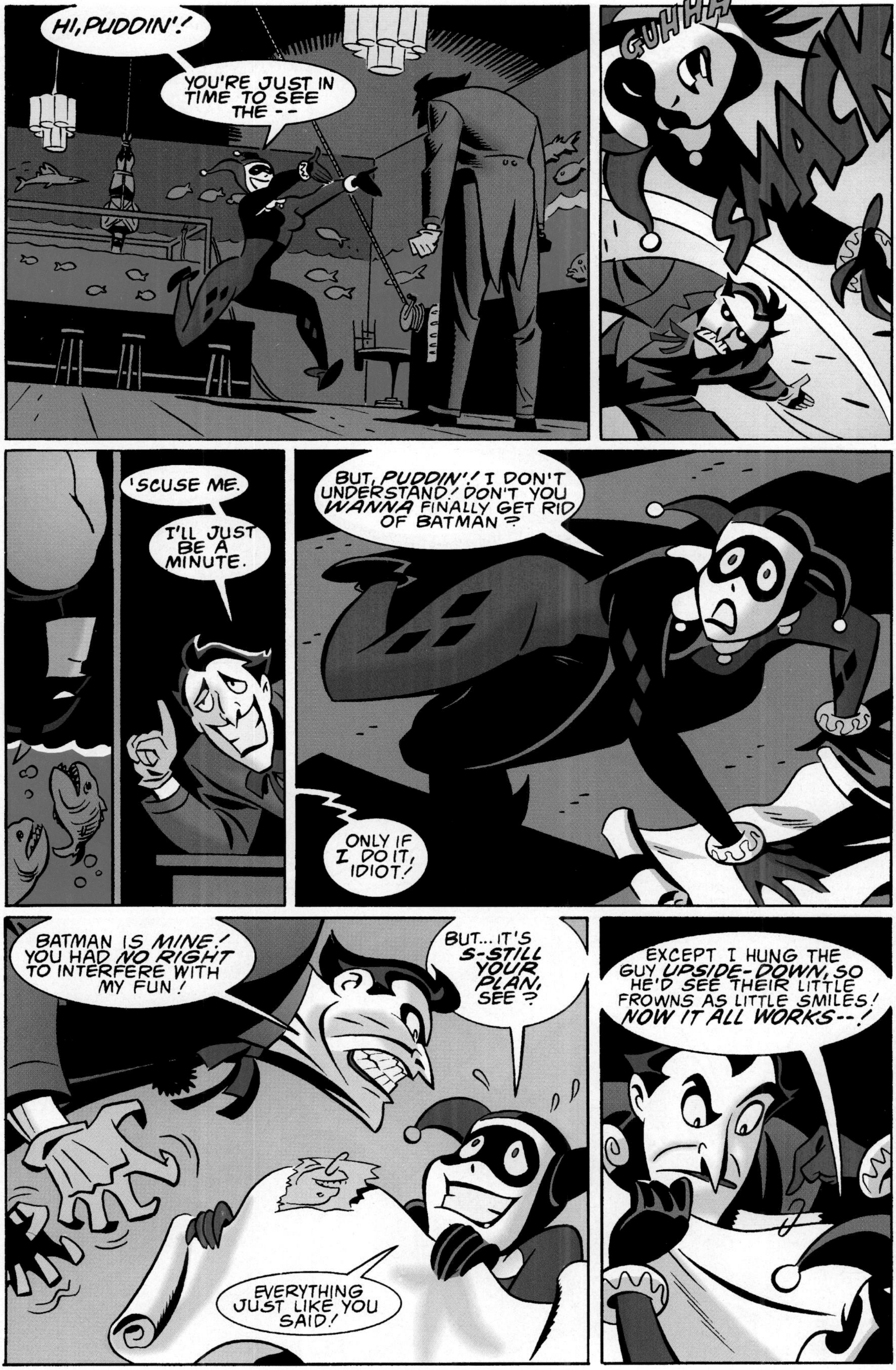
HI, PUDDIN'!
YOU'RE JUST IN TIME TO SEE THE --
GUHHH
SMACK!
'SCUSE ME.
I'LL JUST BE A MINUTE.
BUT, PUDDIN'! I DON'T UNDERSTAND! DON'T YOU WANNA FINALLY GET RID OF BATMAN?
ONLY IF I DO IT, IDIOT!
BATMAN IS MINE! YOU HAD NO RIGHT TO INTERFERE WITH MY FUN!
BUT... IT'S S-STILL YOUR PLAN, SEE?
EVERYTHING JUST LIKE YOU SAID!
EXCEPT I HUNG THE GUY UPSIDE-DOWN, SO HE'D SEE THEIR LITTLE FROWNS AS LITTLE SMILES! NOW IT ALL WORKS--!

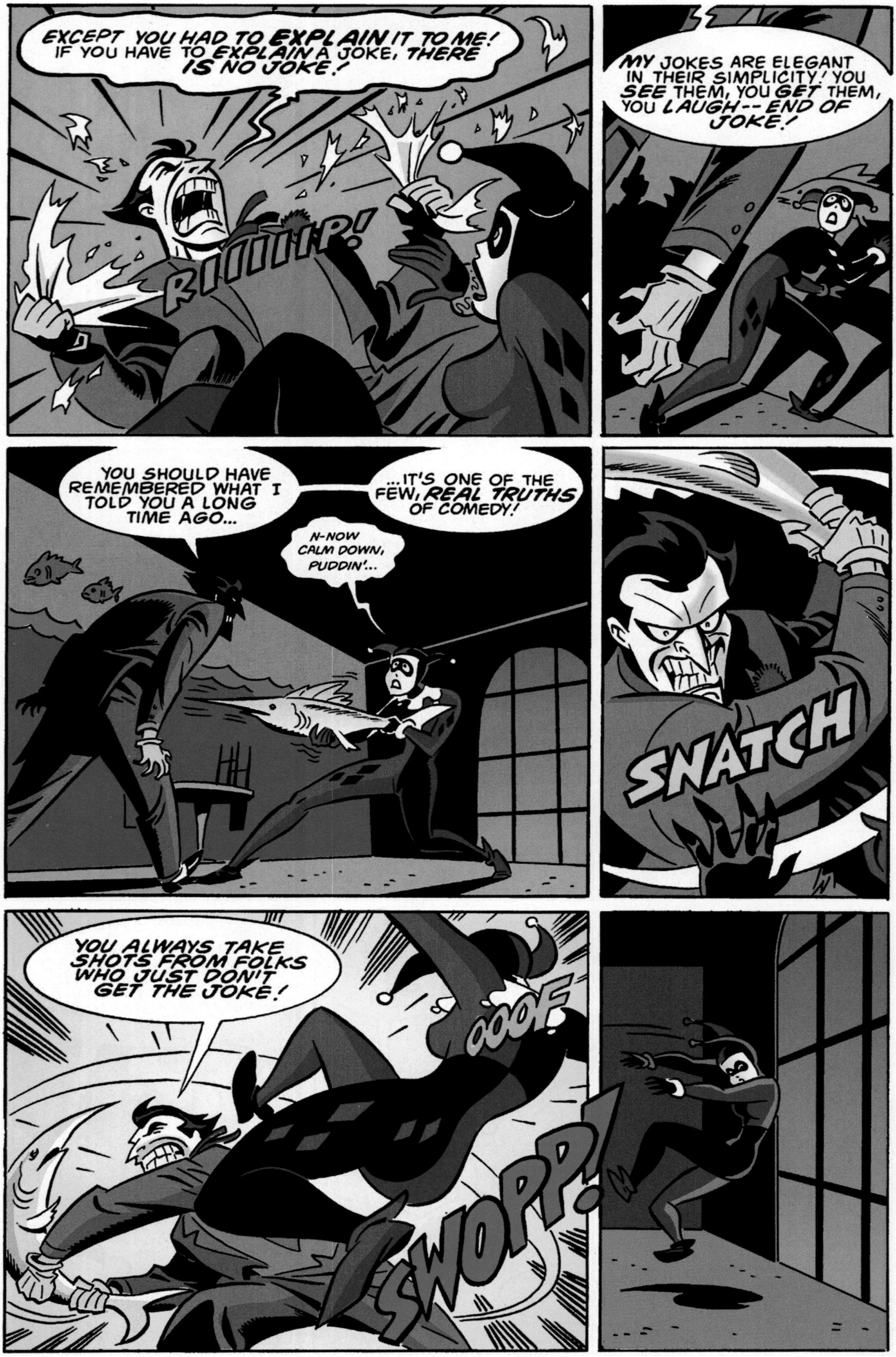
EXCEPT YOU HAD TO EXPLAIN IT TO ME! IF YOU HAVE TO EXPLAIN A JOKE, THERE IS NO JOKE!
RIIIIIIP!
MY JOKES ARE ELEGANT IN THEIR SIMPLICITY! YOU SEE THEM, YOU GET THEM, YOU LAUGH-- END OF JOKE!
YOU SHOULD HAVE REMEMBERED WHAT I TOLD YOU A LONG TIME AGO...
...IT'S ONE OF THE FEW, REAL TRUTHS OF COMEDY!
N-NOW CALM DOWN, PUDDIN'...
SNATCH
YOU ALWAYS TAKE SHOTS FROM FOLKS WHO JUST DON'T GET THE JOKE!
OOOF
SWOPP!

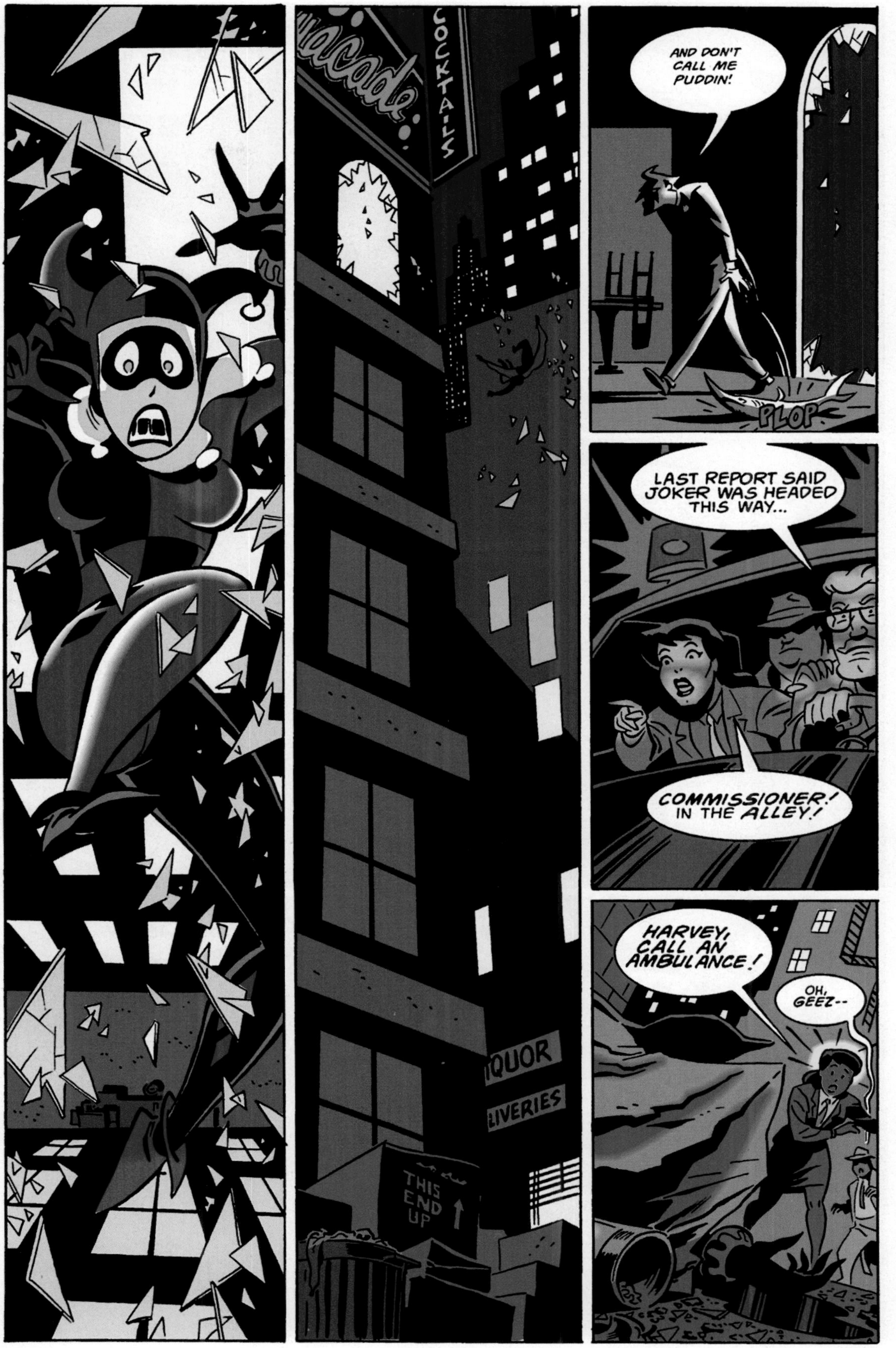
COCKTAILS
AND DON'T CALL ME PUDDIN!
PLOP
LAST REPORT SAID JOKER WAS HEADED THIS WAY...
COMMISSIONER! IN THE ALLEY!
HARVEY, CALL AN AMBULANCE!
OH, GEEZ--
IQUOR
LIVERIES
THIS END UP

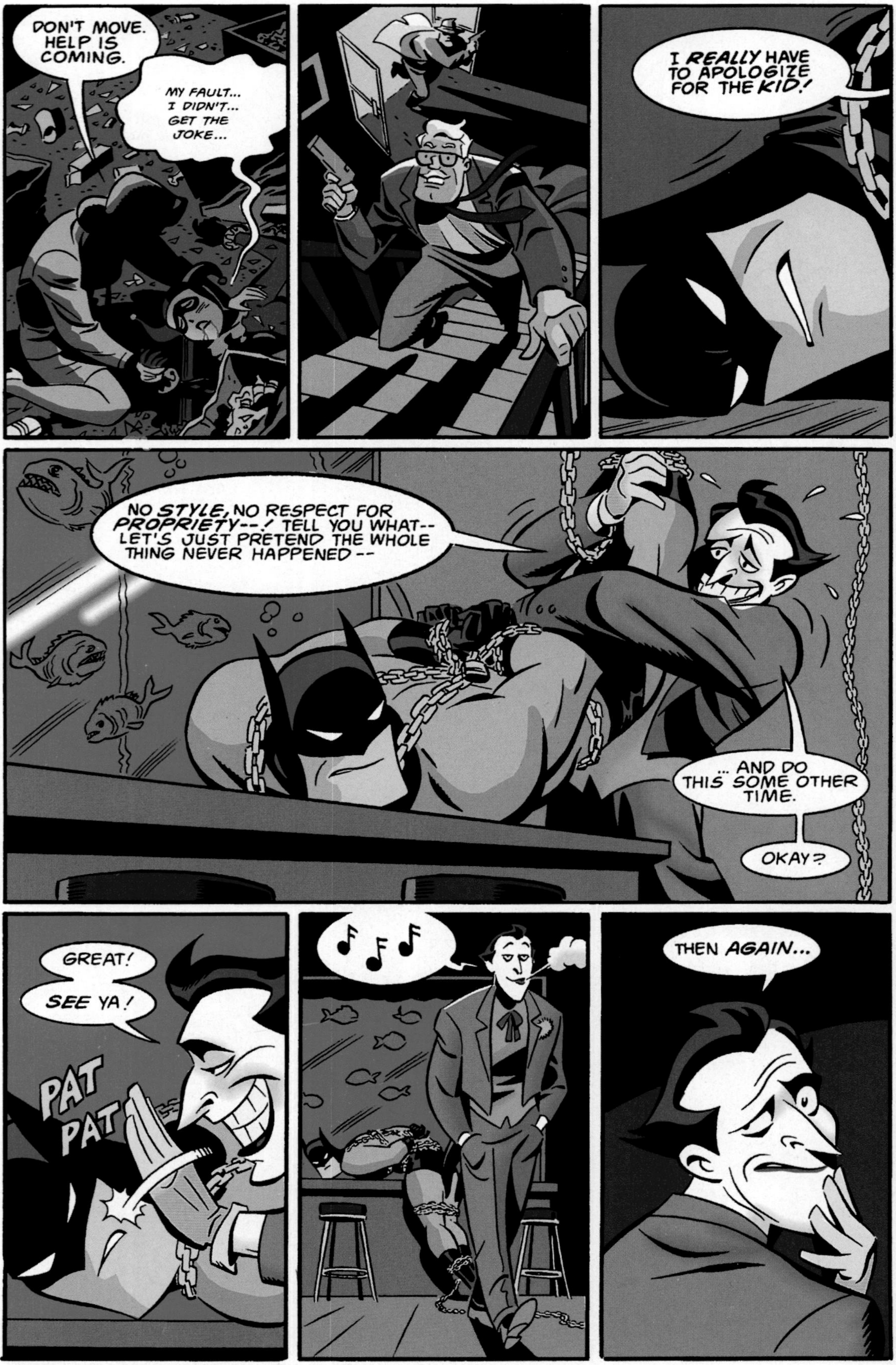
DON'T MOVE. HELP IS COMING.
MY FAULT... I DIDN'T... GET THE JOKE...
I REALLY HAVE TO APOLOGIZE FOR THE KID!
NO STYLE, NO RESPECT FOR PROPRIETY--! TELL YOU WHAT-- LET'S JUST PRETEND THE WHOLE THING NEVER HAPPENED --
... AND DO THIS SOME OTHER TIME.
OKAY?
GREAT!
SEE YA!
PAT PAT
THEN AGAIN...

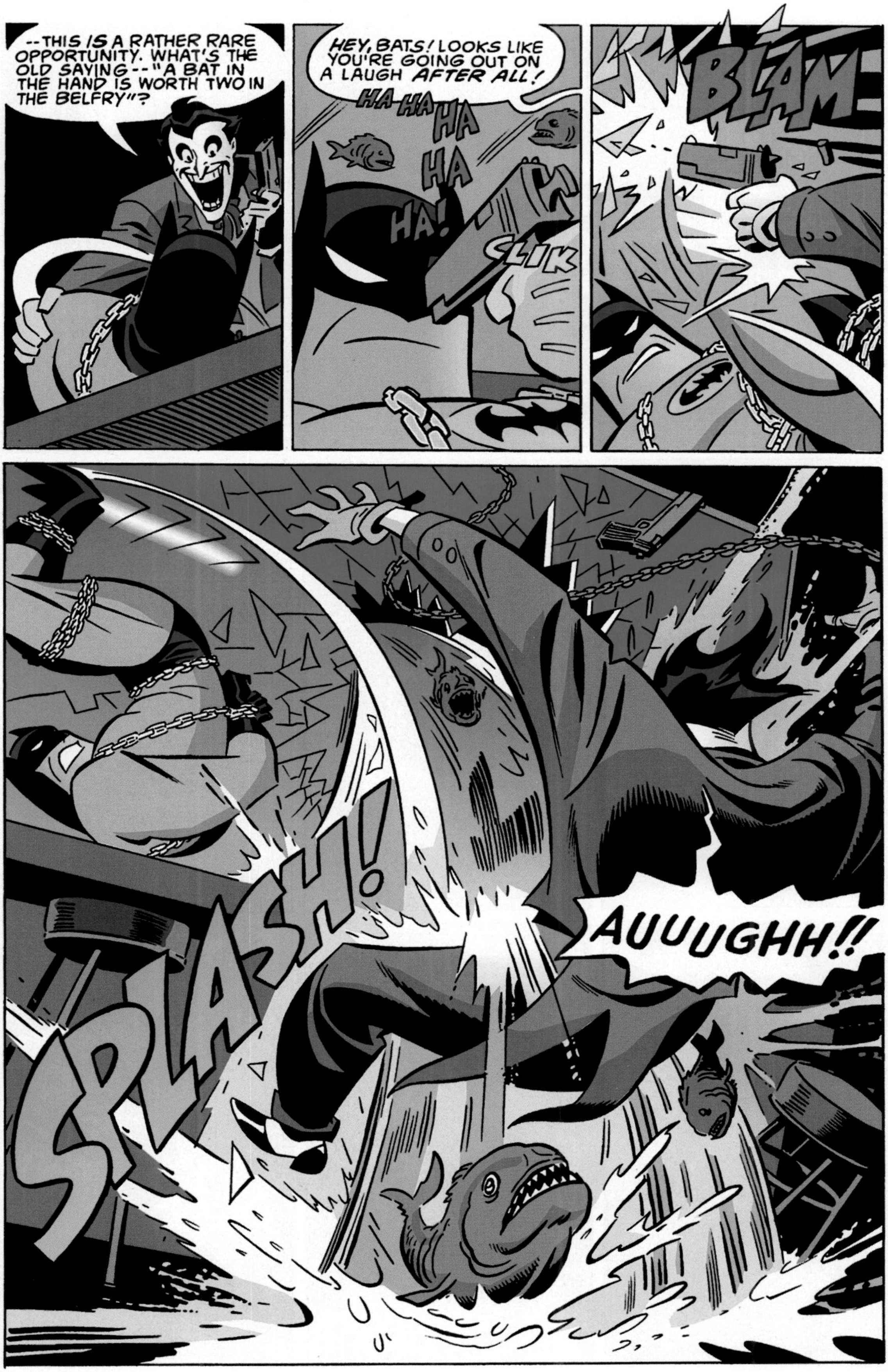

--THIS IS A RATHER RARE OPPORTUNITY. WHAT'S THE OLD SAYING--"A BAT IN THE HAND IS WORTH TWO IN THE BELFRY"?
HEY, BATS! LOOKS LIKE YOU'RE GOING OUT ON A LAUGH AFTER ALL!
HA HA HA HA HA HA!
CLIK
BLAM
SPLASH!
AUUUGHH!!

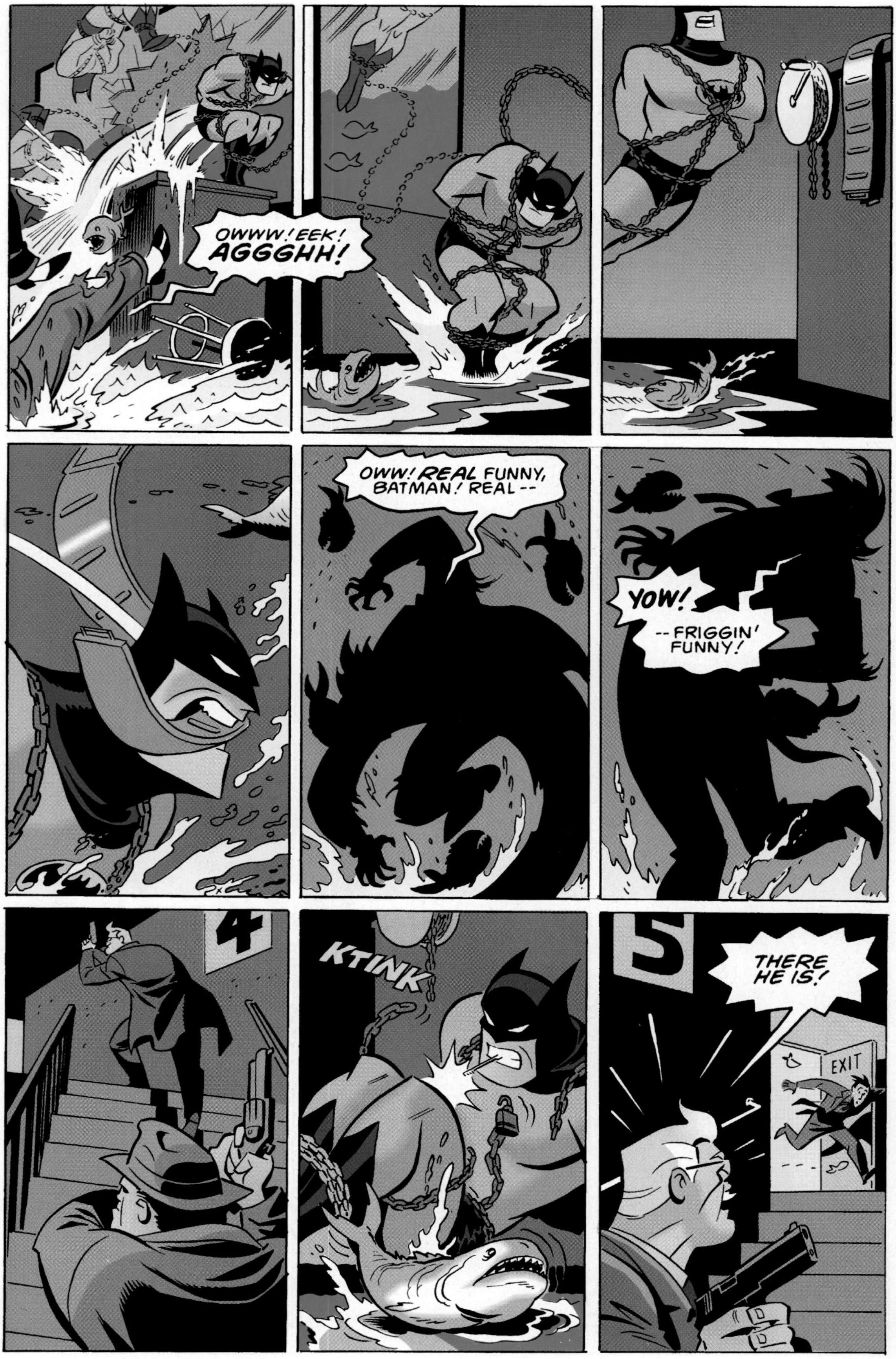
OWWW! EEK! AGGGHH!
OWW! REAL FUNNY, BATMAN! REAL --
YOW!
-- FRIGGIN' FUNNY!
KTINK
EXIT
THERE HE IS!

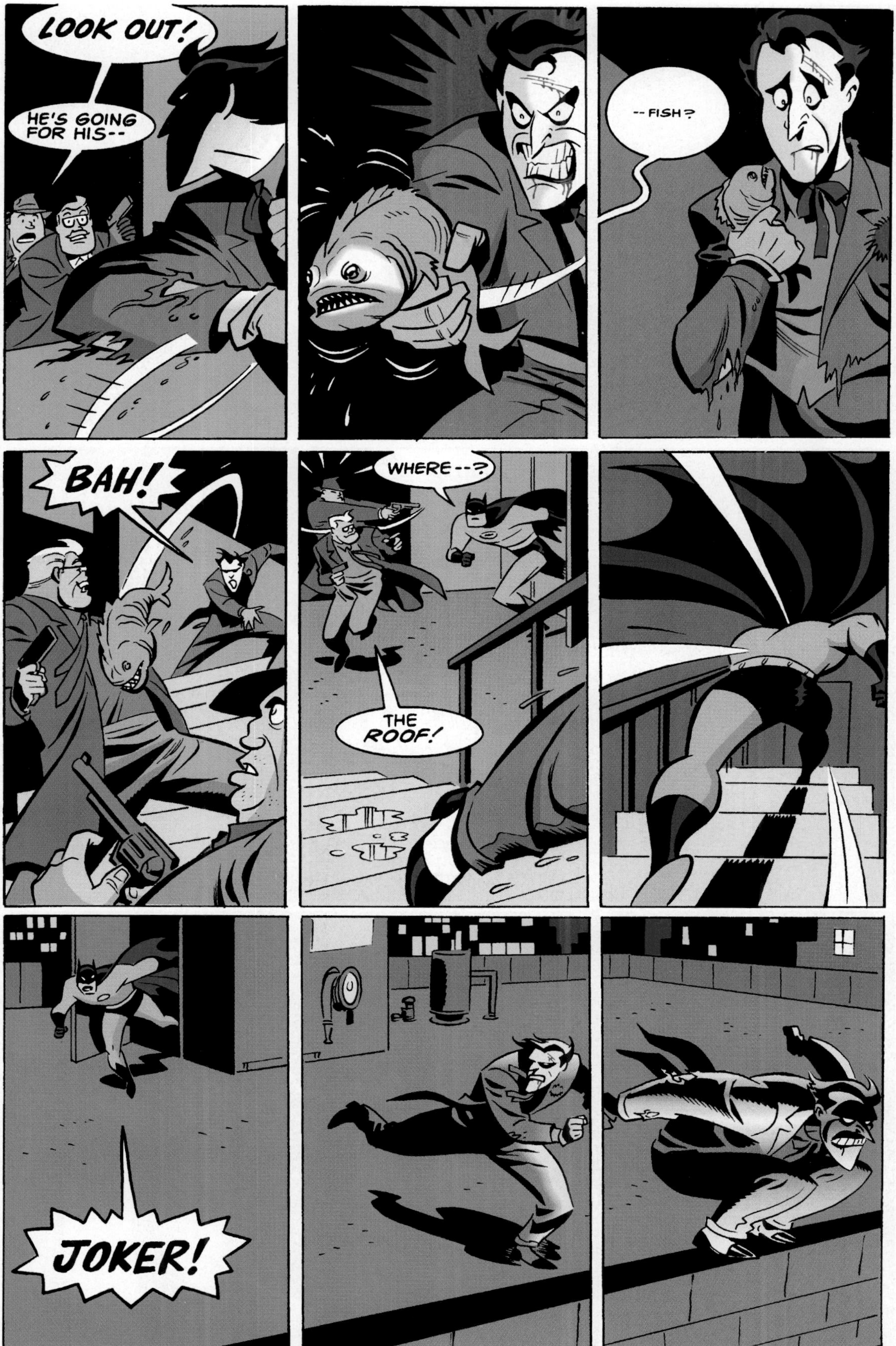
LOOK OUT!
HE'S GOING FOR HIS--
--FISH?
BAH!
WHERE--?
THE ROOF!
JOKER!

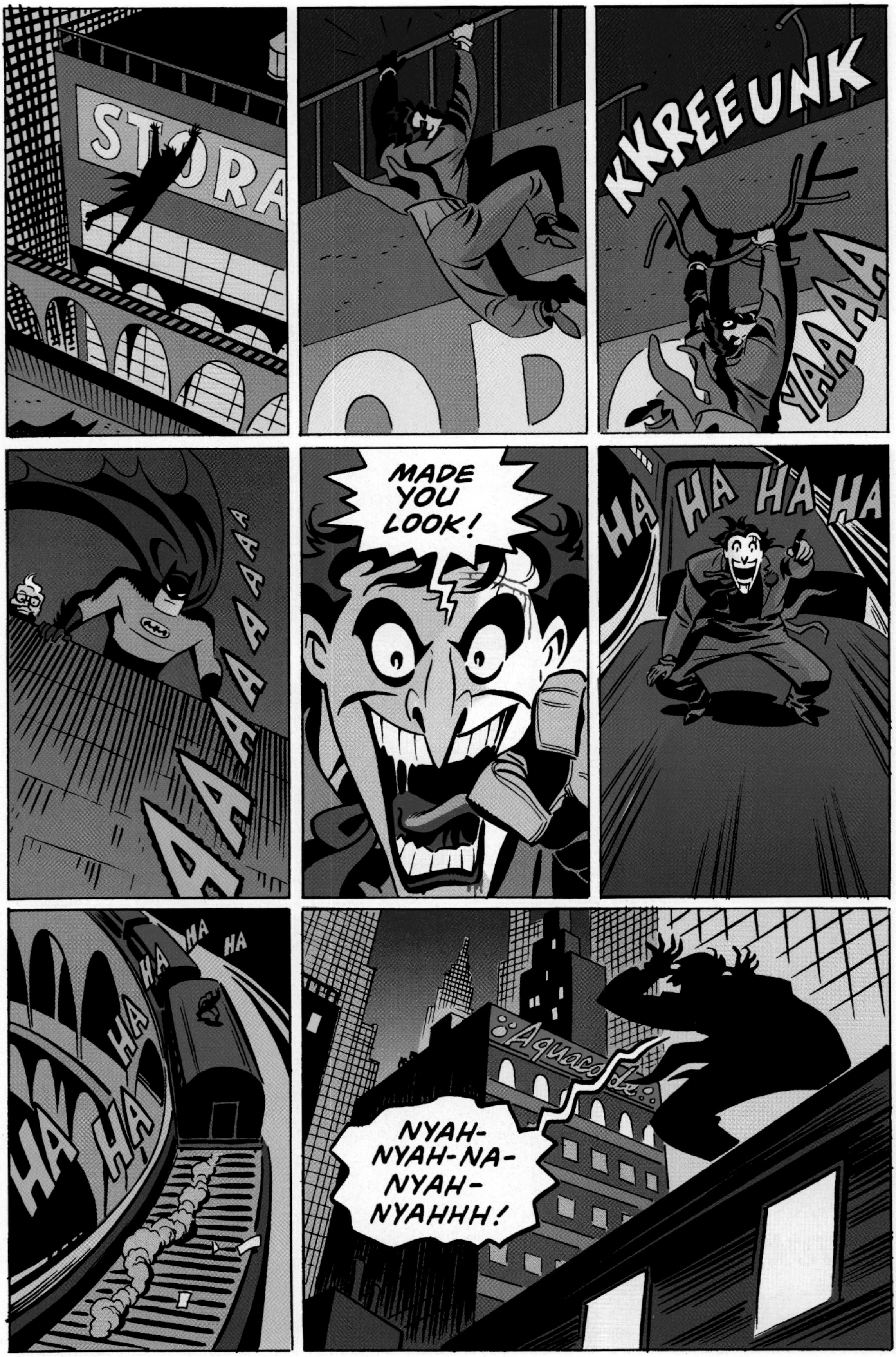
STORA
KKREEUNK
YAAAA
MADE YOU LOOK!
HA HA HA HA
HA HA HA HA HA HA HA HA
NYAH-NYAH-NA-NYAH-NYAHHH!

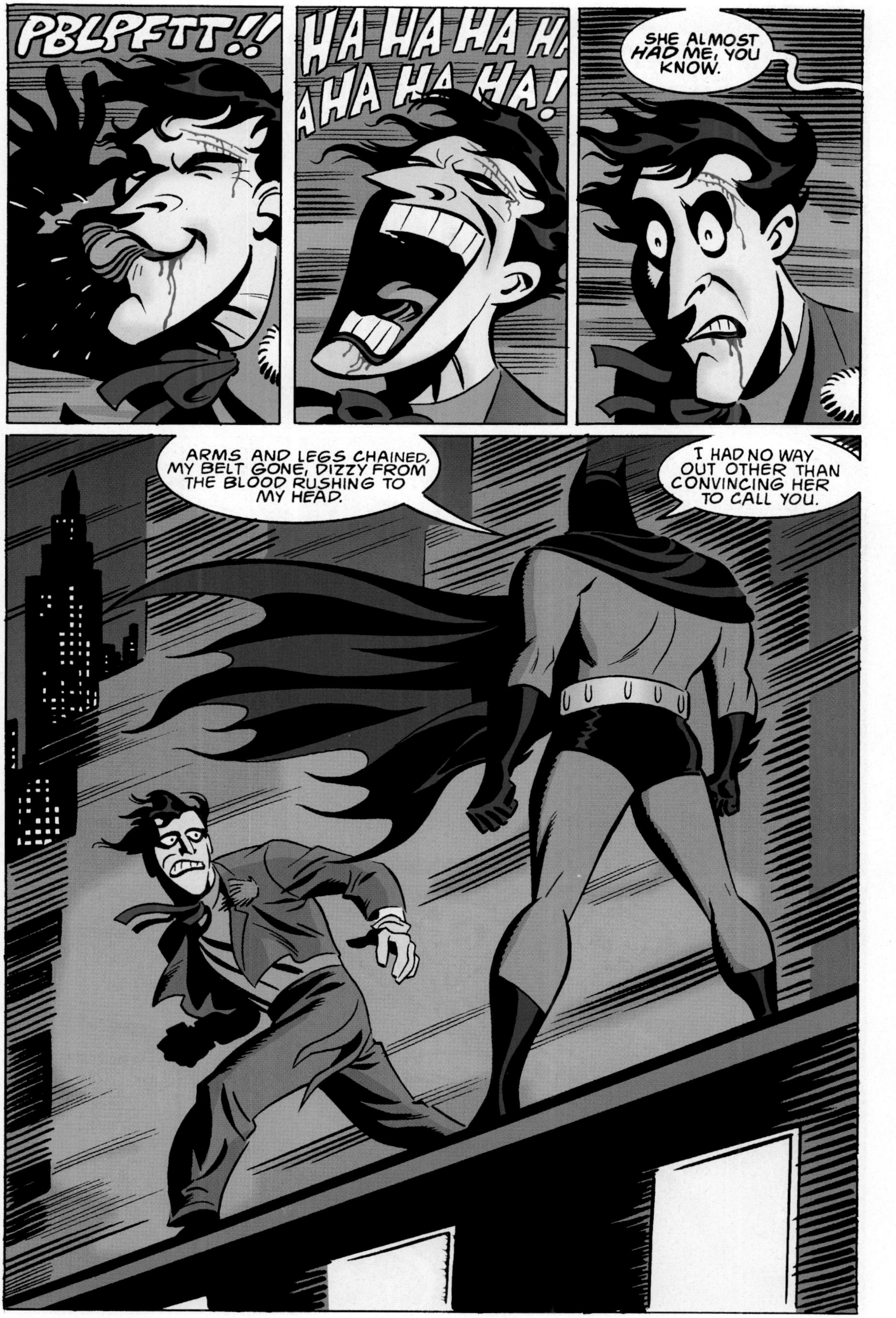
PBLPFTT!!
HA HA HA HA HA HA HA HA HA!
SHE ALMOST HAD ME, YOU KNOW.
ARMS AND LEGS CHAINED, MY BELT GONE, DIZZY FROM THE BLOOD RUSHING TO MY HEAD.
I HAD NO WAY OUT OTHER THAN CONVINCING HER TO CALL YOU.

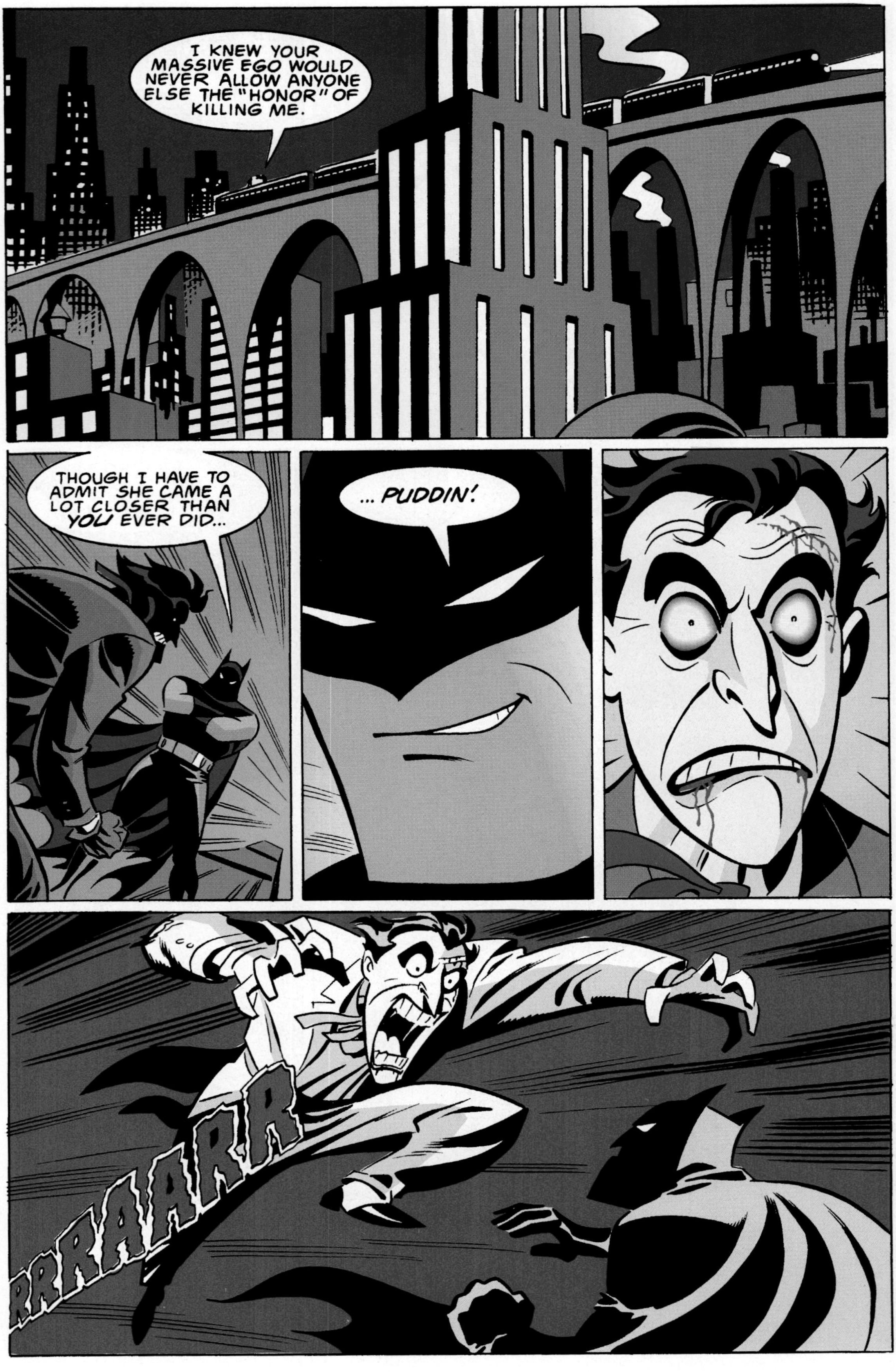
I KNEW YOUR MASSIVE EGO WOULD NEVER ALLOW ANYONE ELSE THE "HONOR" OF KILLING ME.
THOUGH I HAVE TO ADMIT SHE CAME A LOT CLOSER THAN *YOU* EVER DID...
...*PUDDIN'!*
RRRAAARR

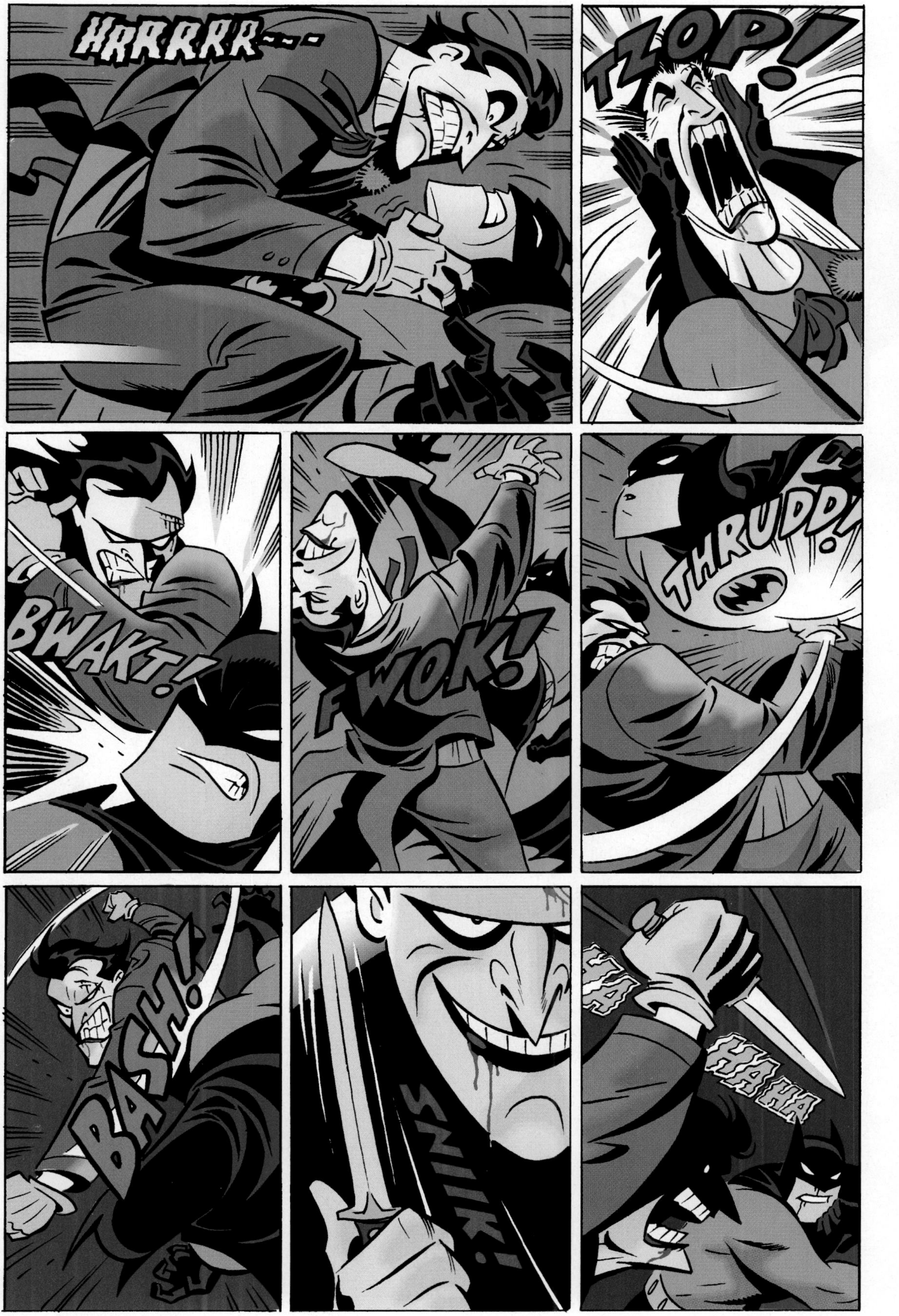

HRRRRRR---
TZOP!
BWAKT!
FWOK!
THRUDD!
BASH!
SNIIK!
HA
HA HA HA

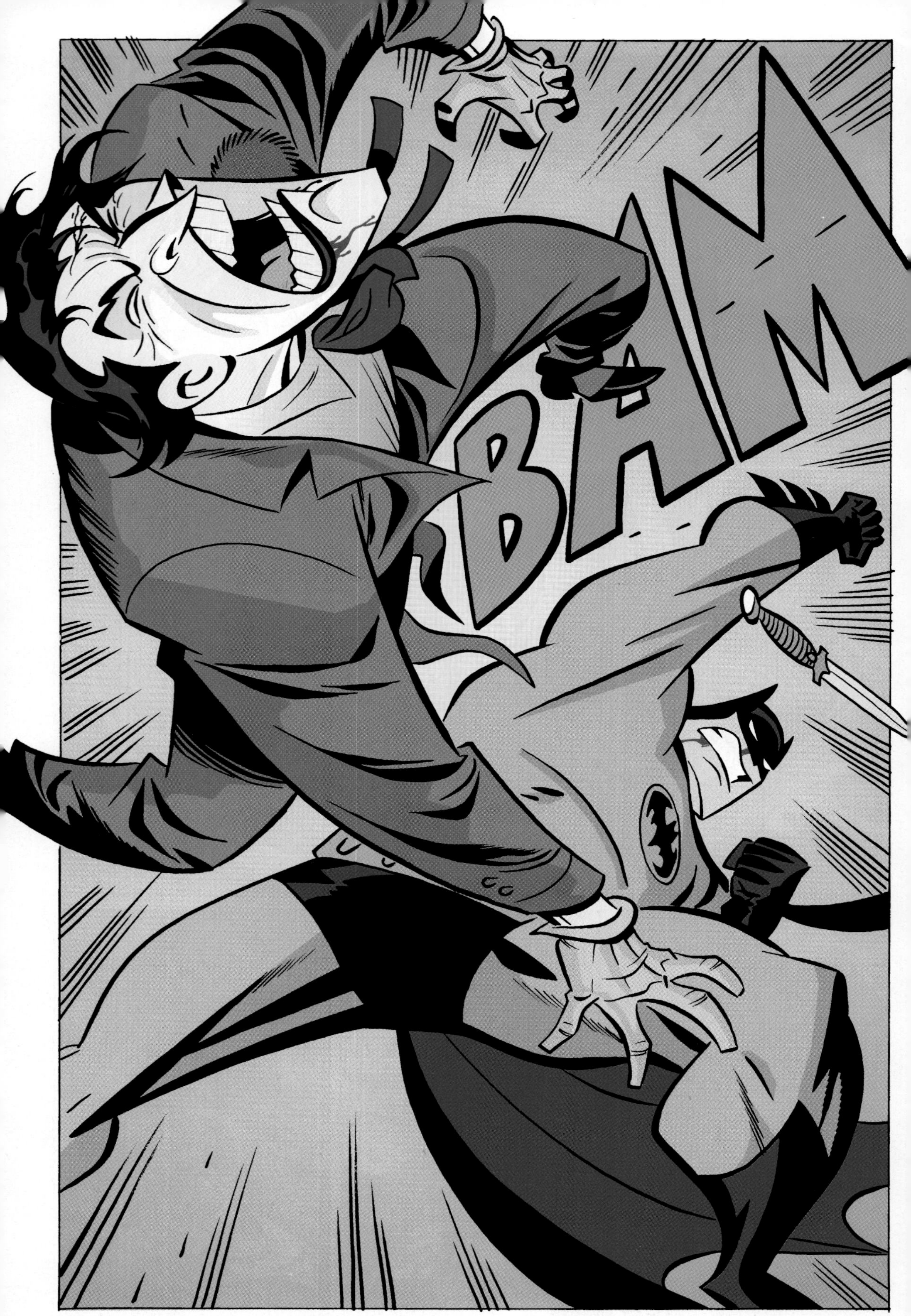
BAM

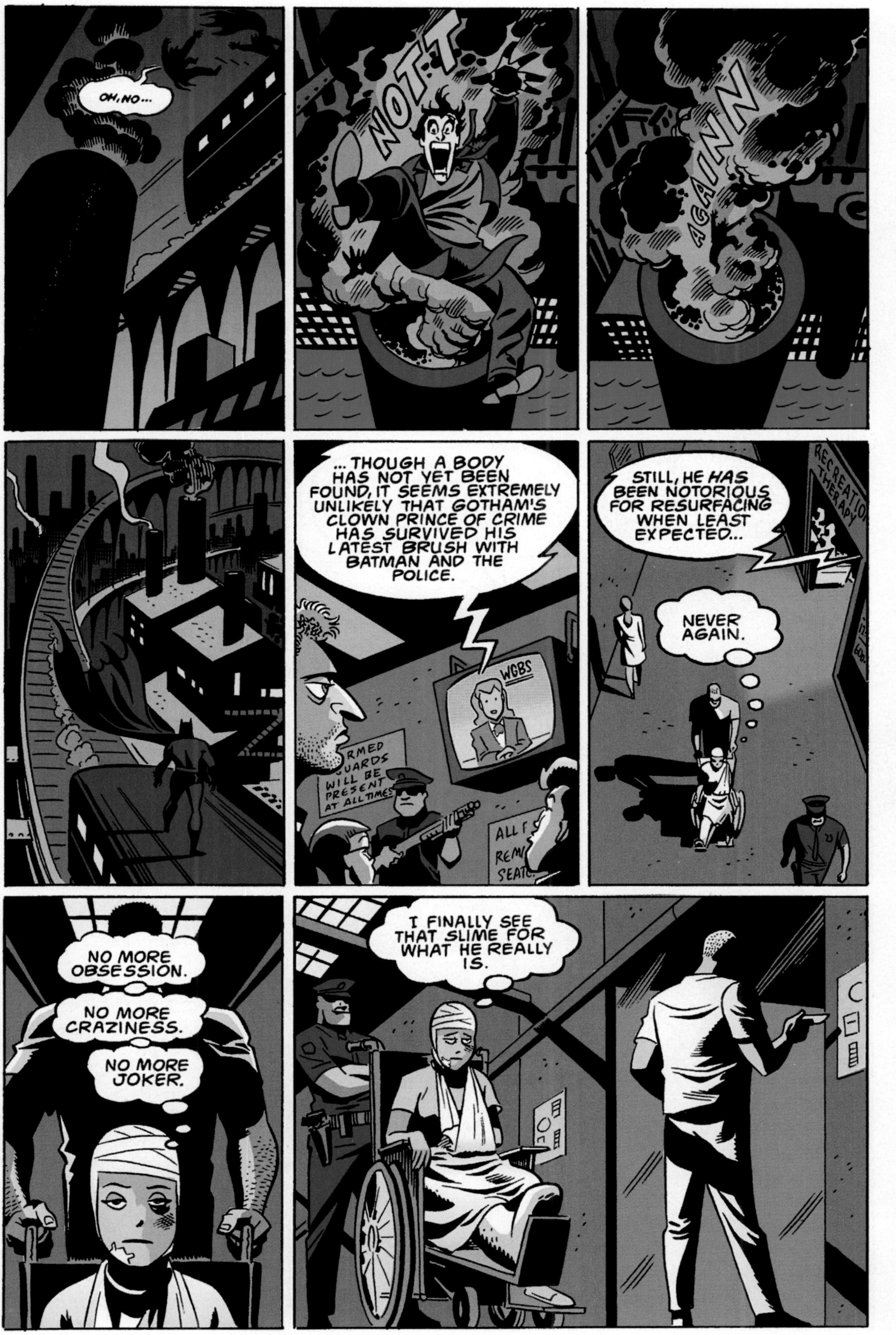
OH, NO...
NOT-T
AGAINN
...THOUGH A BODY HAS NOT YET BEEN FOUND, IT SEEMS EXTREMELY UNLIKELY THAT GOTHAM'S CLOWN PRINCE OF CRIME HAS SURVIVED HIS LATEST BRUSH WITH BATMAN AND THE POLICE.
WGBS
RMED UARDS WILL BE PRESENT AT ALL TIMES
STILL, HE HAS BEEN NOTORIOUS FOR RESURFACING WHEN LEAST EXPECTED...
RECREATION THERAPY
NEVER AGAIN.
NO MORE OBSESSION.
NO MORE CRAZINESS.
NO MORE JOKER.
I FINALLY SEE THAT SLIME FOR WHAT HE REALLY IS.

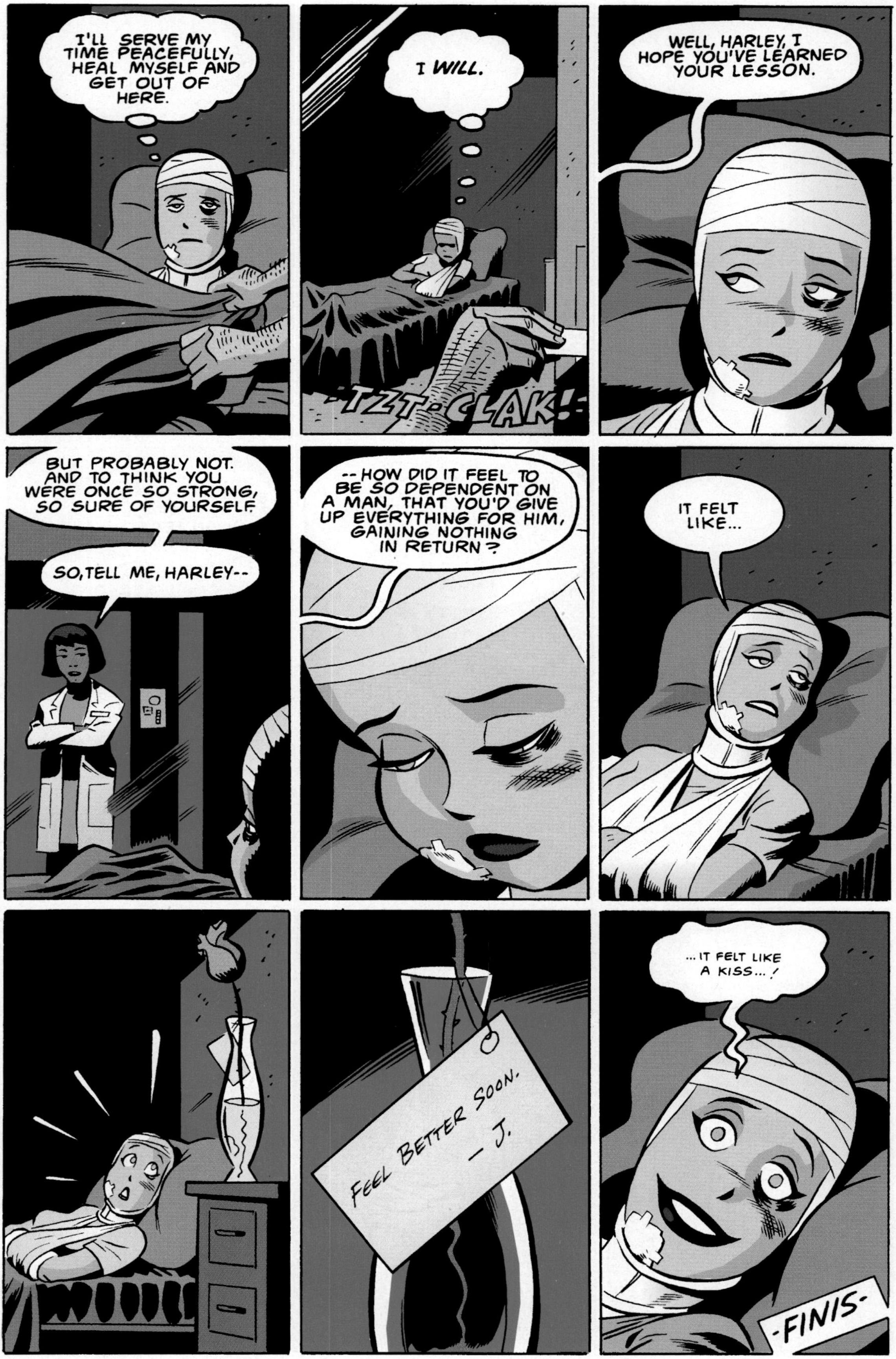
I'LL SERVE MY TIME PEACEFULLY, HEAL MYSELF AND GET OUT OF HERE.
I WILL.
TZT-CLAK!
WELL, HARLEY, I HOPE YOU'VE LEARNED YOUR LESSON.
BUT PROBABLY NOT. AND TO THINK YOU WERE ONCE SO STRONG, SO SURE OF YOURSELF.
SO, TELL ME, HARLEY--
--HOW DID IT FEEL TO BE SO DEPENDENT ON A MAN, THAT YOU'D GIVE UP EVERYTHING FOR HIM, GAINING NOTHING IN RETURN?
IT FELT LIKE...
FEEL BETTER SOON. — J.
...IT FELT LIKE A KISS...!
-FINIS-

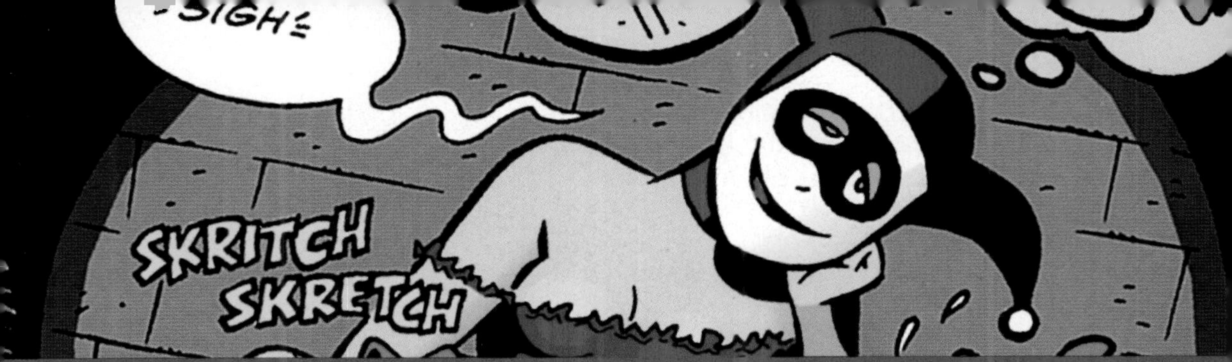
SIGH
SKRITCH
SKRETCH

MAD LOVE COMMENTARY By Bruce Timm

IN THE BEGINNING…

Paul casually mentioned to me one day that he'd figured out Harley Quinn's origin story — turns out the kooky clown-girl was once Joker's *psychiatrist*!

I thought it was a great twist and suggested we do the story as a comic, rather than as an episode of the TV series. We got the go-ahead from DC and plotted the story over several lunches and dinners. In fact, we even used the *setting* of one of those meals in the story. We often ate at a tropical-themed restaurant/bar called "The Paradise" downstairs from the WB Animation offices. The decor was the very definition of "tacky," complete with Day-Glo plastic swordfish on the walls, and it became the abandoned "Aquacade" nightclub, where Harley intends to turn Batman into piranha-chow.

BASED ON A TRUE STORY…

Another instance of "art imitating life" — a mutual friend of ours was stuck in a stormy (but nonviolent) relationship with a guy whose personal obsessions precluded him from returning her unconditional love. I'm happy to report that the "real-life Harley" *did* finally break away from her "Joker" and has been happily married to another man for several years now.

ART IMITATES ART…

As others have pointed out, the shadow of Harvey Kurtzman hangs heavily over this story. It's my opinion that Kurtzman was one of the finest pure storytellers in the history of comics, and freely admit that much of my "meat-and-potatoes"/no-frills storytelling chops derive directly from him. In particular, I definitely had Kurtzman's famous "Missed!… Missed!" sequence from "Batboy and Rubin" in my mind while drawing Joker pacing behind the ringing telephone (p. 55). I redrew that little sequence three or four times 'til I got the Kurtzman-esque rhythm of it *just so*…

It wasn't until about a year ago that I realized I'd subconsciously pinched the staging of Harley's fall out the window from an old issue of *Tomb of Dracula* (#29) drawn by Gene Colan… *D'oh*!

KEITH GIFFEN SAVED MY LIFE…

… or at least my sanity. Initially, I was very intimidated by the prospect of drawing a 64-page comic, at least four times the length of any comic I'd ever done before. One day, I was reading a LEGION OF SUPER-HEROES comic that Keith had plotted and laid out and noticed that every page was structured on a rigid three-tier/nine-panel grid. I figured if I loosely followed that format, I could stop worrying about designing fancy page layouts and just concentrate on telling the story. I traced off the grid from the comic, Xeroxed a stack of copies and did fairly tight "printed size" roughs of the entire story in about two weeks. Once I got started, the work just *flowed* — man, I was *on fire* while roughing out that baby! — slowing down only when I got to the occasional bit of business in Paul's script that either a) interfered with the rhythm/pacing of the story, b) just didn't seem "right" to me, or c) I just plain didn't feel like drawing! Fortunately, Paul is the ideal collaborator — he loved all the weird little touches I added, and readily agreed to the edits I made.

Once the roughs were approved by DC, I then blew them up on the Xerox machine and traced/inked them onto Bristol board with a lightbox. All the compositions, backgrounds, and spot-blacks, etc. were thoroughly worked out on the thumbnails, so the final inking *should* have gone quickly. But as this was my mainstream comics debut, I *sweated* over the inks, wanting them to be pristine. Glen Murakami pitched in as the deadline approached, inking about five pages toward the end, and several pages were printed directly from the roughs, just tightened up a bit… thank God for Wite-Out!

And thank God for Keith Giffen.

I HATE FISH…

Paul actually bought me a stuffed piranha to use as reference. It was a sweet, typically "Dini-esque" thing for him to do, and it really *was* a big help, but *man* was that thing *disgusting*! It sat on a shelf in my office for years afterward, but when we relocated to new digs a few years ago I took the opportunity to toss the hideous beast in the nearest waste bin — sorry, Paul!

NAUGHTY BUT NICE...

Editor Scott Peterson was a wee bit nervous about some of the "sexier" elements of the story, mostly in the "Harley's Inept Seduction" sequence. I talked him into running most of it "as is" — Harley could keep her nightie as long as it was red, not any kind of see-through "flesh" color, and he reluctantly signed off on her provocative poses in the first two panels of page 21. Panel 3 *was* redrawn at his request — I thought Paul's "rev up your Harley" line was brilliantly "punny," and had drawn her as if she were riding an old-style chopper, leaning back with her feet in the air. It looked more "goofy" than "dirty" to me, but I agreed to tone it down.

THE "LOVE" I LOST...

Paul's biggest "weakness" as a writer is that he often writes *too much* "good stuff." Among the scenes that didn't make it past my pencil:

Joker is riding an elaborate miniature fun-house roller coaster in his hideout while going over some of his favorite death-trap plans. I thought it detracted from Joker's intense concentration (no time for fun, gotta kill Batman!), it went on too long, and come *on*, like I'm really gonna design and draw a miniature fun-house roller coaster! Less *is* more... especially if you're lazy, or on a tight deadline, or both.

Bullock, sent by Gordon to fetch Batman, gets the drop on our hero just as he's trashed an army of thugs in a seedy nightclub. I actually started to draw that scene — it started on the bottom of page 45 — but felt it was an unnecessary tangent, and we were seriously running out of pages by that point. I substituted a single panel of the Bat-signal and before you can say "Holy Instant Exposition," we're right back to the story.

I seem to recall other little changes/edits/deletions, but it was ten years ago, for Pete's sake, I can't remember *everything*...

Incidentally, the "Dentist Office" scene was originally from an episode of the cartoon ("Joker's Wild," maybe?), but was cut for time. We realized it would work here and plunked it in...we *never* let a good idea go to waste!

AND IN THE END...

Years later, we *did* adapt MAD LOVE for the animated series — amazingly, it survived the transition to "children's programming" with most of its innuendo and violence pretty much intact.

Oh, and the comic itself won a few awards and stuff...

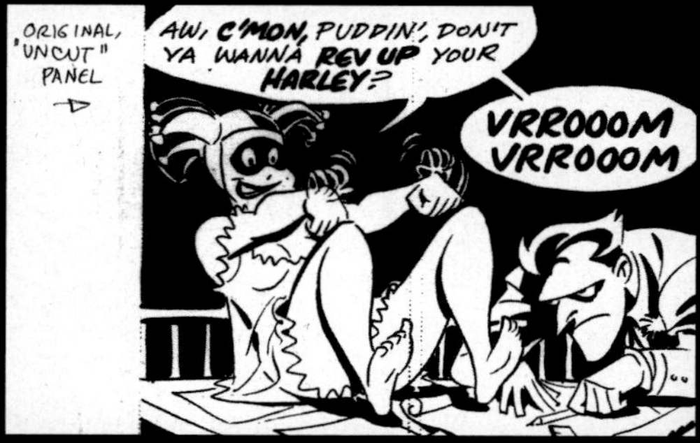
ORIGINAL "UNCUT" PANEL
AW, C'MON, PUDDIN', DON'T YA WANNA REV UP YOUR HARLEY?
VRROOOM VRROOOM

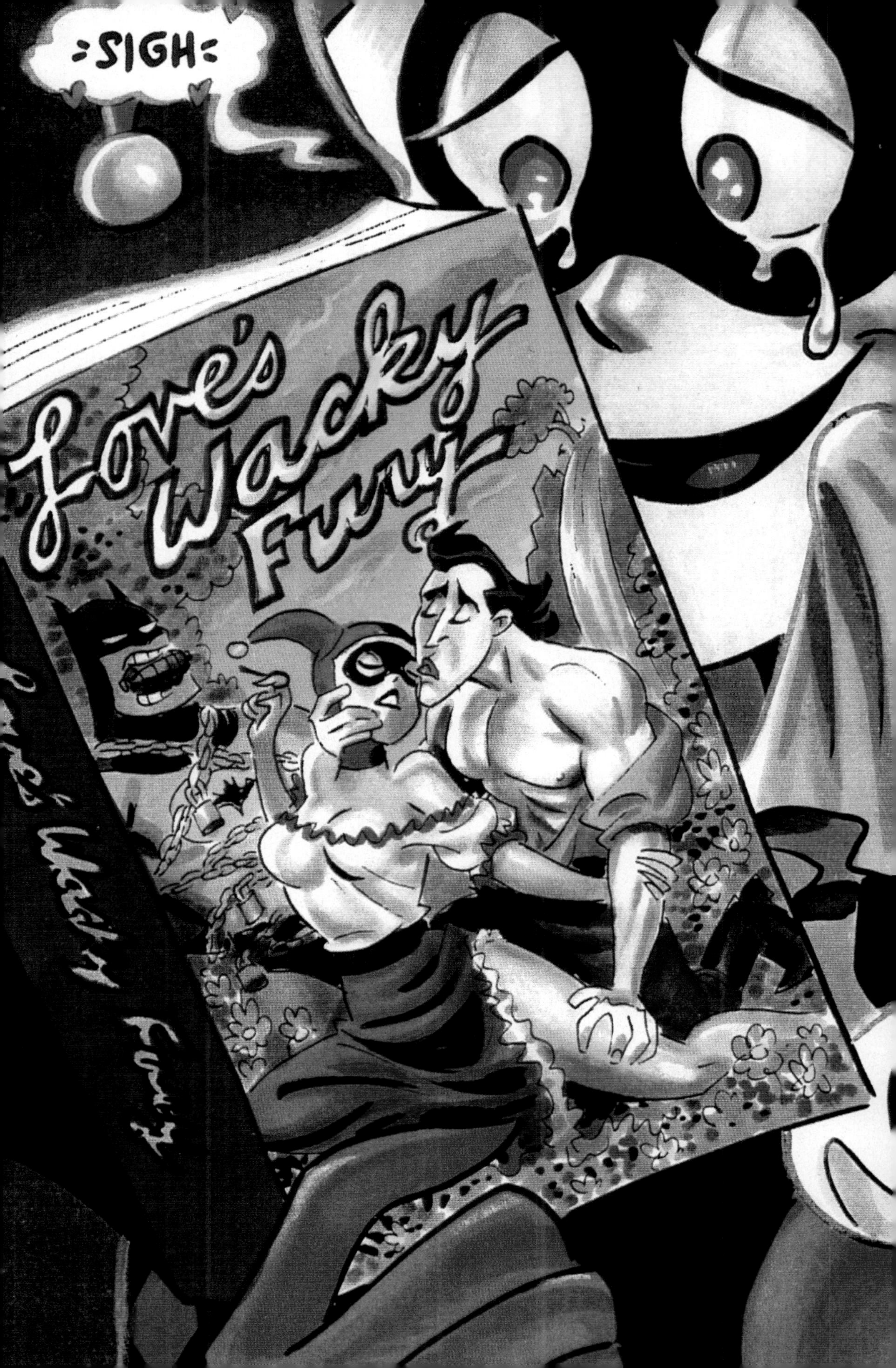
SIGH
Love's Wacky Fury

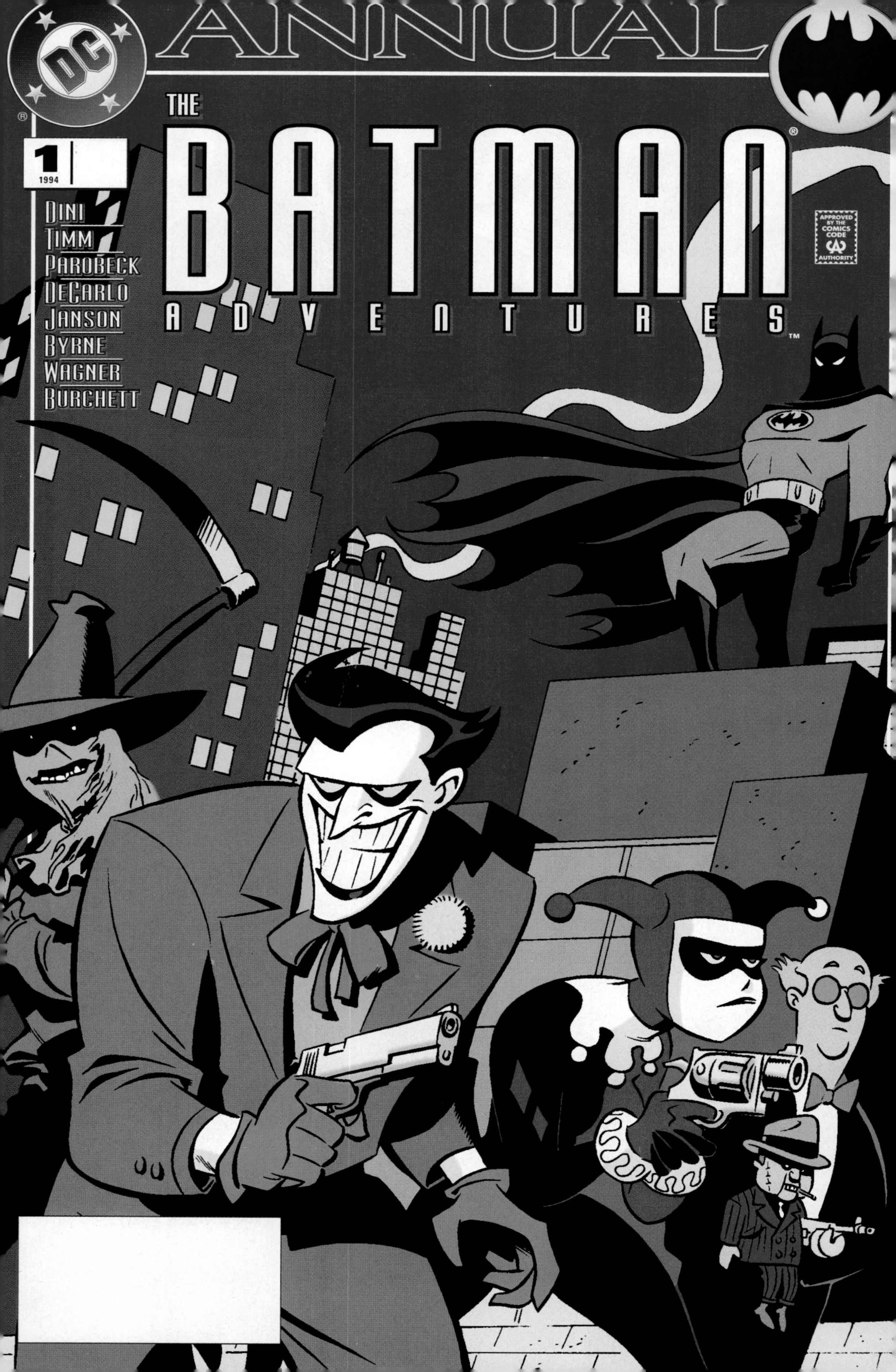
ANNUAL
DC
THE BATMAN ADVENTURES
1
1994
DINI
TIMM
PAROBECK
DECARLO
JANSON
BYRNE
WAGNER
BURCHETT
APPROVED BY THE COMICS CODE AUTHORITY

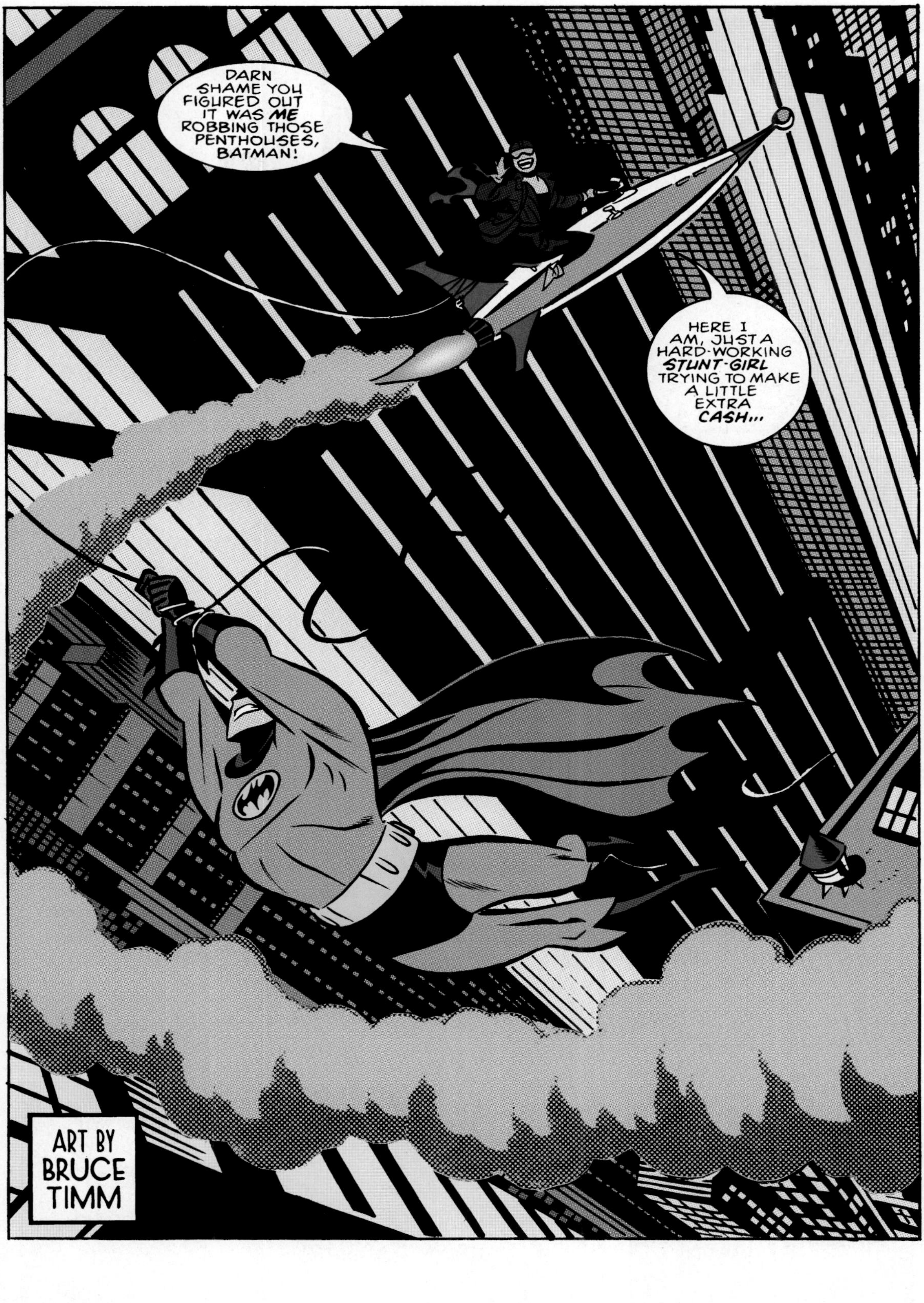
DARN SHAME YOU FIGURED OUT IT WAS ME ROBBING THOSE PENTHOUSES, BATMAN!
HERE I AM, JUST A HARD-WORKING STUNT-GIRL TRYING TO MAKE A LITTLE EXTRA CASH...
ART BY BRUCE TIMM

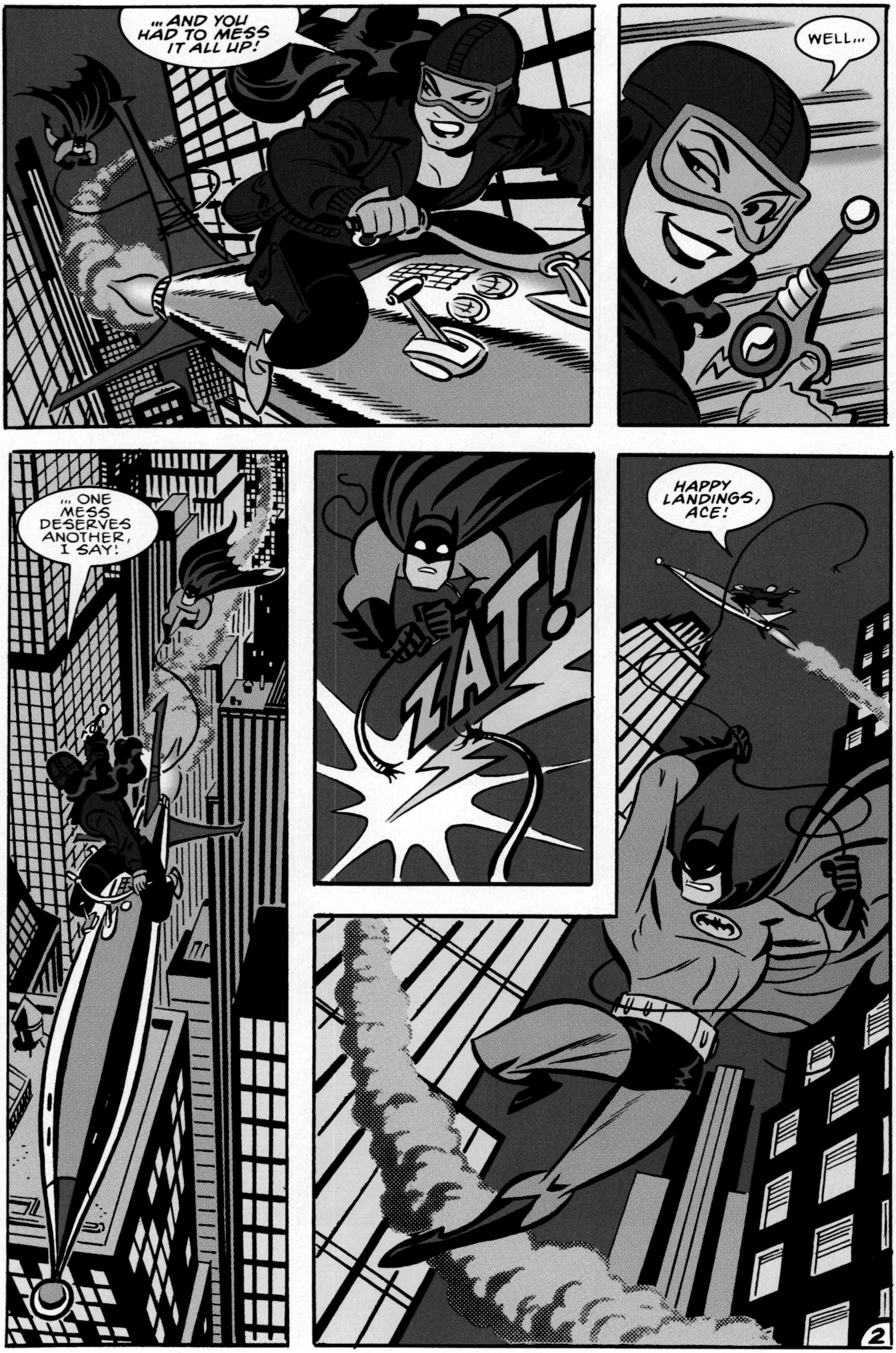
...AND YOU HAD TO MESS IT ALL UP!
WELL...
...ONE MESS DESERVES ANOTHER, I SAY!
ZAT!
HAPPY LANDINGS, ACE!
2

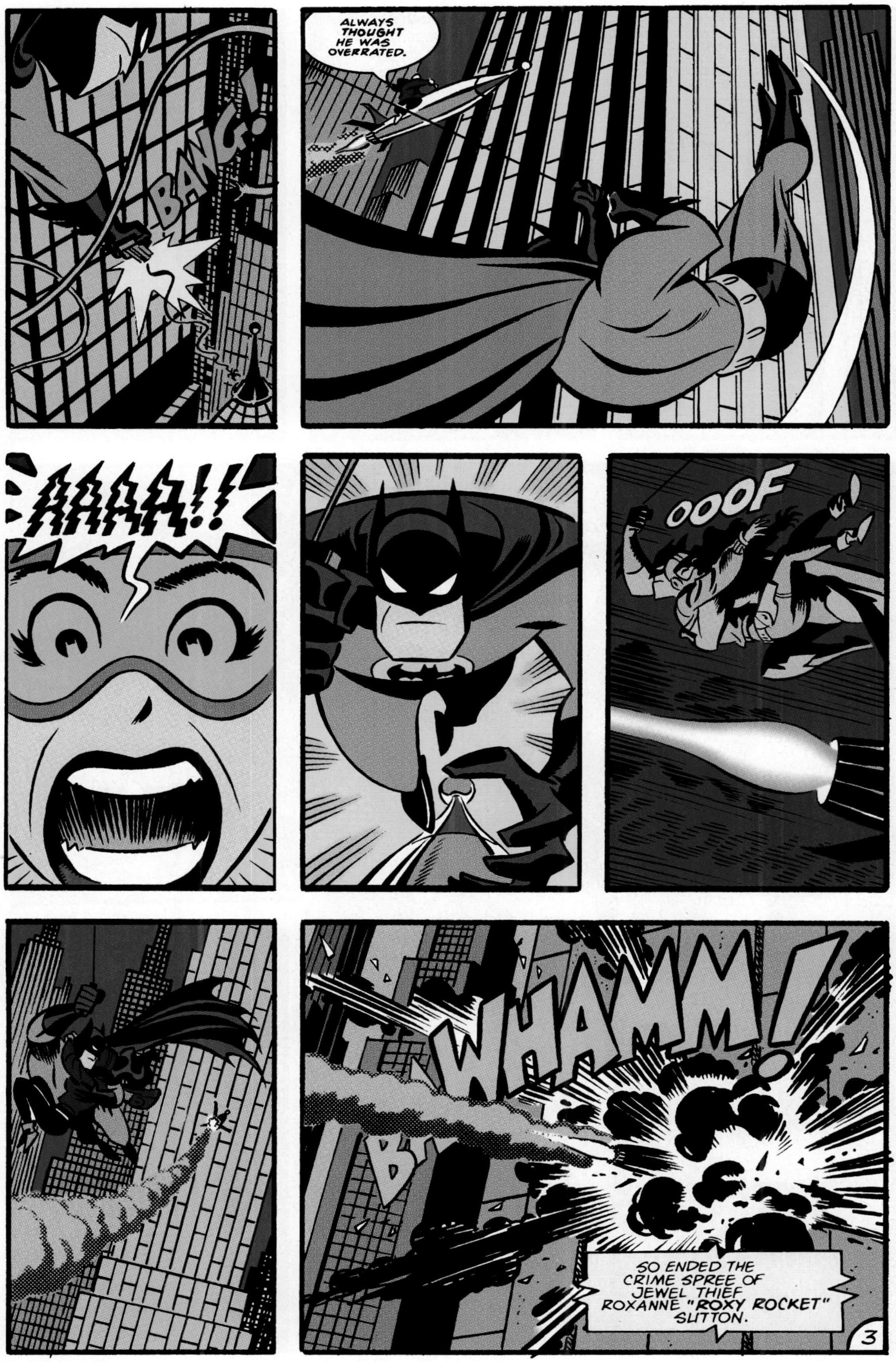
BANG!
ALWAYS THOUGHT HE WAS OVERRATED.
AAAA!!
OOOF
WHAMM!
SO ENDED THE CRIME SPREE OF JEWEL THIEF ROXANNE "ROXY ROCKET" SUTTON.
3

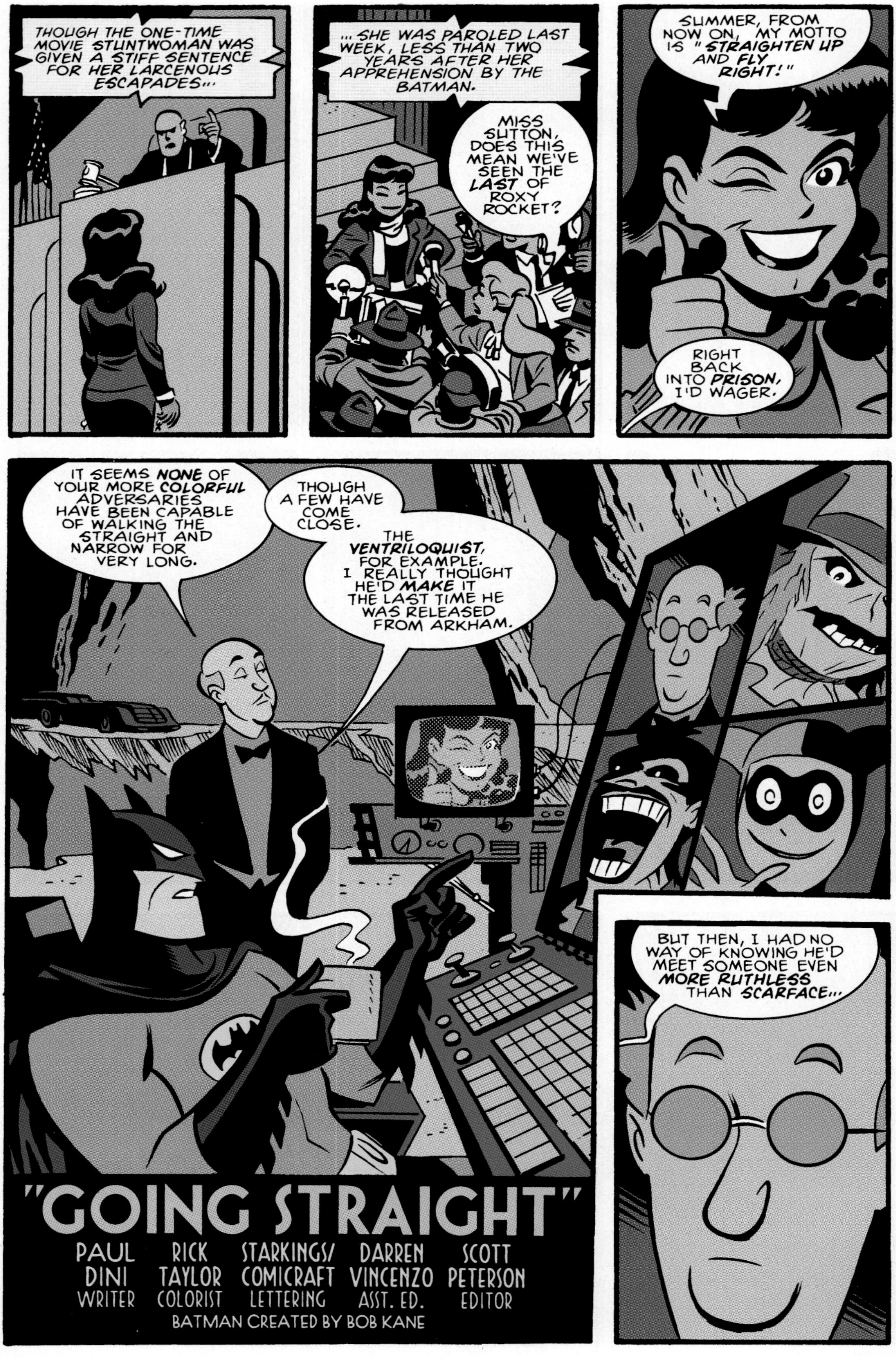
THOUGH THE ONE-TIME MOVIE STUNTWOMAN WAS GIVEN A STIFF SENTENCE FOR HER LARCENOUS ESCAPADES...
...SHE WAS PAROLED LAST WEEK, LESS THAN TWO YEARS AFTER HER APPREHENSION BY THE BATMAN.
MISS SUTTON, DOES THIS MEAN WE'VE SEEN THE LAST OF ROXY ROCKET?
SUMMER, FROM NOW ON, MY MOTTO IS "STRAIGHTEN UP AND FLY RIGHT!"
RIGHT BACK INTO PRISON, I'D WAGER.
IT SEEMS NONE OF YOUR MORE COLORFUL ADVERSARIES HAVE BEEN CAPABLE OF WALKING THE STRAIGHT AND NARROW FOR VERY LONG.
THOUGH A FEW HAVE COME CLOSE.
THE VENTRILOQUIST, FOR EXAMPLE. I REALLY THOUGHT HE'D MAKE IT THE LAST TIME HE WAS RELEASED FROM ARKHAM.
BUT THEN, I HAD NO WAY OF KNOWING HE'D MEET SOMEONE EVEN MORE RUTHLESS THAN SCARFACE...
"GOING STRAIGHT"
PAUL DINI WRITER
RICK TAYLOR COLORIST
STARKINGS/ COMICRAFT LETTERING
DARREN VINCENZO ASST. ED.
SCOTT PETERSON EDITOR
BATMAN CREATED BY BOB KANE

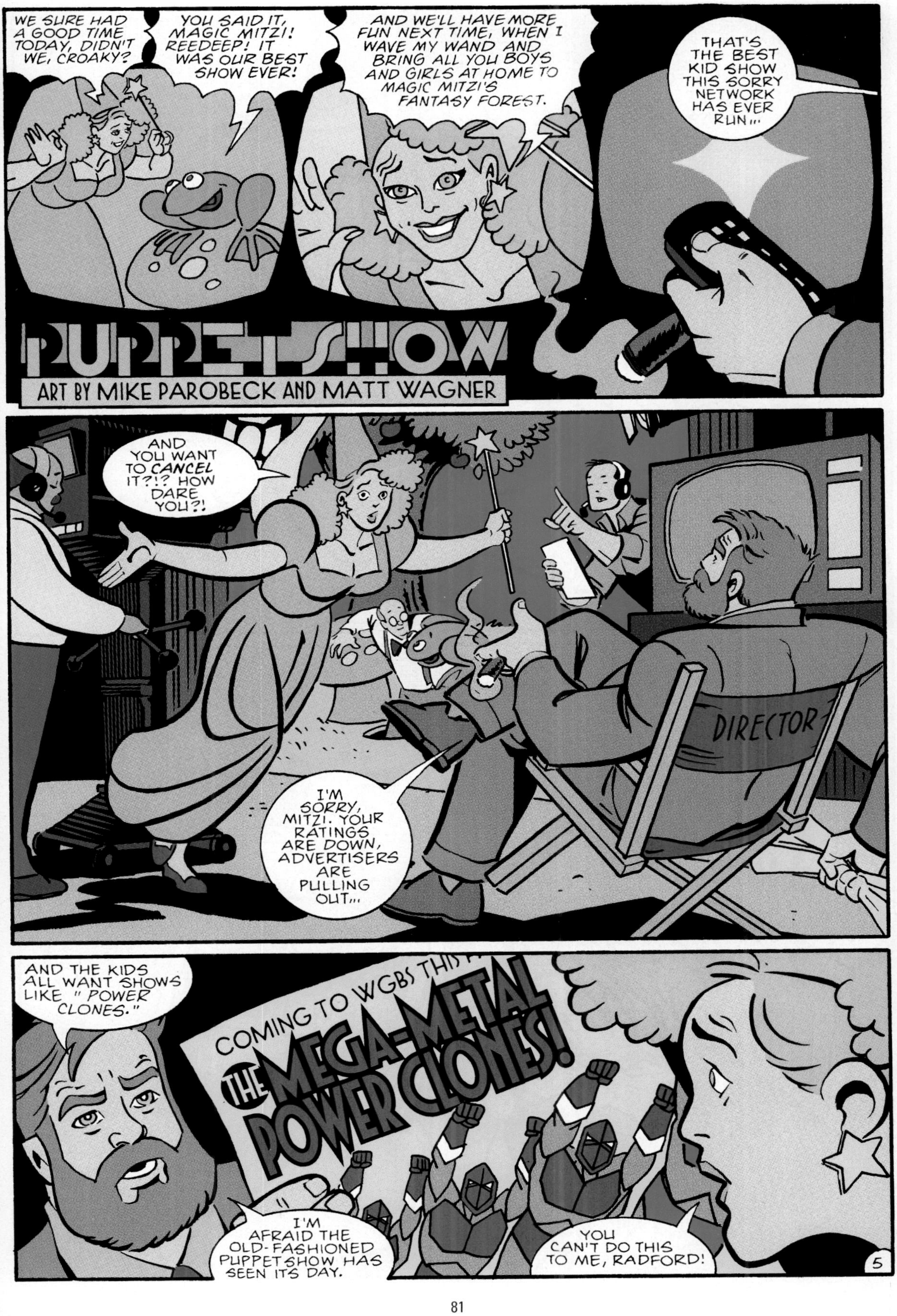

WE SURE HAD A GOOD TIME TODAY, DIDN'T WE, CROAKY?
YOU SAID IT, MAGIC MITZI! REEDEEP! IT WAS OUR BEST SHOW EVER!
AND WE'LL HAVE MORE FUN NEXT TIME, WHEN I WAVE MY WAND AND BRING ALL YOU BOYS AND GIRLS AT HOME TO MAGIC MITZI'S FANTASY FOREST.
THAT'S THE BEST KID SHOW THIS SORRY NETWORK HAS EVER RUN...
PUPPET SHOW
ART BY MIKE PAROBECK AND MATT WAGNER
AND YOU WANT TO CANCEL IT?!? HOW DARE YOU?!
DIRECTOR
I'M SORRY, MITZI. YOUR RATINGS ARE DOWN, ADVERTISERS ARE PULLING OUT...
AND THE KIDS ALL WANT SHOWS LIKE "POWER CLONES."
COMING TO WGBS THIS
THE MEGA-METAL POWER CLONES!
I'M AFRAID THE OLD-FASHIONED PUPPET SHOW HAS SEEN ITS DAY.
YOU CAN'T DO THIS TO ME, RADFORD!
5

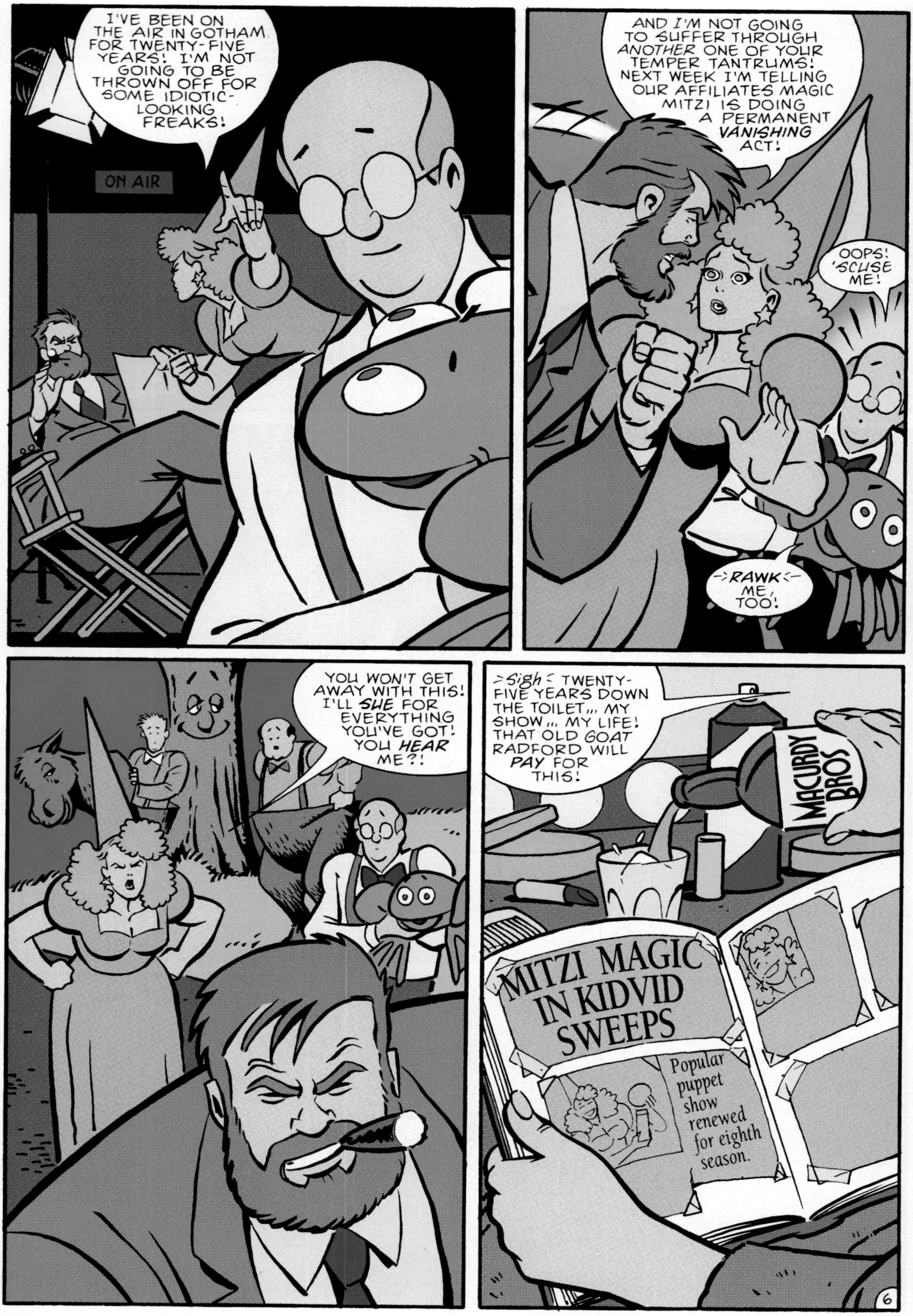

I'VE BEEN ON THE AIR IN GOTHAM FOR TWENTY-FIVE YEARS! I'M NOT GOING TO BE THROWN OFF FOR SOME IDIOTIC-LOOKING FREAKS!
ON AIR
AND I'M NOT GOING TO SUFFER THROUGH ANOTHER ONE OF YOUR TEMPER TANTRUMS! NEXT WEEK I'M TELLING OUR AFFILIATES MAGIC MITZI IS DOING A PERMANENT VANISHING ACT!
OOPS! 'SCUSE ME!
>RAWK< ME, TOO!
YOU WON'T GET AWAY WITH THIS! I'LL SUE FOR EVERYTHING YOU'VE GOT! YOU HEAR ME?!
>Sigh< TWENTY-FIVE YEARS DOWN THE TOILET... MY SHOW... MY LIFE! THAT OLD GOAT RADFORD WILL PAY FOR THIS!
MACURDY BROS
MITZI MAGIC IN KIDVID SWEEPS
Popular puppet show renewed for eighth season.
6

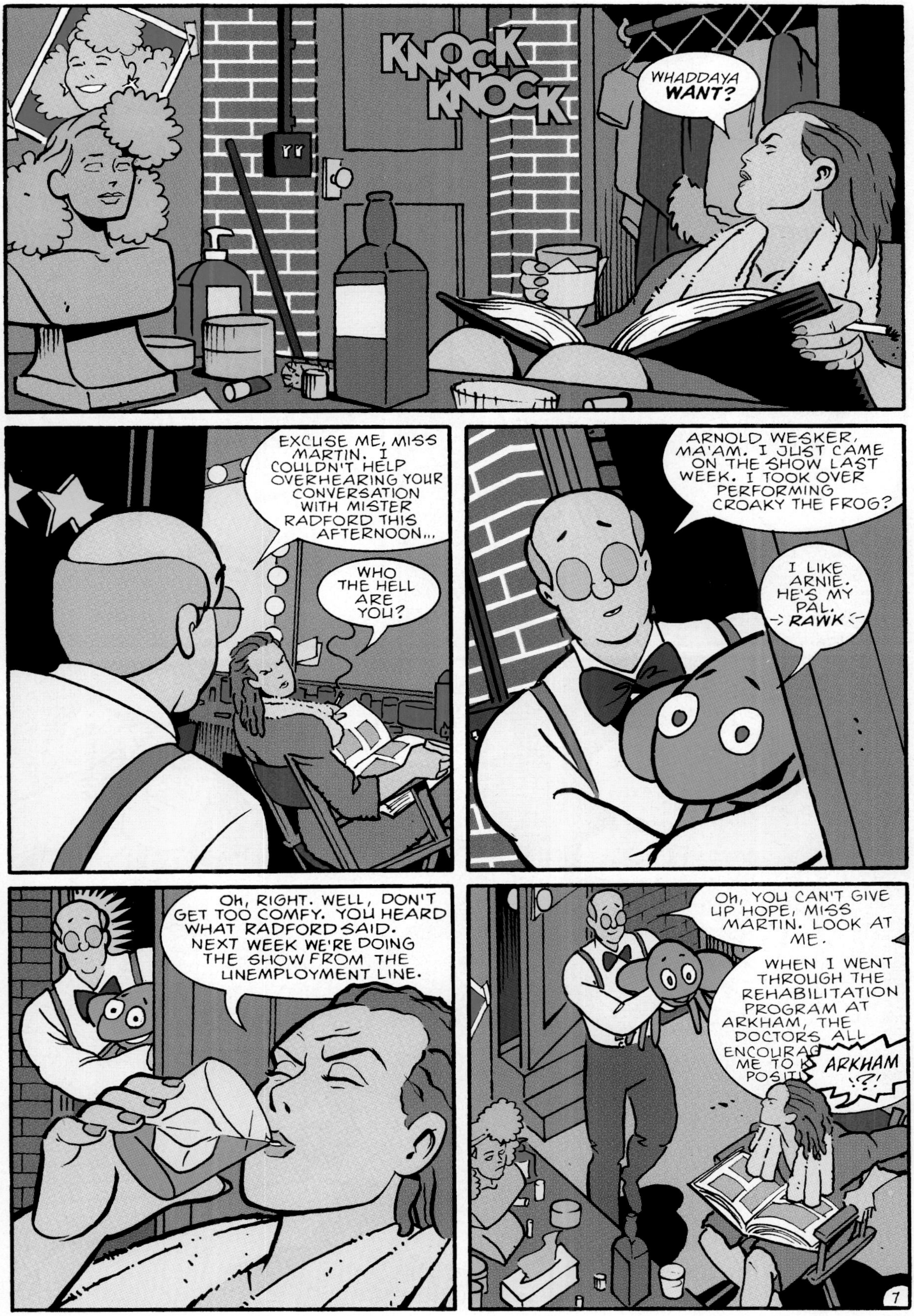
KNOCK KNOCK
WHADDAYA WANT?
EXCUSE ME, MISS MARTIN. I COULDN'T HELP OVERHEARING YOUR CONVERSATION WITH MISTER RADFORD THIS AFTERNOON...
WHO THE HELL ARE YOU?
ARNOLD WESKER, MA'AM. I JUST CAME ON THE SHOW LAST WEEK. I TOOK OVER PERFORMING CROAKY THE FROG?
I LIKE ARNIE. HE'S MY PAL. RAWK
OH, RIGHT. WELL, DON'T GET TOO COMFY. YOU HEARD WHAT RADFORD SAID. NEXT WEEK WE'RE DOING THE SHOW FROM THE UNEMPLOYMENT LINE.
OH, YOU CAN'T GIVE UP HOPE, MISS MARTIN. LOOK AT ME.
WHEN I WENT THROUGH THE REHABILITATION PROGRAM AT ARKHAM, THE DOCTORS ALL ENCOURAG
ME TO K
POSITI
ARKHAM !?!
7

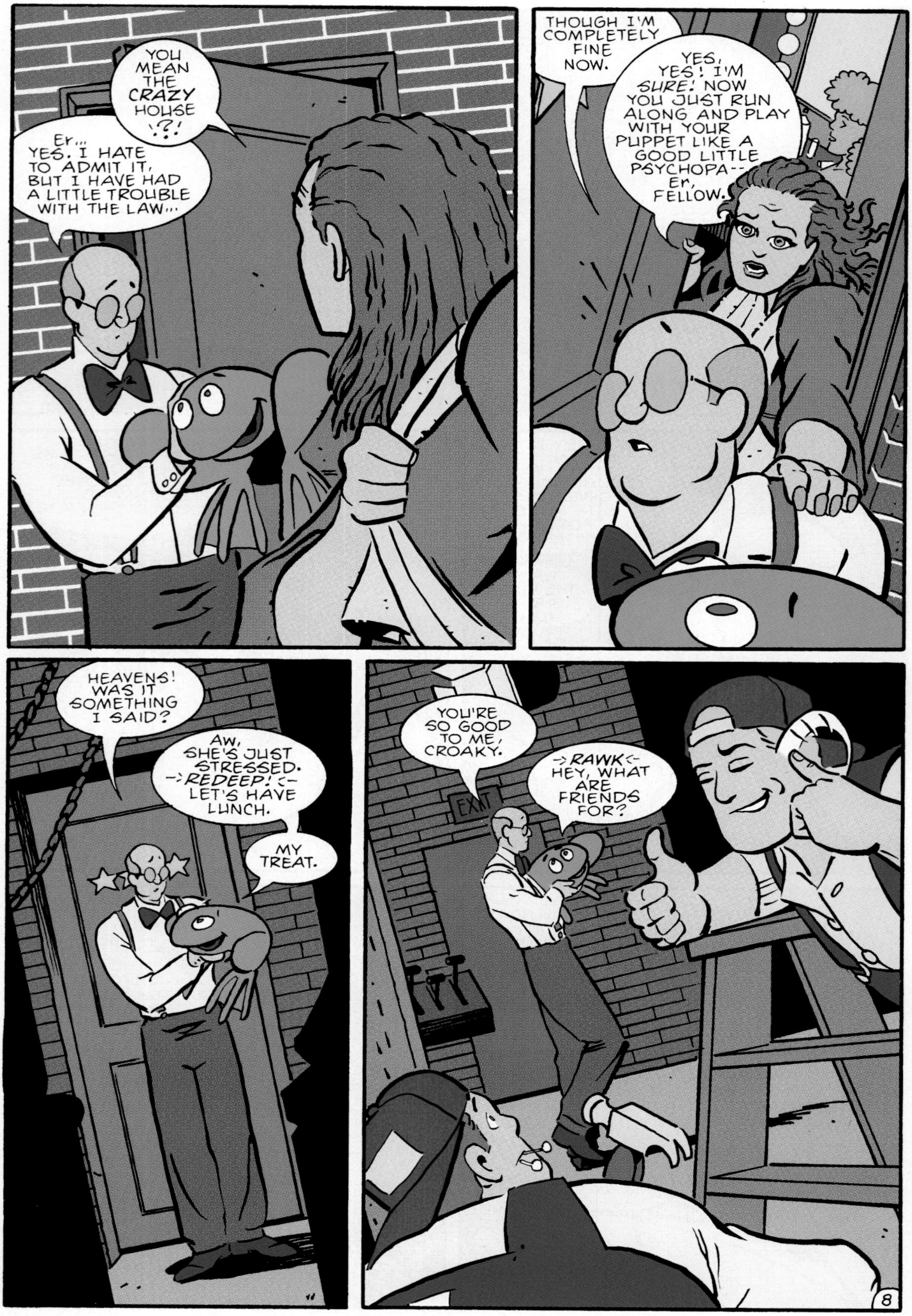
YOU MEAN THE CRAZY HOUSE ?!
Er... YES. I HATE TO ADMIT IT, BUT I HAVE HAD A LITTLE TROUBLE WITH THE LAW...
THOUGH I'M COMPLETELY FINE NOW.
YES, YES! I'M SURE! NOW YOU JUST RUN ALONG AND PLAY WITH YOUR PUPPET LIKE A GOOD LITTLE PSYCHOPA-- Er, FELLOW.
HEAVENS! WAS IT SOMETHING I SAID?
AW, SHE'S JUST STRESSED. REDEEP! LET'S HAVE LUNCH.
MY TREAT.
EXIT
YOU'RE SO GOOD TO ME, CROAKY.
RAWK HEY, WHAT ARE FRIENDS FOR?
8

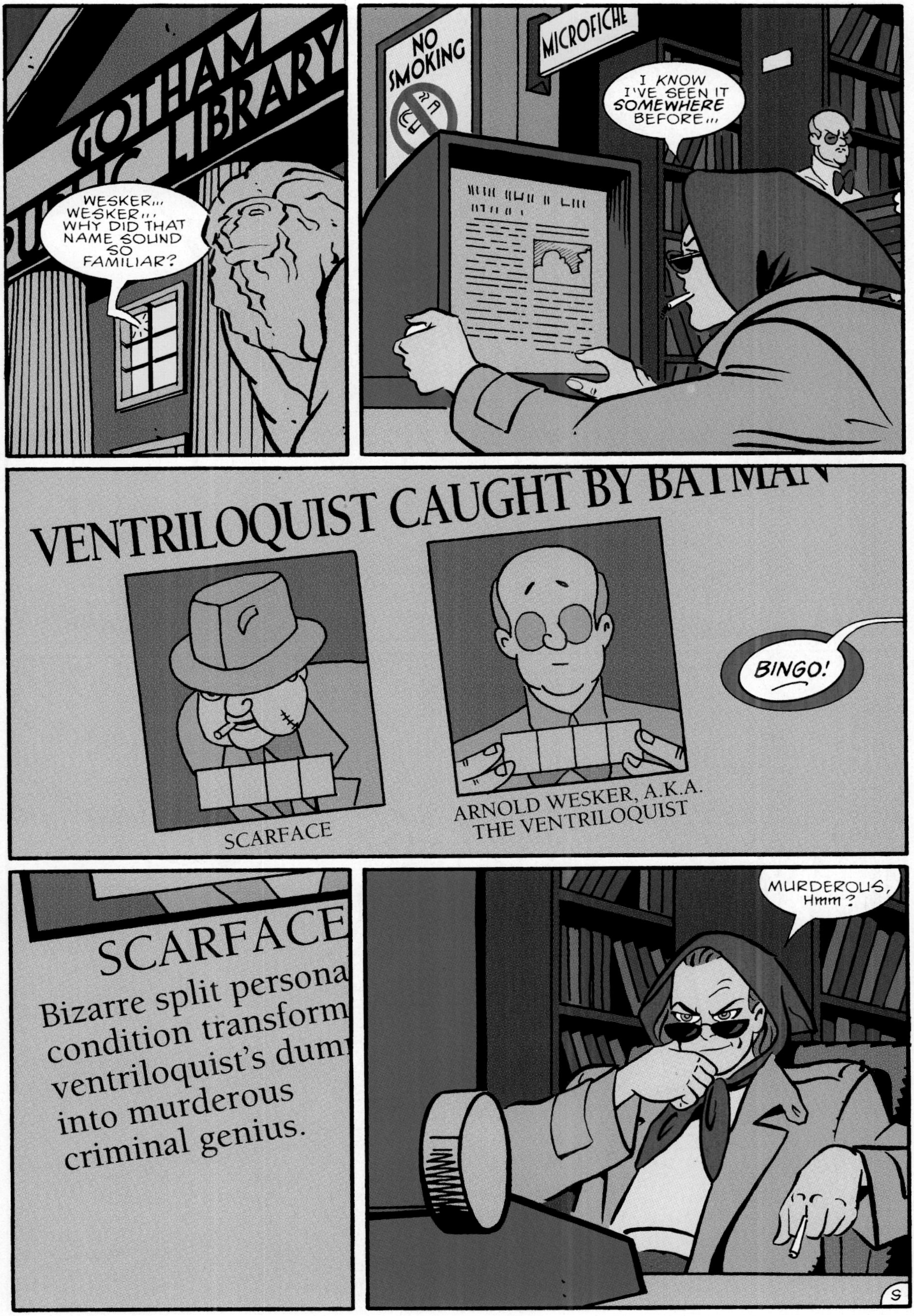
GOTHAM
LIBRARY
WESKER... WESKER... WHY DID THAT NAME SOUND SO FAMILIAR?
NO SMOKING
MICROFICHE
I KNOW I'VE SEEN IT SOMEWHERE BEFORE...
VENTRILOQUIST CAUGHT BY BATMAN
SCARFACE
ARNOLD WESKER, A.K.A. THE VENTRILOQUIST
BINGO!
SCARFACE
Bizarre split persona
condition transform
ventriloquist's dum
into murderous
criminal genius.
MURDEROUS, Hmm?

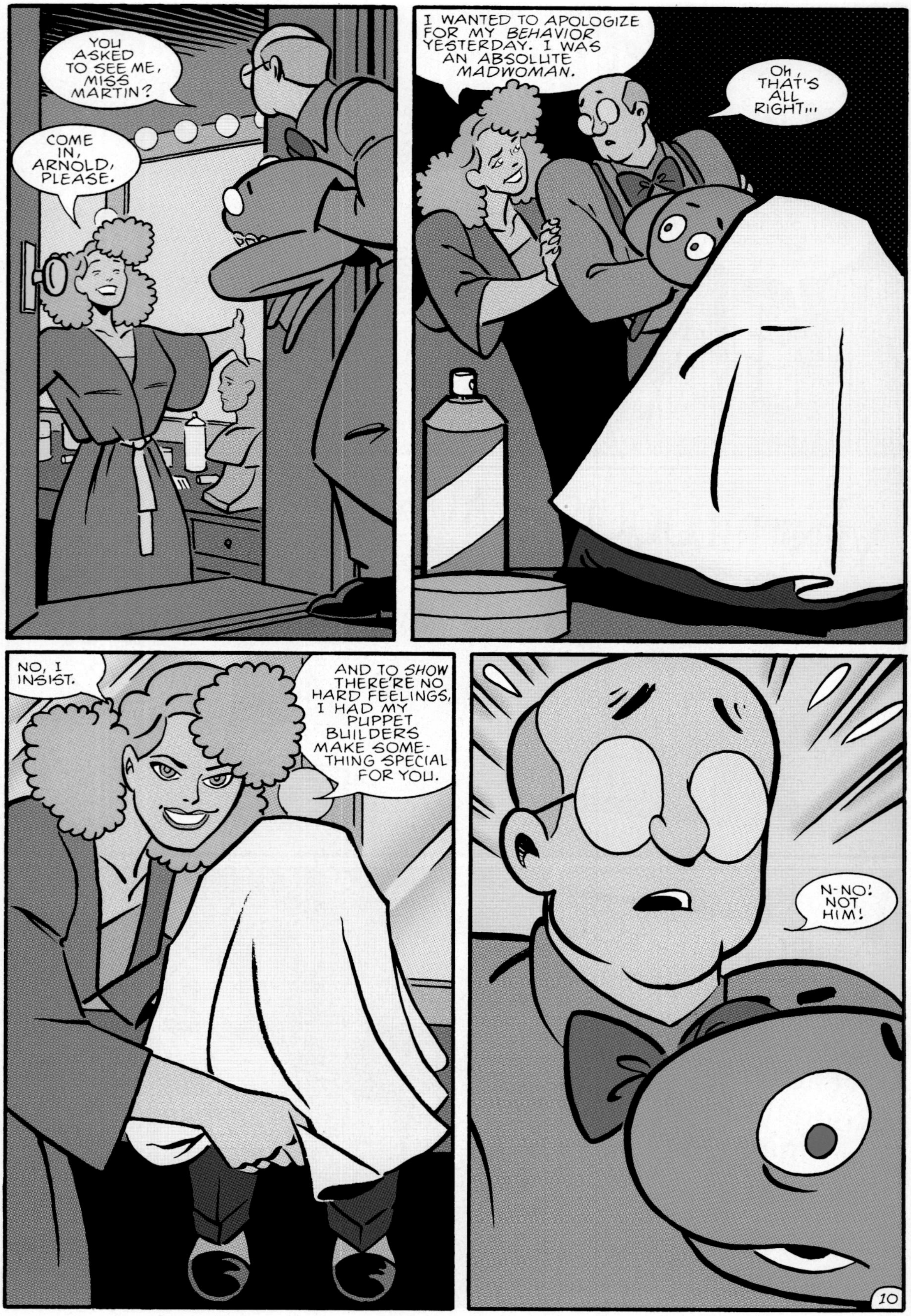
YOU ASKED TO SEE ME, MISS MARTIN?
COME IN, ARNOLD, PLEASE.
I WANTED TO APOLOGIZE FOR MY *BEHAVIOR* YESTERDAY. I WAS AN ABSOLUTE *MADWOMAN*.
Oh, THAT'S ALL RIGHT...
NO, I INSIST.
AND TO *SHOW* THERE'RE NO HARD FEELINGS, I HAD MY PUPPET BUILDERS MAKE SOME-THING SPECIAL FOR YOU.
N-NO! NOT HIM!
10

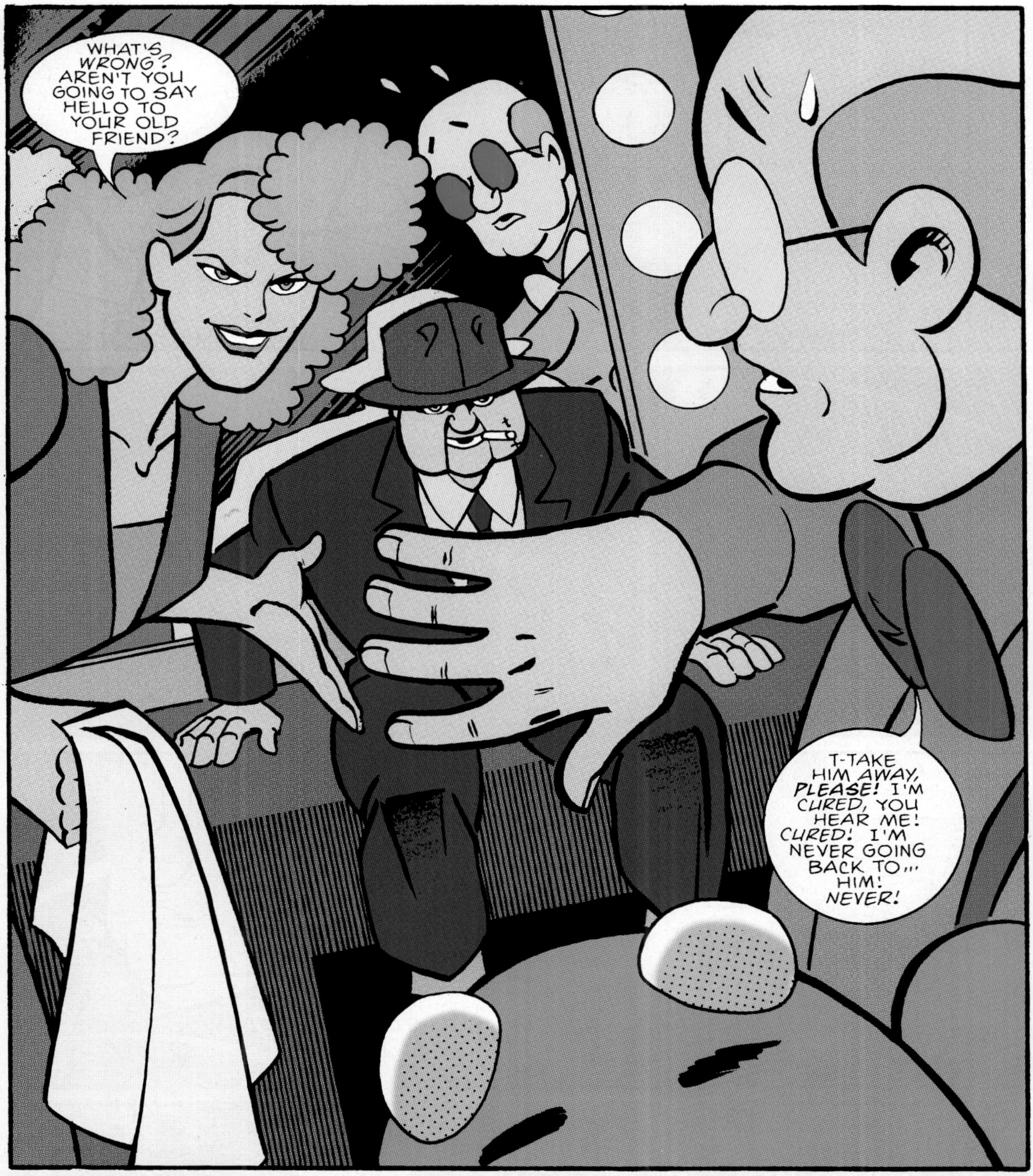
WHAT'S WRONG? AREN'T YOU GOING TO SAY HELLO TO YOUR OLD FRIEND?
T-TAKE HIM AWAY, PLEASE! I'M CURED, YOU HEAR ME! CURED! I'M NEVER GOING BACK TO... HIM! NEVER!

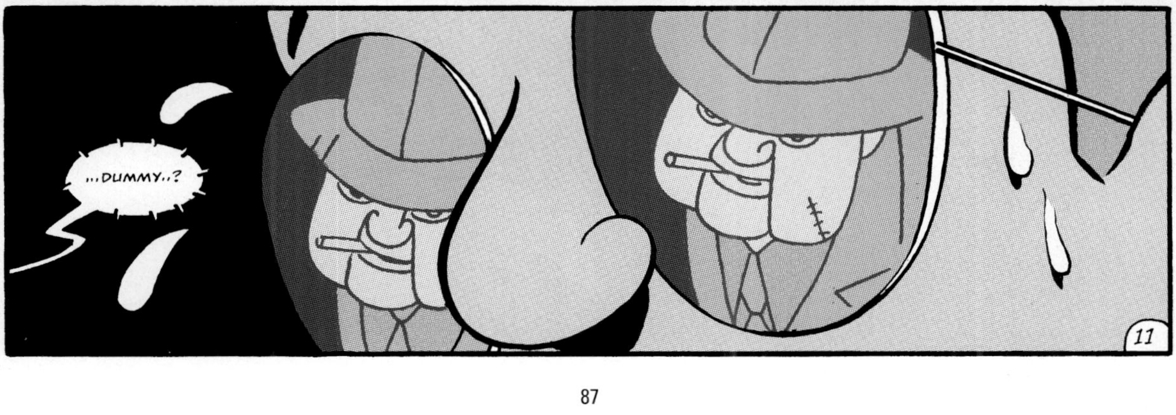
...DUMMY..?
11

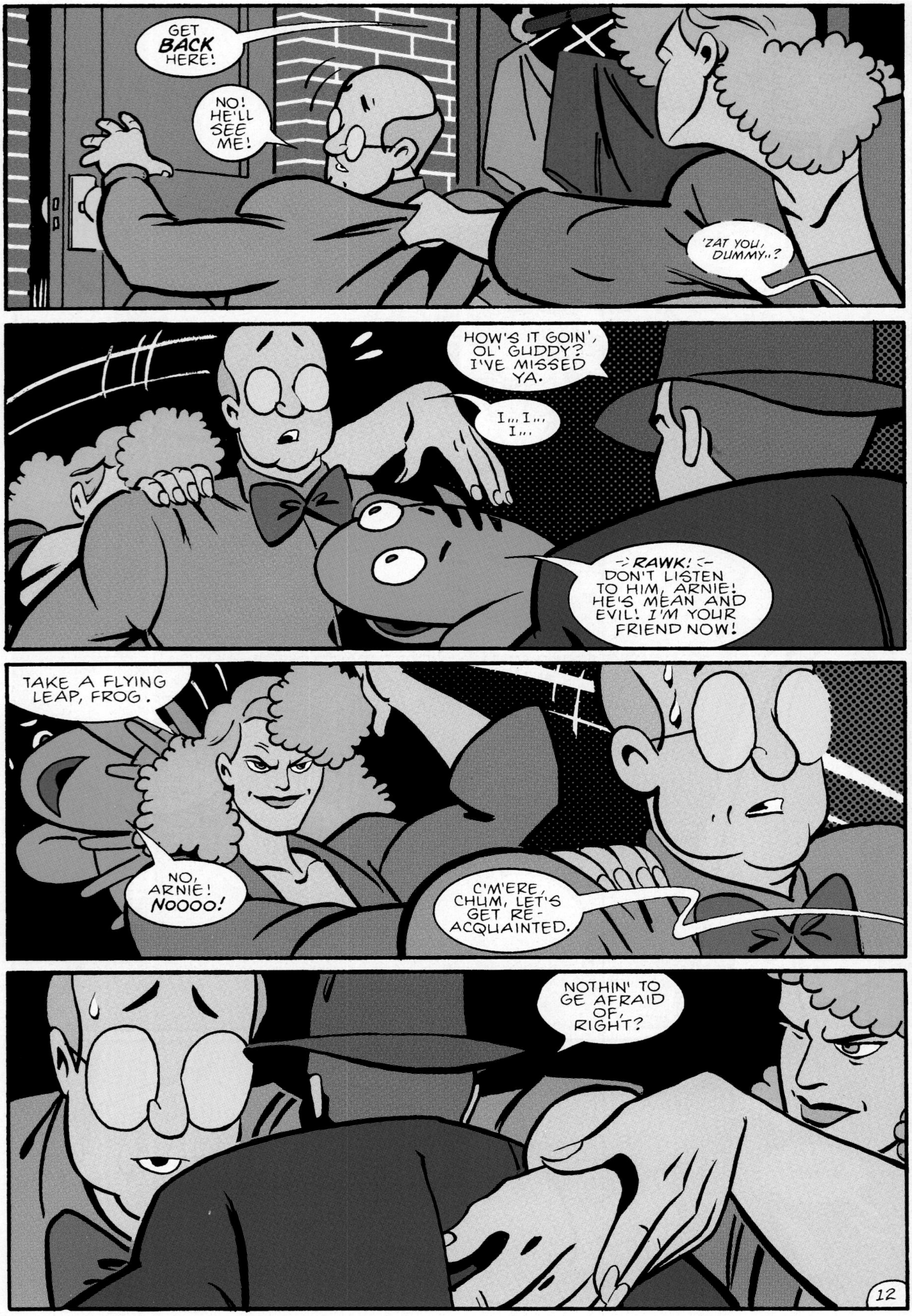
GET BACK HERE!
NO! HE'LL SEE ME!
'ZAT YOU, DUMMY..?
HOW'S IT GOIN', OL' GUDDY? I'VE MISSED YA.
I..., I..., I...
RAWK! DON'T LISTEN TO HIM, ARNIE! HE'S MEAN AND EVIL! I'M YOUR FRIEND NOW!
TAKE A FLYING LEAP, FROG.
NO, ARNIE! NOOOO!
C'M'ERE, CHUM, LET'S GET RE-ACQUAINTED.
NOTHIN' TO GE AFRAID OF, RIGHT?
12

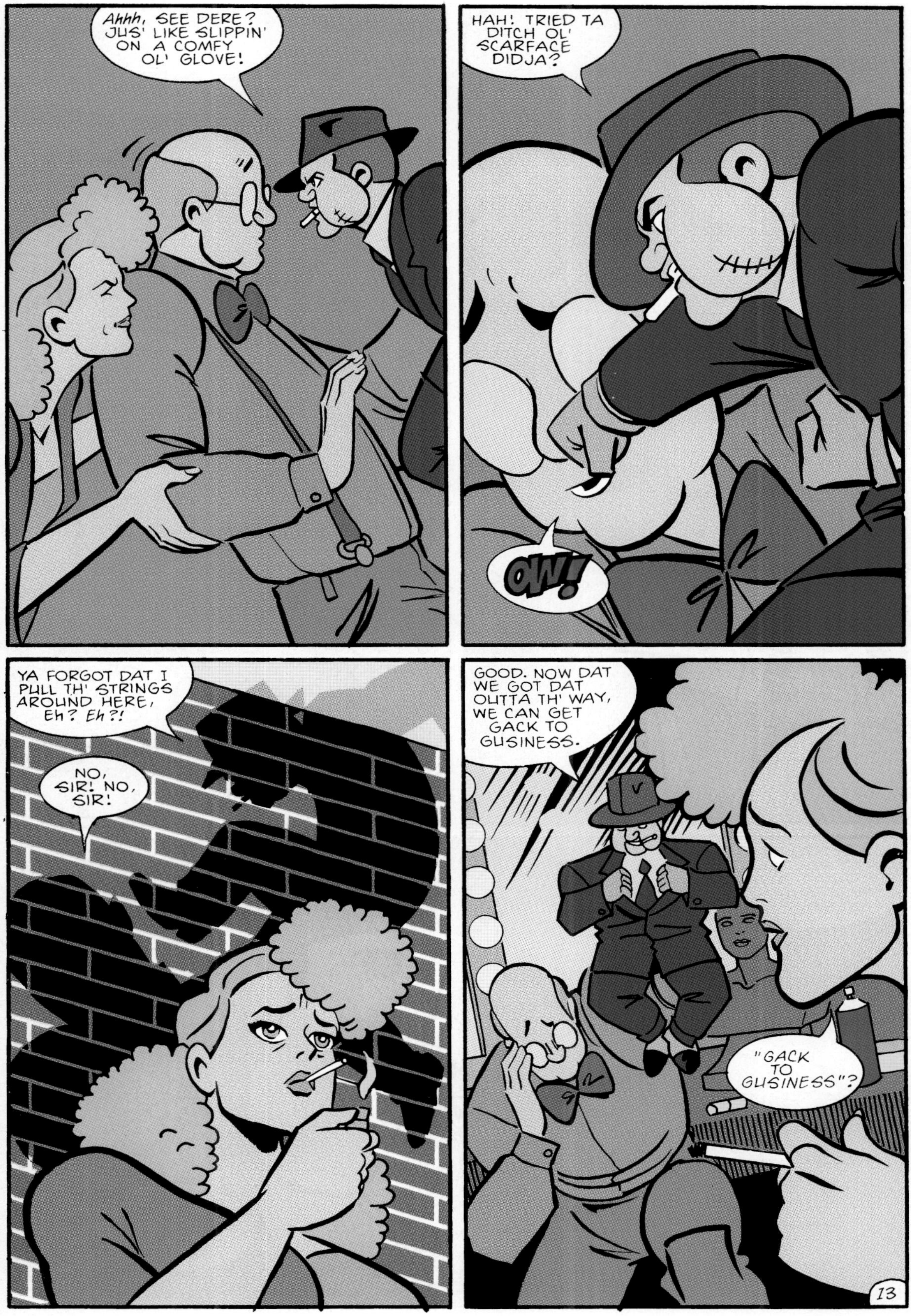
Ahhh, SEE DERE? JUS' LIKE SLIPPIN' ON A COMFY OL' GLOVE!
HAH! TRIED TA DITCH OL' SCARFACE DIDJA?
OW!
YA FORGOT DAT I PULL TH' STRINGS AROUND HERE, Eh? Eh?!
NO, SIR! NO, SIR!
GOOD. NOW DAT WE GOT DAT OUTTA TH' WAY, WE CAN GET GACK TO GUSINESS.
"GACK TO GUSINESS"?
13

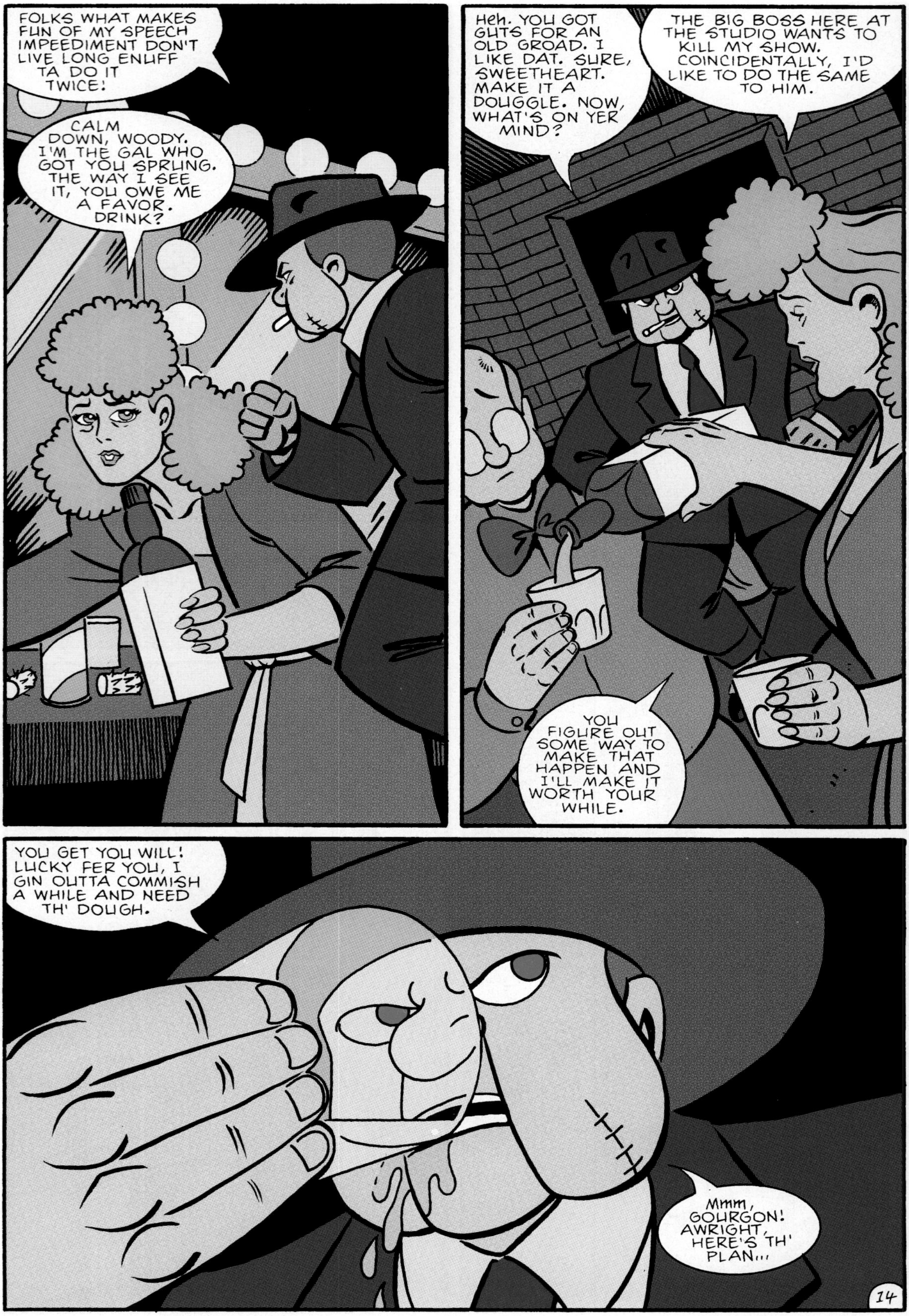
FOLKS WHAT MAKES FUN OF MY SPEECH IMPEEDIMENT DON'T LIVE LONG ENUFF TA DO IT TWICE!
CALM DOWN, WOODY. I'M THE GAL WHO GOT YOU SPRUNG. THE WAY I SEE IT, YOU OWE ME A FAVOR. DRINK?
Heh. YOU GOT GUTS FOR AN OLD GROAD. I LIKE DAT. SURE, SWEETHEART. MAKE IT A DOUGGLE. NOW, WHAT'S ON YER MIND?
THE BIG BOSS HERE AT THE STUDIO WANTS TO KILL MY SHOW. COINCIDENTALLY, I'D LIKE TO DO THE SAME TO HIM.
YOU FIGURE OUT SOME WAY TO MAKE THAT HAPPEN AND I'LL MAKE IT WORTH YOUR WHILE.
YOU GET YOU WILL! LUCKY FER YOU, I GIN OUTTA COMMISH A WHILE AND NEED TH' DOUGH.
Mmm, GOURGON! AWRIGHT, HERE'S TH' PLAN...
14

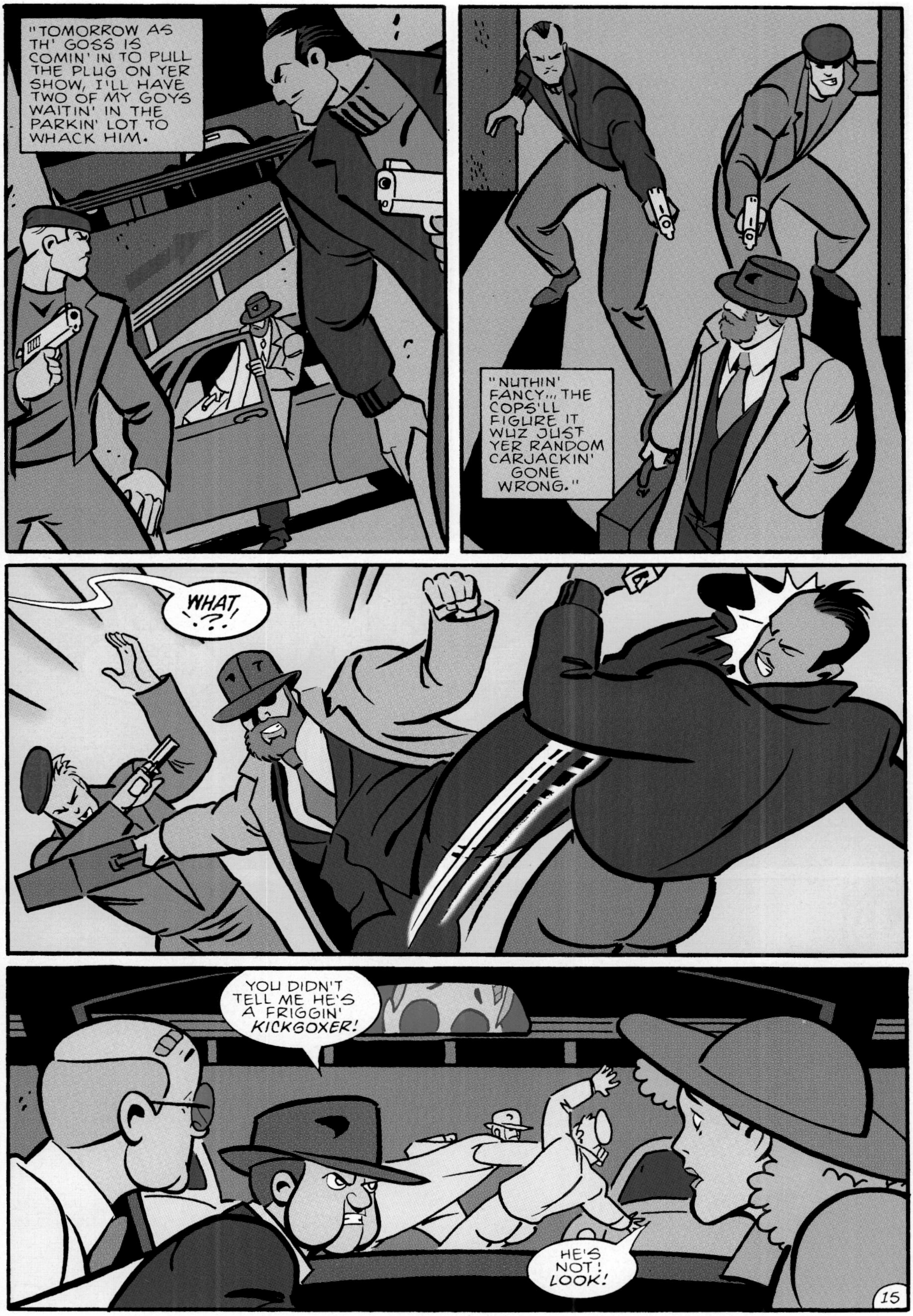
"TOMORROW AS TH' GOSS IS COMIN' IN TO PULL THE PLUG ON YER SHOW, I'LL HAVE TWO OF MY GOYS WAITIN' IN THE PARKIN' LOT TO WHACK HIM.
"NUTHIN' FANCY... THE COPS'LL FIGURE IT WUZ JUST YER RANDOM CARJACKIN' GONE WRONG."
WHAT, !?!
YOU DIDN'T TELL ME HE'S A FRIGGIN' KICKGOXER!
HE'S NOT! LOOK!
15

Oh, GREAT!

LAST THING I NEED IS THAT *FREAK* DRAGGIN' ME GACK TO THE JOINT! GET ME OUTTA HERE, DUMMY!

BUT WHAT ABOUT ME?

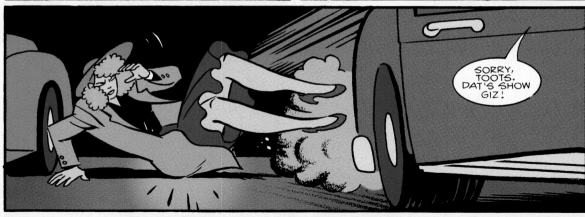

SORRY, TOOTS. DAT'S SHOW GIZ!

16

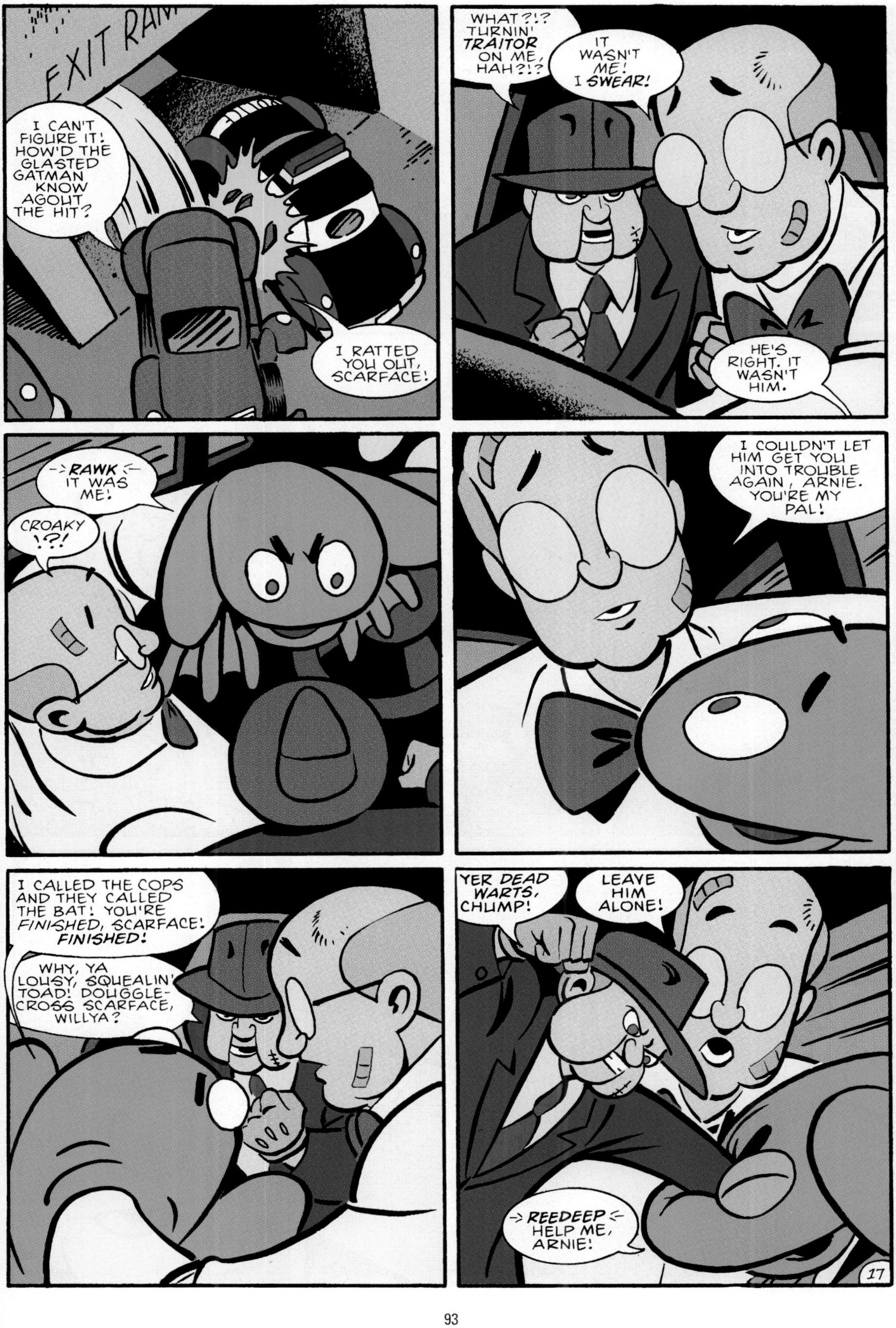
EXIT RAM
I CAN'T FIGURE IT! HOW'D THE GLASTED GATMAN KNOW AGOUT THE HIT?
I RATTED YOU OUT, SCARFACE!
WHAT?!? TURNIN' TRAITOR ON ME, HAH?!?
IT WASN'T ME! I SWEAR!
HE'S RIGHT. IT WASN'T HIM.
RAWK IT WAS ME!
CROAKY !?!
I COULDN'T LET HIM GET YOU INTO TROUBLE AGAIN, ARNIE. YOU'RE MY PAL!
I CALLED THE COPS AND THEY CALLED THE BAT! YOU'RE FINISHED, SCARFACE! FINISHED!
WHY, YA LOUSY, SQUEALIN' TOAD! DOUGGLE-CROSS SCARFACE, WILLYA?
YER DEAD WARTS, CHUMP!
LEAVE HIM ALONE!
REEDEEP HELP ME, ARNIE!
17

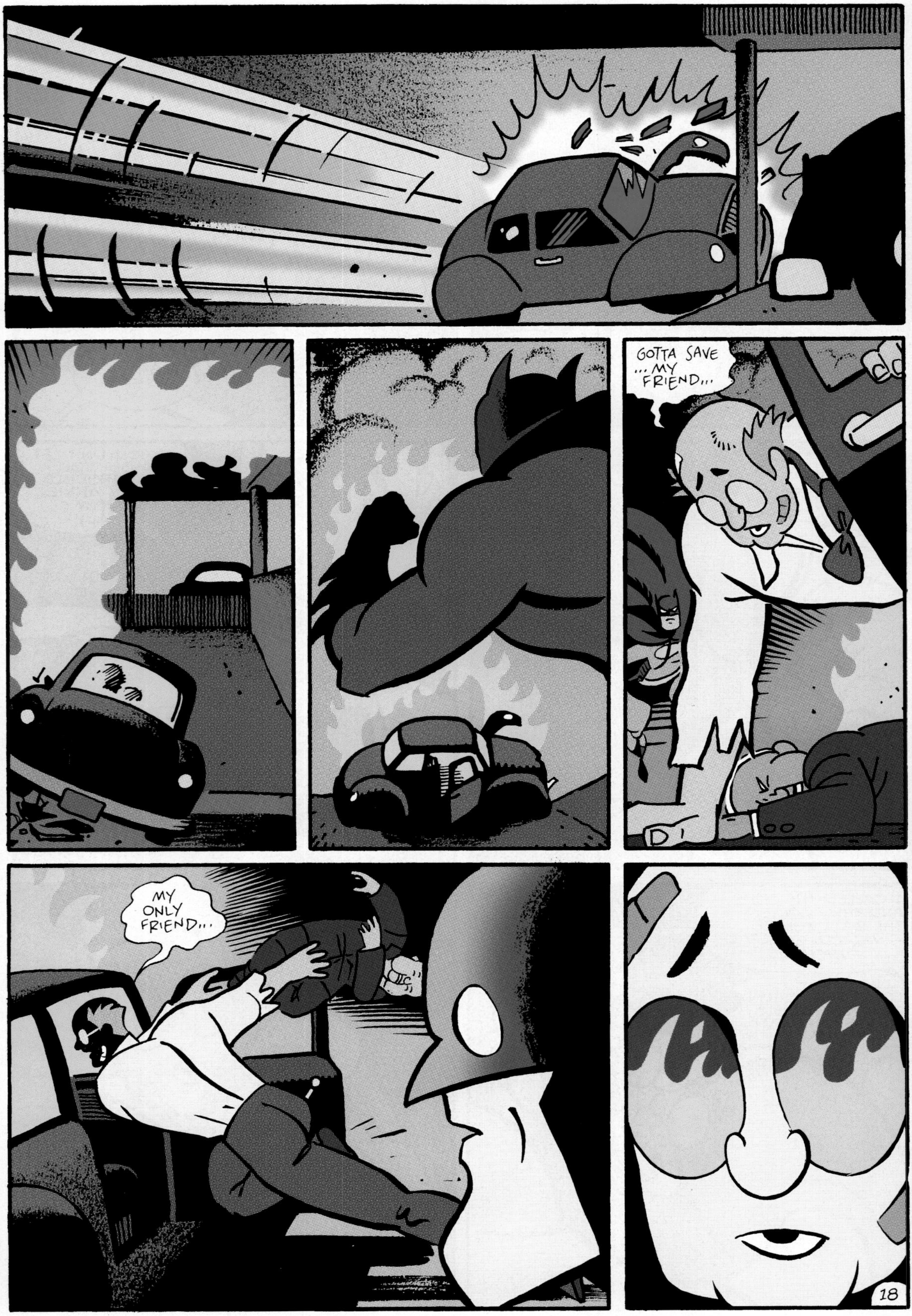
GOTTA SAVE ...MY FRIEND...
MY ONLY FRIEND...
18

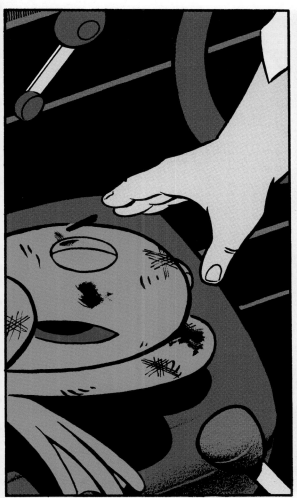

...DUMMY...

COMING, MISTER SCARFACE.

19

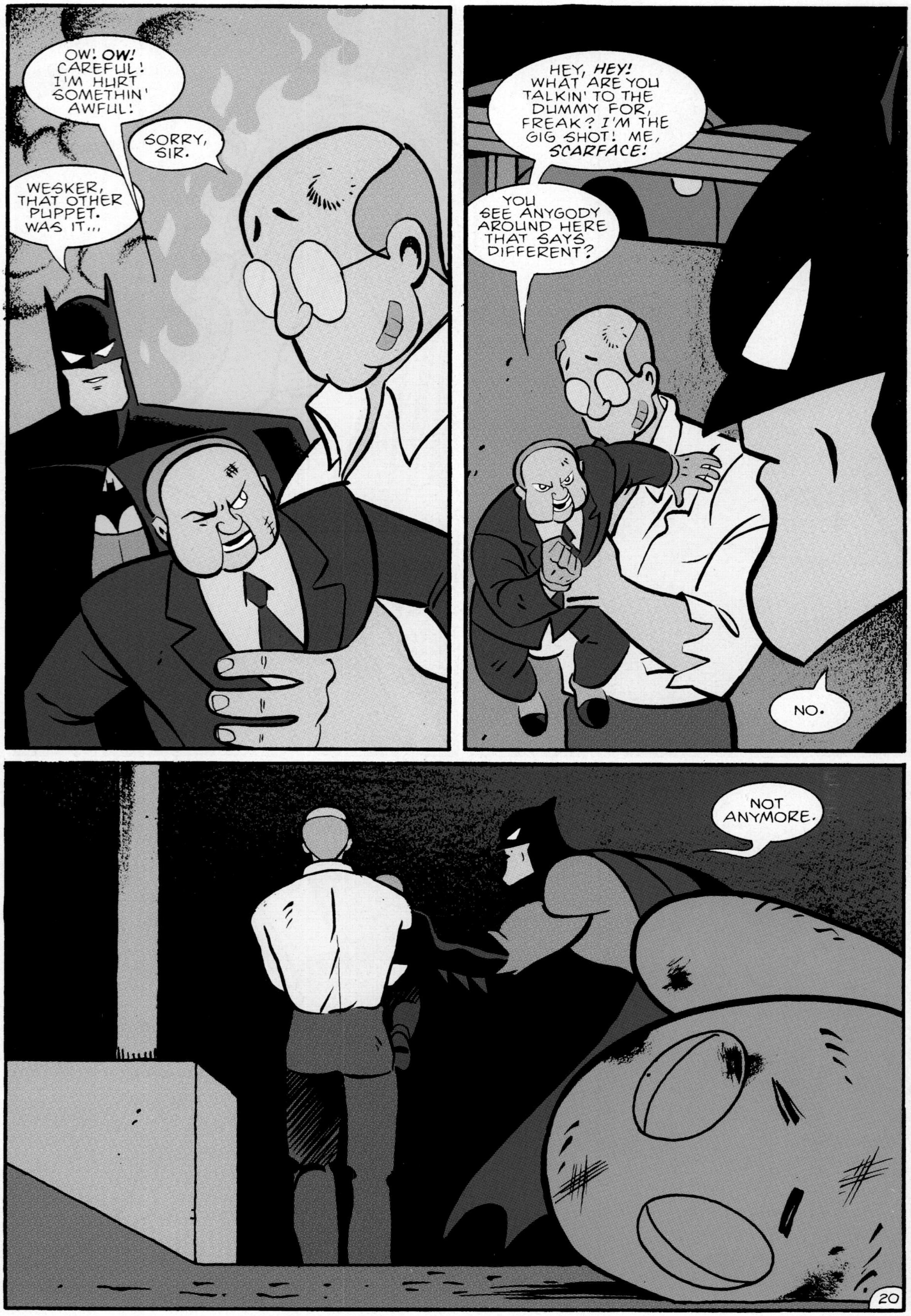

OW! OW! CAREFUL! I'M HURT SOMETHIN' AWFUL!
SORRY, SIR.
WESKER, THAT OTHER PUPPET. WAS IT...
HEY, HEY! WHAT ARE YOU TALKIN' TO THE DUMMY FOR, FREAK? I'M THE GIG SHOT! ME, SCARFACE!
YOU SEE ANYGODY AROUND HERE THAT SAYS DIFFERENT?
NO.
NOT ANYMORE.
20

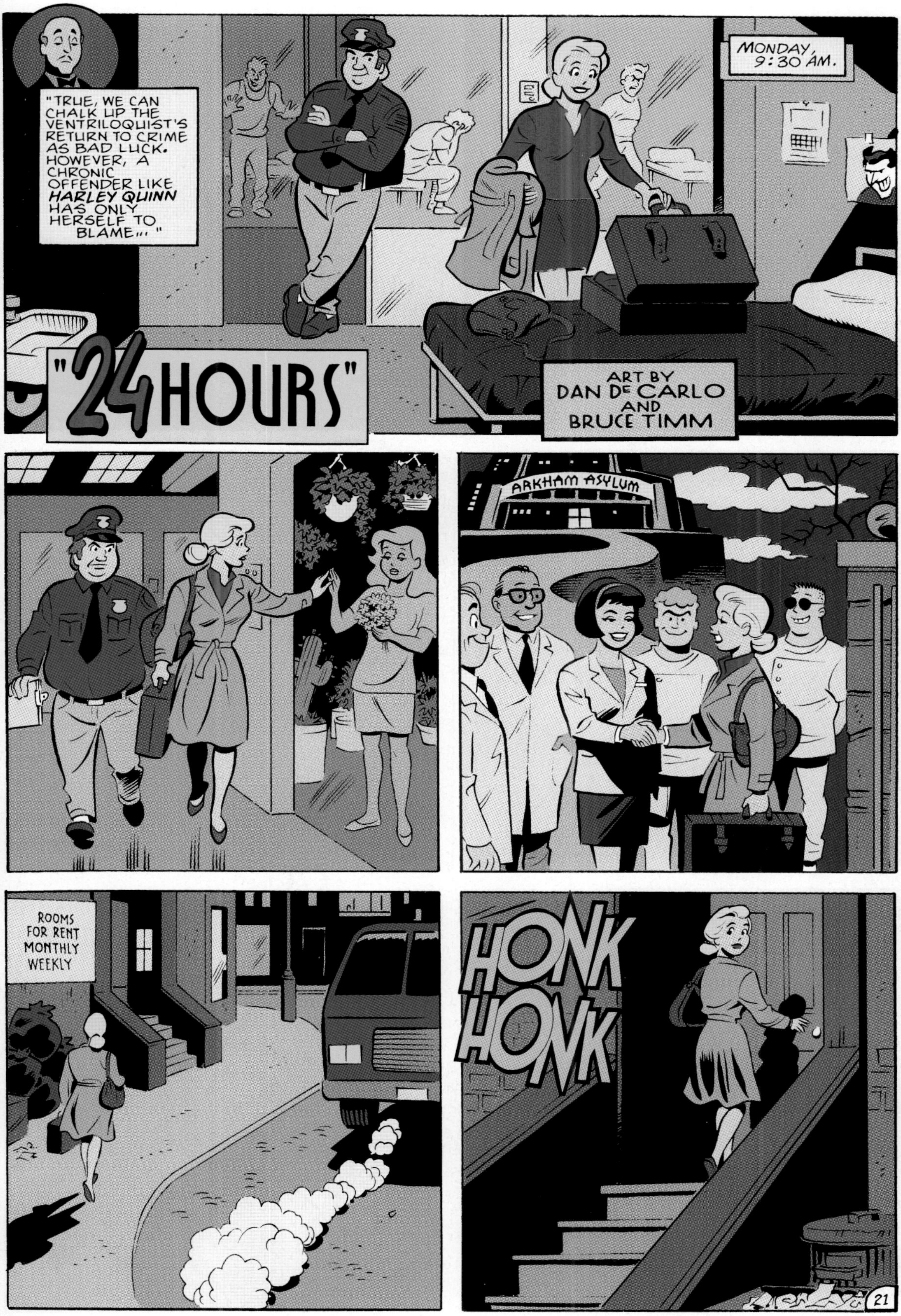
"TRUE, WE CAN CHALK UP THE VENTRILOQUIST'S RETURN TO CRIME AS BAD LUCK. HOWEVER, A CHRONIC OFFENDER LIKE HARLEY QUINN HAS ONLY HERSELF TO BLAME..."
MONDAY, 9:30 AM.
"24 HOURS"
ART BY DAN DeCARLO AND BRUCE TIMM
ARKHAM ASYLUM
ROOMS FOR RENT MONTHLY WEEKLY
HONK HONK
21

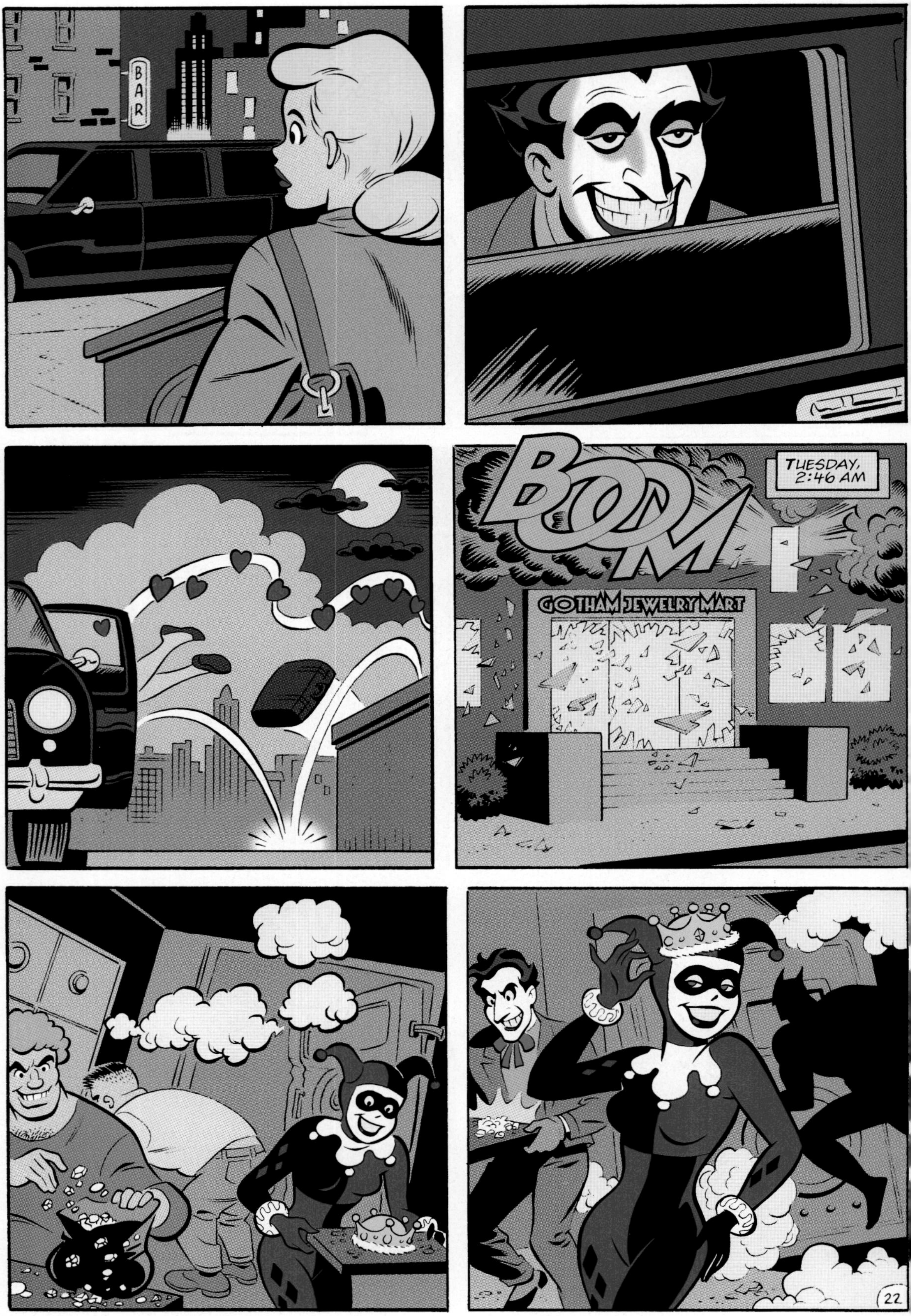
BAR
BOOM
TUESDAY, 2:46 AM
GOTHAM JEWELRY MART
22

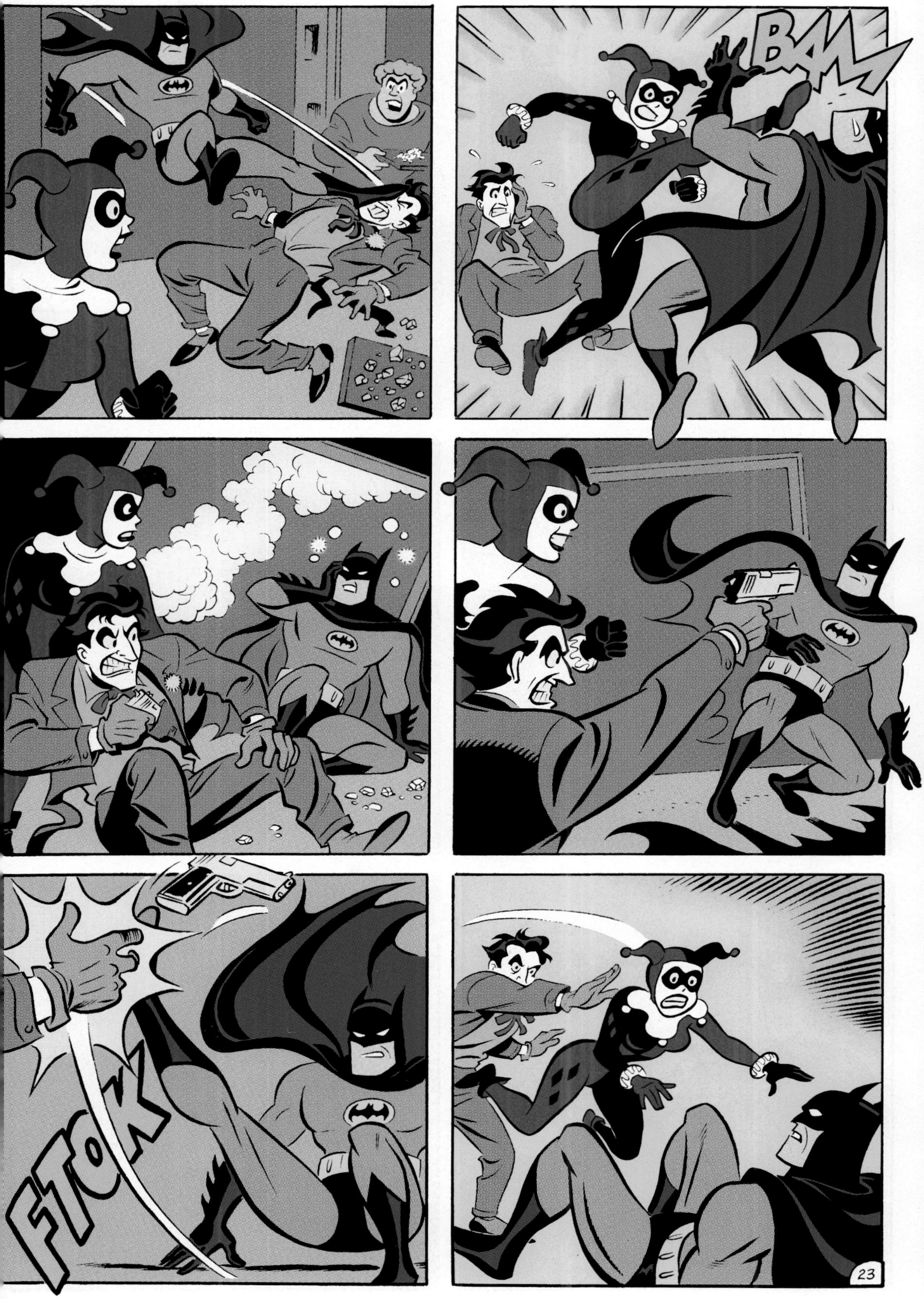
BAM
FTOK
23

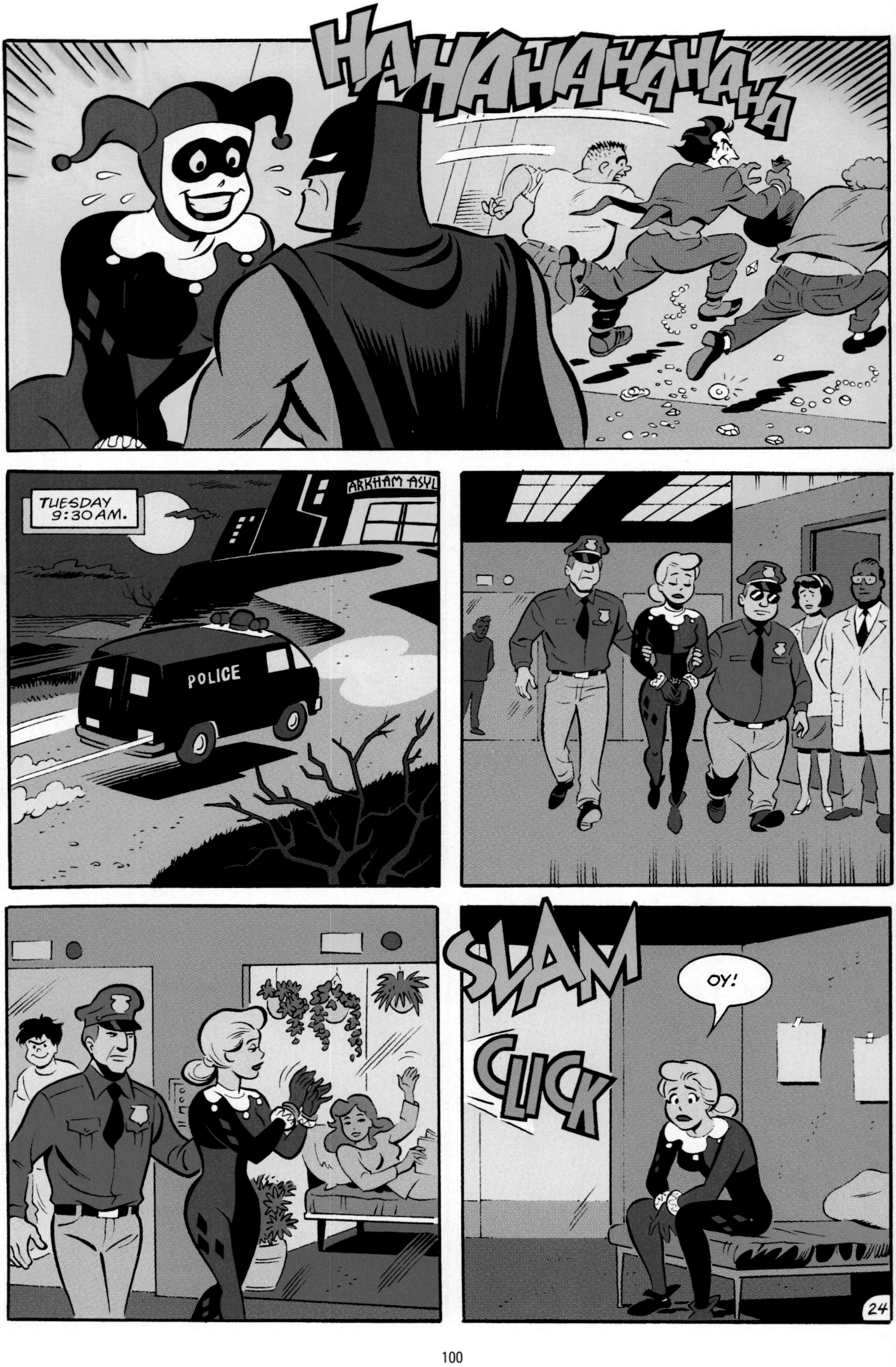
HAHAHAHAHAHAHAHA
TUESDAY 9:30 AM.
ARKHAM ASYL
POLICE
SLAM
CLICK
OY!
24

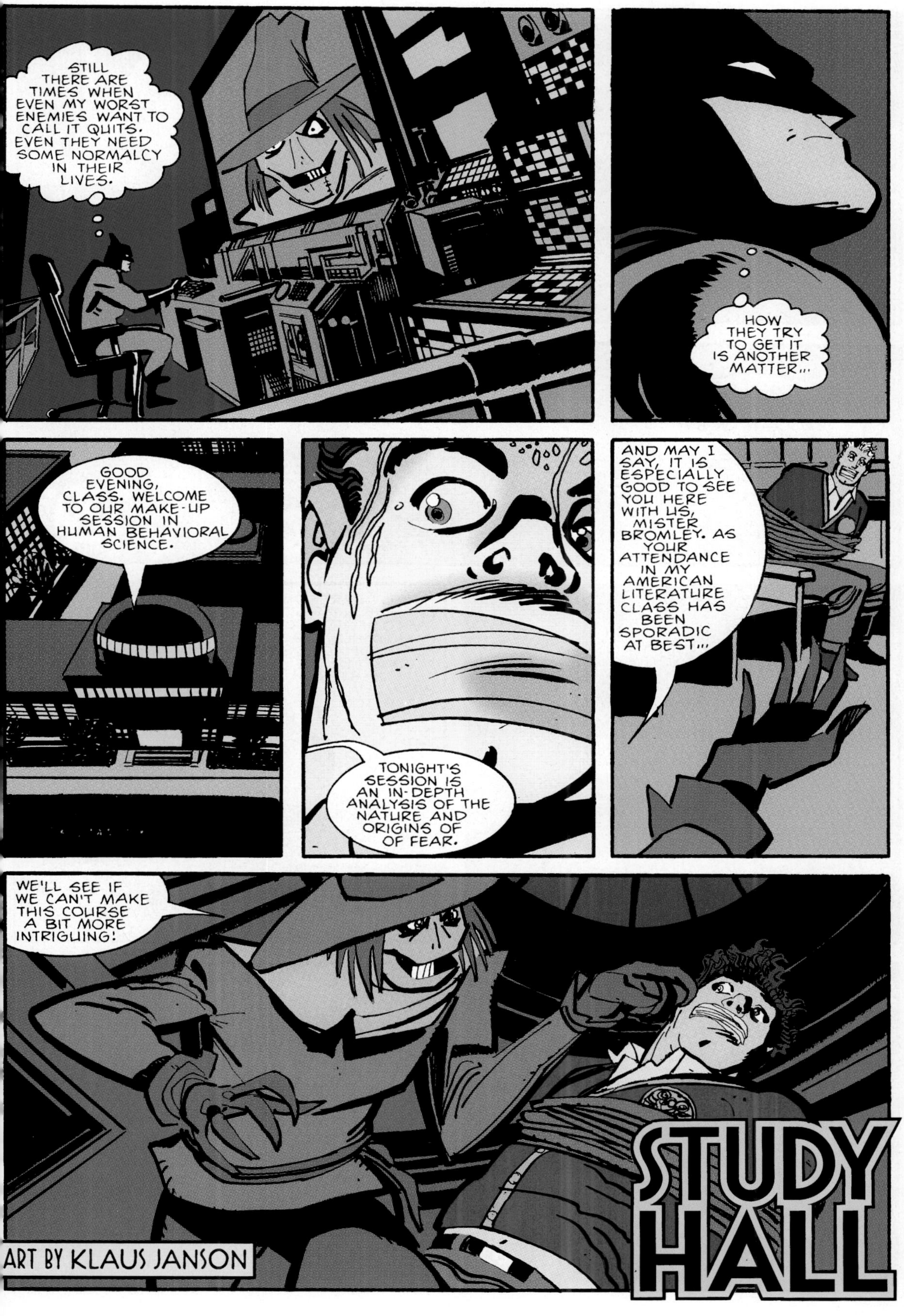
STILL THERE ARE TIMES WHEN EVEN MY WORST ENEMIES WANT TO CALL IT QUITS. EVEN THEY NEED SOME NORMALCY IN THEIR LIVES.
HOW THEY TRY TO GET IT IS ANOTHER MATTER...
GOOD EVENING, CLASS. WELCOME TO OUR MAKE-UP SESSION IN HUMAN BEHAVIORAL SCIENCE.
TONIGHT'S SESSION IS AN IN-DEPTH ANALYSIS OF THE NATURE AND ORIGINS OF FEAR.
AND MAY I SAY, IT IS ESPECIALLY GOOD TO SEE YOU HERE WITH US, MISTER BROMLEY. AS YOUR ATTENDANCE IN MY AMERICAN LITERATURE CLASS HAS BEEN SPORADIC AT BEST...
WE'LL SEE IF WE CAN'T MAKE THIS COURSE A BIT MORE INTRIGUING!
STUDY HALL
ART BY KLAUS JANSON

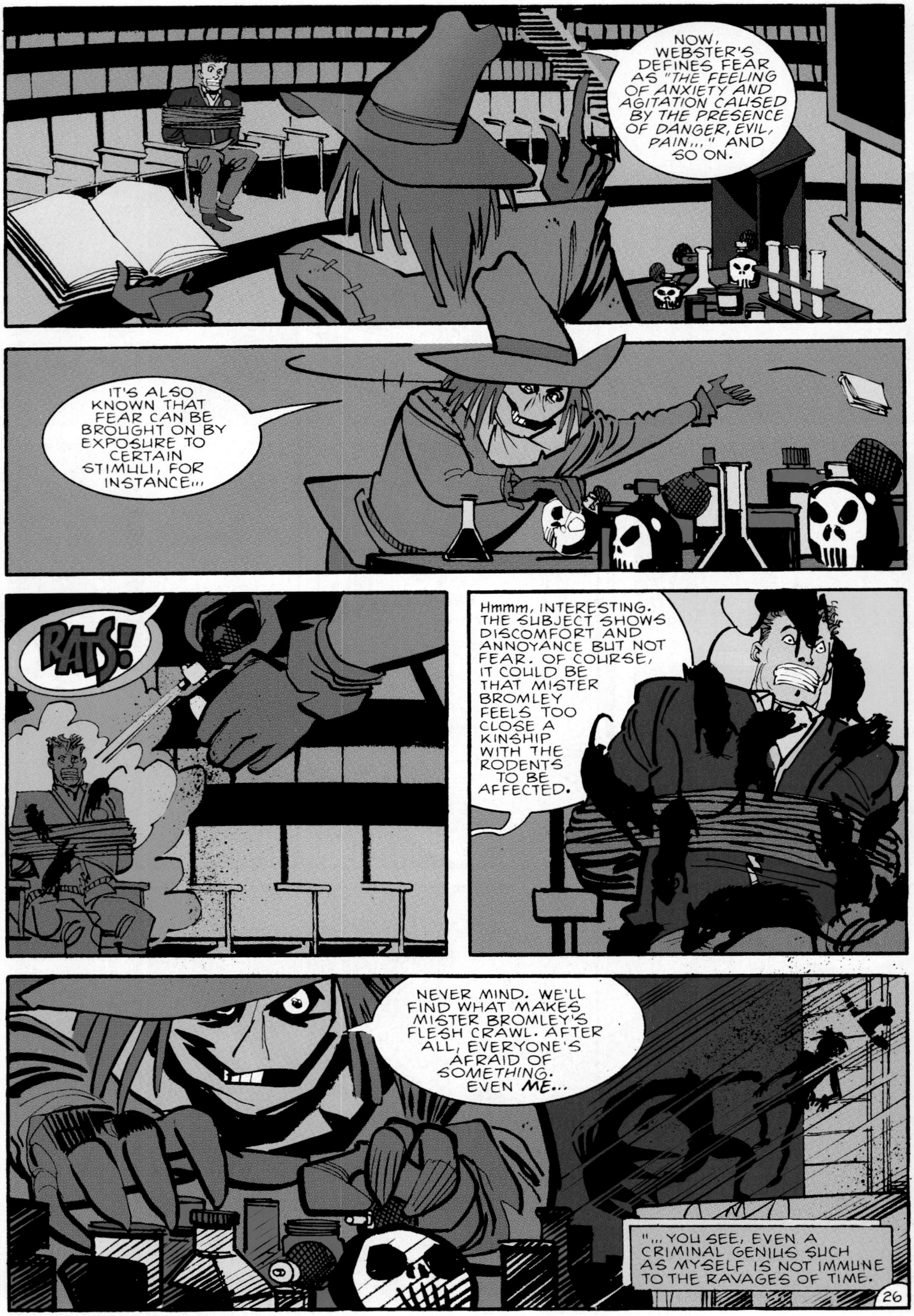
NOW, WEBSTER'S DEFINES FEAR AS "THE FEELING OF ANXIETY AND AGITATION CAUSED BY THE PRESENCE OF DANGER, EVIL, PAIN...," AND SO ON.
IT'S ALSO KNOWN THAT FEAR CAN BE BROUGHT ON BY EXPOSURE TO CERTAIN STIMULI, FOR INSTANCE...
RATS!
Hmmm, INTERESTING. THE SUBJECT SHOWS DISCOMFORT AND ANNOYANCE BUT NOT FEAR. OF COURSE, IT COULD BE THAT MISTER BROMLEY FEELS TOO CLOSE A KINSHIP WITH THE RODENTS TO BE AFFECTED.
NEVER MIND. WE'LL FIND WHAT MAKES MISTER BROMLEY'S FLESH CRAWL. AFTER ALL, EVERYONE'S AFRAID OF SOMETHING. EVEN ME...
"...YOU SEE, EVEN A CRIMINAL GENIUS SUCH AS MYSELF IS NOT IMMUNE TO THE RAVAGES OF TIME.
26

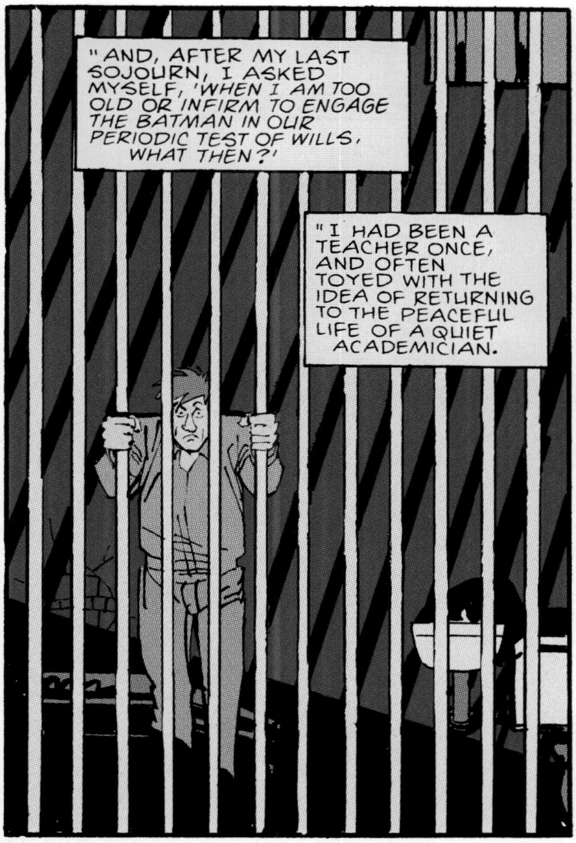
"AND, AFTER MY LAST SOJOURN, I ASKED MYSELF, 'WHEN I AM TOO OLD OR INFIRM TO ENGAGE THE BATMAN IN OUR PERIODIC TEST OF WILLS, WHAT THEN?'
"I HAD BEEN A TEACHER ONCE, AND OFTEN TOYED WITH THE IDEA OF RETURNING TO THE PEACEFUL LIFE OF A QUIET ACADEMICIAN.

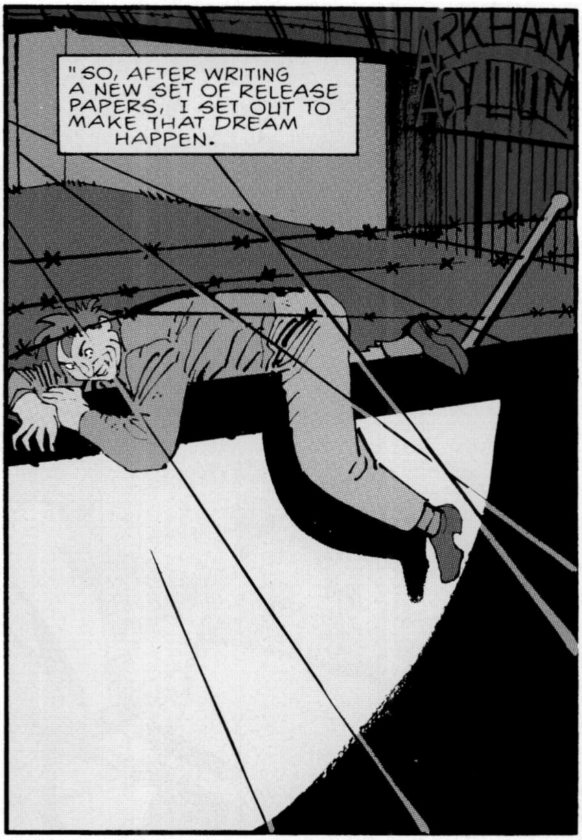
ARKHAM ASYLUM
"SO, AFTER WRITING A NEW SET OF RELEASE PAPERS, I SET OUT TO MAKE THAT DREAM HAPPEN.

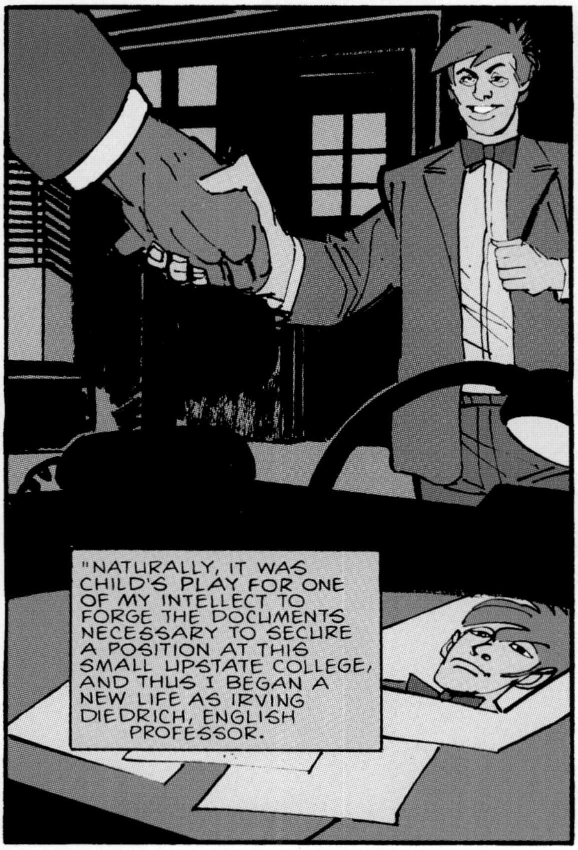
"NATURALLY, IT WAS CHILD'S PLAY FOR ONE OF MY INTELLECT TO FORGE THE DOCUMENTS NECESSARY TO SECURE A POSITION AT THIS SMALL UPSTATE COLLEGE, AND THUS I BEGAN A NEW LIFE AS IRVING DIEDRICH, ENGLISH PROFESSOR.

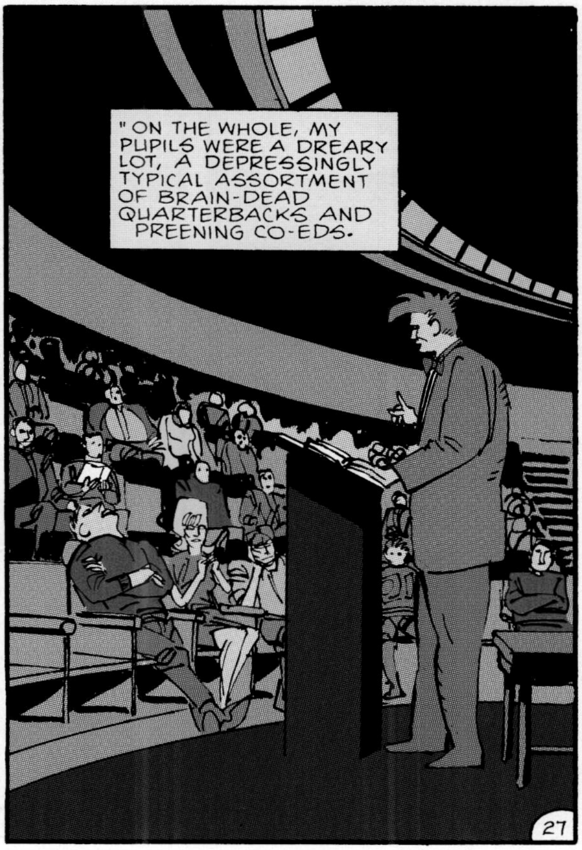
"ON THE WHOLE, MY PUPILS WERE A DREARY LOT, A DEPRESSINGLY TYPICAL ASSORTMENT OF BRAIN-DEAD QUARTERBACKS AND PREENING CO-EDS.
27

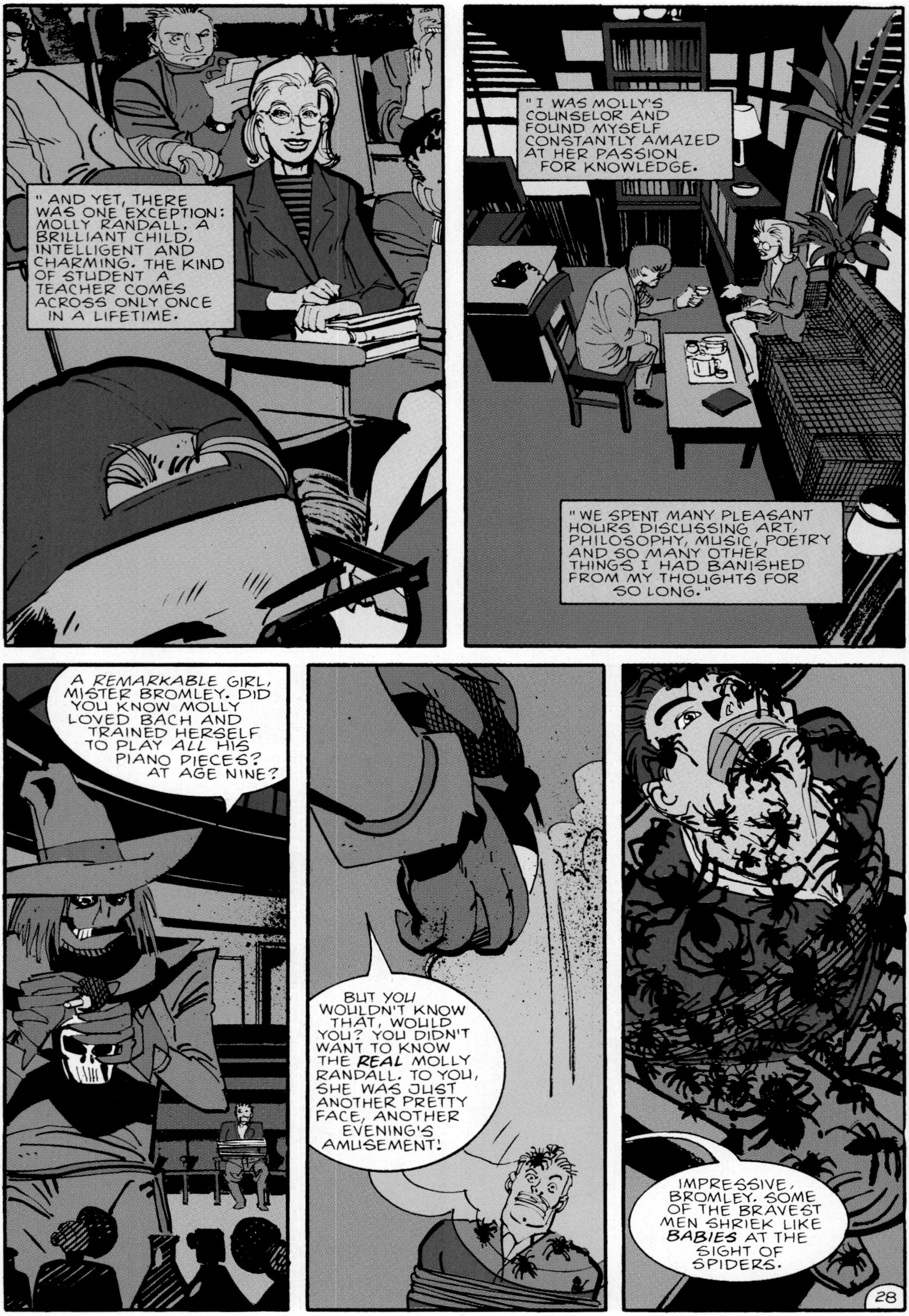
"AND YET, THERE WAS ONE EXCEPTION: MOLLY RANDALL. A BRILLIANT CHILD, INTELLIGENT AND CHARMING. THE KIND OF STUDENT A TEACHER COMES ACROSS ONLY ONCE IN A LIFETIME.
"I WAS MOLLY'S COUNSELOR AND FOUND MYSELF CONSTANTLY AMAZED AT HER PASSION FOR KNOWLEDGE.
"WE SPENT MANY PLEASANT HOURS DISCUSSING ART, PHILOSOPHY, MUSIC, POETRY AND SO MANY OTHER THINGS I HAD BANISHED FROM MY THOUGHTS FOR SO LONG."
A *REMARKABLE* GIRL, MISTER BROMLEY. DID YOU KNOW MOLLY LOVED BACH AND TRAINED HERSELF TO PLAY *ALL* HIS PIANO PIECES? AT AGE NINE?
BUT *YOU* WOULDN'T KNOW THAT, WOULD YOU? YOU DIDN'T WANT TO KNOW THE ***REAL*** MOLLY RANDALL. TO YOU, SHE WAS JUST ANOTHER PRETTY FACE, ANOTHER EVENING'S AMUSEMENT!
IMPRESSIVE, BROMLEY. SOME OF THE BRAVEST MEN SHRIEK LIKE ***BABIES*** AT THE SIGHT OF SPIDERS.
28

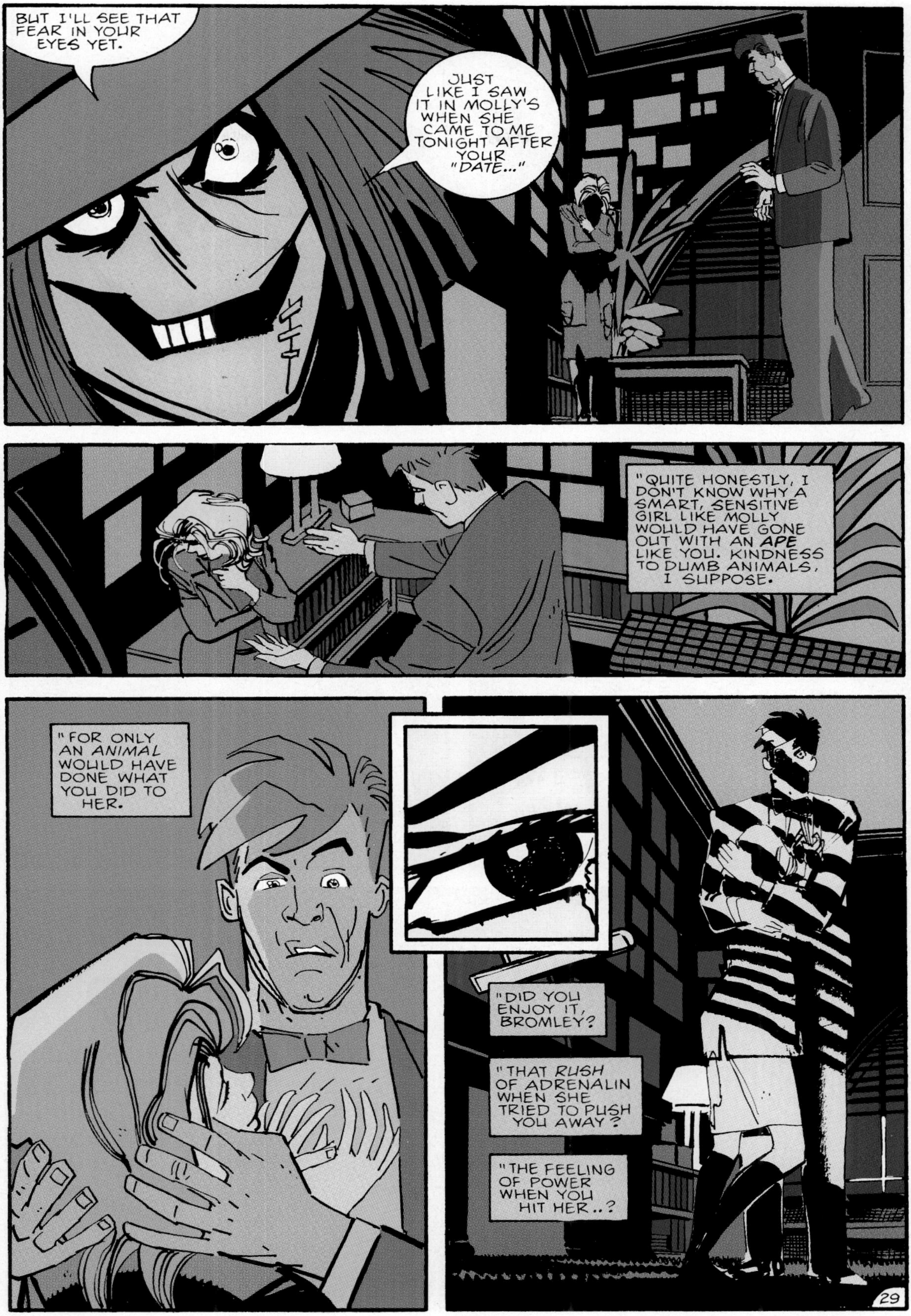

BUT I'LL SEE THAT FEAR IN YOUR EYES YET.
JUST LIKE I SAW IT IN MOLLY'S WHEN SHE CAME TO ME TONIGHT AFTER YOUR "DATE..."
"QUITE HONESTLY, I DON'T KNOW WHY A SMART, SENSITIVE GIRL LIKE MOLLY WOULD HAVE GONE OUT WITH AN APE LIKE YOU. KINDNESS TO DUMB ANIMALS, I SUPPOSE.
"FOR ONLY AN ANIMAL WOULD HAVE DONE WHAT YOU DID TO HER.
"DID YOU ENJOY IT, BROMLEY?
"THAT RUSH OF ADRENALIN WHEN SHE TRIED TO PUSH YOU AWAY?
"THE FEELING OF POWER WHEN YOU HIT HER..?
29

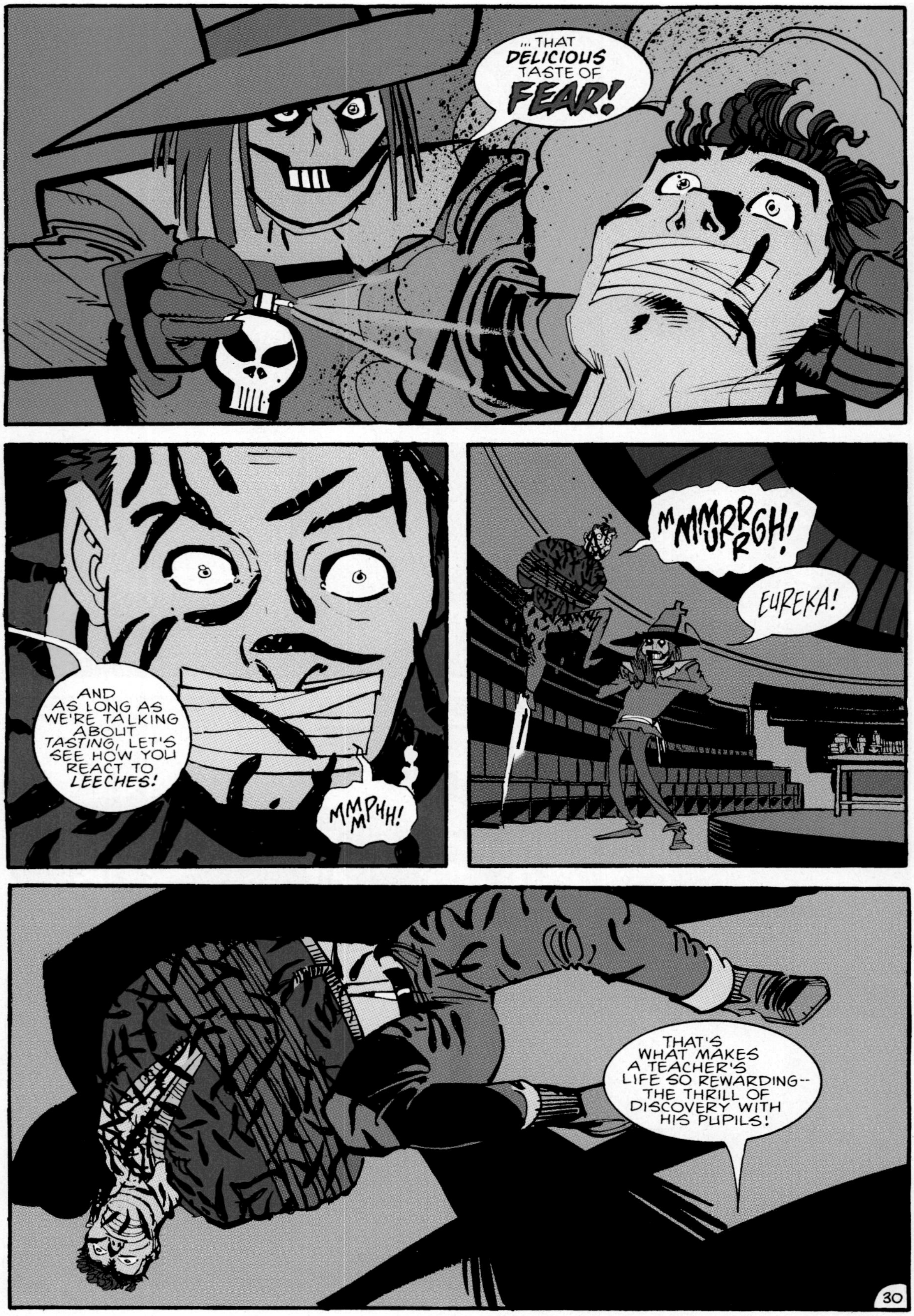
...THAT DELICIOUS TASTE OF FEAR!
AND AS LONG AS WE'RE TALKING ABOUT TASTING, LET'S SEE HOW YOU REACT TO LEECHES!
MMMPHH!
MMMMRRGH! URR
EUREKA!
THAT'S WHAT MAKES A TEACHER'S LIFE SO REWARDING-- THE THRILL OF DISCOVERY WITH HIS PUPILS!
30

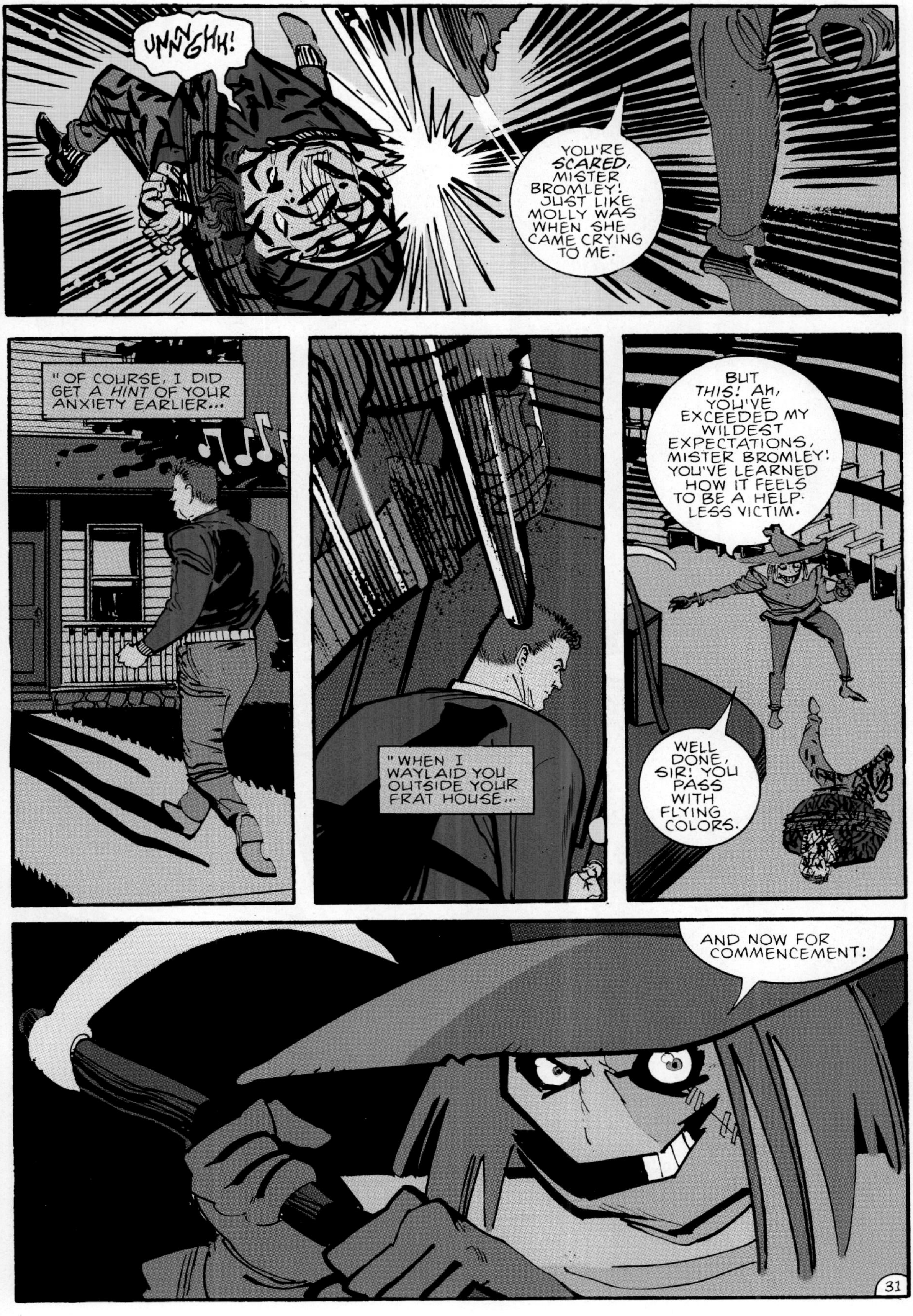
UNNNGHH!
YOU'RE SCARED, MISTER BROMLEY! JUST LIKE MOLLY WAS WHEN SHE CAME CRYING TO ME.
"OF COURSE, I DID GET A HINT OF YOUR ANXIETY EARLIER...
"WHEN I WAYLAID YOU OUTSIDE YOUR FRAT HOUSE...
BUT THIS! AH, YOU'VE EXCEEDED MY WILDEST EXPECTATIONS, MISTER BROMLEY! YOU'VE LEARNED HOW IT FEELS TO BE A HELPLESS VICTIM.
WELL DONE, SIR! YOU PASS WITH FLYING COLORS.
AND NOW FOR COMMENCEMENT!
31

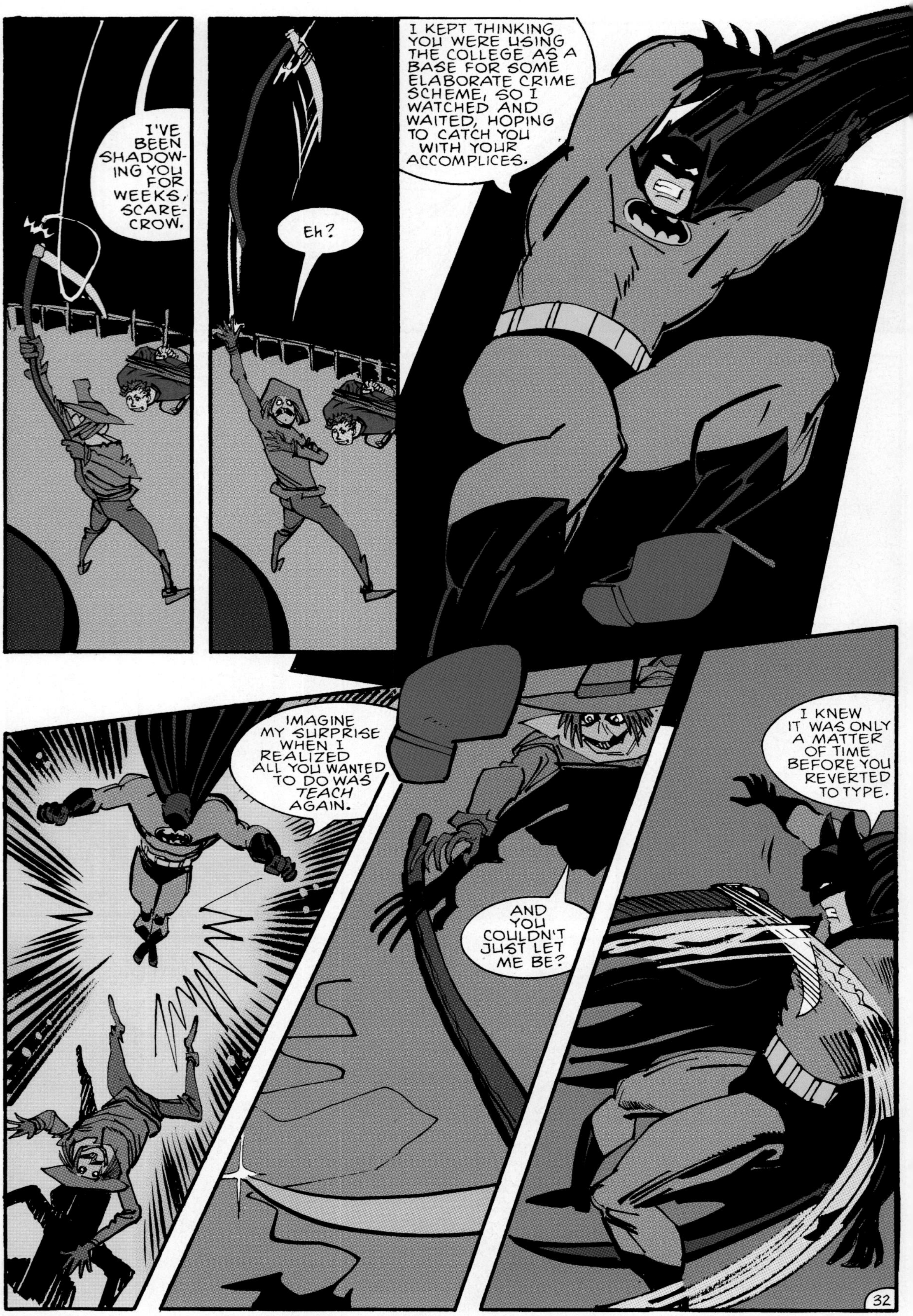
I'VE BEEN SHADOWING YOU FOR WEEKS, SCARECROW.
Eh?
I KEPT THINKING YOU WERE USING THE COLLEGE AS A BASE FOR SOME ELABORATE CRIME SCHEME, SO I WATCHED AND WAITED, HOPING TO CATCH YOU WITH YOUR ACCOMPLICES.
IMAGINE MY SURPRISE WHEN I REALIZED ALL YOU WANTED TO DO WAS *TEACH* AGAIN.
AND YOU COULDN'T JUST LET ME BE?
I KNEW IT WAS ONLY A MATTER OF TIME BEFORE YOU REVERTED TO TYPE.
32

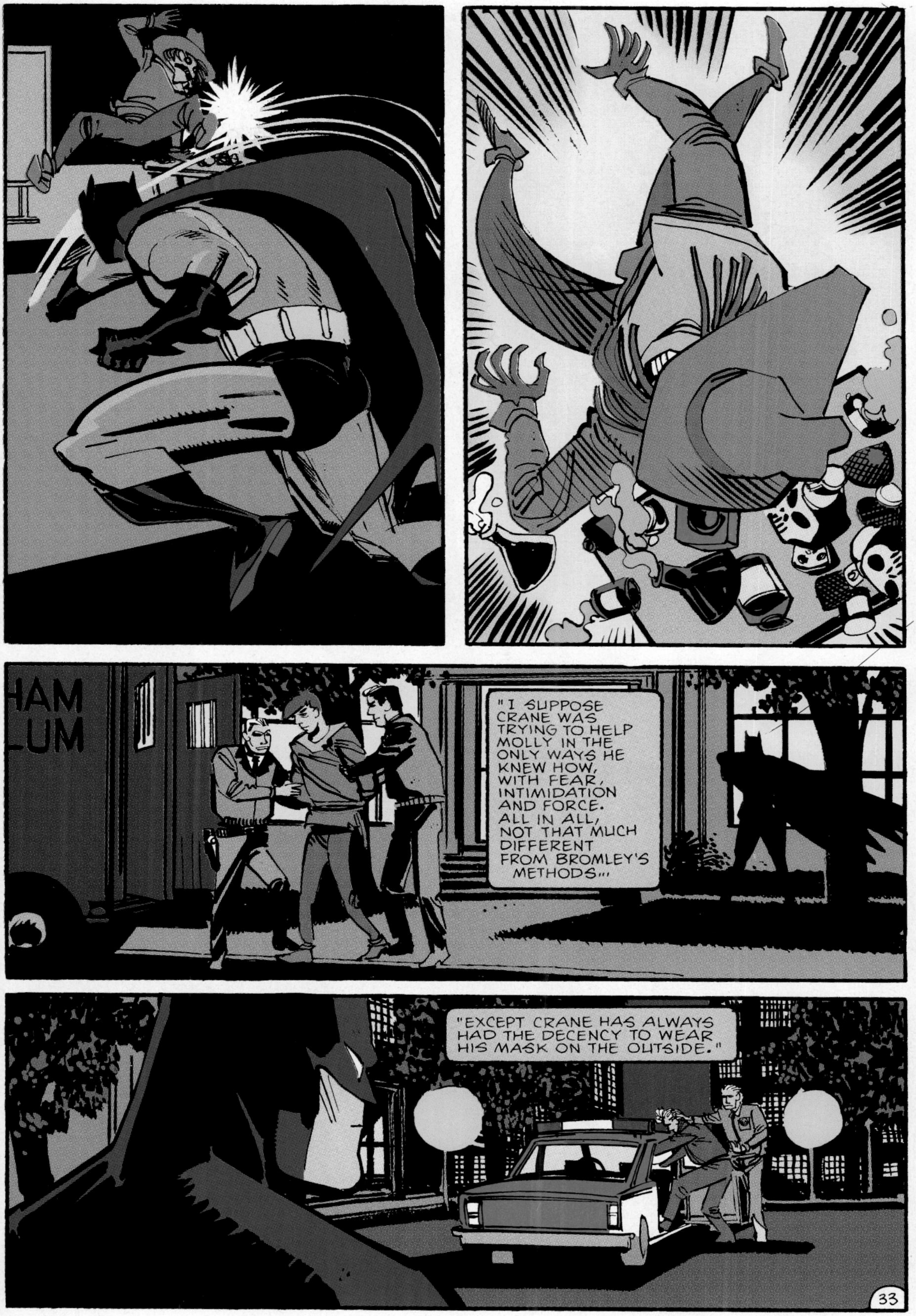
HAM
LUM
"I SUPPOSE CRANE WAS TRYING TO HELP MOLLY IN THE ONLY WAYS HE KNEW HOW, WITH FEAR, INTIMIDATION AND FORCE. ALL IN ALL, NOT THAT MUCH DIFFERENT FROM BROMLEY'S METHODS...
"EXCEPT CRANE HAS ALWAYS HAD THE DECENCY TO WEAR HIS MASK ON THE OUTSIDE."
33

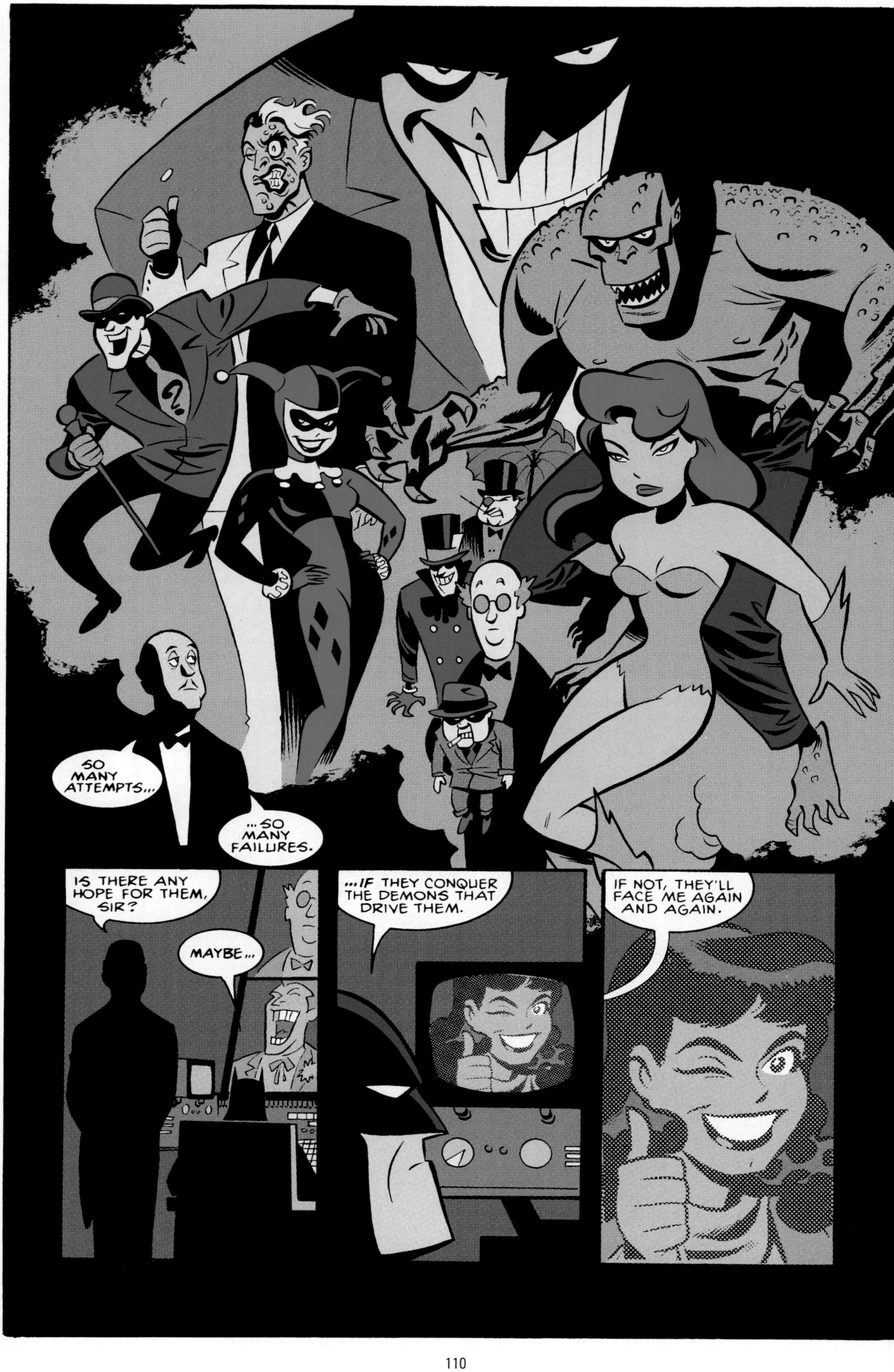
SO MANY ATTEMPTS...
...SO MANY FAILURES.
IS THERE ANY HOPE FOR THEM, SIR?
MAYBE...
...IF THEY CONQUER THE DEMONS THAT DRIVE THEM.
IF NOT, THEY'LL FACE ME AGAIN AND AGAIN.

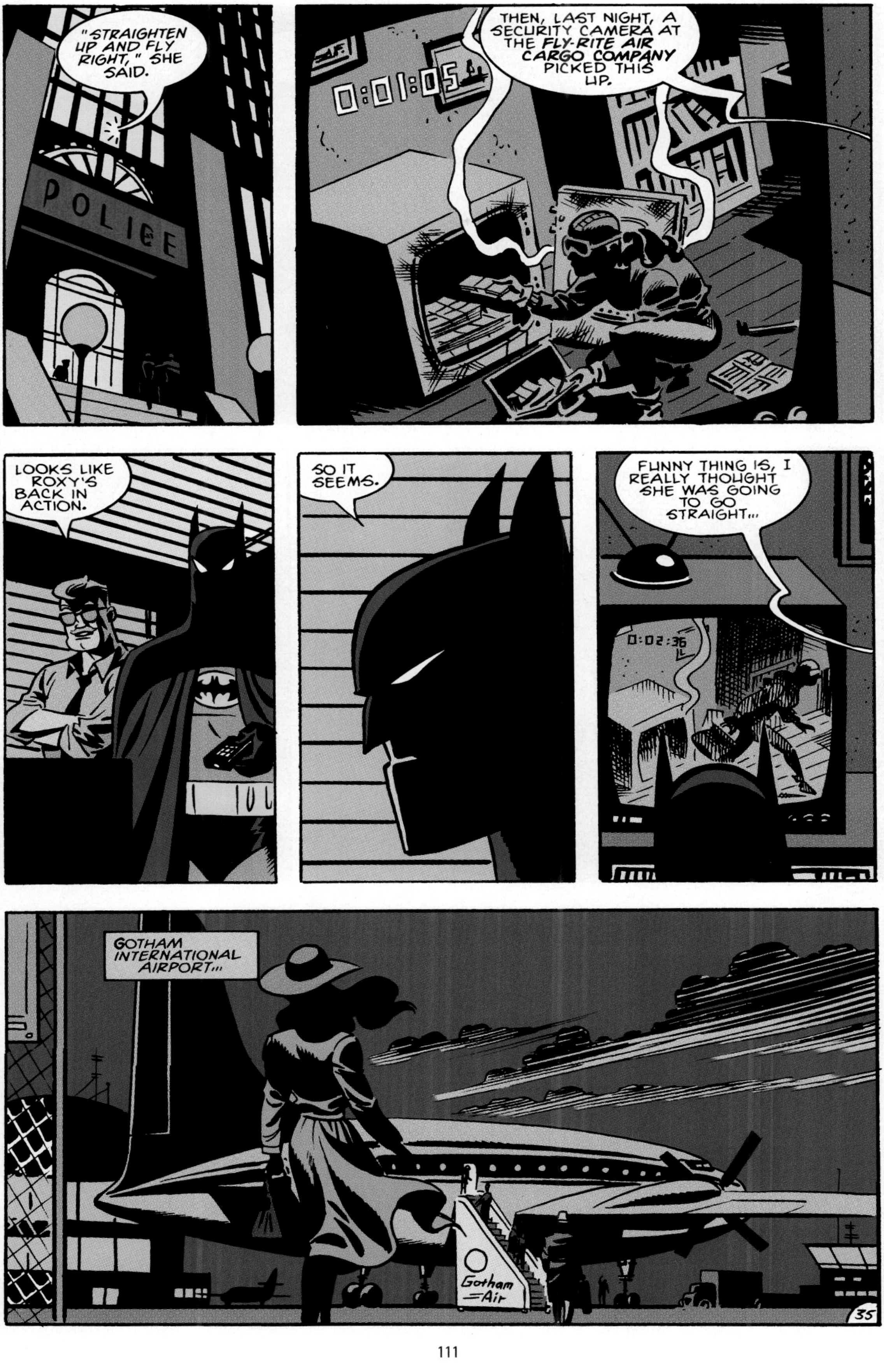
"STRAIGHTEN UP AND FLY RIGHT," SHE SAID.
THEN, LAST NIGHT, A SECURITY CAMERA AT THE FLY-RITE AIR CARGO COMPANY PICKED THIS UP.
0:01:05
LOOKS LIKE ROXY'S BACK IN ACTION.
SO IT SEEMS.
FUNNY THING IS, I REALLY THOUGHT SHE WAS GOING TO GO STRAIGHT...
0:02:36
GOTHAM INTERNATIONAL AIRPORT...
Gotham Air
35

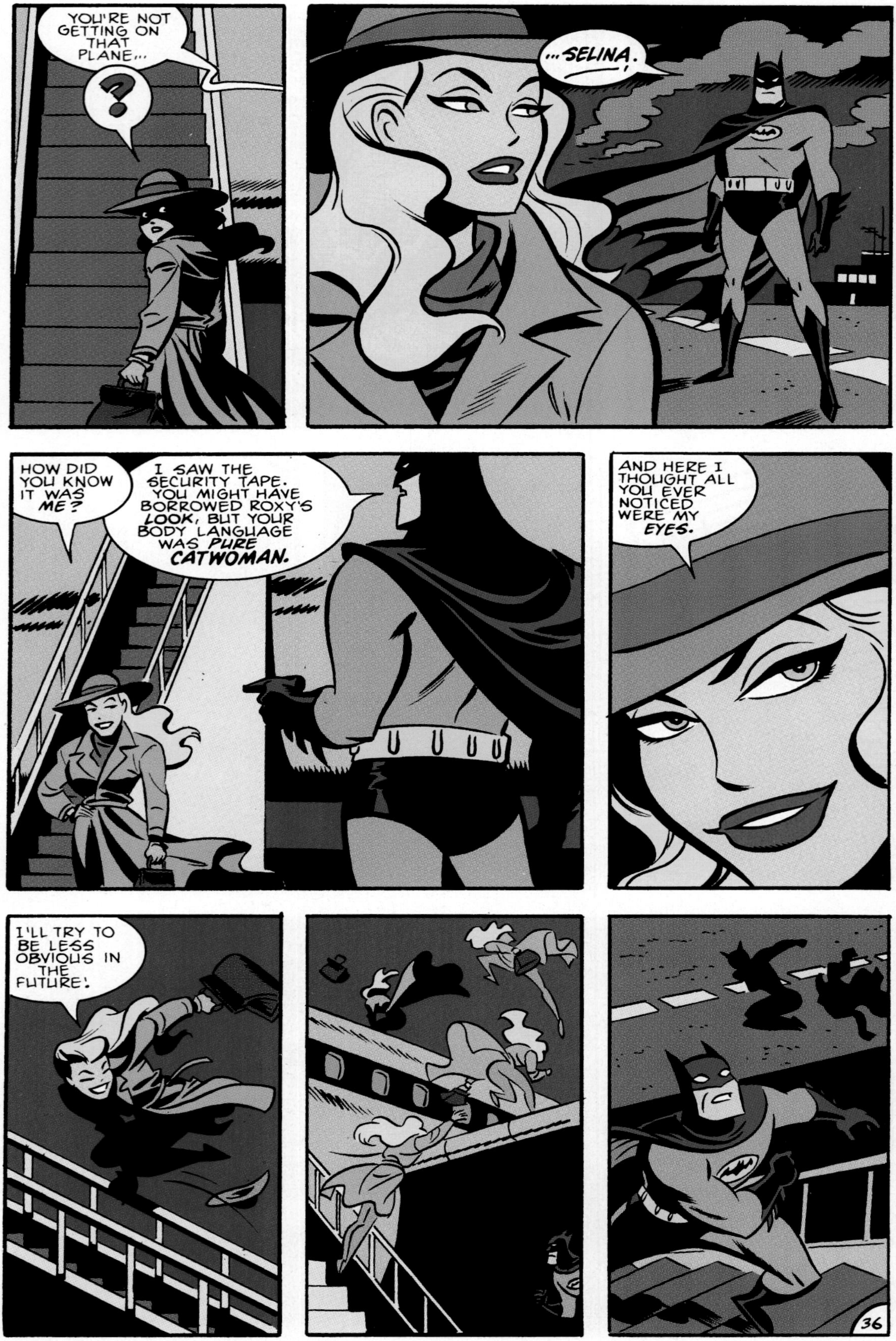
YOU'RE NOT GETTING ON THAT PLANE...
?
...SELINA.
HOW DID YOU KNOW IT WAS ME?
I SAW THE SECURITY TAPE. YOU MIGHT HAVE BORROWED ROXY'S LOOK, BUT YOUR BODY LANGUAGE WAS PURE CATWOMAN.
AND HERE I THOUGHT ALL YOU EVER NOTICED WERE MY EYES.
I'LL TRY TO BE LESS OBVIOUS IN THE FUTURE!
36

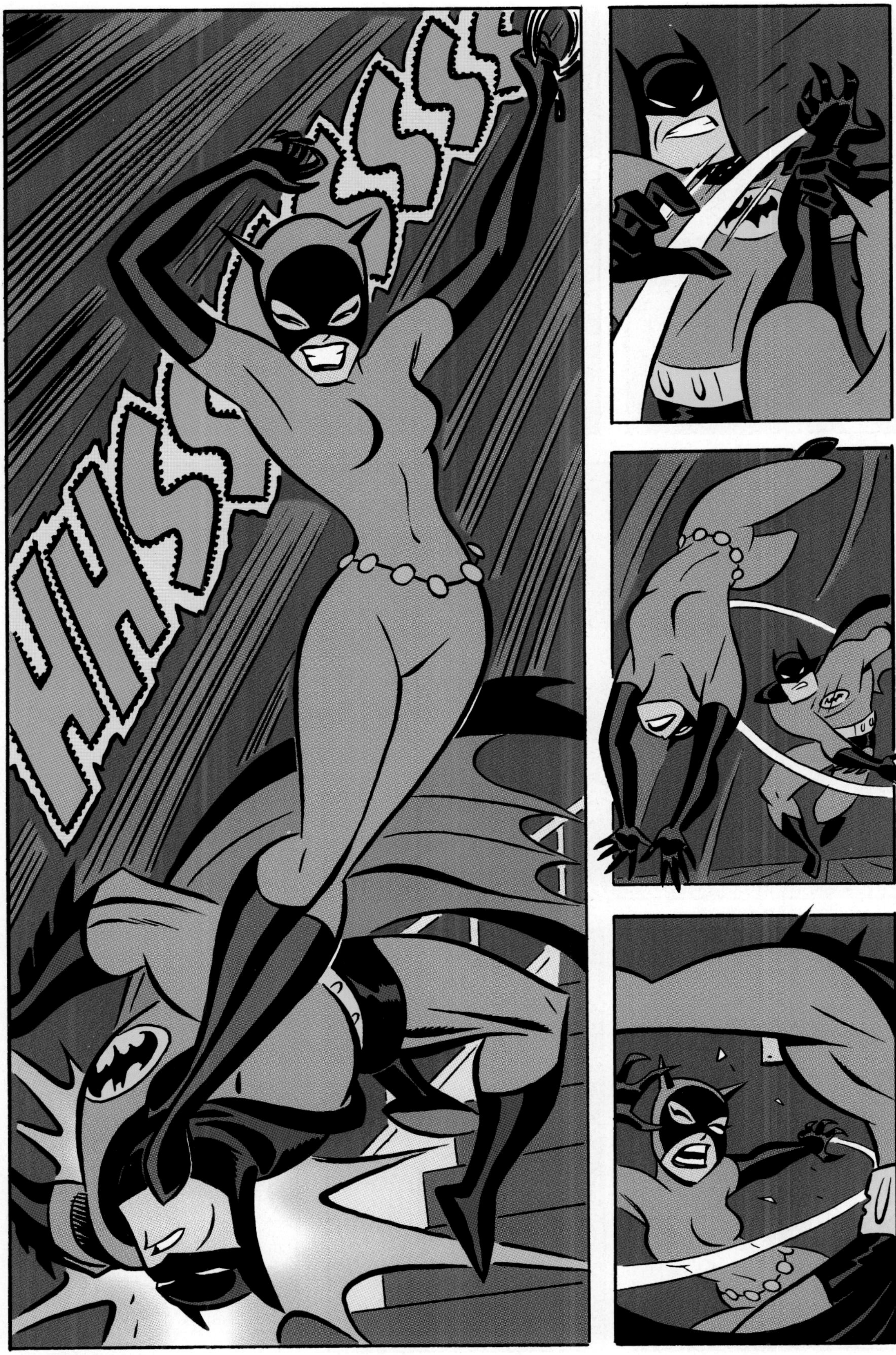
HHSSSSS

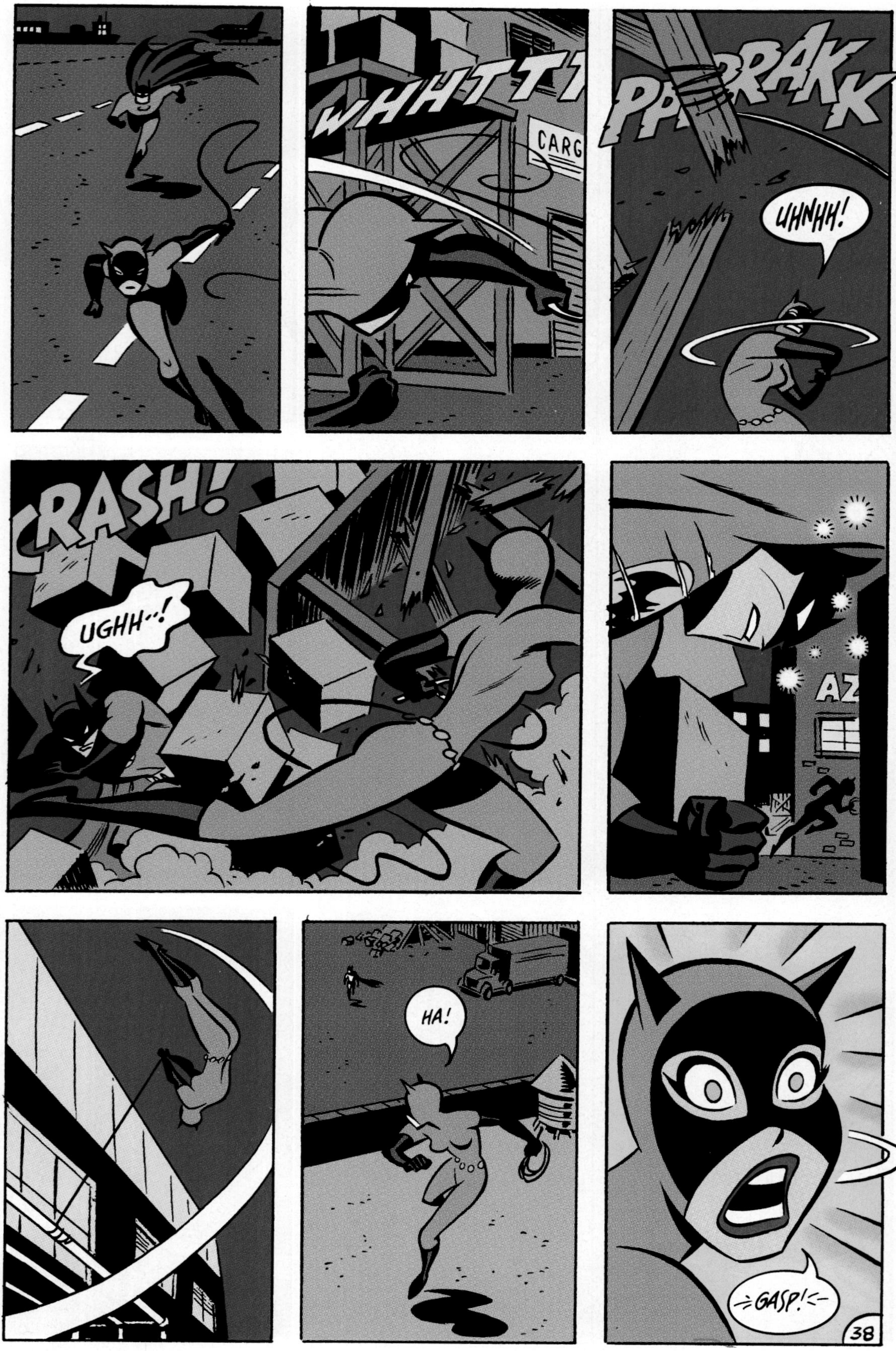

WHHTTT
CARG
PPBRAKK
UHNHH!
CRASH!
UGHH--!
AZ
HA!
GASP!
38

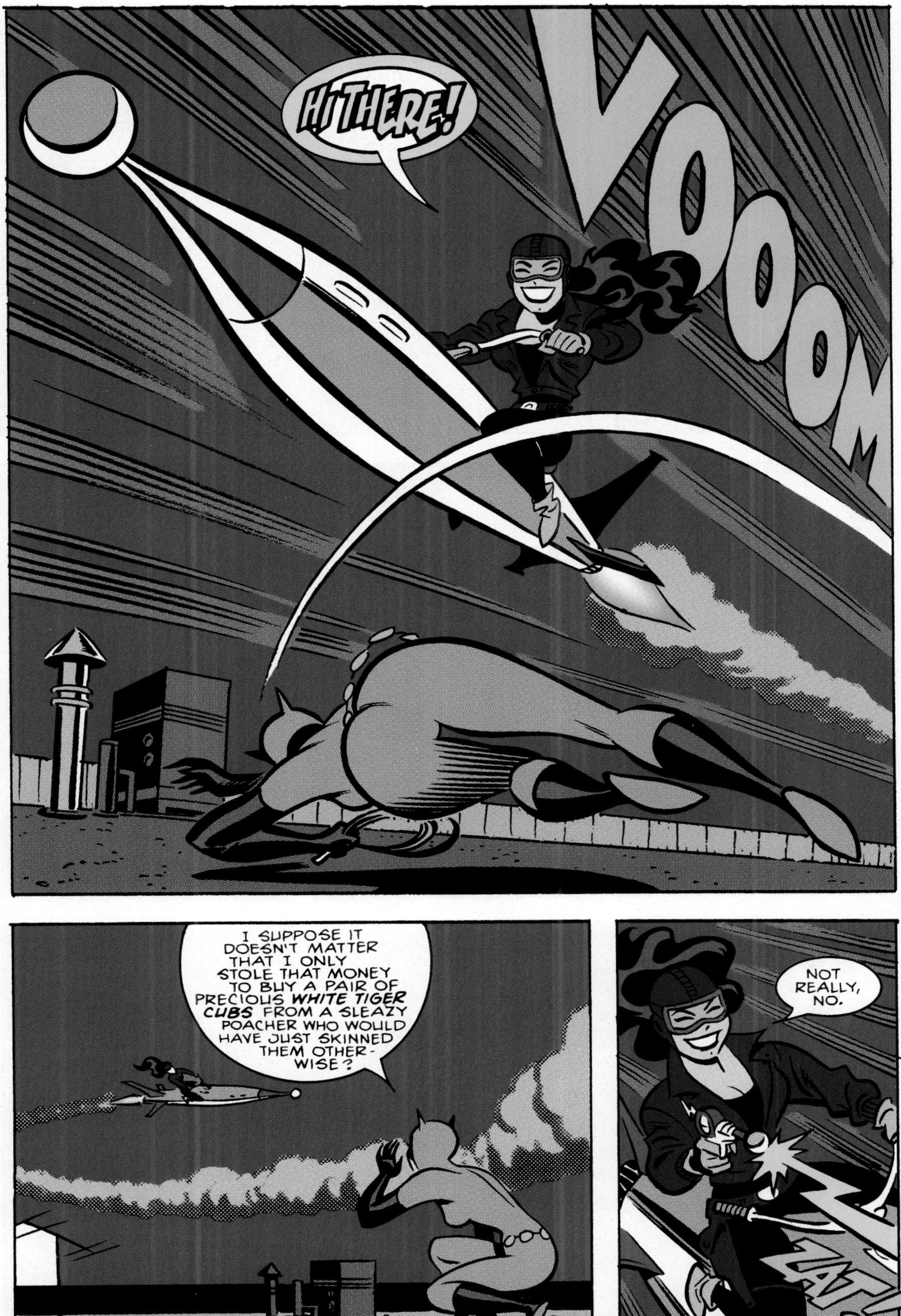
HI THERE!
VOOOOM
I SUPPOSE IT DOESN'T MATTER THAT I ONLY STOLE THAT MONEY TO BUY A PAIR OF PRECIOUS WHITE TIGER CUBS FROM A SLEAZY POACHER WHO WOULD HAVE JUST SKINNED THEM OTHER-WISE?
NOT REALLY, NO.
ZAT!
39

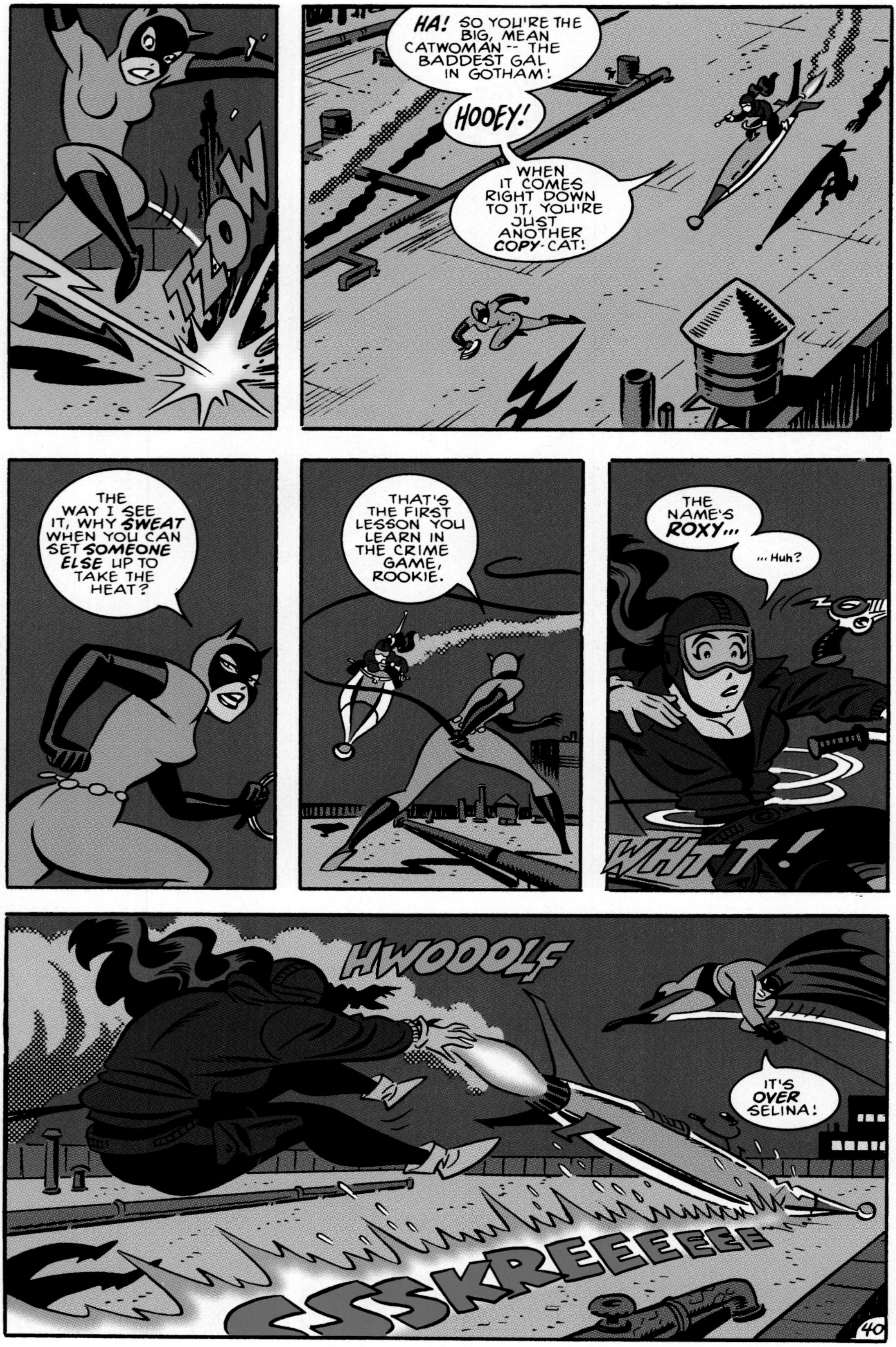
TZOW
HA! SO YOU'RE THE BIG, MEAN CATWOMAN -- THE BADDEST GAL IN GOTHAM!
HOOEY!
WHEN IT COMES RIGHT DOWN TO IT, YOU'RE JUST ANOTHER COPY-CAT!
THE WAY I SEE IT, WHY SWEAT WHEN YOU CAN SET SOMEONE ELSE UP TO TAKE THE HEAT?
THAT'S THE FIRST LESSON YOU LEARN IN THE CRIME GAME, ROOKIE.
THE NAME'S ROXY...
...Huh?
WHTT!
HWOOOLF
IT'S OVER SELINA!
CSSKREEEEEEE
40

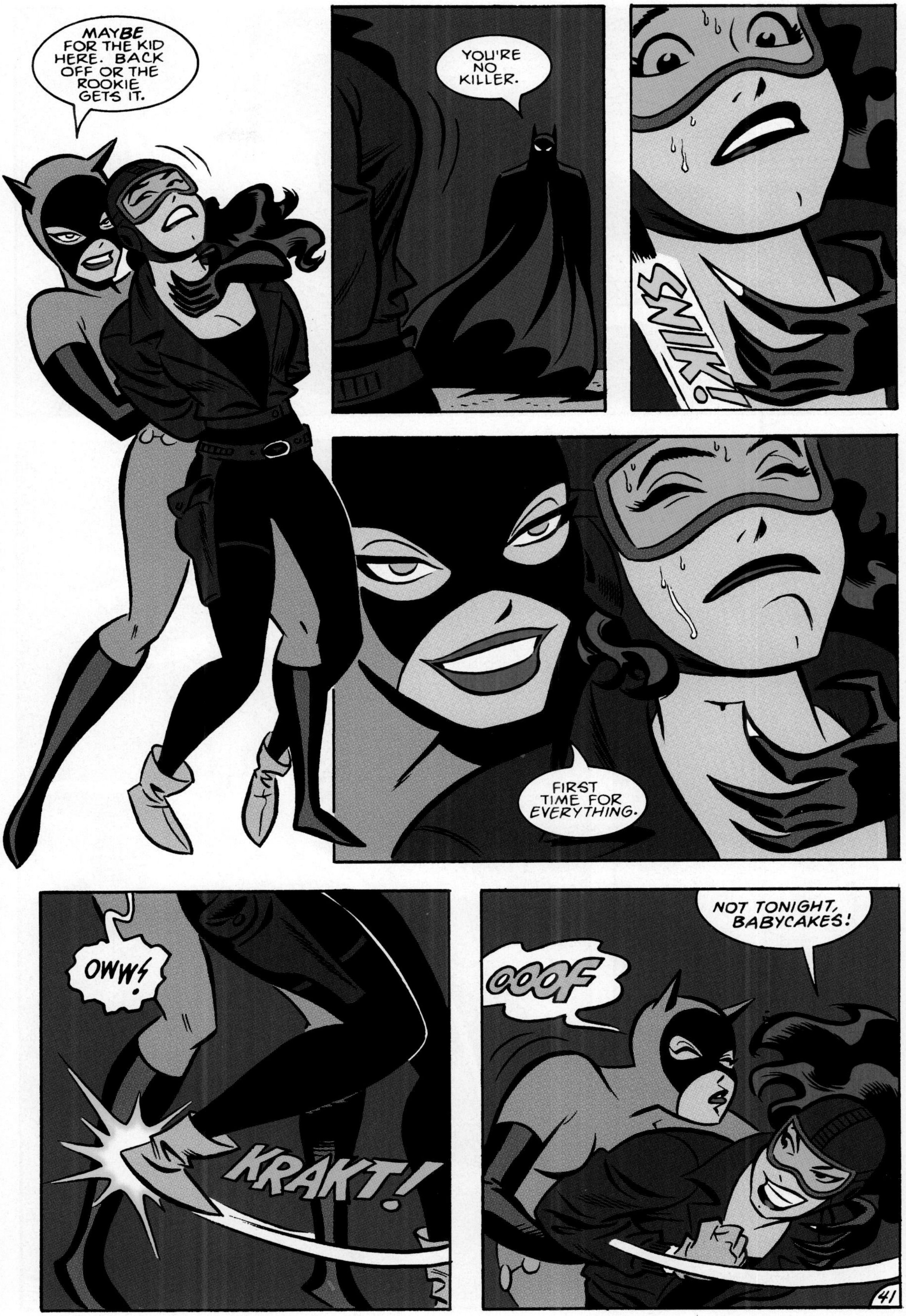

MAYBE FOR THE KID HERE. BACK OFF OR THE ROOKIE GETS IT.
YOU'RE NO KILLER.
SNIK!
FIRST TIME FOR EVERYTHING.
OWW!
KRAKT!
OOOF
NOT TONIGHT, BABYCAKES!
41

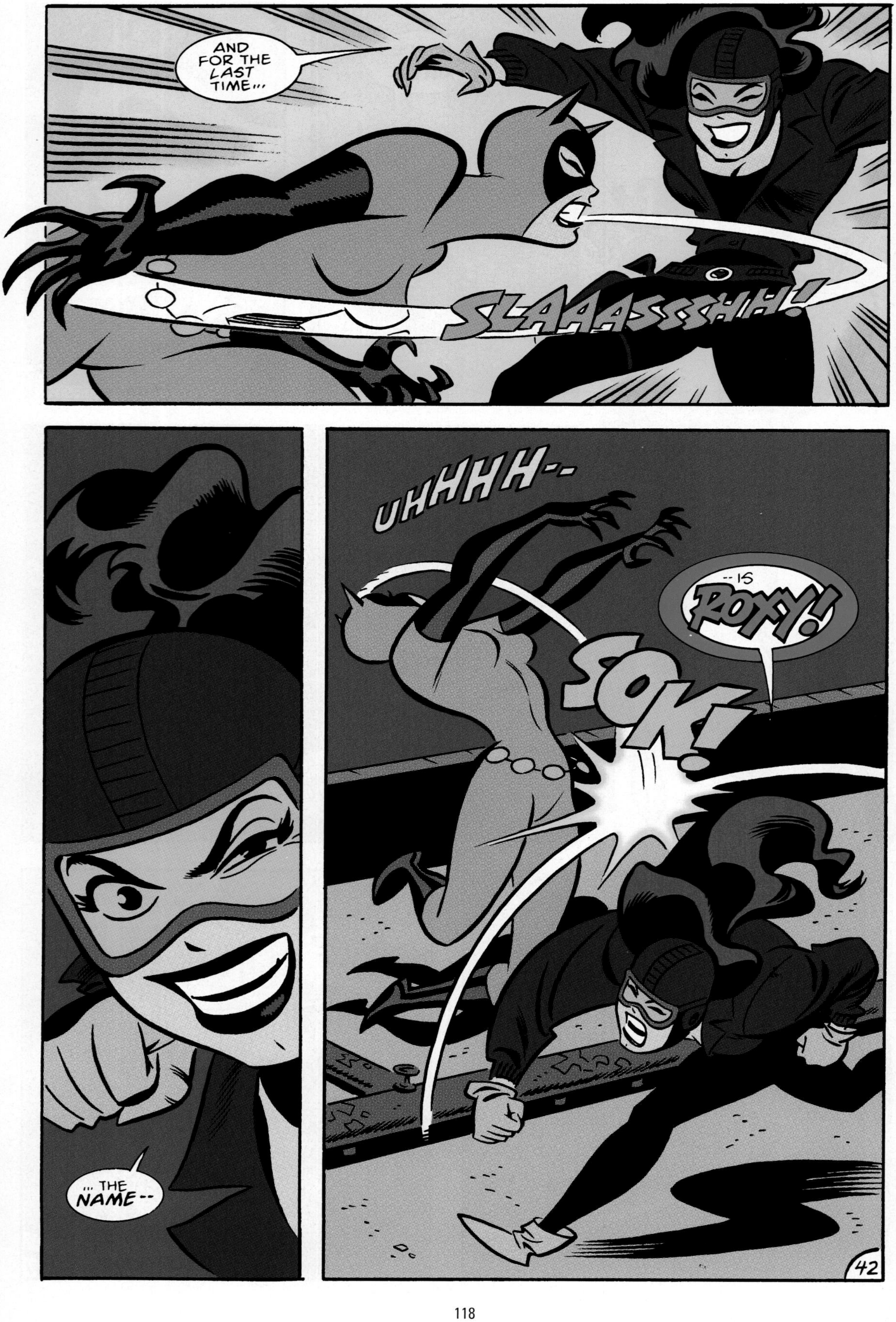
AND FOR THE LAST TIME...
SLAAASSSHH!
... THE NAME--
UHHHH--
--IS ROXY!
SOK!
42

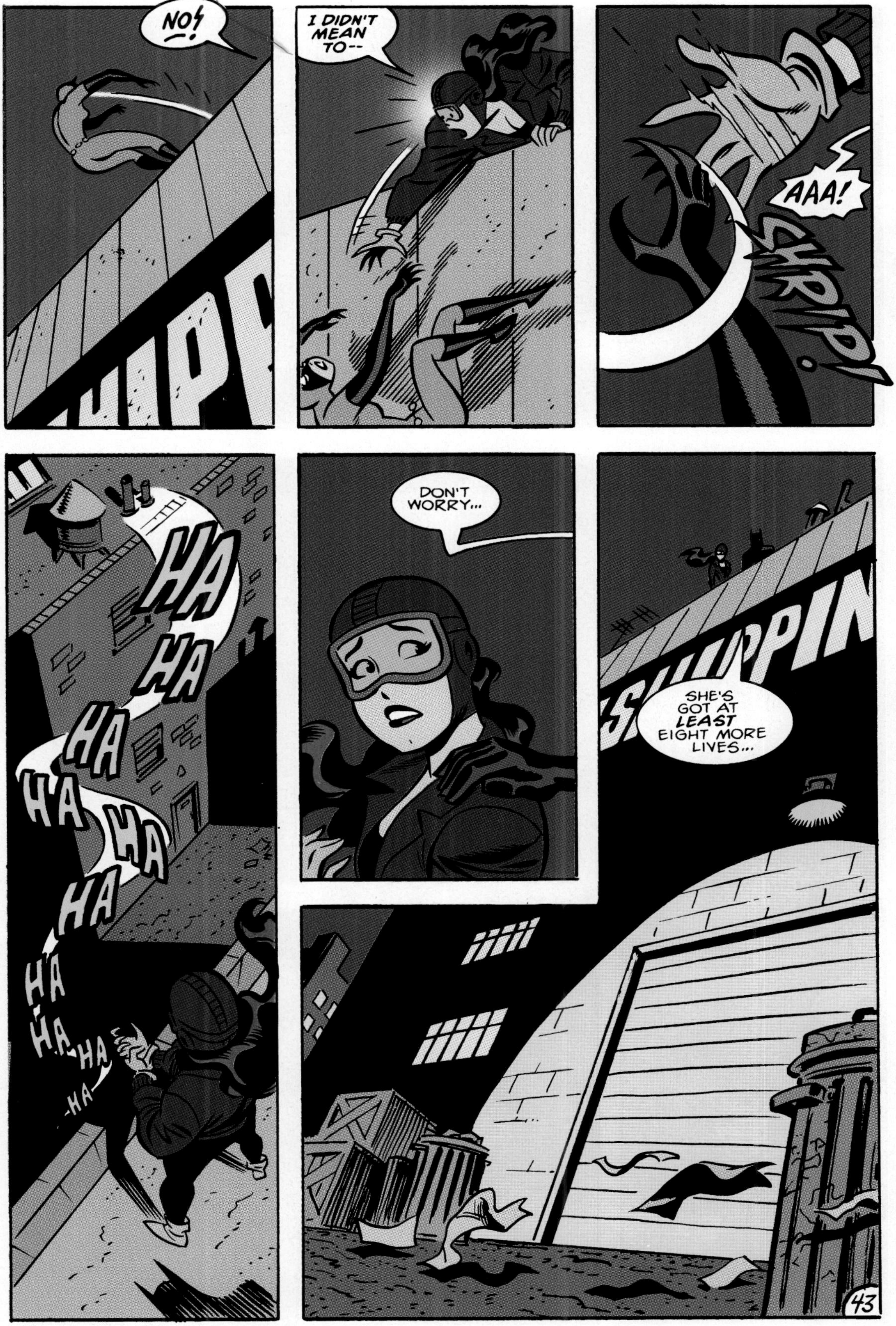
NO!
I DIDN'T MEAN TO--
AAA!
SHRIP!
HA HA HA HA HA HA HA HA HA HA -HA
DON'T WORRY...
SHE'S GOT AT LEAST EIGHT MORE LIVES...
43

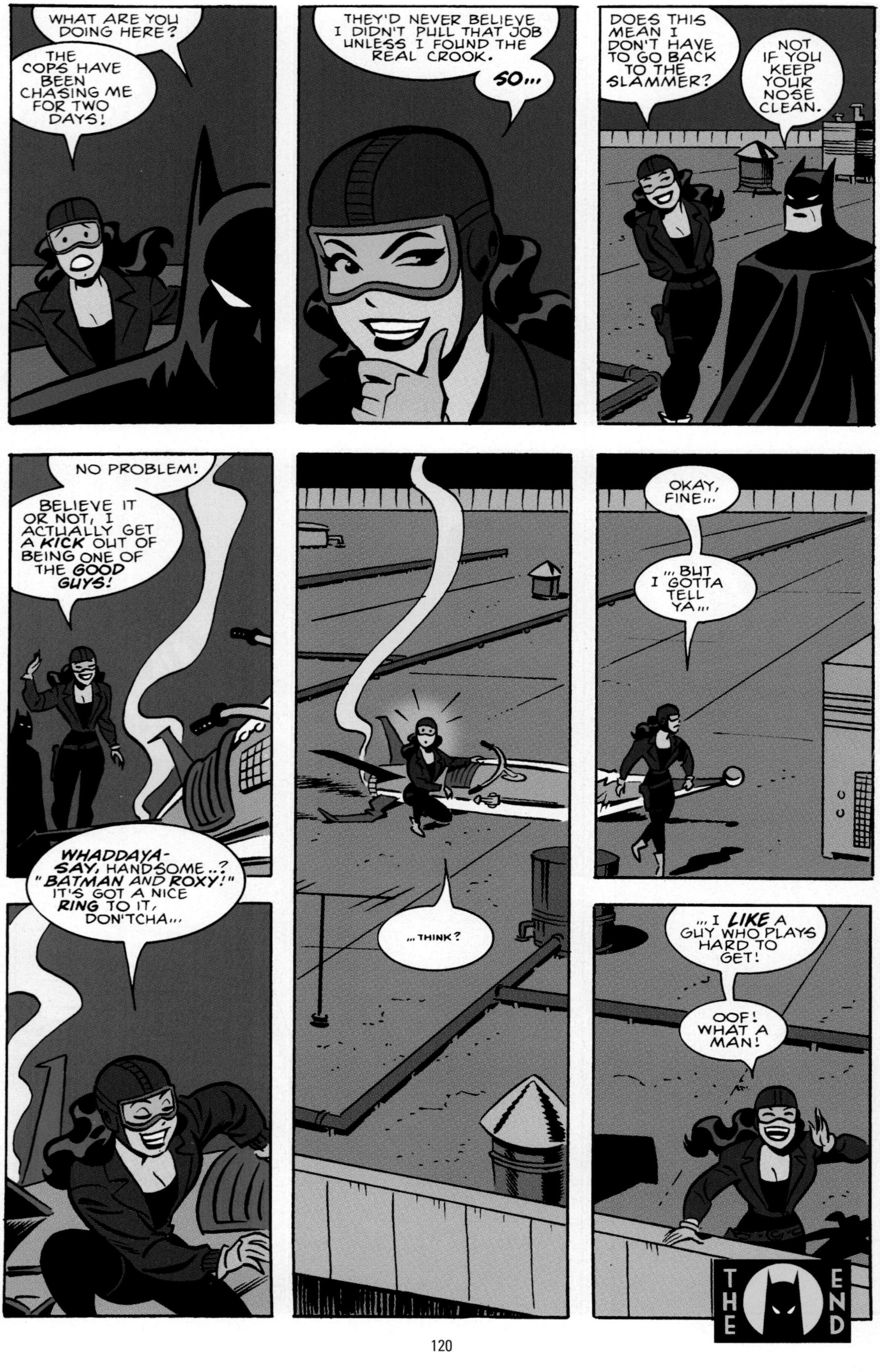
WHAT ARE YOU DOING HERE?
THE COPS HAVE BEEN CHASING ME FOR TWO DAYS!
THEY'D NEVER BELIEVE I DIDN'T PULL THAT JOB UNLESS I FOUND THE REAL CROOK.
SO...
DOES THIS MEAN I DON'T HAVE TO GO BACK TO THE SLAMMER?
NOT IF YOU KEEP YOUR NOSE CLEAN.
NO PROBLEM!
BELIEVE IT OR NOT, I ACTUALLY GET A KICK OUT OF BEING ONE OF THE GOOD GUYS!
OKAY, FINE...
...BUT I GOTTA TELL YA...
WHADDAYA-SAY, HANDSOME..? "BATMAN AND ROXY!" IT'S GOT A NICE RING TO IT, DON'TCHA...
...THINK?
...I LIKE A GUY WHO PLAYS HARD TO GET!
OOF! WHAT A MAN!
THE END

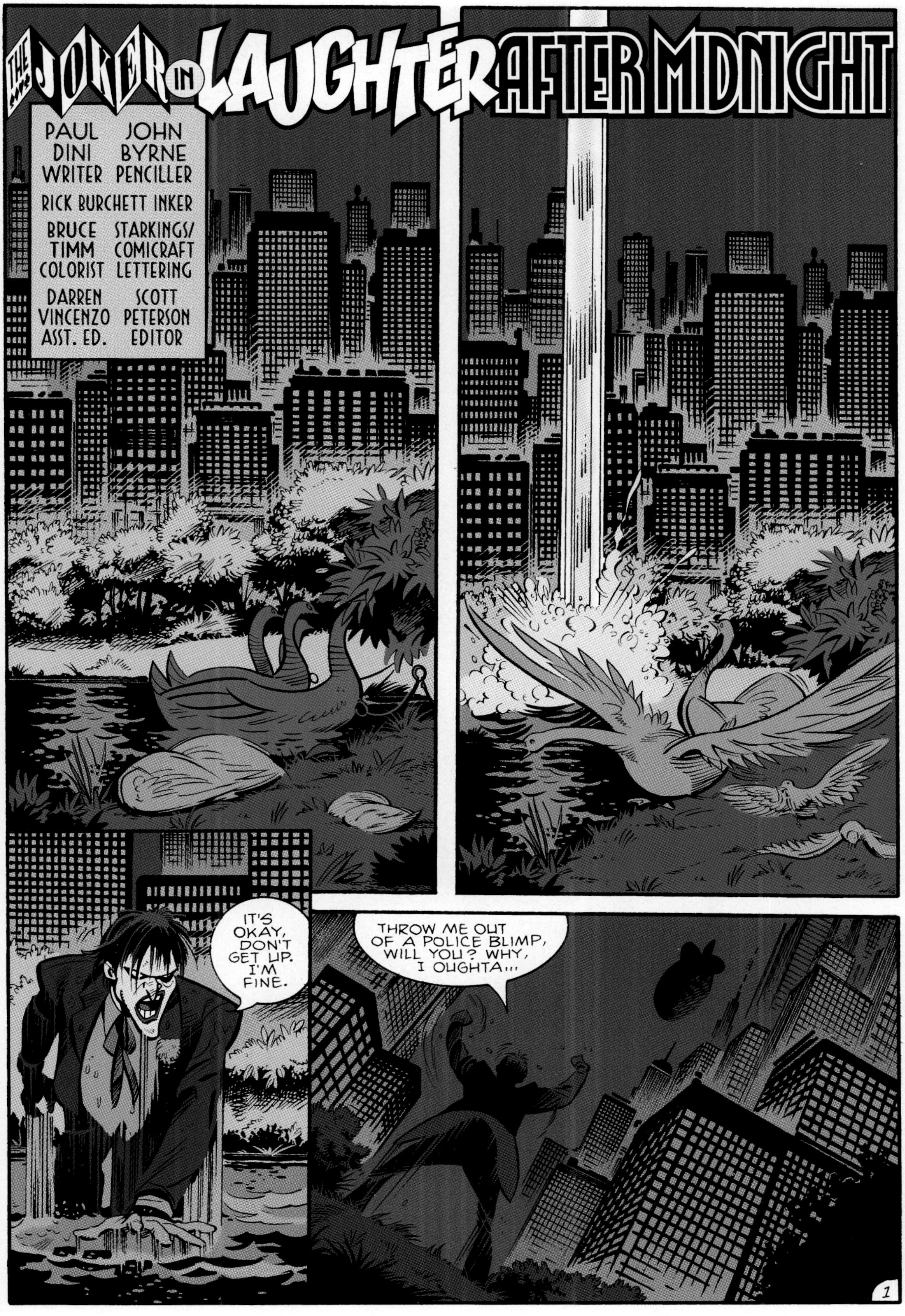
THE JOKER IN
LAUGHTER AFTER MIDNIGHT
PAUL DINI WRITER
JOHN BYRNE PENCILLER
RICK BURCHETT INKER
BRUCE TIMM COLORIST
STARKINGS/ COMICRAFT LETTERING
DARREN VINCENZO ASST. ED.
SCOTT PETERSON EDITOR
IT'S OKAY, DON'T GET UP. I'M FINE.
THROW ME OUT OF A POLICE BLIMP, WILL YOU? WHY, I OUGHTA...
1

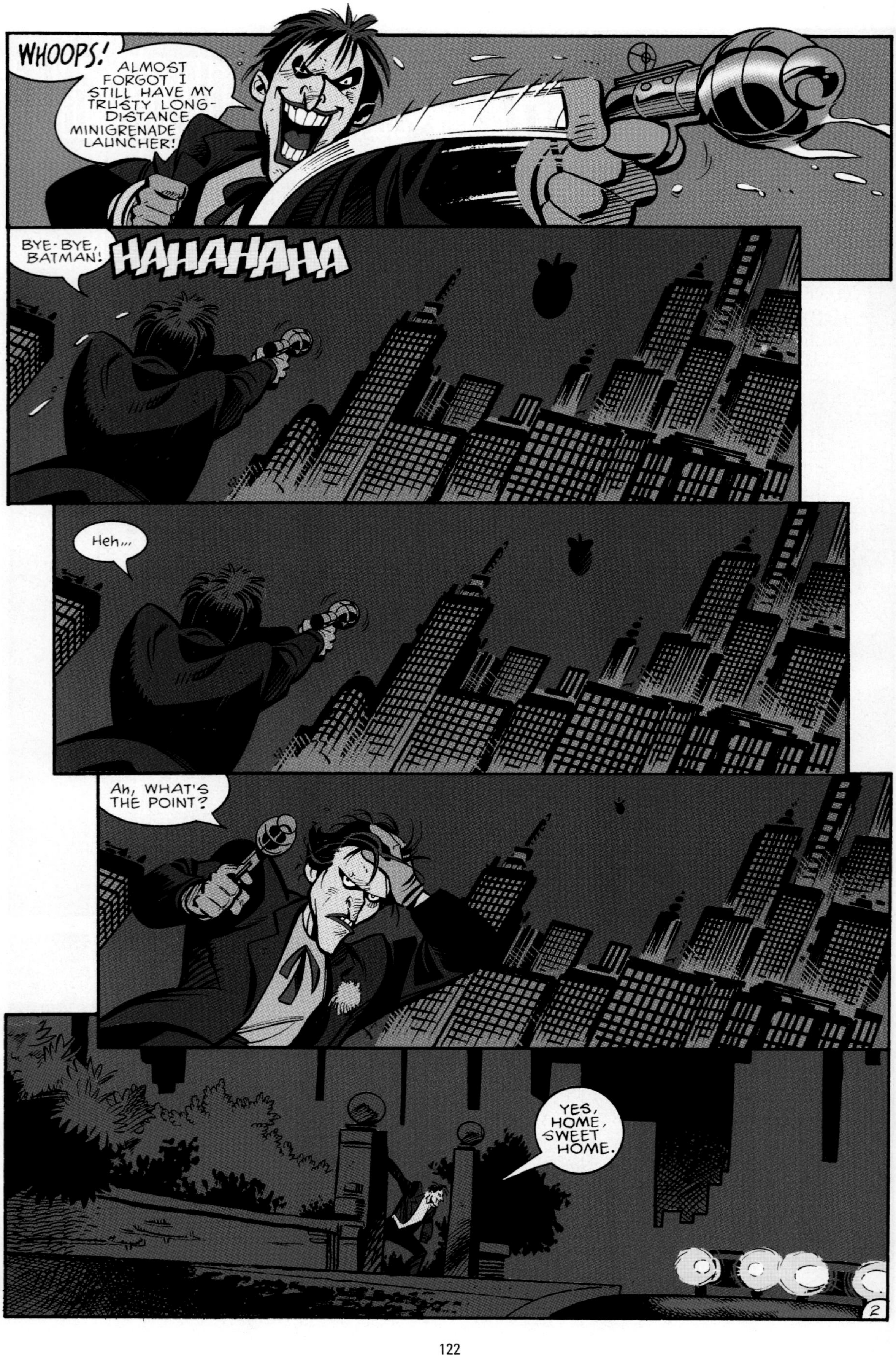
WHOOPS!
ALMOST FORGOT I STILL HAVE MY TRUSTY LONG-DISTANCE MINIGRENADE LAUNCHER!
BYE-BYE, BATMAN!
HAHAHAHA
Heh,,,
Ah, WHAT'S THE POINT?
YES, HOME, SWEET HOME.
2

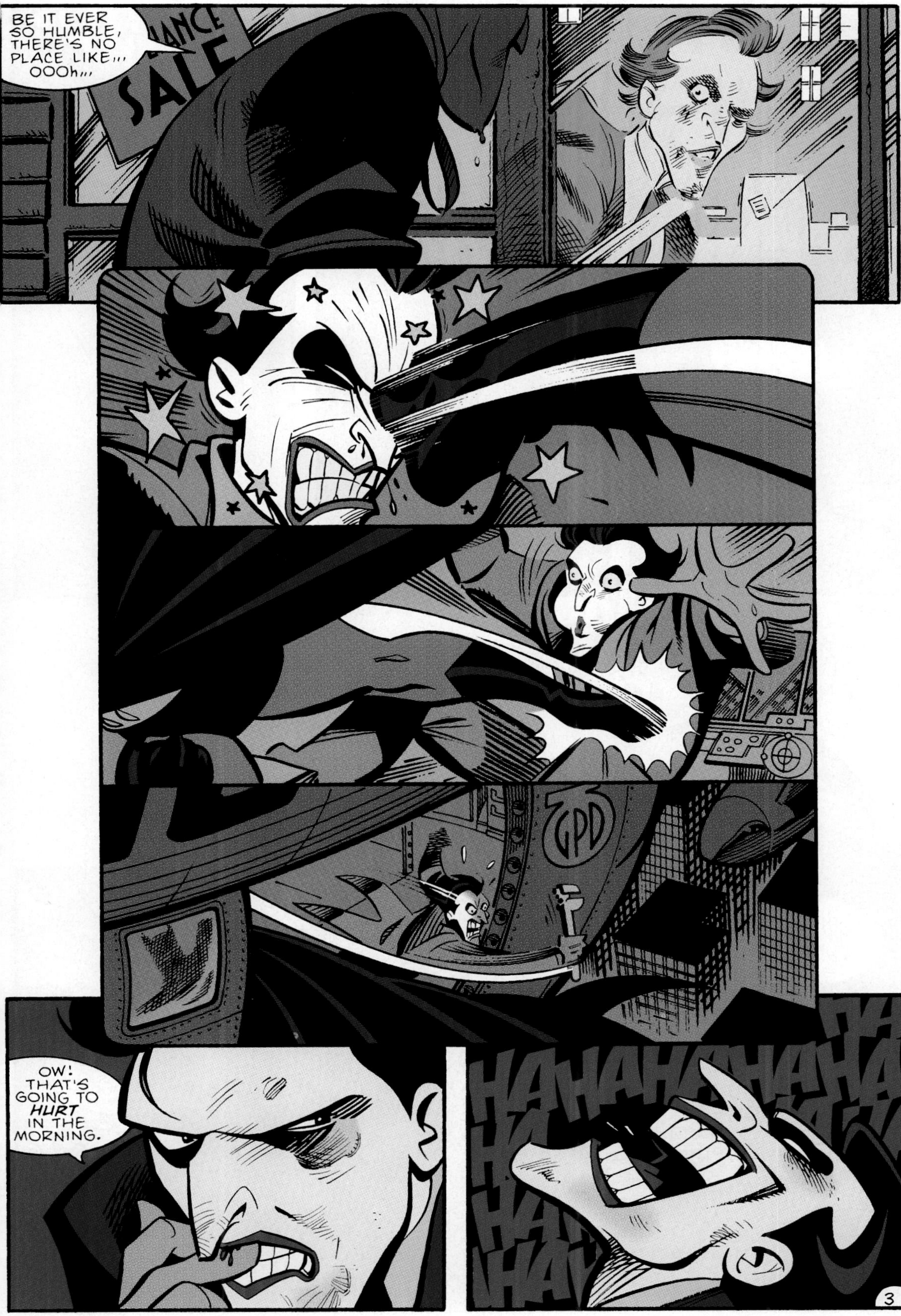
BE IT EVER SO HUMBLE, THERE'S NO PLACE LIKE... OOOh...
SALE
GPD
OW! THAT'S GOING TO HURT IN THE MORNING.
HAHAHAHAHA
3

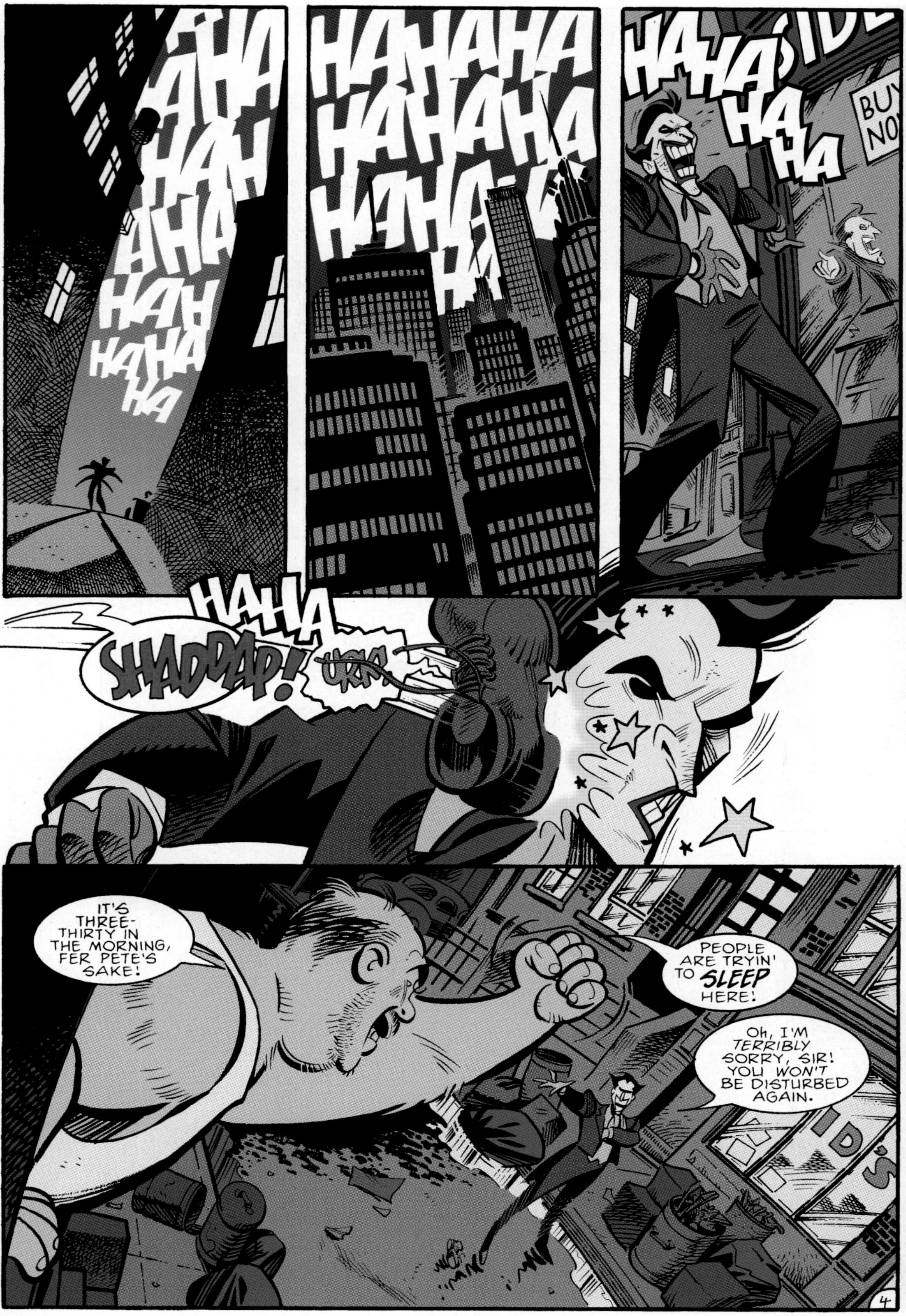
HAHAHA
HAHAHA
HAHAHA
HAHA
HA
HA
BUY NO
HAHA
SHADDAP!
URK!
IT'S THREE-THIRTY IN THE MORNING, FER PETE'S SAKE!
PEOPLE ARE TRYIN' TO SLEEP HERE!
Oh, I'M TERRIBLY SORRY, SIR! YOU WON'T BE DISTURBED AGAIN.
4

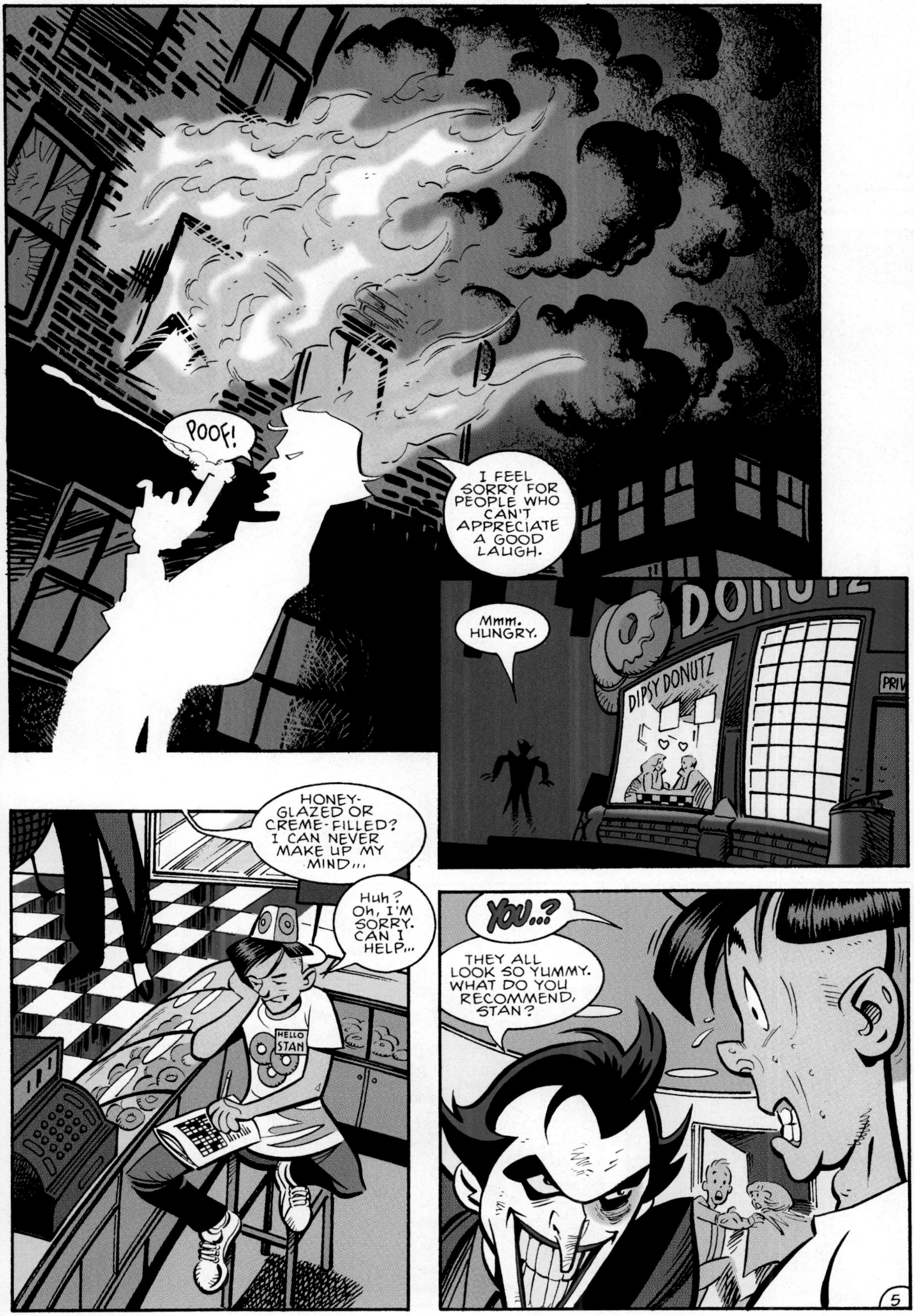
POOF!
I FEEL SORRY FOR PEOPLE WHO CAN'T APPRECIATE A GOOD LAUGH.
DONUTZ
Mmm. HUNGRY.
DIPSY DONUTZ
PRIV
HONEY-GLAZED OR CREME-FILLED? I CAN NEVER MAKE UP MY MIND...
Huh? Oh, I'M SORRY. CAN I HELP...
HELLO STAN
YOU..?
THEY ALL LOOK SO YUMMY. WHAT DO YOU RECOMMEND, STAN?
5

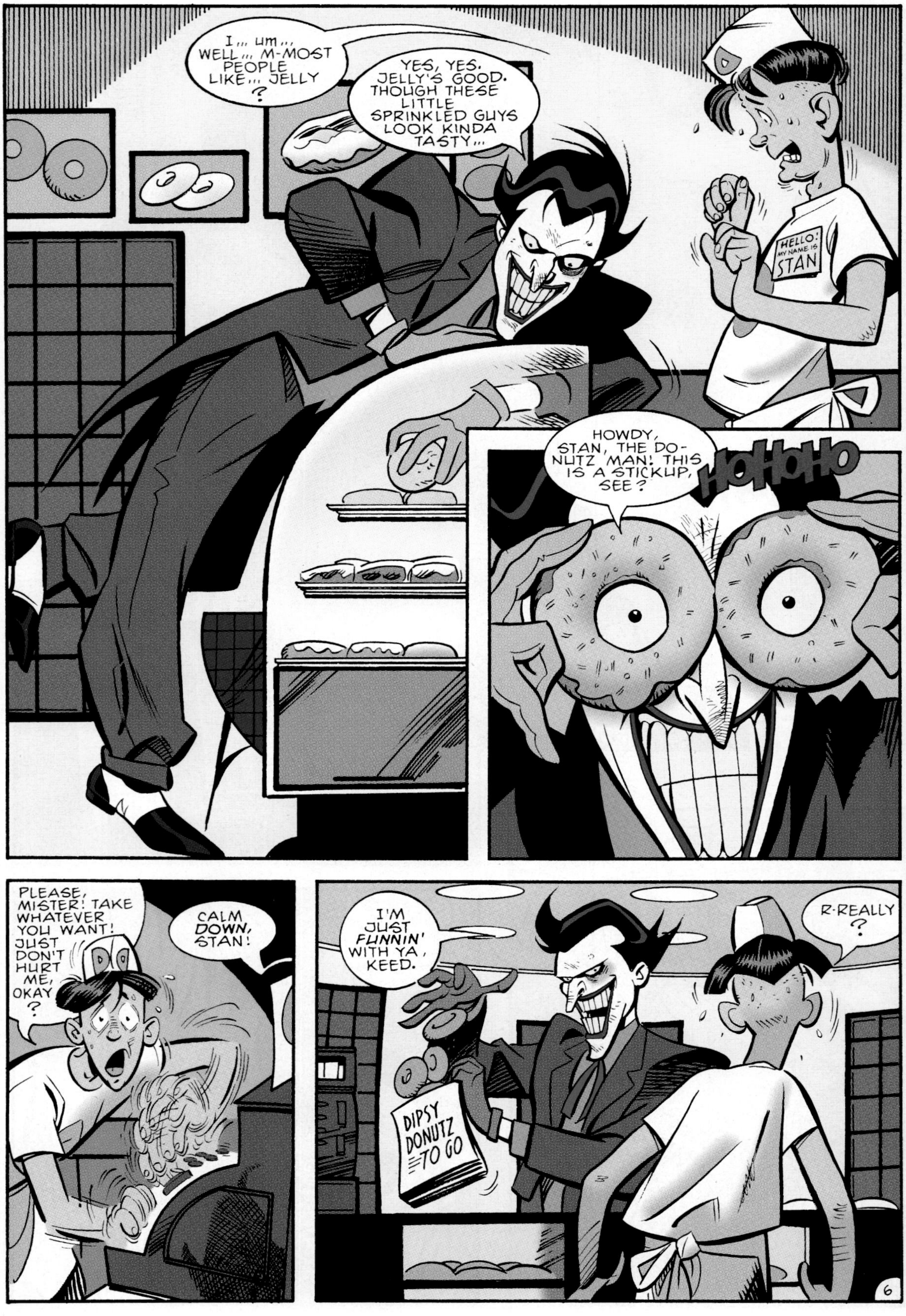

I... UM... WELL... M-MOST PEOPLE LIKE... JELLY?
YES, YES. JELLY'S GOOD. THOUGH THESE LITTLE SPRINKLED GUYS LOOK KINDA TASTY...
HELLO! MY NAME IS STAN
HOWDY, STAN, THE DO-NUTZ MAN! THIS IS A STICKUP, SEE?
HOHOHO
PLEASE, MISTER! TAKE WHATEVER YOU WANT! JUST DON'T HURT ME, OKAY?
CALM DOWN, STAN!
I'M JUST FUNNIN' WITH YA, KEED.
R-REALLY?
DIPSY DONUTZ TO GO
6

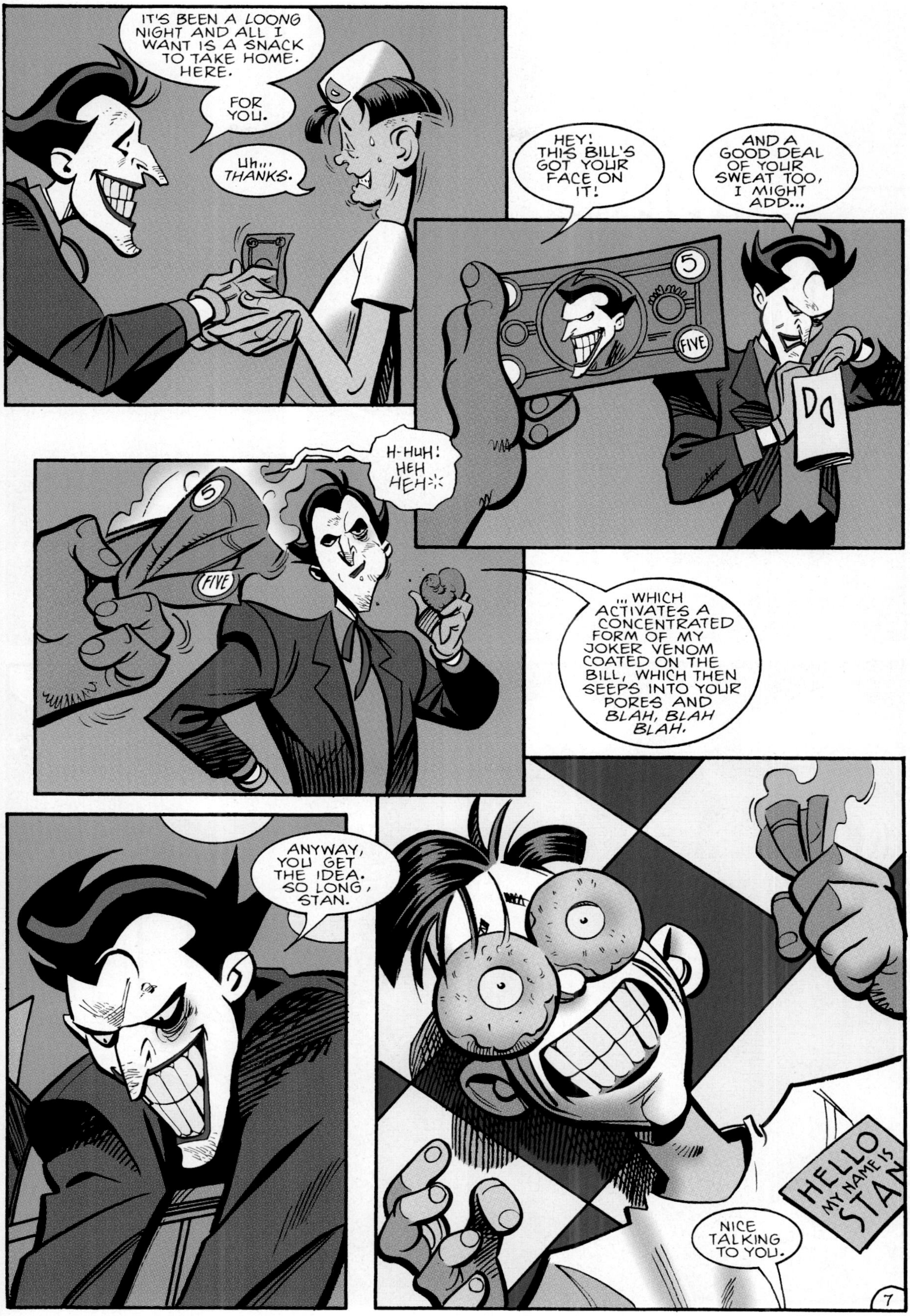
IT'S BEEN A LOONG NIGHT AND ALL I WANT IS A SNACK TO TAKE HOME. HERE.
FOR YOU.
UH... THANKS.
HEY! THIS BILL'S GOT YOUR FACE ON IT!
AND A GOOD DEAL OF YOUR SWEAT TOO, I MIGHT ADD...
5
FIVE
H-HUH! HEH HEH!
...WHICH ACTIVATES A CONCENTRATED FORM OF MY JOKER VENOM COATED ON THE BILL, WHICH THEN SEEPS INTO YOUR PORES AND BLAH, BLAH BLAH.
ANYWAY, YOU GET THE IDEA. SO LONG, STAN.
HELLO MY NAME IS STAN
NICE TALKING TO YOU.
7

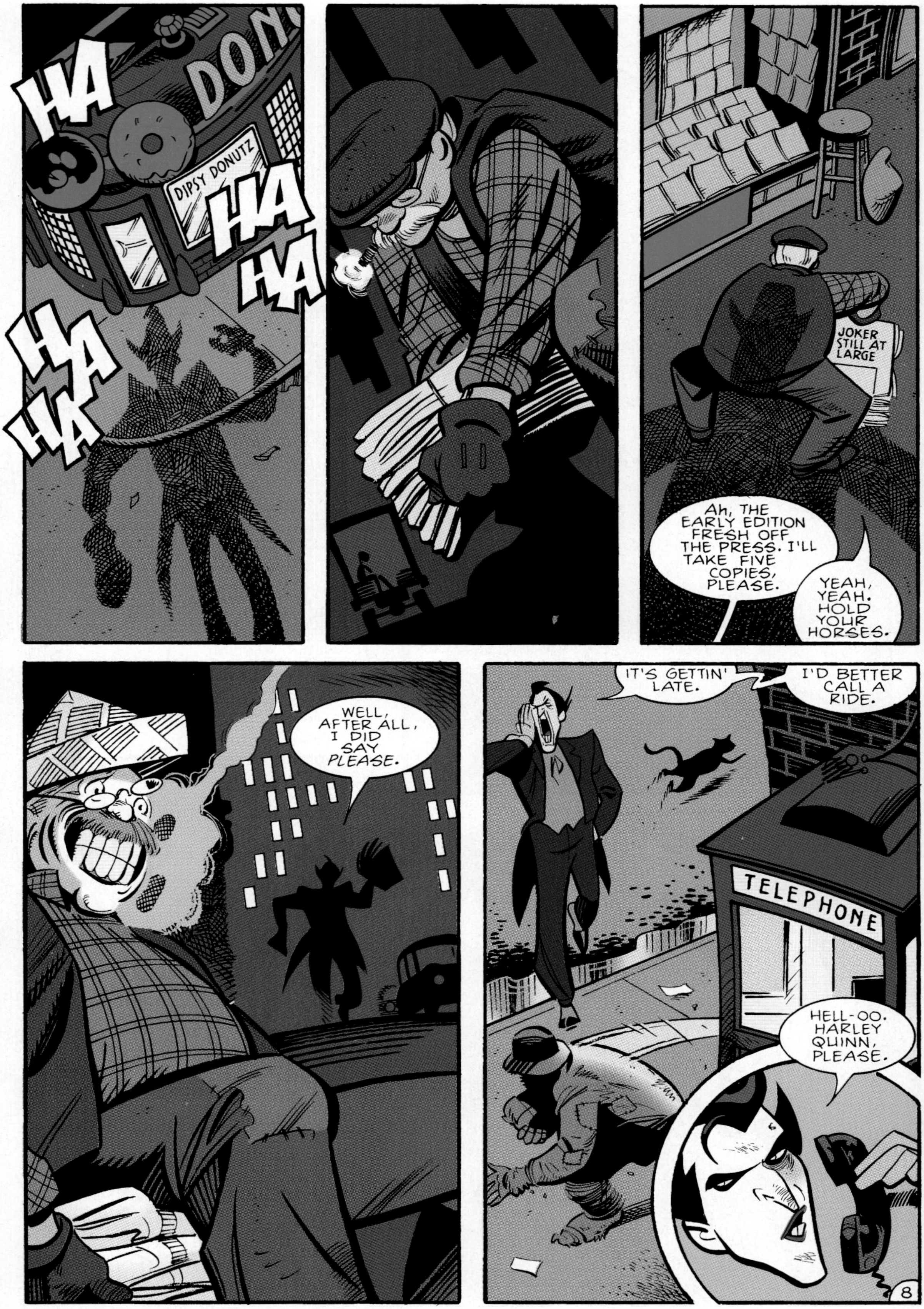
HA
DONU
DIPSY DONUTZ
HA
HA
HA
HA
HA
JOKER STILL AT LARGE
Ah, THE EARLY EDITION FRESH OFF THE PRESS. I'LL TAKE FIVE COPIES, PLEASE.
YEAH, YEAH. HOLD YOUR HORSES.
WELL, AFTER ALL, I DID SAY PLEASE.
IT'S GETTIN' LATE.
I'D BETTER CALL A RIDE.
TELEPHONE
HELL-OO. HARLEY QUINN, PLEASE.
8

JOKER STILL AT LARGE

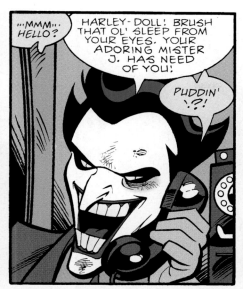

"...MMM... HELLO?"

HARLEY-DOLL! BRUSH THAT OL' SLEEP FROM YOUR EYES. YOUR ADORING MISTER J. HAS NEED OF YOU!

PUDDIN'\?!

YES, I *KNOW* YOU'RE *EXCITED,* BUT PAY ATTENTION. I WANT YOU TO GET A CAR AND COME DOWNTOWN AND PICK ME UP. THERE'S A GOOD GIRL.

Umm... I DON'T THINK I CAN.

WHAT? WHY NOT?!

WELL...

ASK HIM WHERE HE IS!

HOLY JOE!

THAT'S NO EXCUSE, BLAST IT!

POLICE

OKAY, JOKER! PUT DOWN THE PHONE AND GET THOSE HANDS IN THE AIR.

OH, PLEASE. I'M REALLY IN NO MOOD FOR THIS TONIGHT.

HELLO?

9

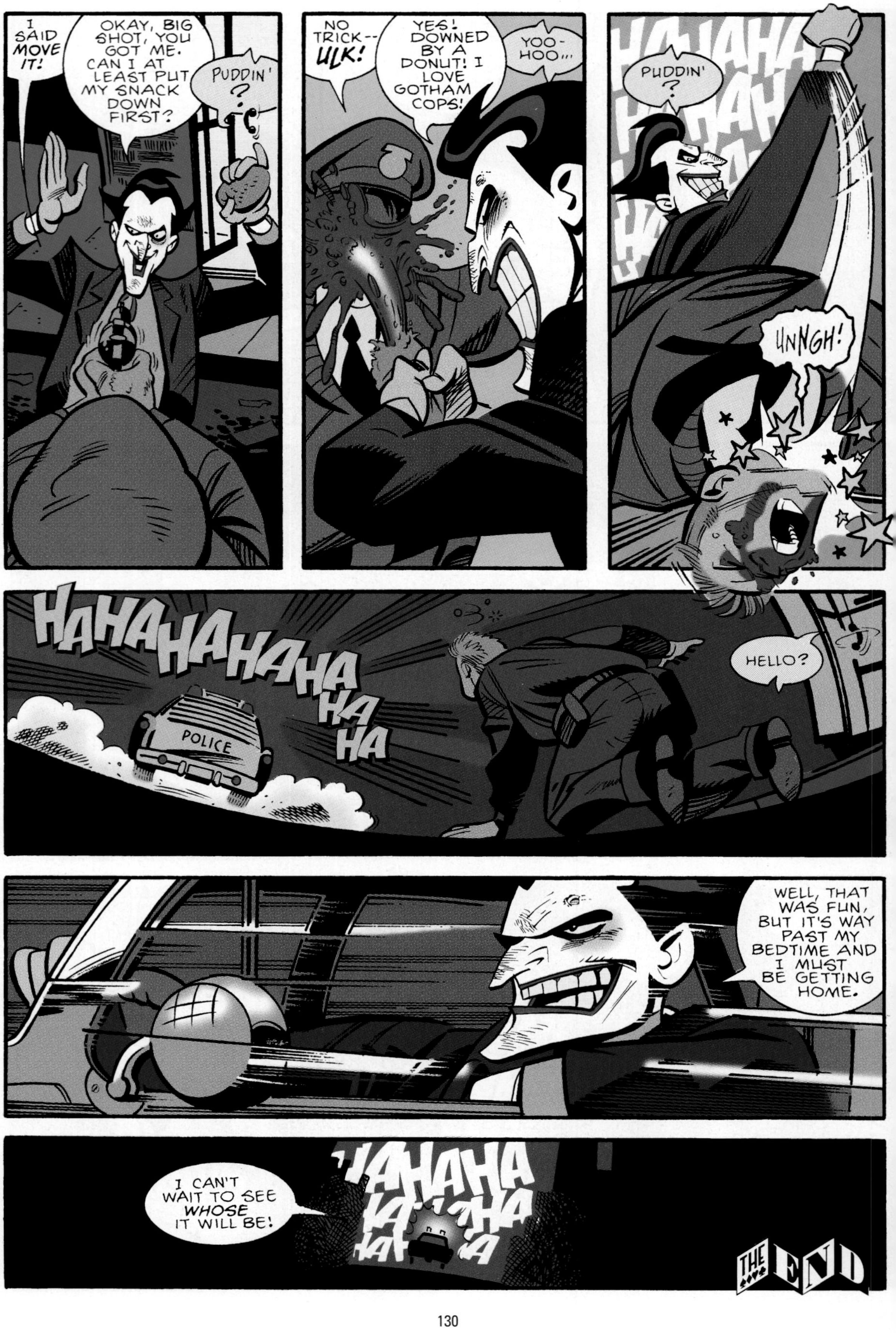
I SAID MOVE IT!
OKAY, BIG SHOT, YOU GOT ME. CAN I AT LEAST PUT MY SNACK DOWN FIRST?
PUDDIN' ?
NO TRICK-- ULK!
YES! DOWNED BY A DONUT! I LOVE GOTHAM COPS!
YOO-HOO...
HAHAHA
PUDDIN' ?
UNNGH!
HAHAHAHAHAHA HA HA HA
POLICE
HELLO?
WELL, THAT WAS FUN, BUT IT'S WAY PAST MY BEDTIME AND I MUST BE GETTING HOME.
I CAN'T WAIT TO SEE WHOSE IT WILL BE!
THE END

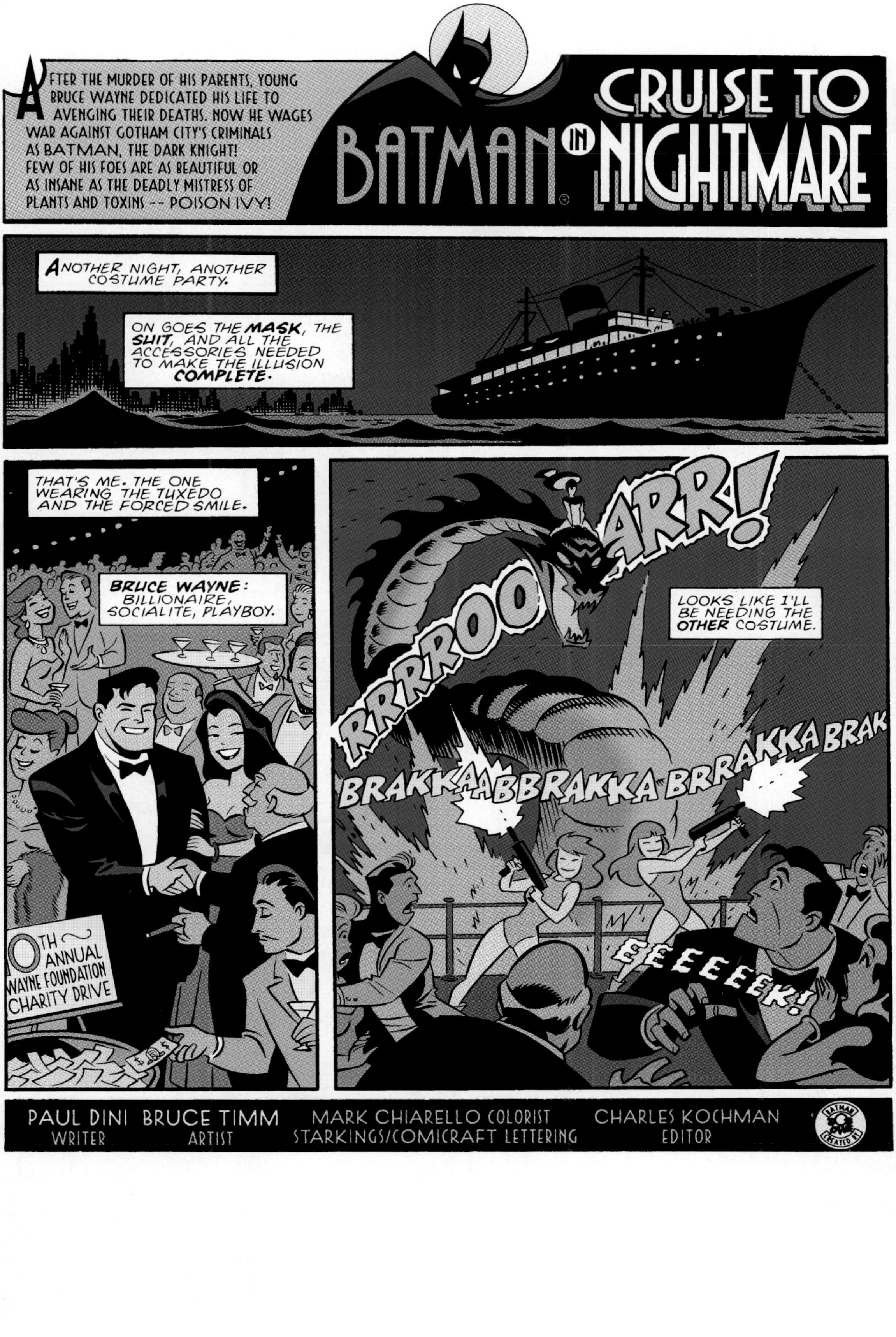

AFTER THE MURDER OF HIS PARENTS, YOUNG BRUCE WAYNE DEDICATED HIS LIFE TO AVENGING THEIR DEATHS. NOW HE WAGES WAR AGAINST GOTHAM CITY'S CRIMINALS AS BATMAN, THE DARK KNIGHT! FEW OF HIS FOES ARE AS BEAUTIFUL OR AS INSANE AS THE DEADLY MISTRESS OF PLANTS AND TOXINS -- POISON IVY!
BATMAN® IN CRUISE TO NIGHTMARE
ANOTHER NIGHT, ANOTHER COSTUME PARTY.
ON GOES THE MASK, THE SUIT, AND ALL THE ACCESSORIES NEEDED TO MAKE THE ILLUSION COMPLETE.
THAT'S ME. THE ONE WEARING THE TUXEDO AND THE FORCED SMILE.
BRUCE WAYNE: BILLIONAIRE, SOCIALITE, PLAYBOY.
0TH ANNUAL WAYNE FOUNDATION CHARITY DRIVE
RRRROO ARR!
LOOKS LIKE I'LL BE NEEDING THE OTHER COSTUME.
BRAKKAABBRAKKA BRRAKKA BRAK
EEEEEEK!
PAUL DINI WRITER
BRUCE TIMM ARTIST
MARK CHIARELLO COLORIST
STARKINGS/COMICRAFT LETTERING
CHARLES KOCHMAN EDITOR

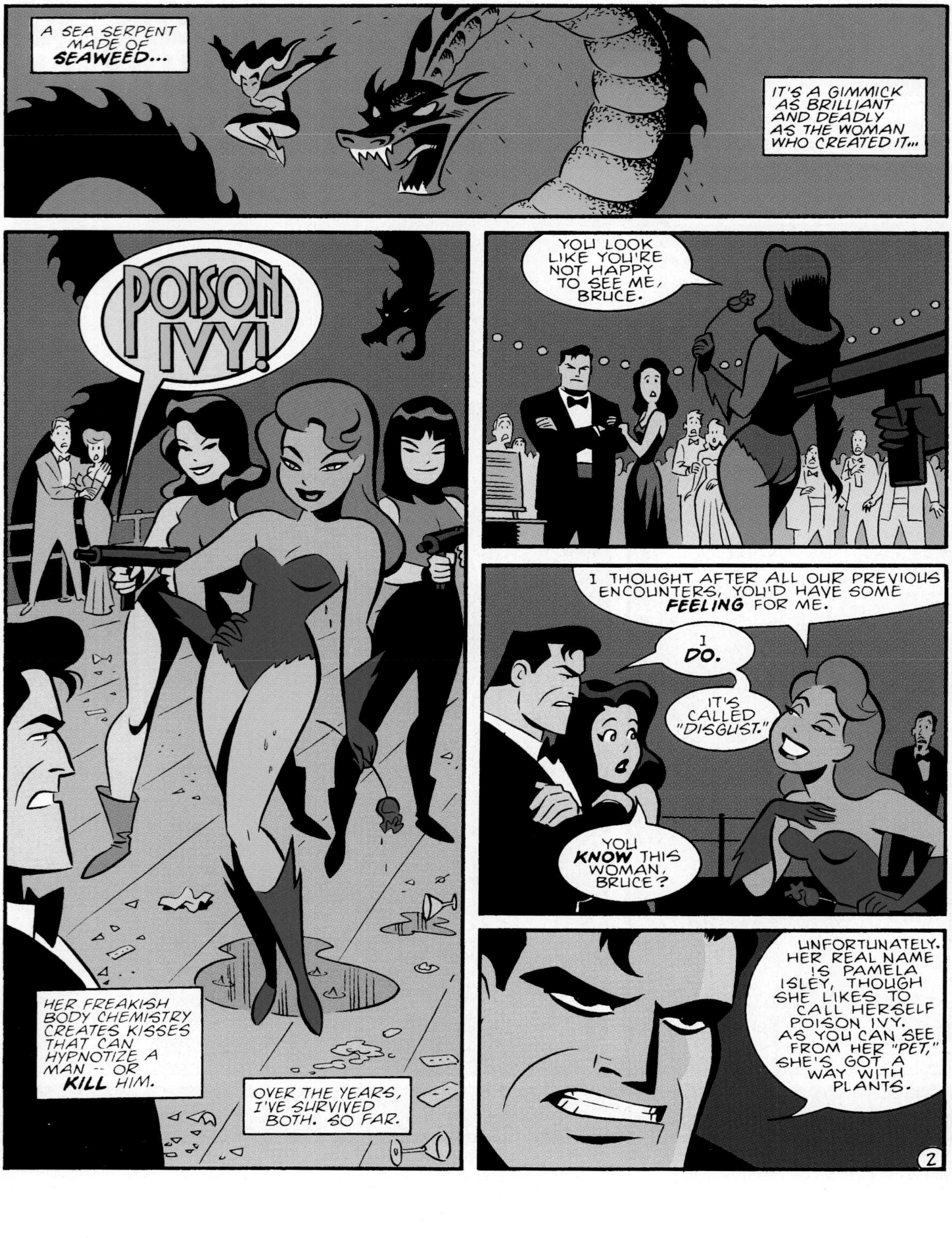
A SEA SERPENT MADE OF SEAWEED...
IT'S A GIMMICK AS BRILLIANT AND DEADLY AS THE WOMAN WHO CREATED IT...
POISON IVY!
HER FREAKISH BODY CHEMISTRY CREATES KISSES THAT CAN HYPNOTIZE A MAN -- OR KILL HIM.
OVER THE YEARS, I'VE SURVIVED BOTH. SO FAR.
YOU LOOK LIKE YOU'RE NOT HAPPY TO SEE ME, BRUCE.
I THOUGHT AFTER ALL OUR PREVIOUS ENCOUNTERS, YOU'D HAVE SOME FEELING FOR ME.
I DO.
IT'S CALLED "DISGUST."
YOU KNOW THIS WOMAN, BRUCE?
UNFORTUNATELY. HER REAL NAME IS PAMELA ISLEY, THOUGH SHE LIKES TO CALL HERSELF POISON IVY. AS YOU CAN SEE FROM HER "PET," SHE'S GOT A WAY WITH PLANTS.
2

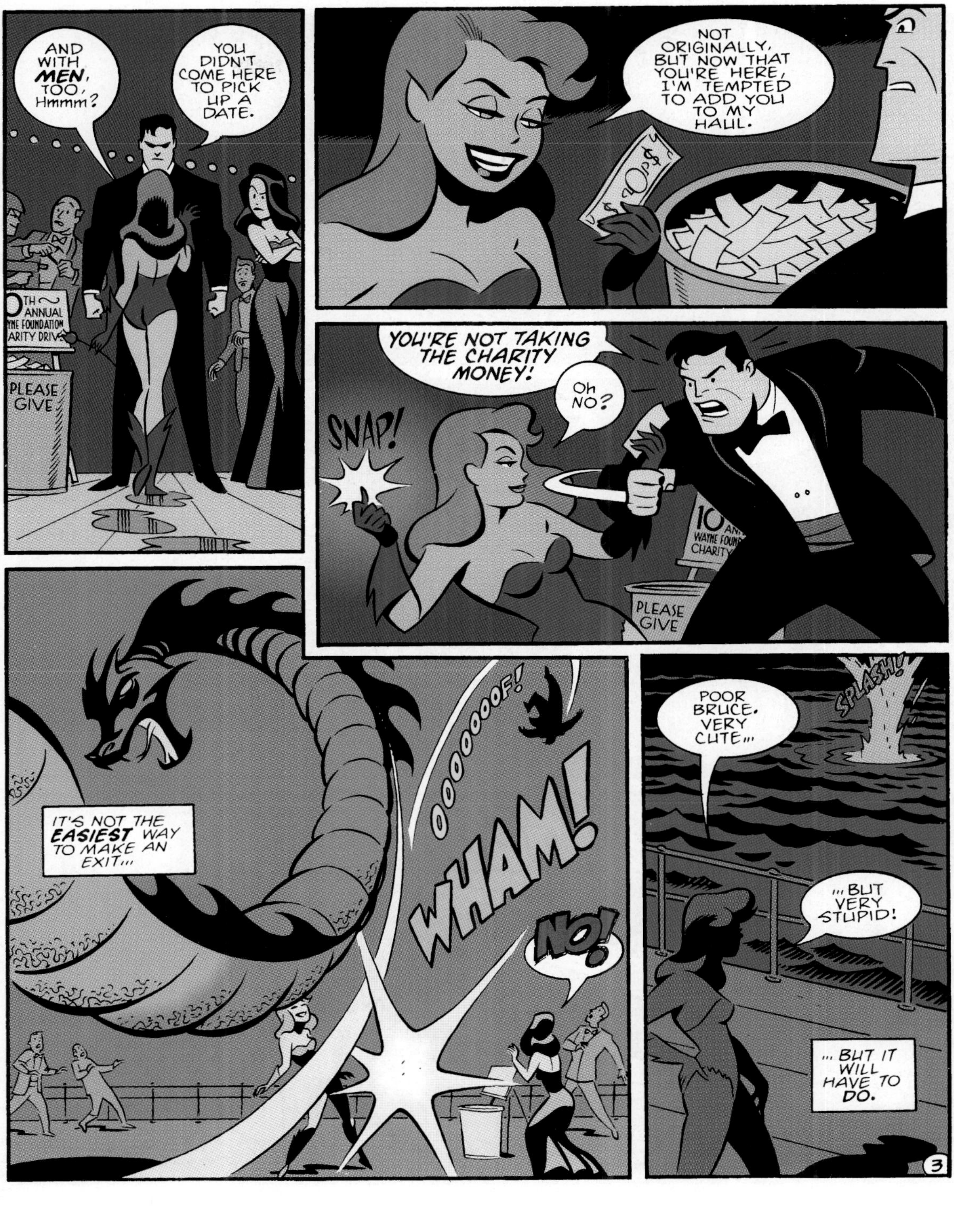
AND WITH MEN, TOO, Hmmm?
YOU DIDN'T COME HERE TO PICK UP A DATE.
0TH ANNUAL WAYNE FOUNDATION ARITY DRIV
PLEASE GIVE
NOT ORIGINALLY, BUT NOW THAT YOU'RE HERE, I'M TEMPTED TO ADD YOU TO MY HAUL.
YOU'RE NOT TAKING THE CHARITY MONEY!
Oh NO?
SNAP!
PLEASE GIVE
IT'S NOT THE EASIEST WAY TO MAKE AN EXIT...
OOOOOOOOF!
WHAM!
NO!
SPLASH!
POOR BRUCE. VERY CUTE...
...BUT VERY STUPID!
...BUT IT WILL HAVE TO DO.
3

BANG!

YOU HEARTLESS WITCH! YOU JUST MURDERED A MAN IN COLD BLOOD!

WHAT'S YOUR POINT?

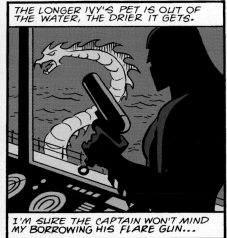

THE LONGER IVY'S PET IS OUT OF THE WATER, THE DRIER IT GETS.

I'M SURE THE CAPTAIN WON'T MIND MY BORROWING HIS FLARE GUN...

ARROOOO

FWOOM!

POP!

HEY!

WHAT GIVES?

4

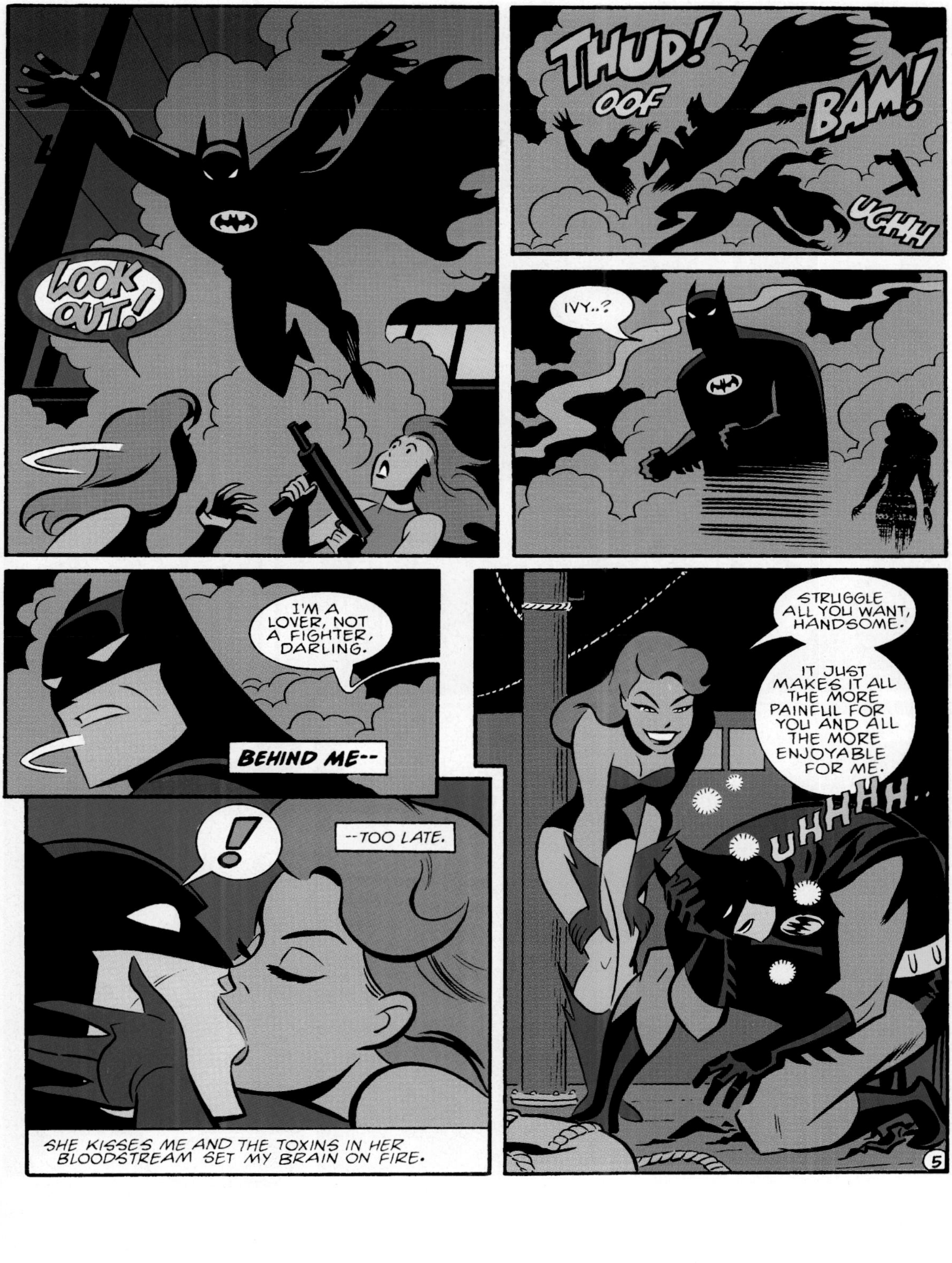
LOOK OUT!
THUD!
OOF
BAM!
UGHH
IVY..?
I'M A LOVER, NOT A FIGHTER, DARLING.
BEHIND ME--
--TOO LATE.
!
SHE KISSES ME AND THE TOXINS IN HER BLOODSTREAM SET MY BRAIN ON FIRE.
STRUGGLE ALL YOU WANT, HANDSOME.
IT JUST MAKES IT ALL THE MORE PAINFUL FOR YOU AND ALL THE MORE ENJOYABLE FOR ME.
UHHHH..
5

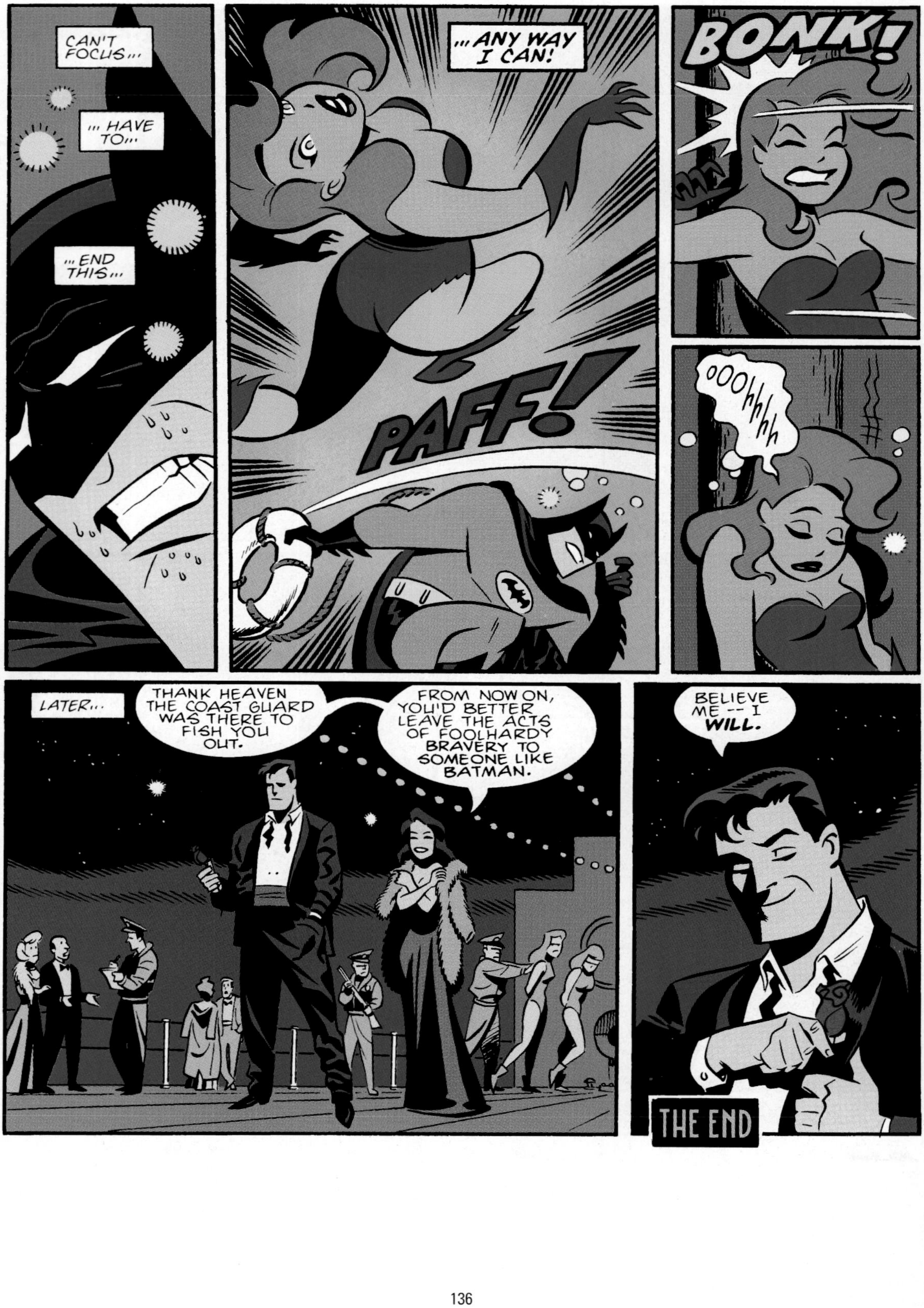

CAN'T FOCUS...
...HAVE TO...
...END THIS...
...ANY WAY I CAN!
PAFF!
BONK!
OOOhhhh
LATER...
THANK HEAVEN THE COAST GUARD WAS THERE TO FISH YOU OUT.
FROM NOW ON, YOU'D BETTER LEAVE THE ACTS OF FOOLHARDY BRAVERY TO SOMEONE LIKE BATMAN.
BELIEVE ME -- I **WILL.**
THE END

MAYFIELD'S DEPARTMENT STORE, DECEMBER 3RD...
Quality TIES
IT'S PERFECT! DAD WILL LOVE IT.
GOSH! I KNOW SOME KIDS ARE SCARED OF SANTA, BUT THAT POOR CHILD SOUNDS ABSOLUTELY TERRIFIED!
Ahhhh, YA BIG CRY-BABY --
HURRP
NEXT!
Oh, I DON'T BELIEVE IT!
MEET
-5-30PM
DONUTS

JOLLY OL' ST. NICHOLAS

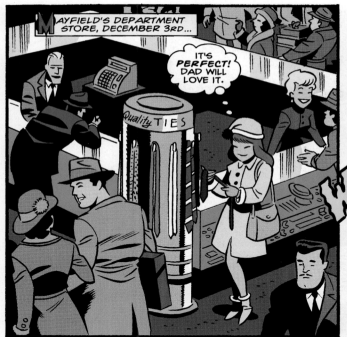

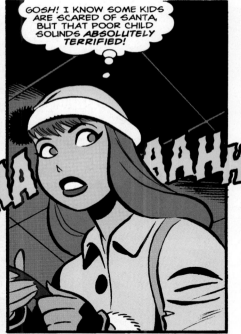

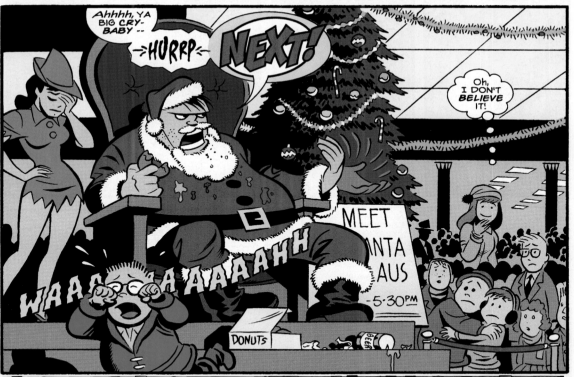

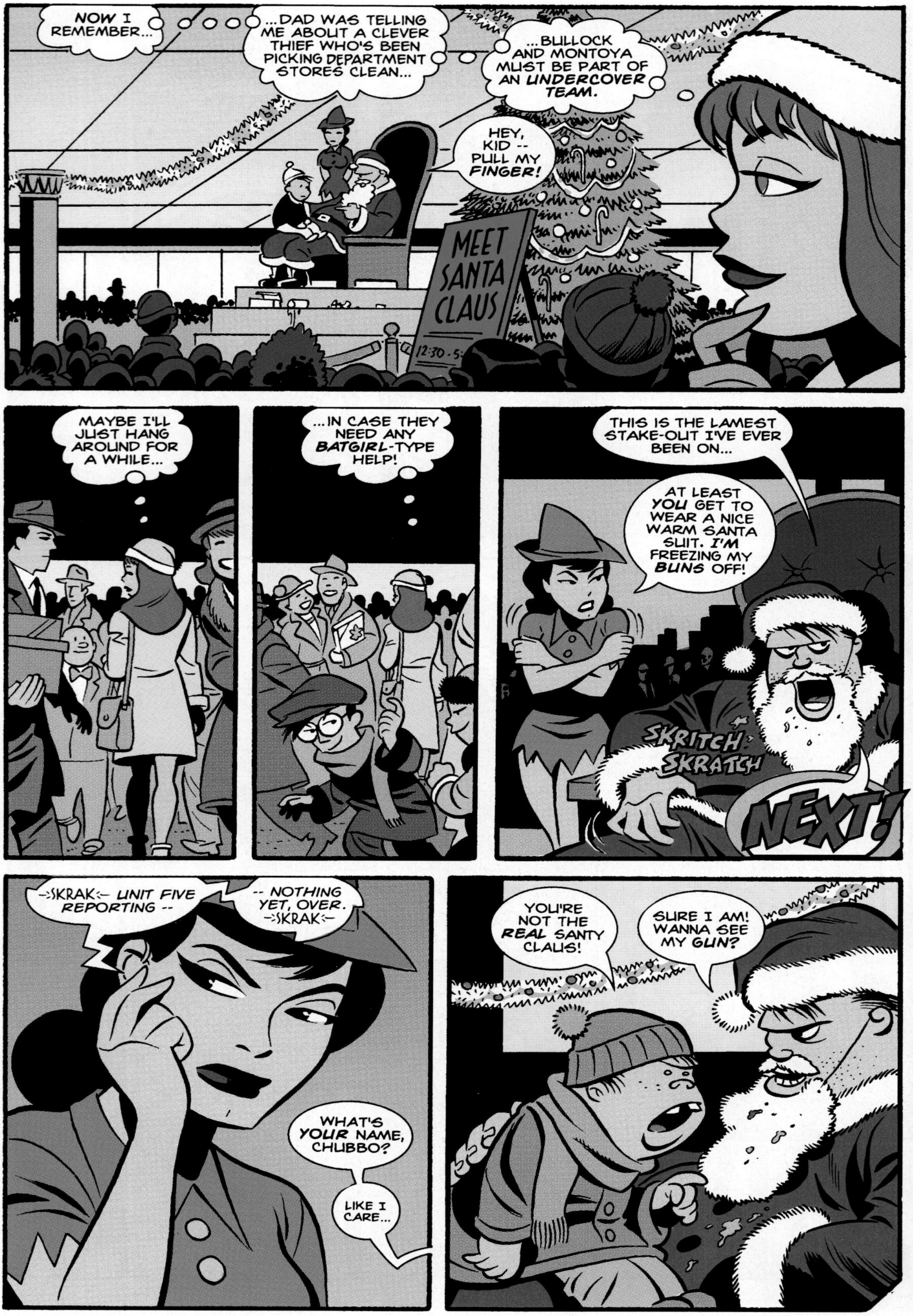
NOW I REMEMBER...
...DAD WAS TELLING ME ABOUT A CLEVER THIEF WHO'S BEEN PICKING DEPARTMENT STORES CLEAN...
...BULLOCK AND MONTOYA MUST BE PART OF AN UNDERCOVER TEAM.
HEY, KID -- PULL MY FINGER!
MEET SANTA CLAUS
MAYBE I'LL JUST HANG AROUND FOR A WHILE...
...IN CASE THEY NEED ANY BATGIRL-TYPE HELP!
THIS IS THE LAMEST STAKE-OUT I'VE EVER BEEN ON...
AT LEAST YOU GET TO WEAR A NICE WARM SANTA SUIT. I'M FREEZING MY BUNS OFF!
SKRITCH SKRATCH
NEXT!
-SKRAK- UNIT FIVE REPORTING --
-- NOTHING YET, OVER. -SKRAK-
WHAT'S YOUR NAME, CHUBBO?
LIKE I CARE...
YOU'RE NOT THE REAL SANTY CLAUS!
SURE I AM! WANNA SEE MY GUN?

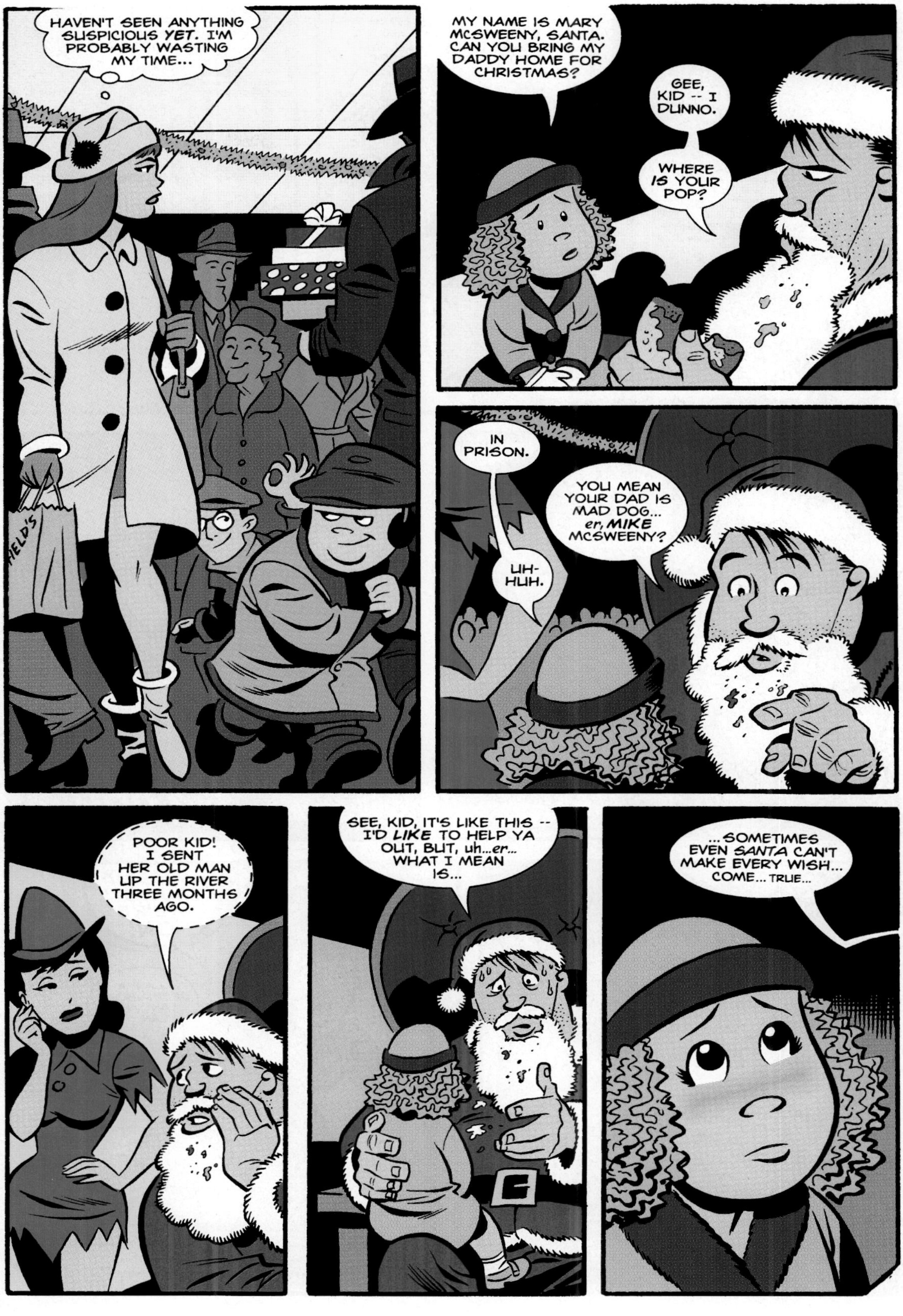
HAVEN'T SEEN ANYTHING SUSPICIOUS YET. I'M PROBABLY WASTING MY TIME...
MY NAME IS MARY McSWEENY, SANTA. CAN YOU BRING MY DADDY HOME FOR CHRISTMAS?
GEE, KID -- I DUNNO.
WHERE IS YOUR POP?
IN PRISON.
YOU MEAN YOUR DAD IS MAD DOG... er, MIKE McSWEENY?
UH-HUH.
HIELD'S
POOR KID! I SENT HER OLD MAN UP THE RIVER THREE MONTHS AGO.
SEE, KID, IT'S LIKE THIS -- I'D LIKE TO HELP YA OUT, BUT, uh...er... WHAT I MEAN IS...
...SOMETIMES EVEN SANTA CAN'T MAKE EVERY WISH... COME... TRUE...

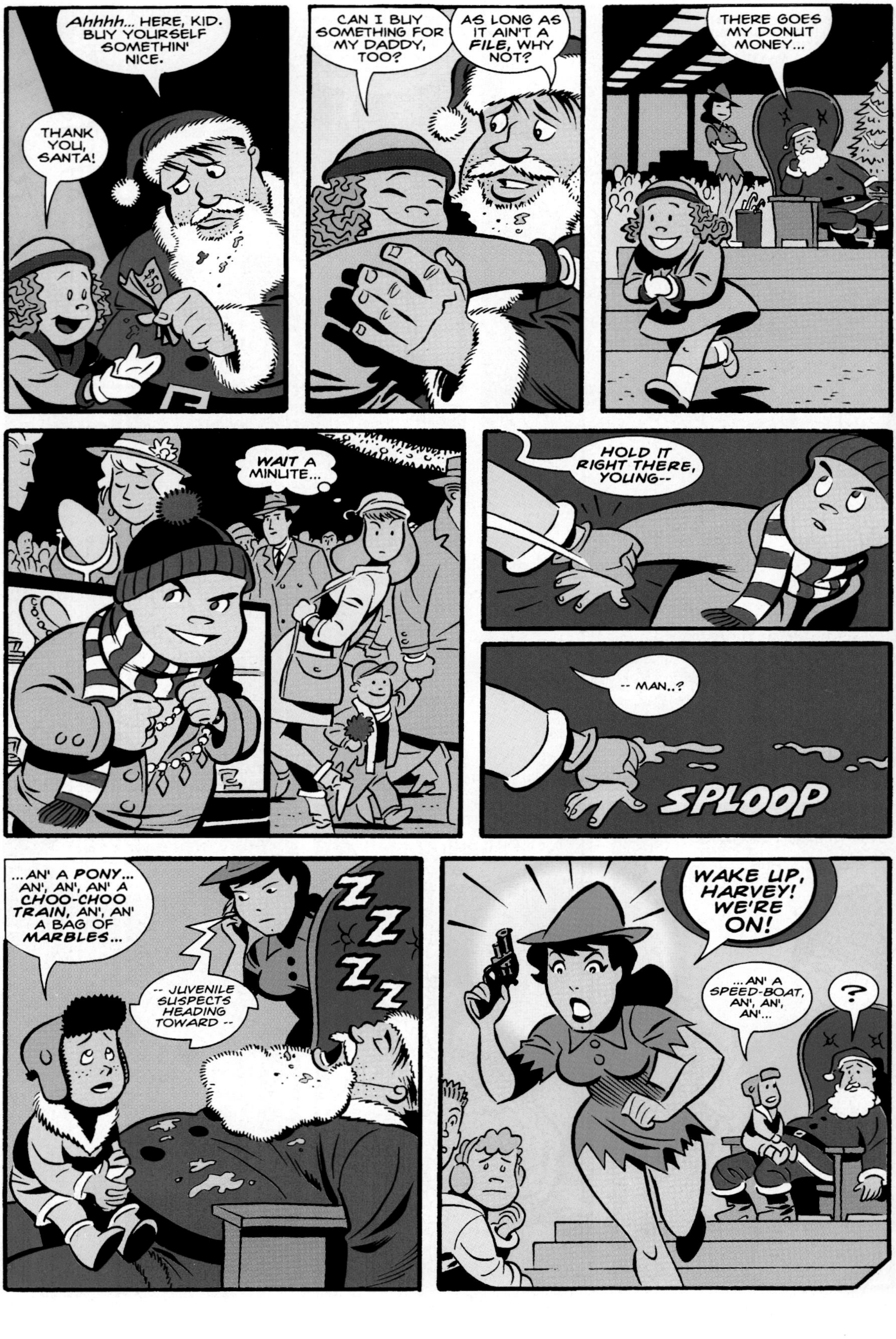
Ahhhh... HERE, KID. BUY YOURSELF SOMETHIN' NICE.
THANK YOU, SANTA!
CAN I BUY SOMETHING FOR MY DADDY, TOO?
AS LONG AS IT AIN'T A FILE, WHY NOT?
THERE GOES MY DONUT MONEY...
WAIT A MINUTE...
HOLD IT RIGHT THERE, YOUNG--
-- MAN..?
SPLOOP
...AN' A PONY... AN', AN', AN' A CHOO-CHOO TRAIN, AN', AN' A BAG OF MARBLES...
-- JUVENILE SUSPECTS HEADING TOWARD --
Z Z Z Z
WAKE UP, HARVEY! WE'RE ON!
...AN' A SPEED-BOAT, AN', AN', AN'...
?

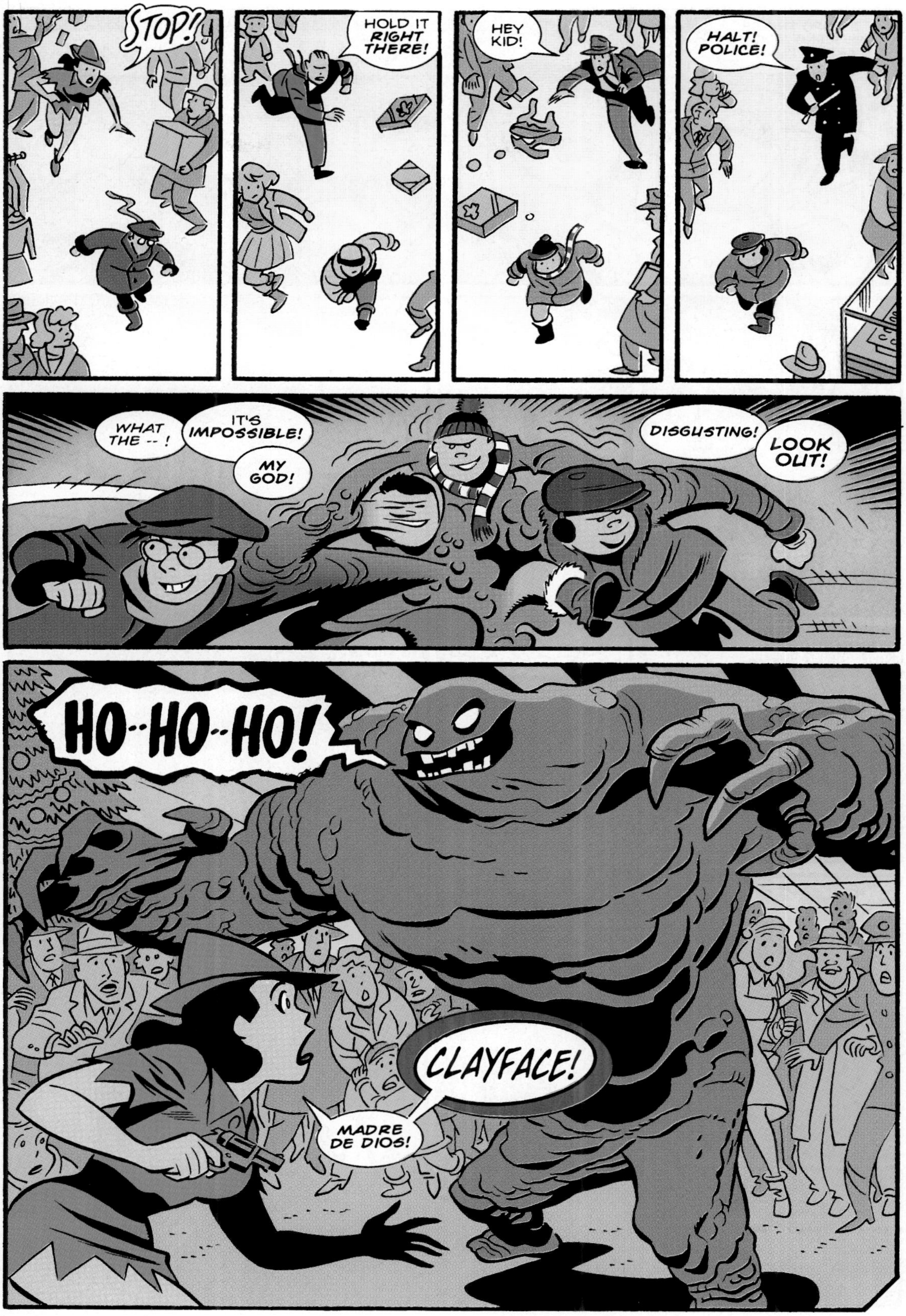
STOP!
HOLD IT RIGHT THERE!
HEY KID!
HALT! POLICE!
WHAT THE -- !
IT'S IMPOSSIBLE!
MY GOD!
DISGUSTING!
LOOK OUT!
HO-HO-HO!
CLAYFACE!
MADRE DE DIOS!

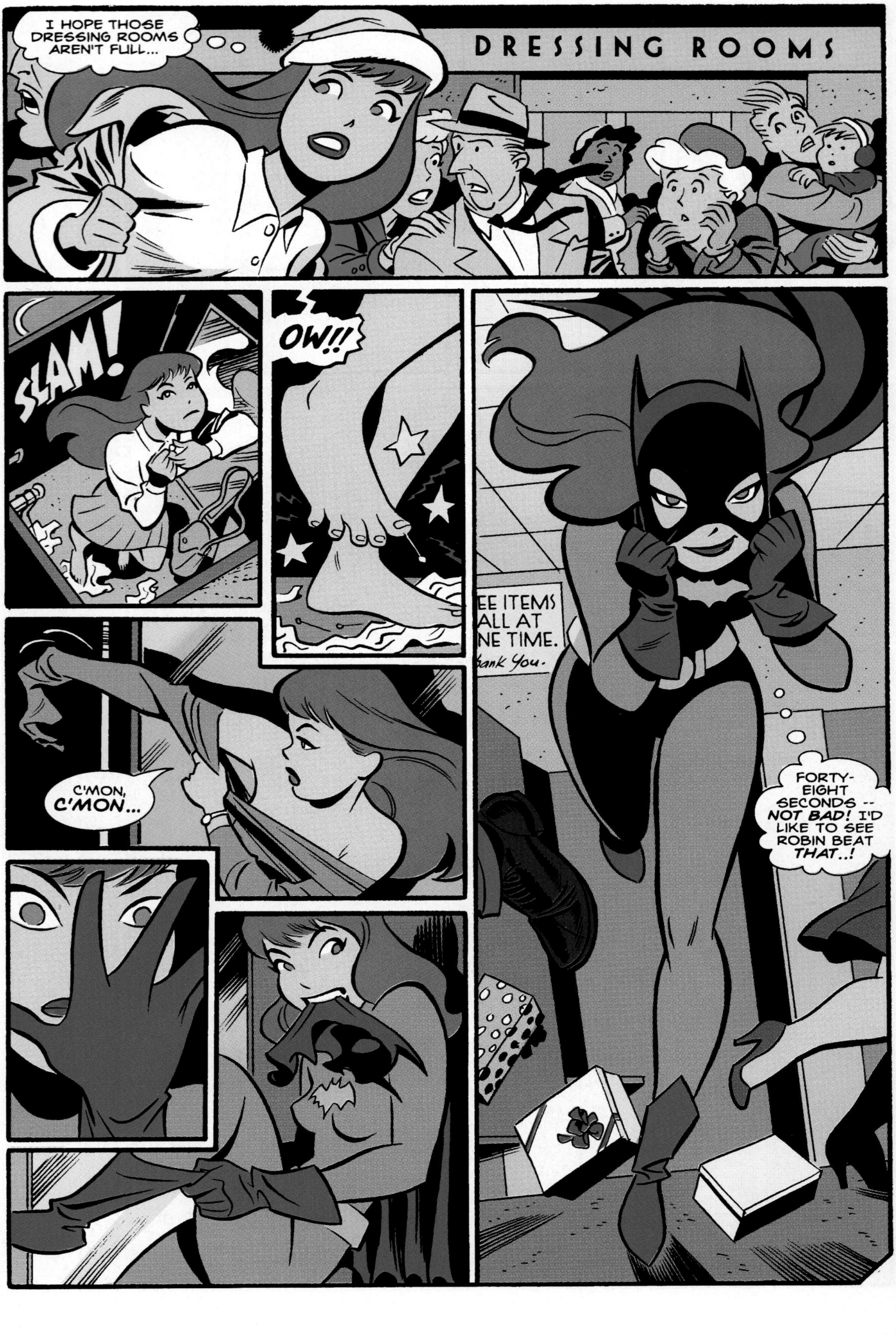
I HOPE THOSE DRESSING ROOMS AREN'T FULL...
DRESSING ROOMS
SLAM!
OW!!
EE ITEMS
ALL AT
NE TIME.
hank You.
C'MON, C'MON...
FORTY-EIGHT SECONDS -- NOT BAD! I'D LIKE TO SEE ROBIN BEAT THAT..!

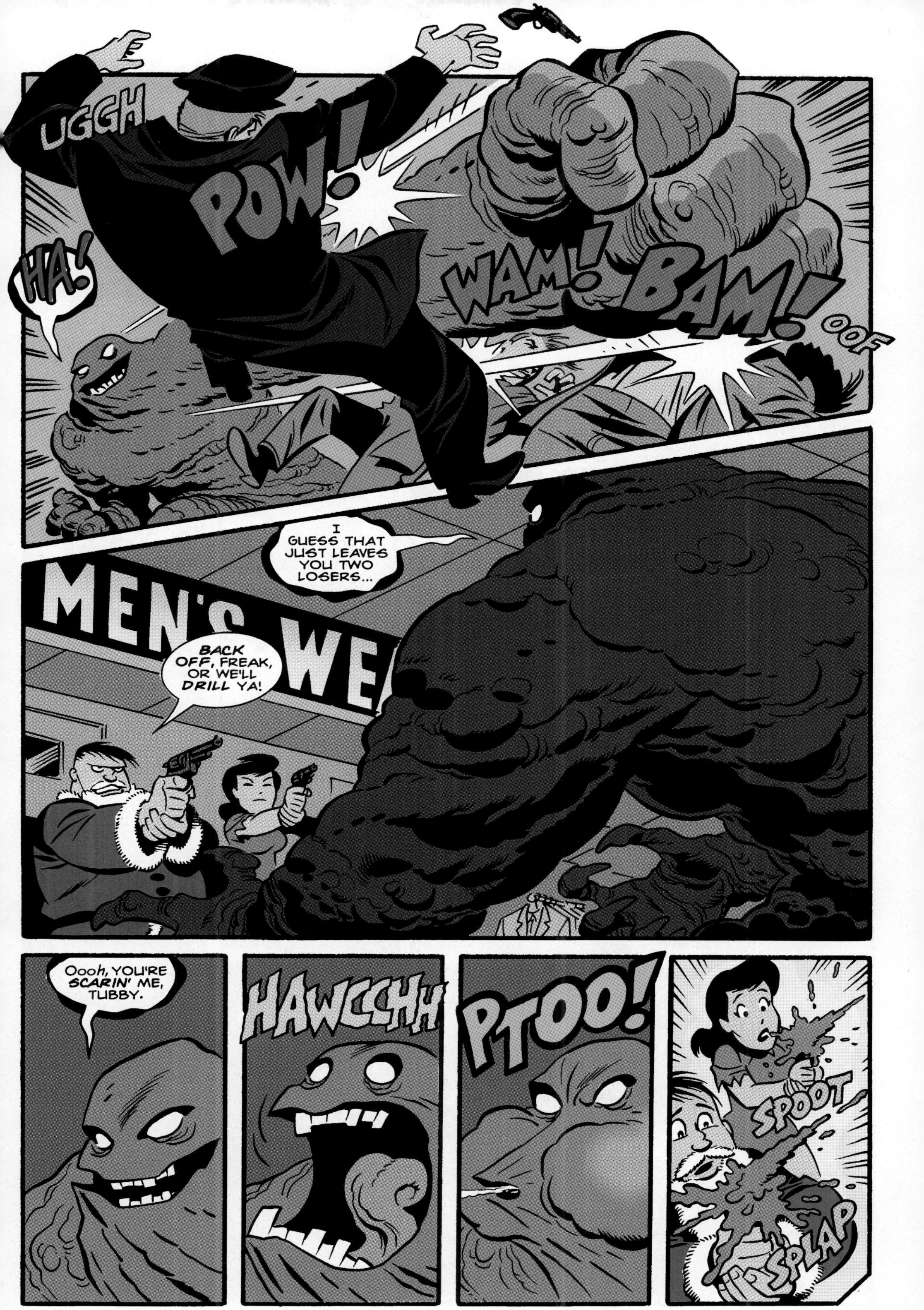
UGGH
POW!
HA!
WAM!
BAM!
OOF
I GUESS THAT JUST LEAVES YOU TWO LOSERS...
MEN'S WE
BACK OFF, FREAK, OR WE'LL DRILL YA!
Oooh, YOU'RE SCARIN' ME, TUBBY.
HAWCCHH
PTOO!
SPOOT
SPLAP

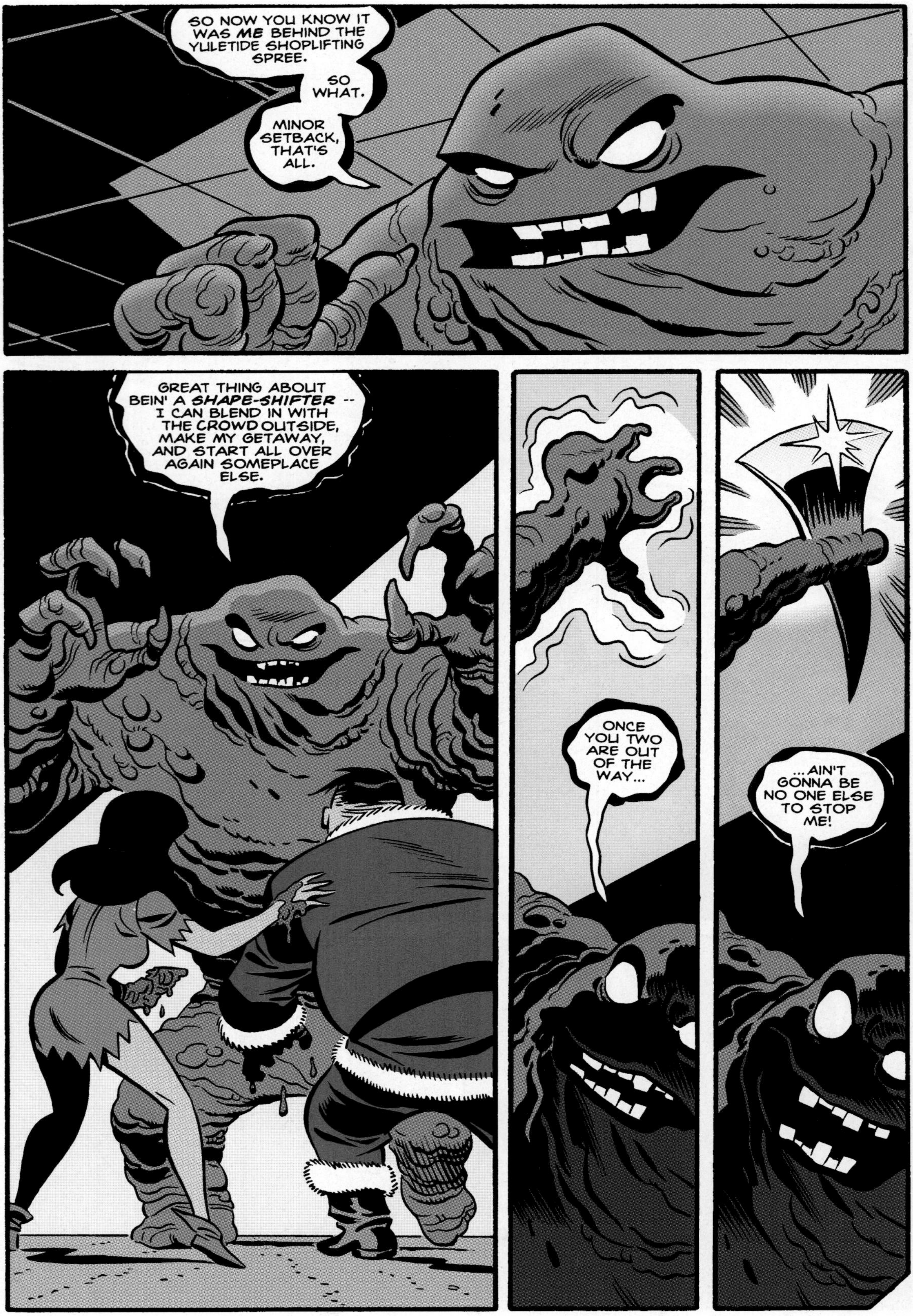
SO NOW YOU KNOW IT WAS *ME* BEHIND THE YULETIDE SHOPLIFTING SPREE.
SO WHAT.
MINOR SETBACK, THAT'S ALL.
GREAT THING ABOUT BEIN' A *SHAPE-SHIFTER* -- I CAN BLEND IN WITH THE CROWD OUTSIDE, MAKE MY GETAWAY, AND START ALL OVER AGAIN SOMEPLACE ELSE.
ONCE YOU TWO ARE OUT OF THE WAY...
...AIN'T GONNA BE NO ONE ELSE TO STOP ME!

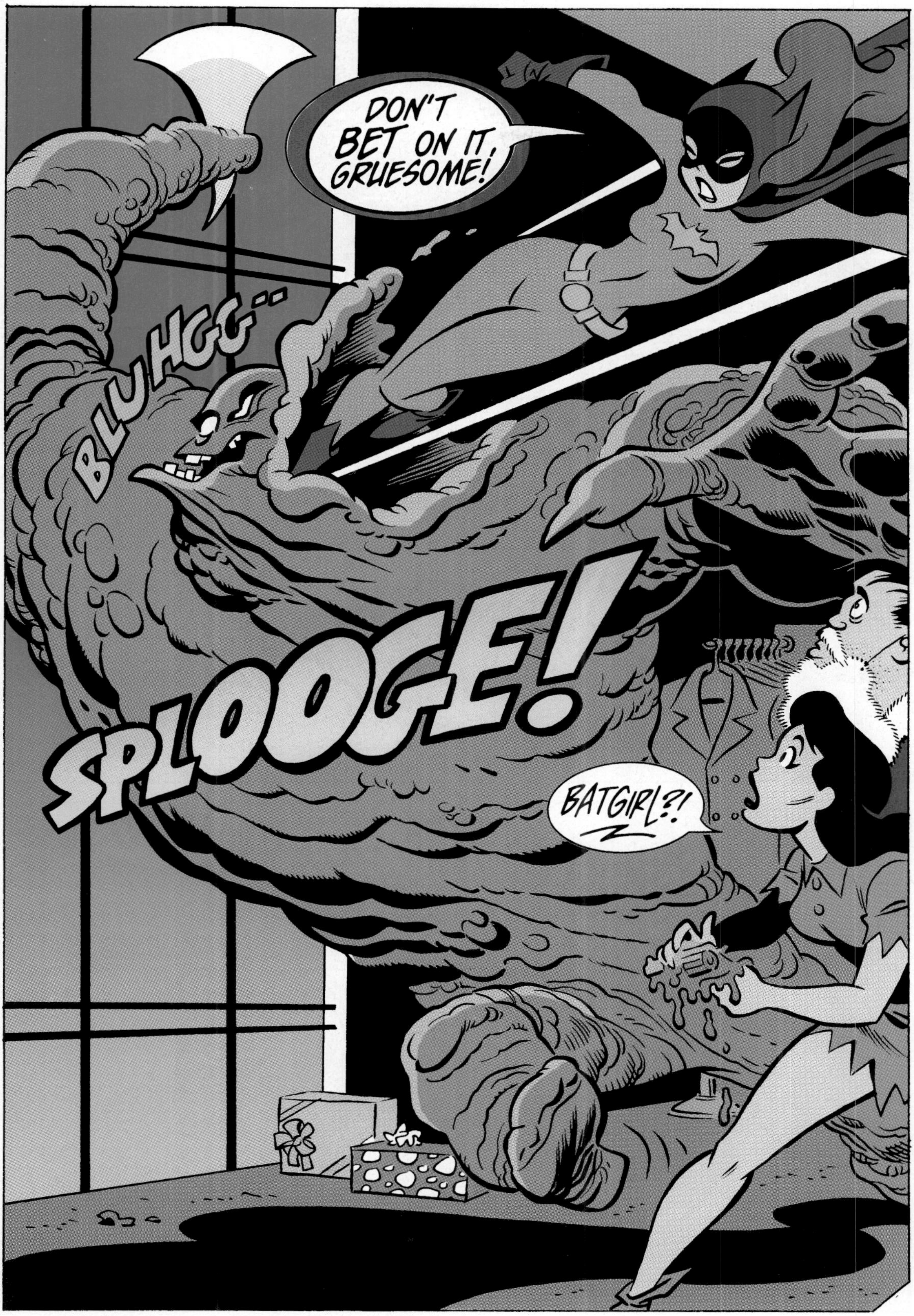
DON'T BET ON IT, GRUESOME!
BLUHGG--
SPLOOGE!
BATGIRL?!

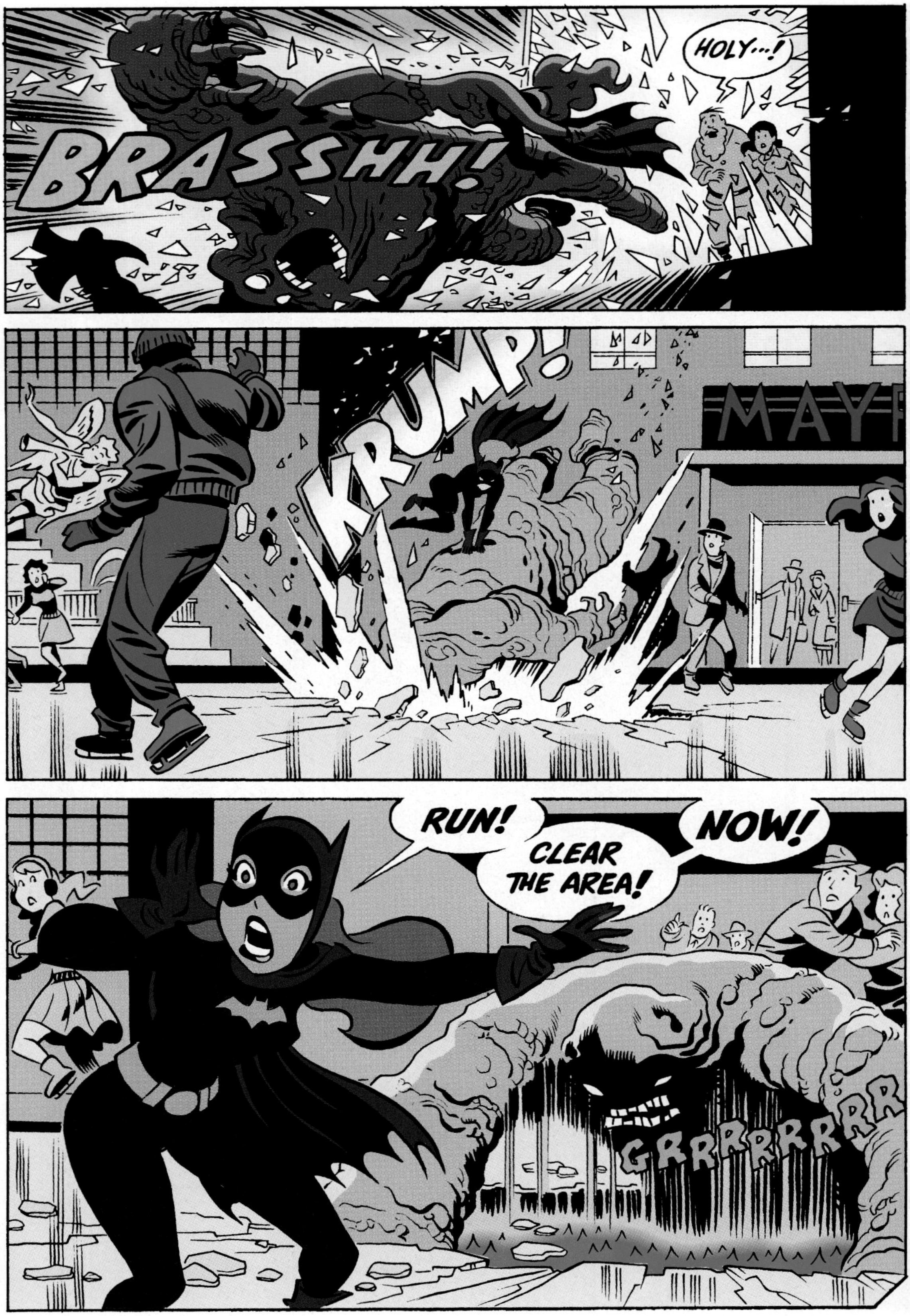
HOLY...!
BRASSHH!
KRUMP!
MAY
RUN!
CLEAR THE AREA!
NOW!
GRRRRRRRR

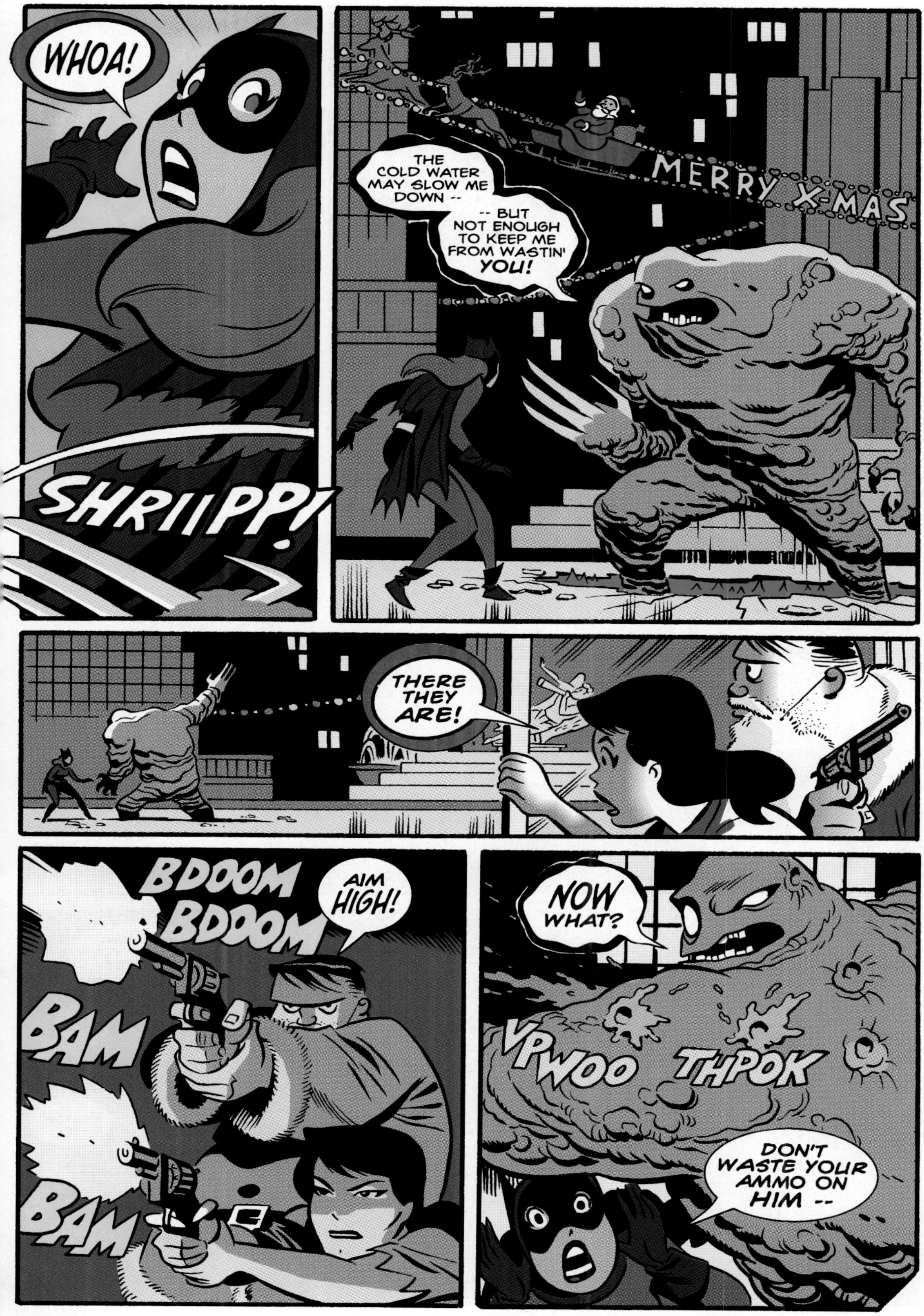
WHOA!
SHRIIPP!
MERRY X-MAS
THE COLD WATER MAY SLOW ME DOWN --
-- BUT NOT ENOUGH TO KEEP ME FROM WASTIN' YOU!
THERE THEY ARE!
BDOOM
BDOOM
AIM HIGH!
BAM
BAM
NOW WHAT?
VPWOO
THPOK
DON'T WASTE YOUR AMMO ON HIM --

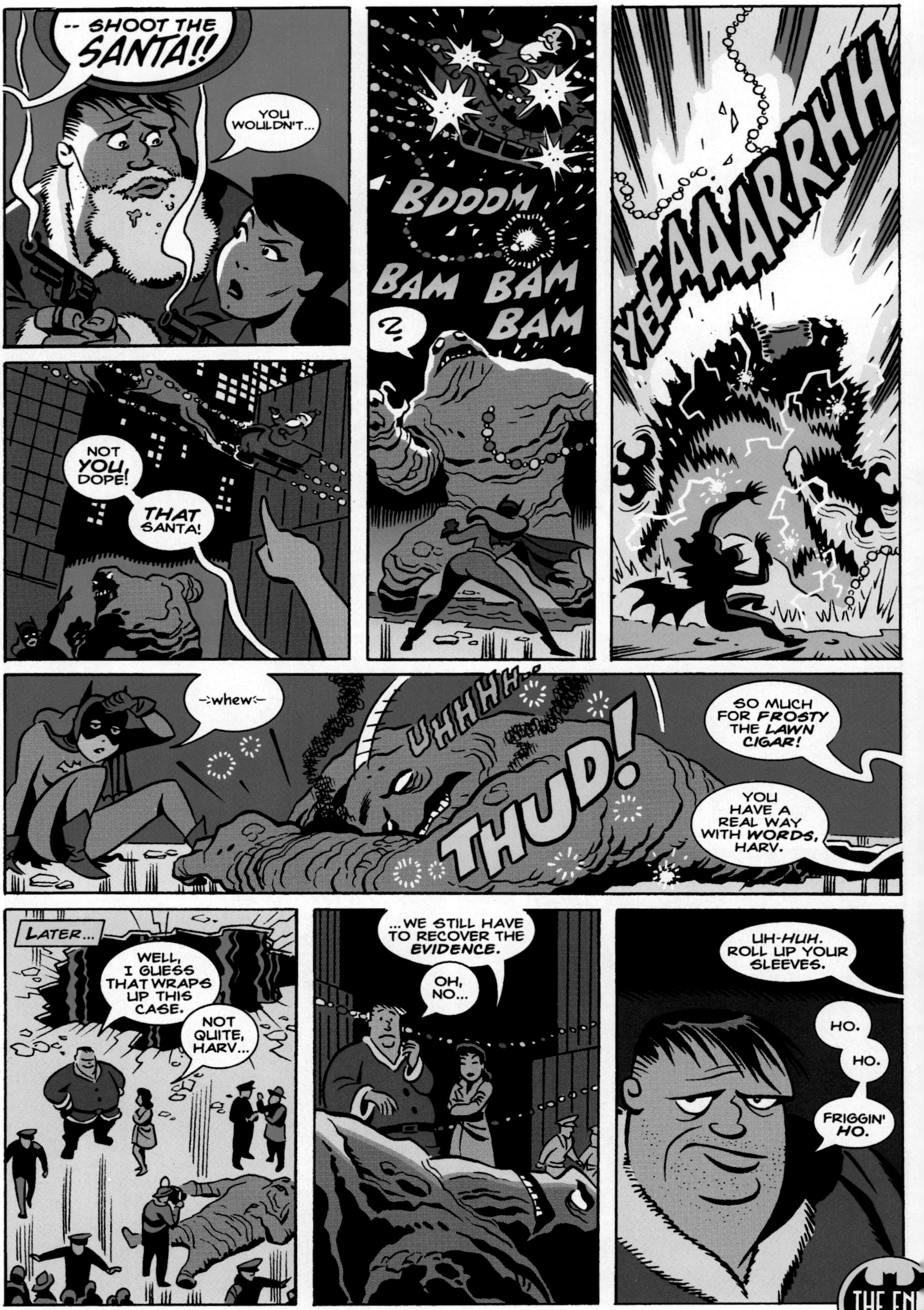

-- SHOOT THE SANTA!!
YOU WOULDN'T...
NOT YOU, DOPE!
THAT SANTA!
BDOOM
BAM BAM BAM
?
YEEAAAARRHH
-whew-
UHHHHH-
THUD!
SO MUCH FOR FROSTY THE LAWN CIGAR!
YOU HAVE A REAL WAY WITH WORDS, HARV.
LATER...
WELL, I GUESS THAT WRAPS UP THIS CASE.
NOT QUITE, HARV...
...WE STILL HAVE TO RECOVER THE EVIDENCE.
OH, NO...
UH-HUH. ROLL UP YOUR SLEEVES.
HO.
HO.
FRIGGIN' HO.
THE EN

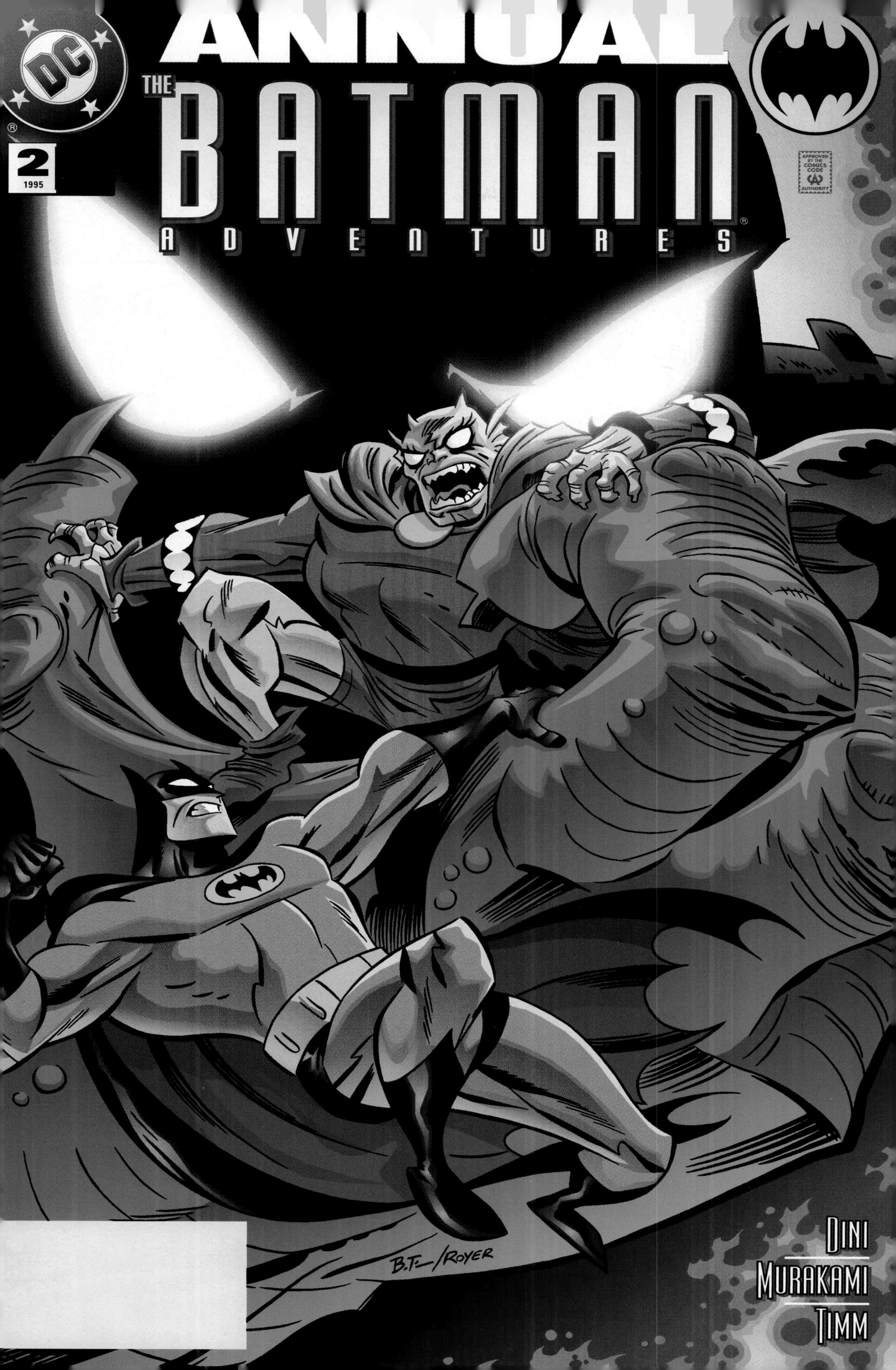

ANNUAL
THE BATMAN ADVENTURES
2
1995
APPROVED BY THE COMICS CODE AUTHORITY
B.T./ROYER
DINI
MURAKAMI
TIMM

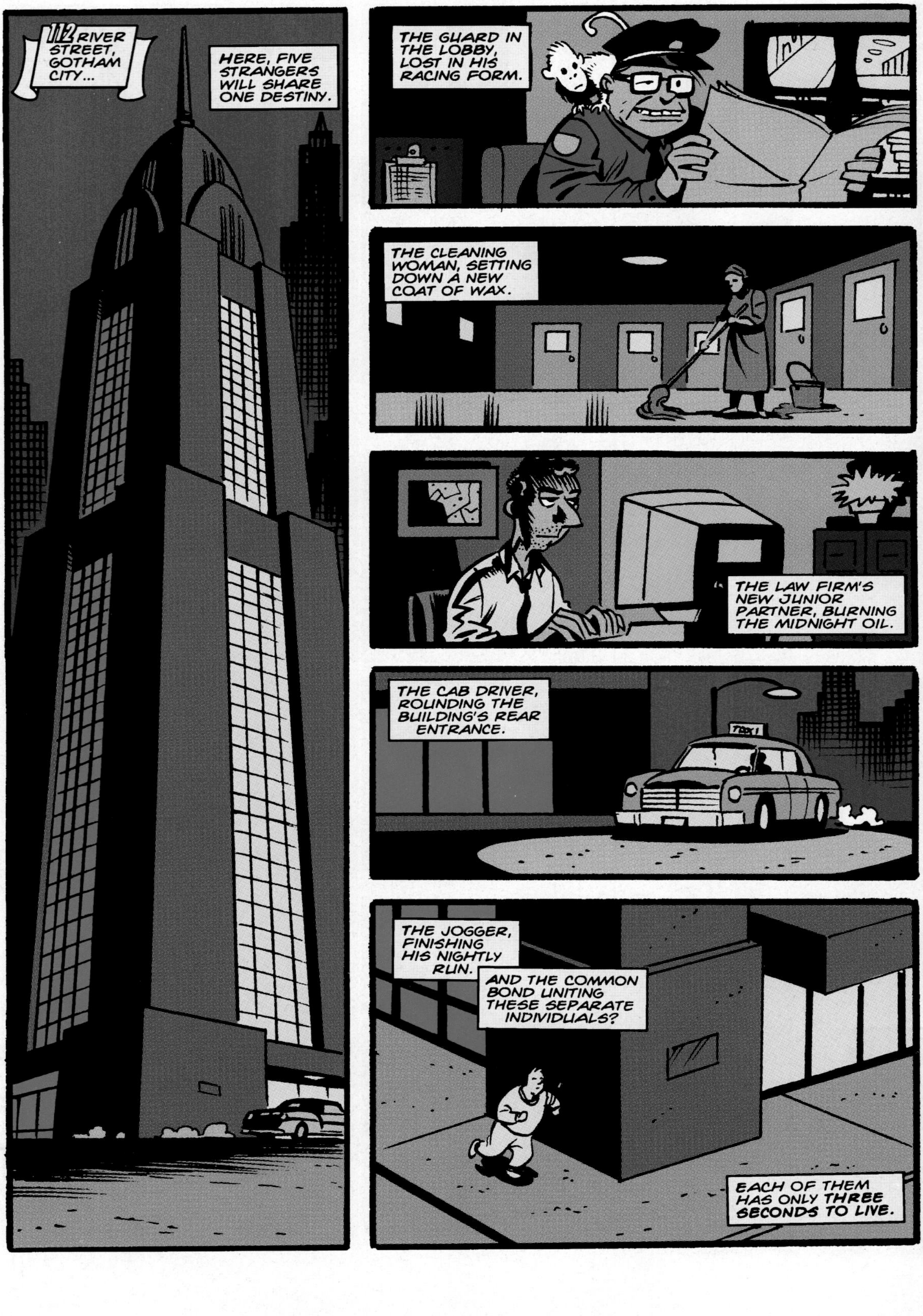
112 RIVER STREET, GOTHAM CITY...
HERE, FIVE STRANGERS WILL SHARE ONE DESTINY.
THE GUARD IN THE LOBBY, LOST IN HIS RACING FORM.
THE CLEANING WOMAN, SETTING DOWN A NEW COAT OF WAX.
THE LAW FIRM'S NEW JUNIOR PARTNER, BURNING THE MIDNIGHT OIL.
THE CAB DRIVER, ROUNDING THE BUILDING'S REAR ENTRANCE.
TAXI
THE JOGGER, FINISHING HIS NIGHTLY RUN.
AND THE COMMON BOND UNITING THESE SEPARATE INDIVIDUALS?
EACH OF THEM HAS ONLY THREE SECONDS TO LIVE.

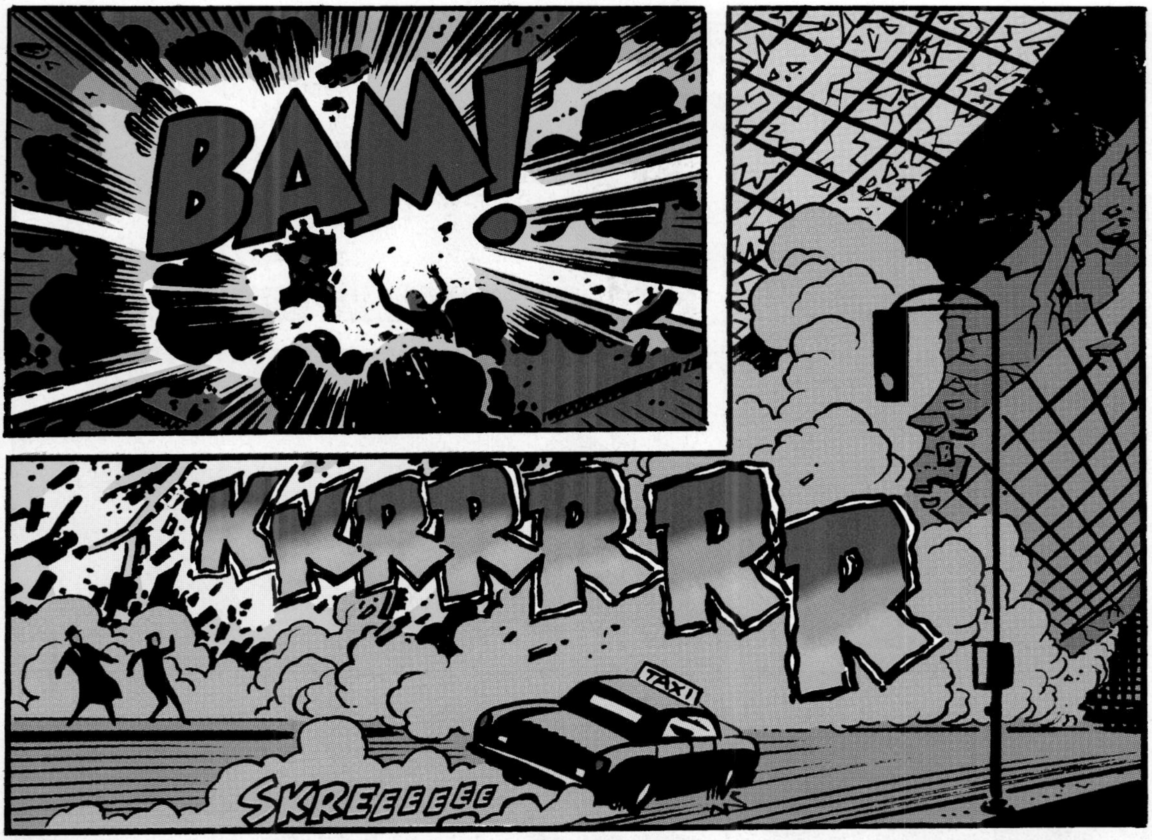
BAM!
KRRRRRR
TAXI
SKREEEEEEE

DEMONS

PAUL DINI
CO-PLOT/WRITER

GLEN MURAKAMI & BRUCE TIMM
CO-PLOT/ART

GLEN MURAKAMI
COLOR

STARKINGS/COMICRAFT
LETTERING

DARREN VINCENZO
ASSOC. EDITOR

SCOTT PETERSON
EDITOR

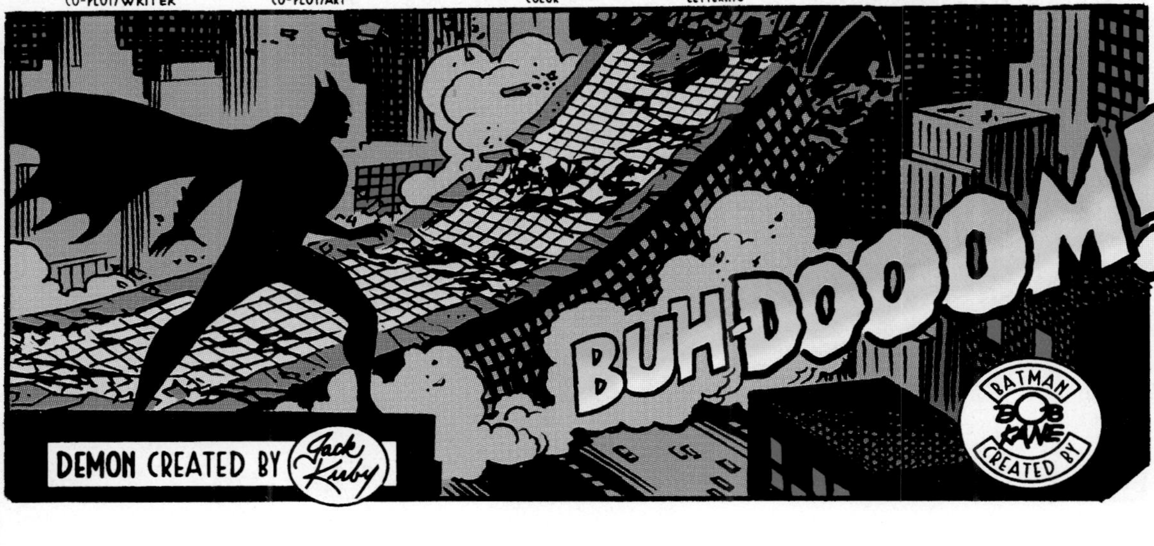
BUH-DOOOOM!
DEMON CREATED BY Jack Kirby
BATMAN CREATED BY BOB KANE

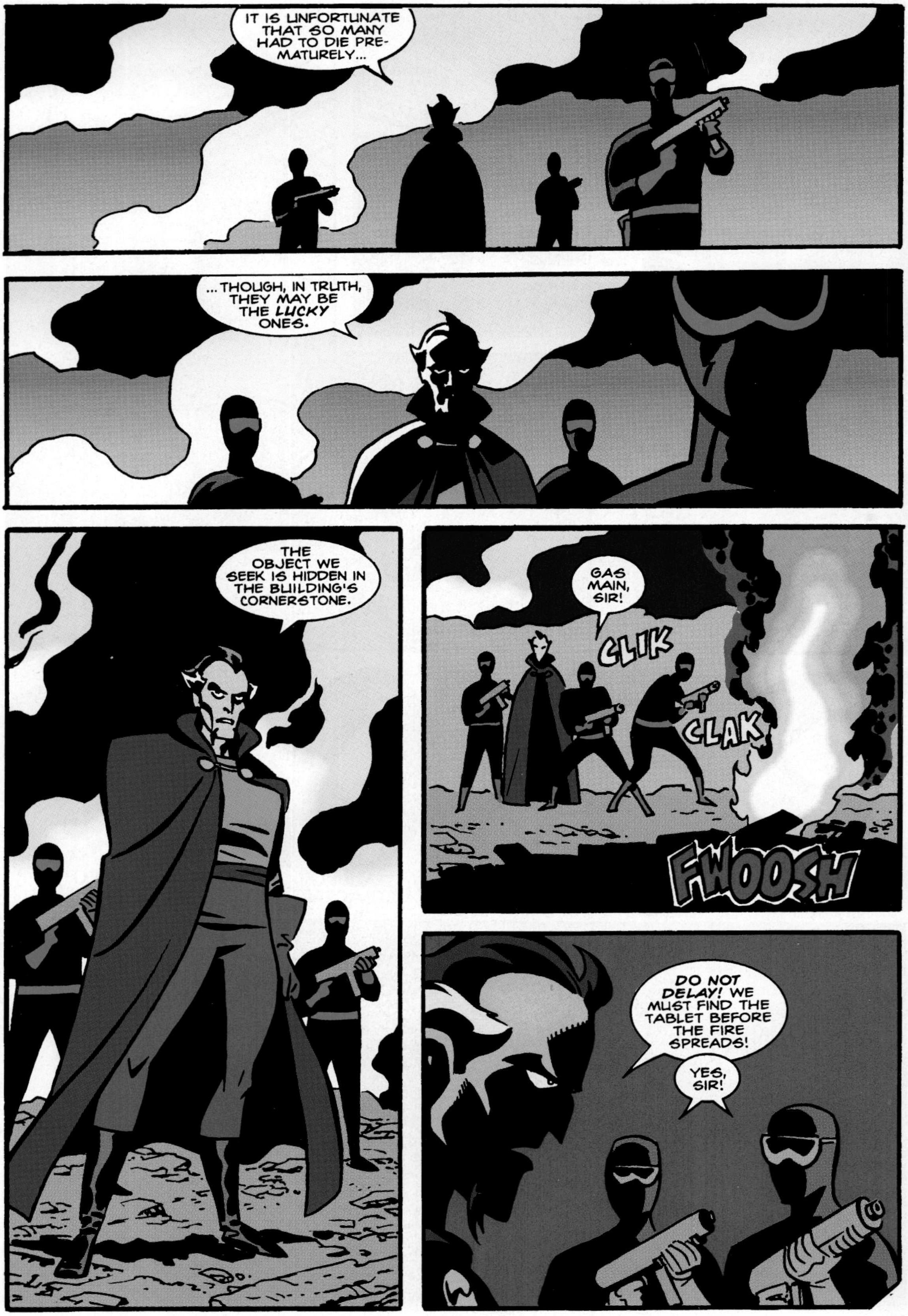
IT IS UNFORTUNATE THAT SO MANY HAD TO DIE PRE-MATURELY...
...THOUGH, IN TRUTH, THEY MAY BE THE *LUCKY* ONES.
THE OBJECT WE SEEK IS HIDDEN IN THE BUILDING'S CORNERSTONE.
GAS MAIN, SIR!
CLIK
CLAK
FWOOSH
DO NOT DELAY! WE MUST FIND THE TABLET BEFORE THE FIRE SPREADS!
YES, SIR!

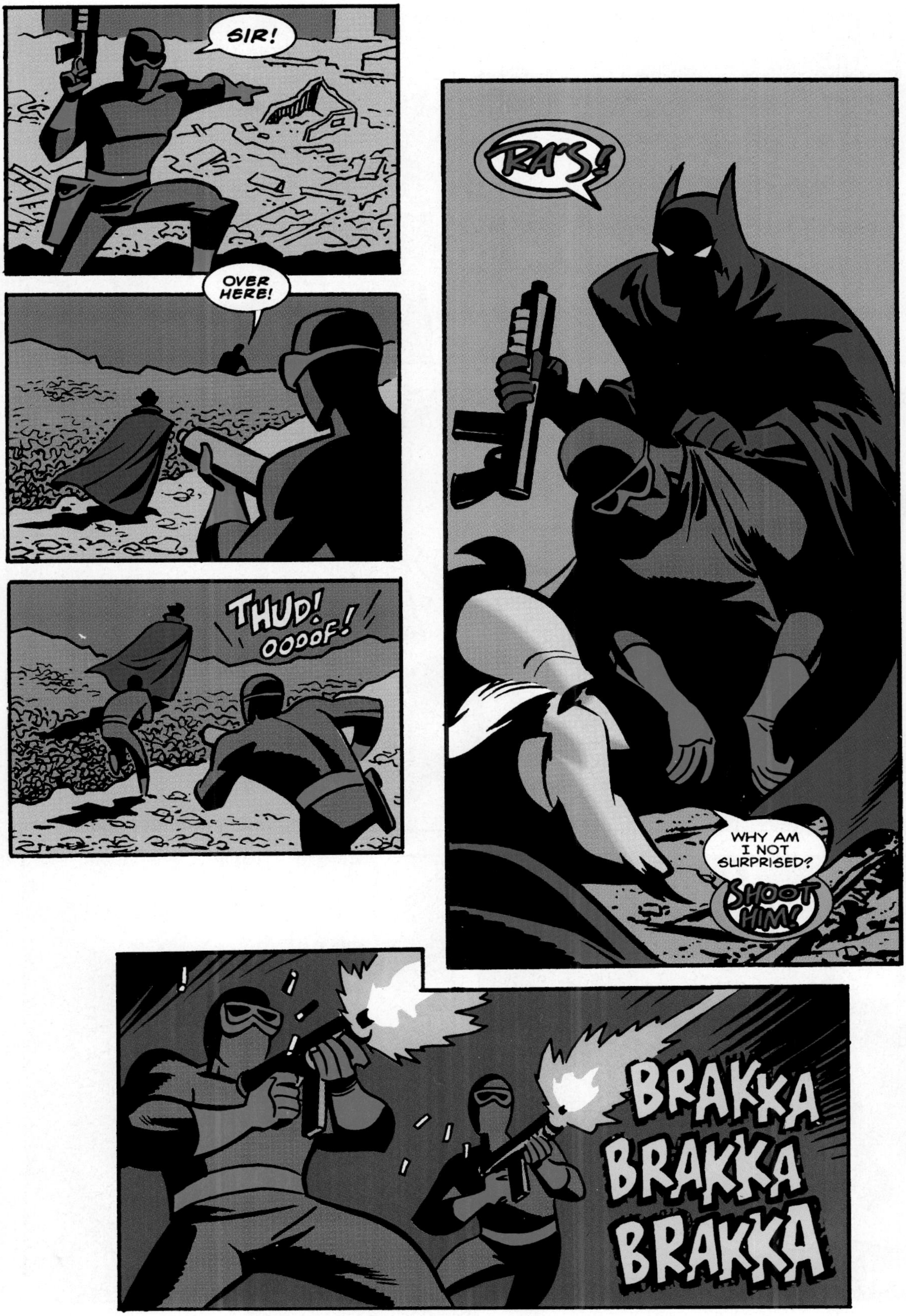

SIR!
OVER HERE!
THUD! OOOOF!
RA'S!
WHY AM I NOT SURPRISED?
SHOOT HIM!
!
BRAKKA BRAKKA BRAKKA

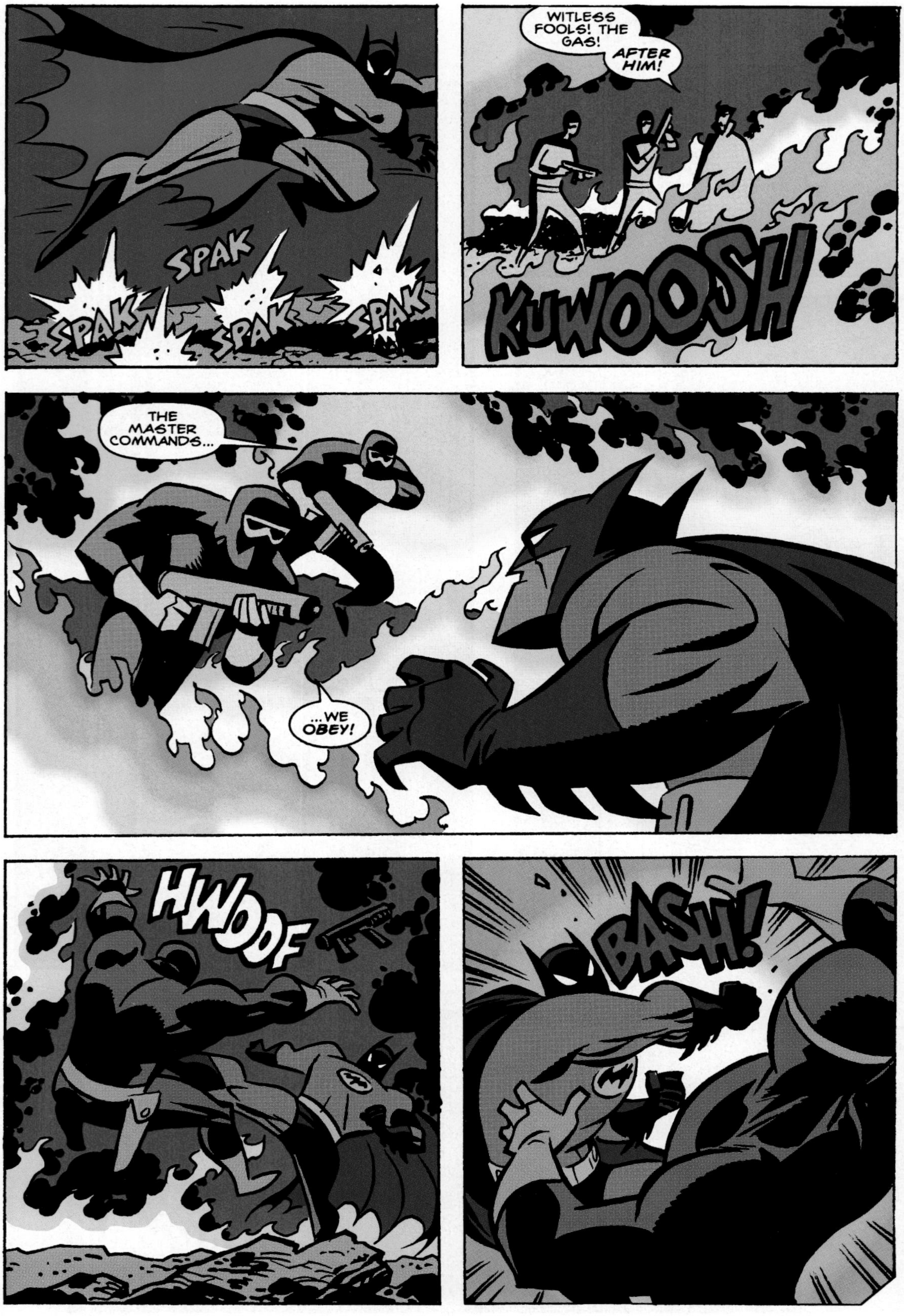

SPAK
SPAK
SPAK
SPAK
WITLESS FOOLS! THE GAS!
AFTER HIM!
KUWOOSH
THE MASTER COMMANDS...
...WE OBEY!
HWOOF
BASH!

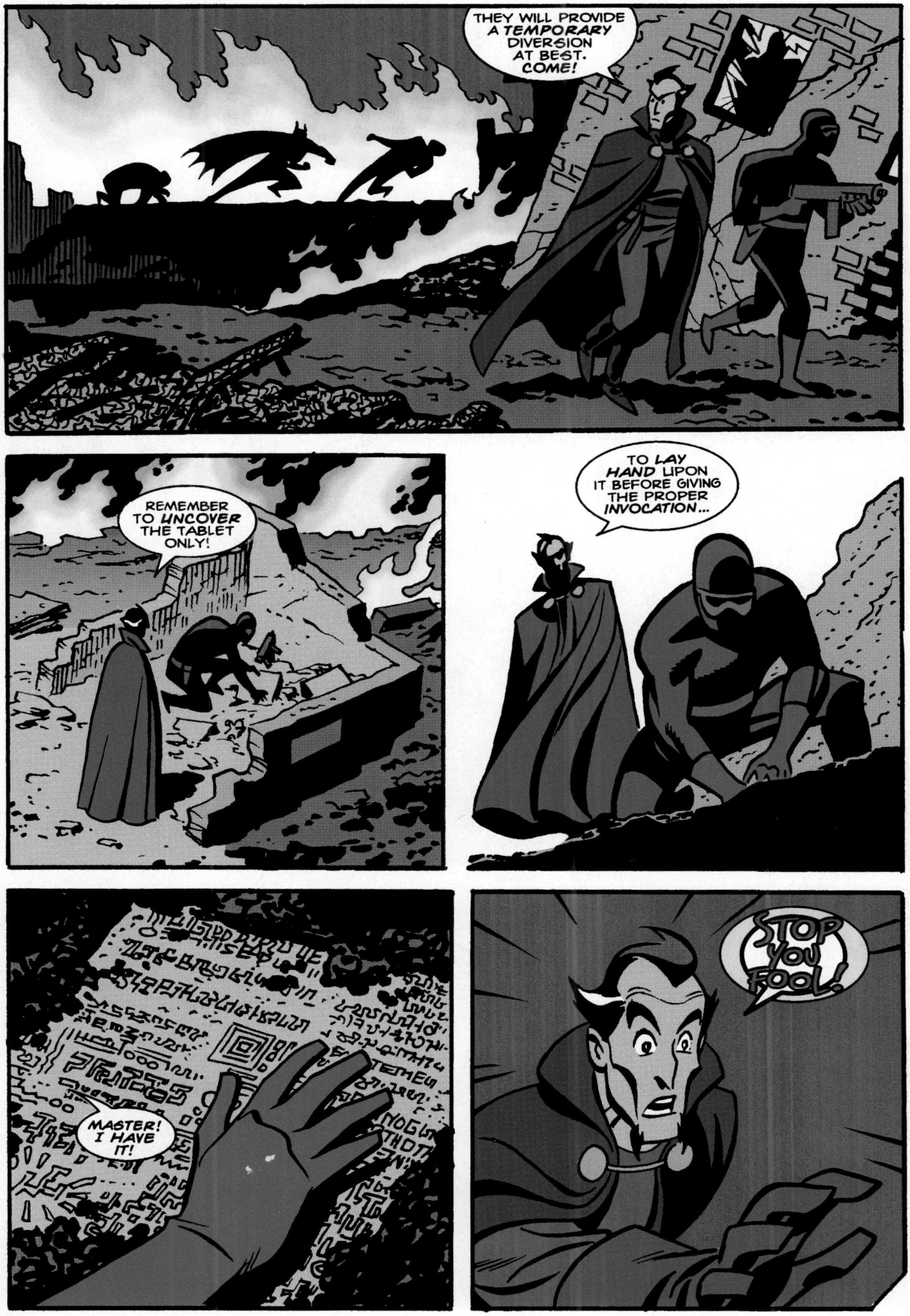
THEY WILL PROVIDE A TEMPORARY DIVERSION AT BEST. COME!
REMEMBER TO UNCOVER THE TABLET ONLY!
TO LAY HAND UPON IT BEFORE GIVING THE PROPER INVOCATION...
MASTER! I HAVE IT!
STOP YOU FOOL!

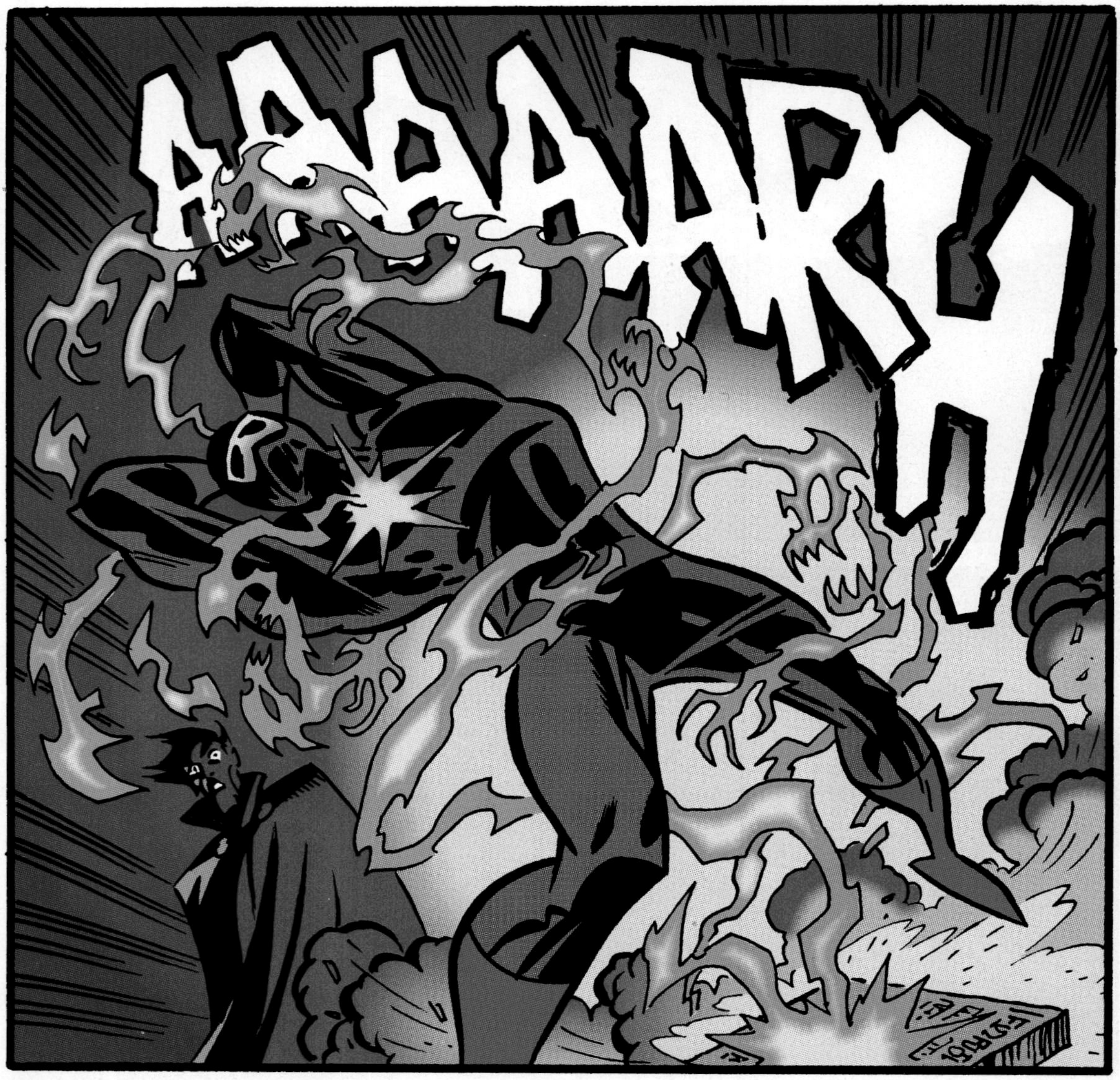
AAAARH!

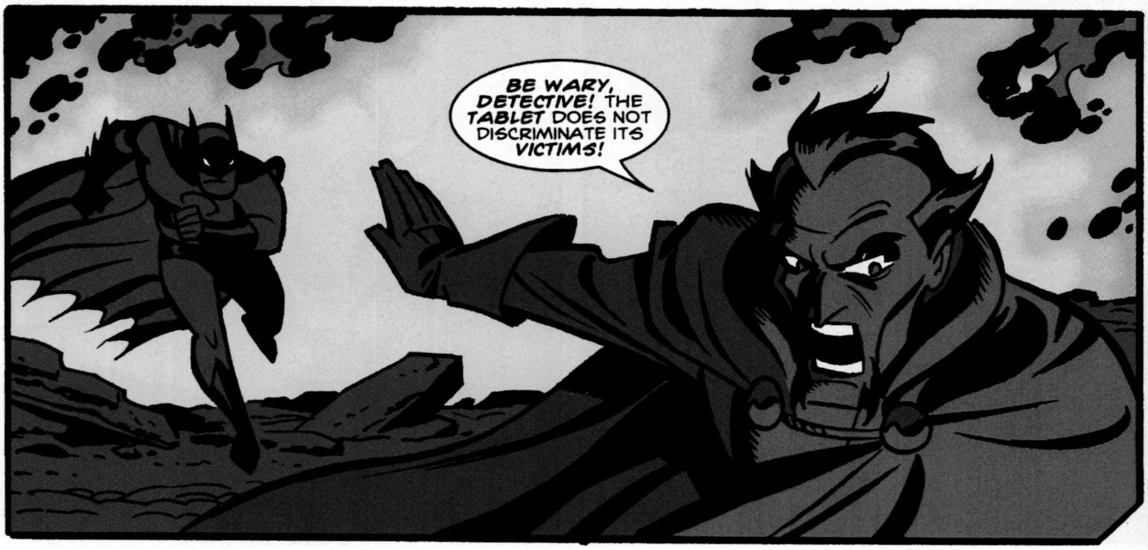
BE WARY, DETECTIVE! THE TABLET DOES NOT DISCRIMINATE ITS VICTIMS!

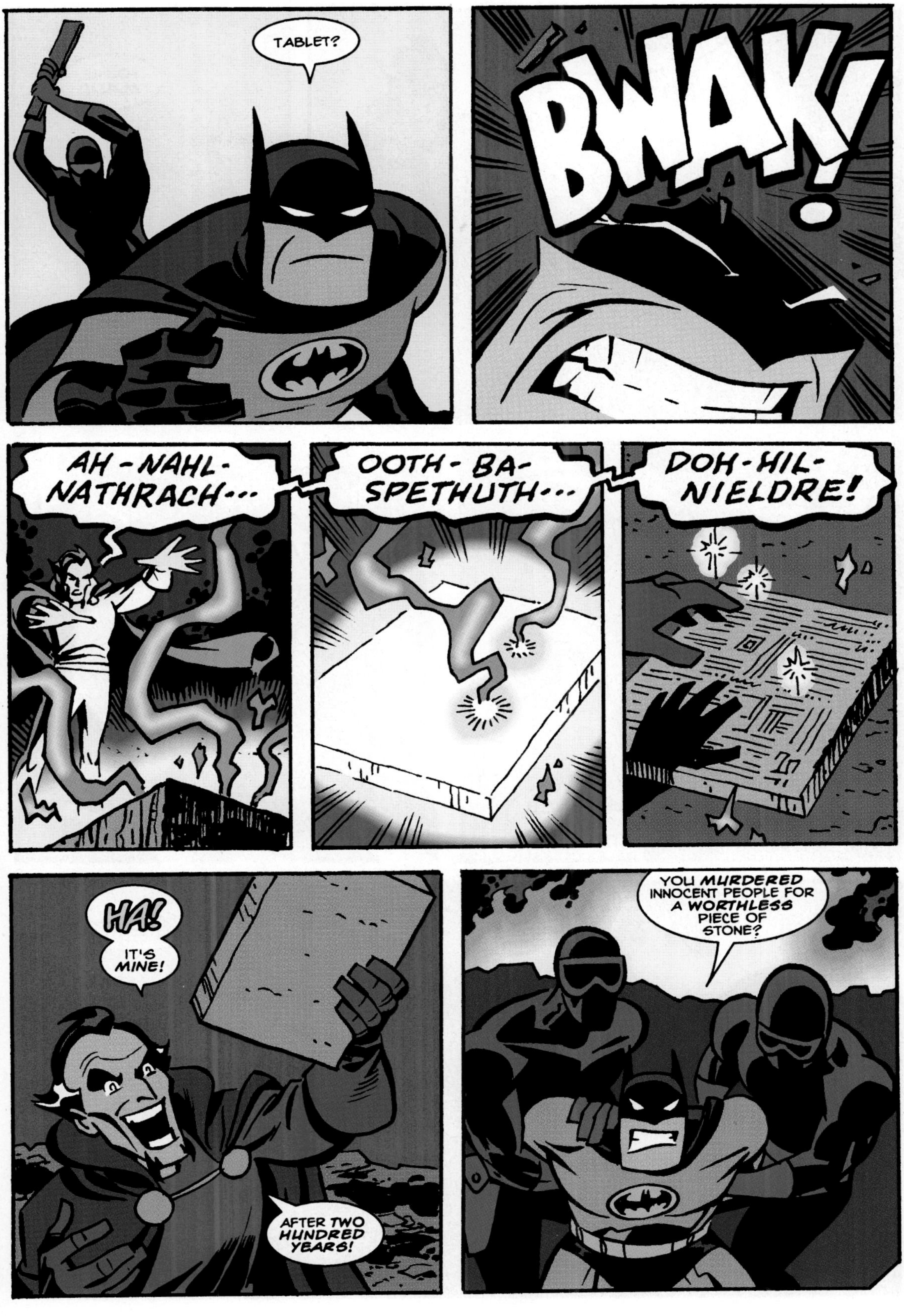
TABLET?
BWAK!
AH-NAHL-NATHRACH...
OOTH-BA-SPETHUTH...
DOH-HIL-NIELDRE!
HA!
IT'S MINE!
AFTER TWO HUNDRED YEARS!
YOU MURDERED INNOCENT PEOPLE FOR A WORTHLESS PIECE OF STONE?

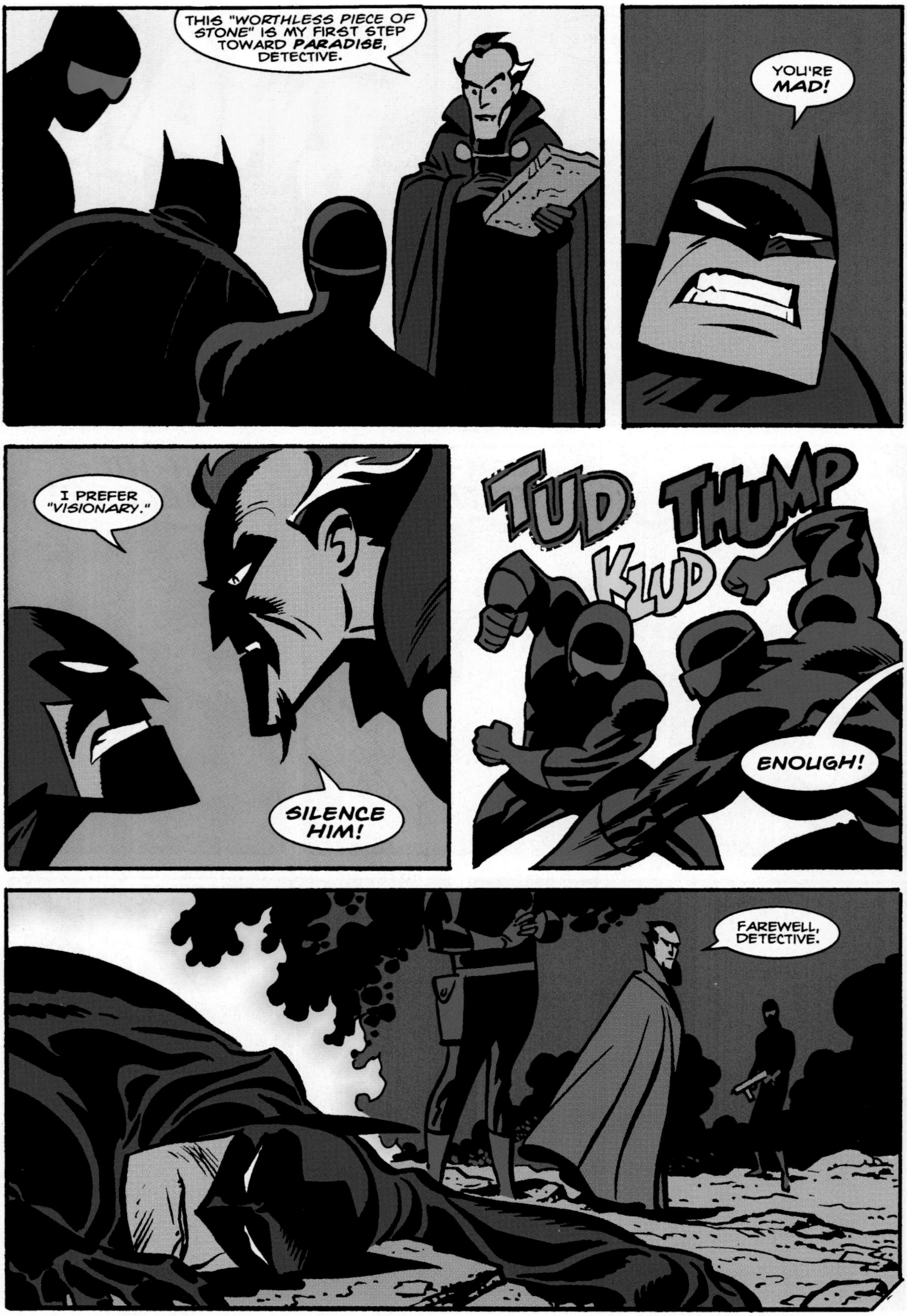
THIS "WORTHLESS PIECE OF STONE" IS MY FIRST STEP TOWARD PARADISE, DETECTIVE.
YOU'RE MAD!
I PREFER "VISIONARY."
SILENCE HIM!
TUD
THUMP
KLUD
ENOUGH!
FAREWELL, DETECTIVE.

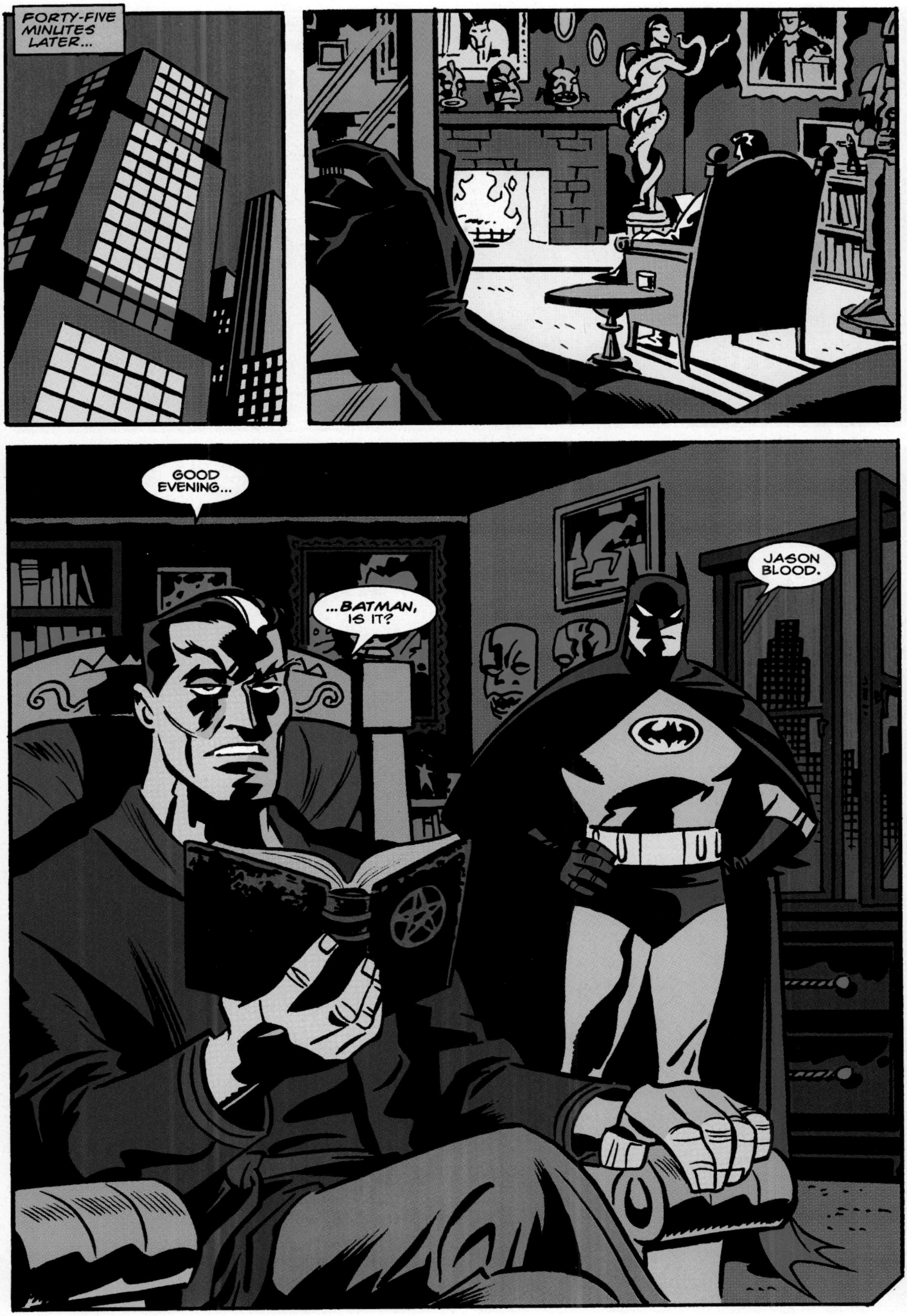
FORTY-FIVE MINUTES LATER...
GOOD EVENING...
...BATMAN, IS IT?
JASON BLOOD.

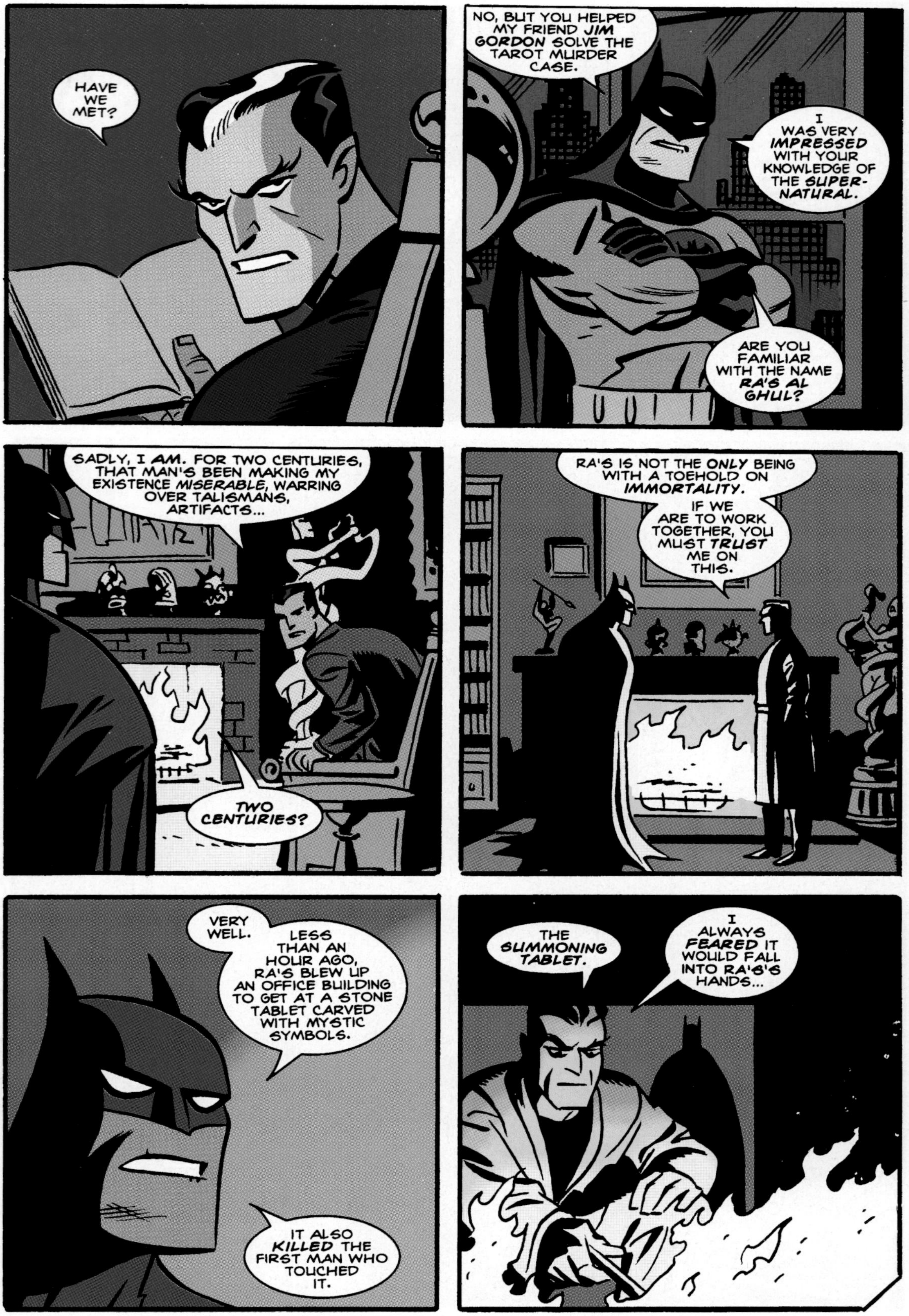
HAVE WE MET?
NO, BUT YOU HELPED MY FRIEND JIM GORDON SOLVE THE TAROT MURDER CASE.
I WAS VERY IMPRESSED WITH YOUR KNOWLEDGE OF THE SUPER-NATURAL.
ARE YOU FAMILIAR WITH THE NAME RA'S AL GHUL?
SADLY, I AM. FOR TWO CENTURIES, THAT MAN'S BEEN MAKING MY EXISTENCE MISERABLE, WARRING OVER TALISMANS, ARTIFACTS...
TWO CENTURIES?
RA'S IS NOT THE ONLY BEING WITH A TOEHOLD ON IMMORTALITY.
IF WE ARE TO WORK TOGETHER, YOU MUST TRUST ME ON THIS.
VERY WELL.
LESS THAN AN HOUR AGO, RA'S BLEW UP AN OFFICE BUILDING TO GET AT A STONE TABLET CARVED WITH MYSTIC SYMBOLS.
IT ALSO KILLED THE FIRST MAN WHO TOUCHED IT.
THE SUMMONING TABLET.
I ALWAYS FEARED IT WOULD FALL INTO RA'S'S HANDS...

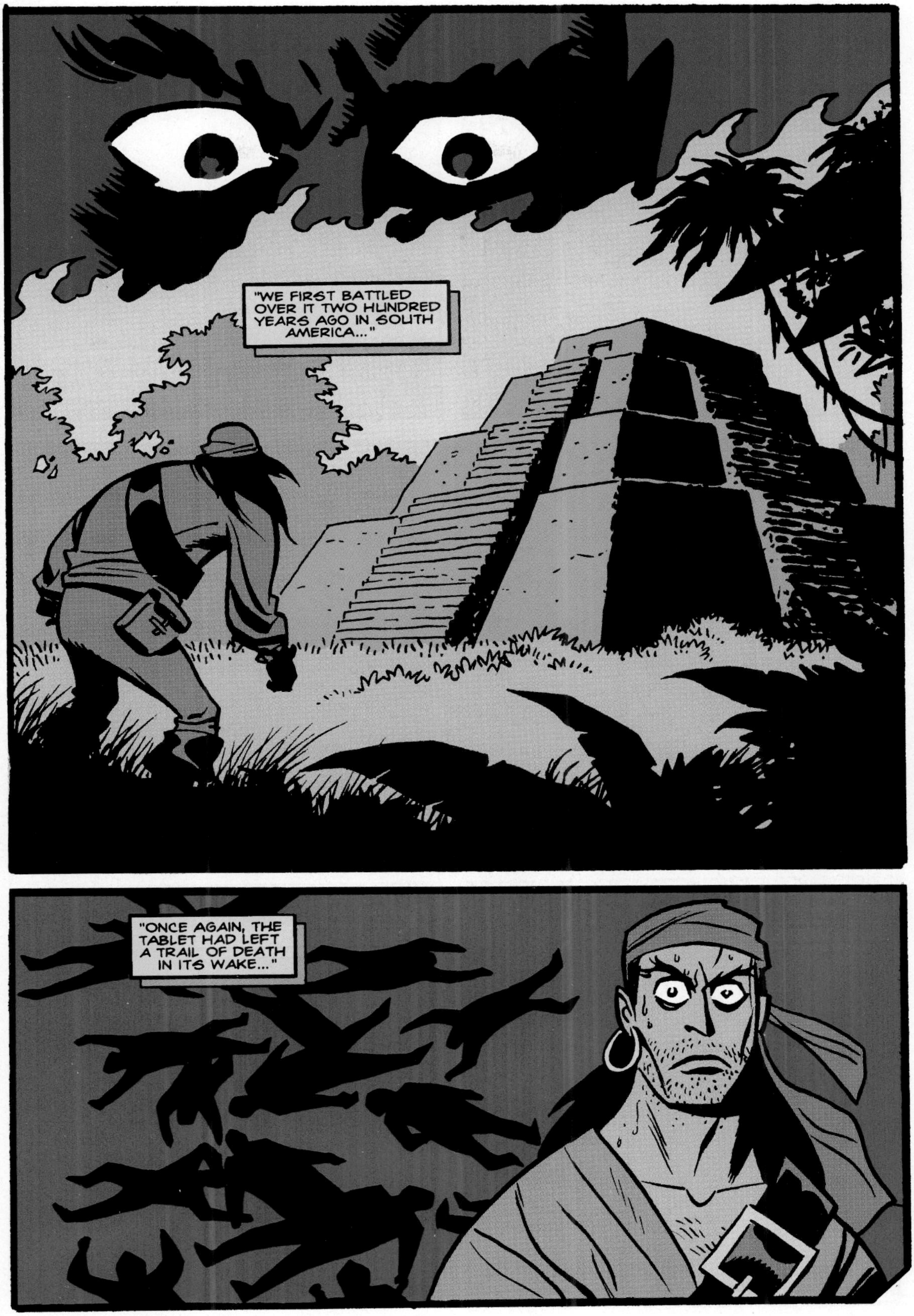
"WE FIRST BATTLED OVER IT TWO HUNDRED YEARS AGO IN SOUTH AMERICA..."
"ONCE AGAIN, THE TABLET HAD LEFT A TRAIL OF DEATH IN ITS WAKE..."

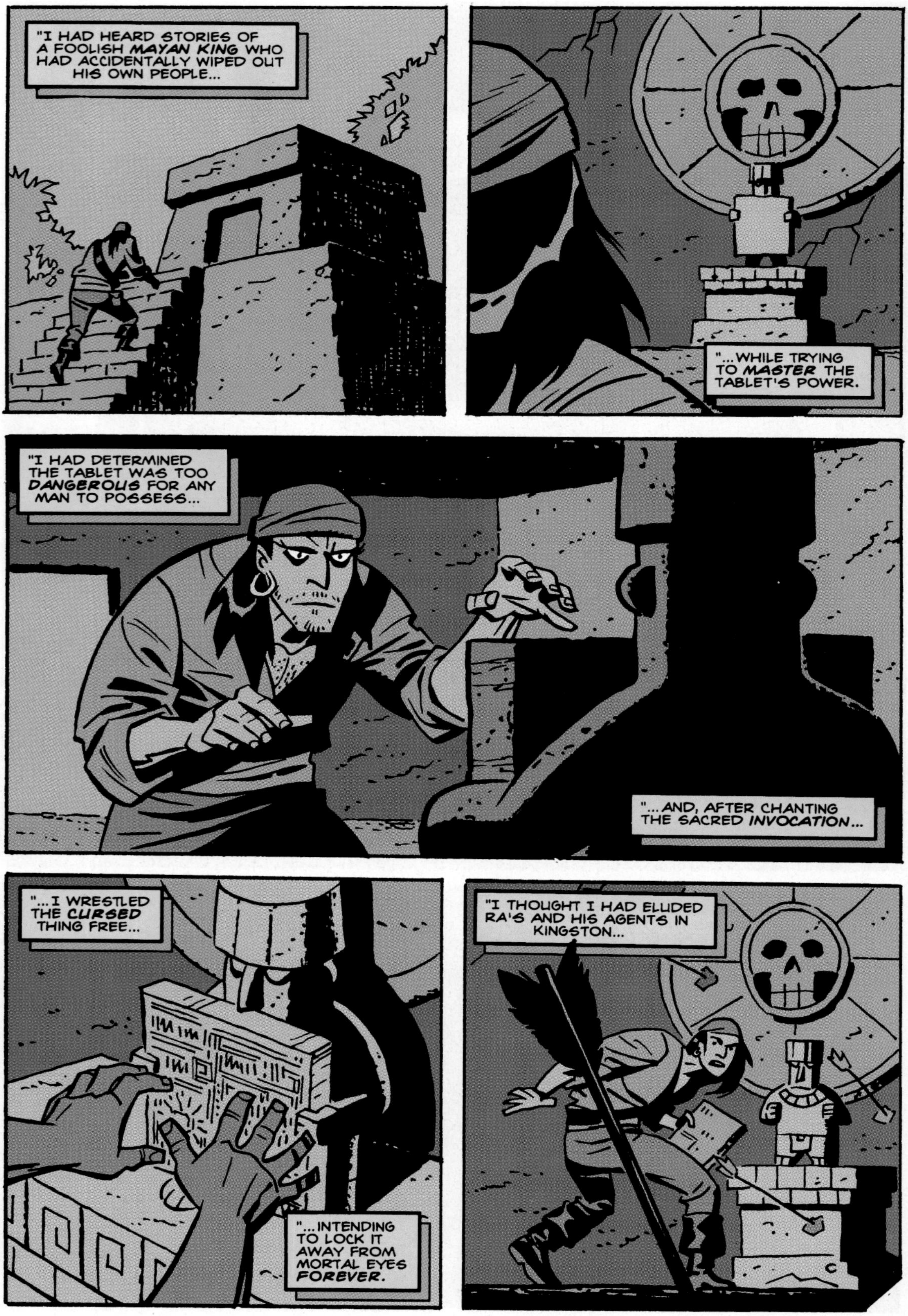
"I HAD HEARD STORIES OF A FOOLISH MAYAN KING WHO HAD ACCIDENTALLY WIPED OUT HIS OWN PEOPLE...
"...WHILE TRYING TO MASTER THE TABLET'S POWER.
"I HAD DETERMINED THE TABLET WAS TOO DANGEROUS FOR ANY MAN TO POSSESS...
"...AND, AFTER CHANTING THE SACRED INVOCATION...
"...I WRESTLED THE CURSED THING FREE...
"...INTENDING TO LOCK IT AWAY FROM MORTAL EYES FOREVER.
"I THOUGHT I HAD ELUDED RA'S AND HIS AGENTS IN KINGSTON...

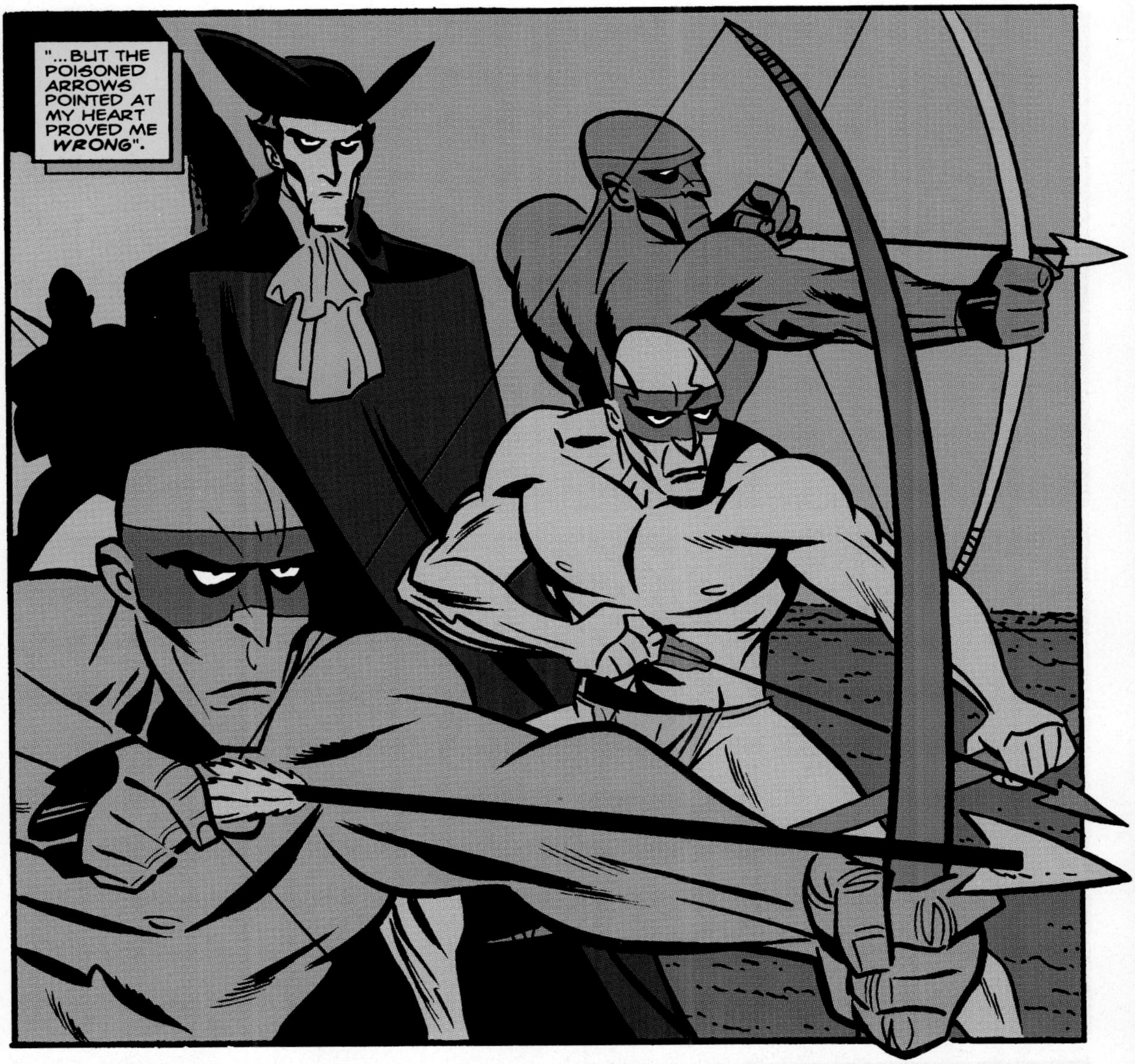
"...BUT THE POISONED ARROWS POINTED AT MY HEART PROVED ME WRONG".

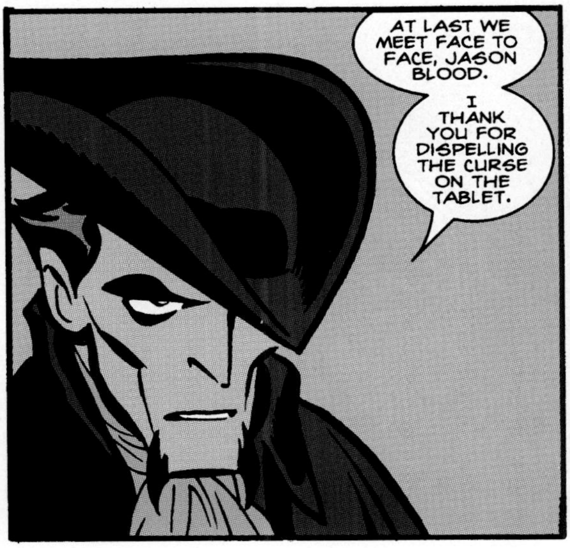
AT LAST WE MEET FACE TO FACE, JASON BLOOD.
I THANK YOU FOR DISPELLING THE CURSE ON THE TABLET.

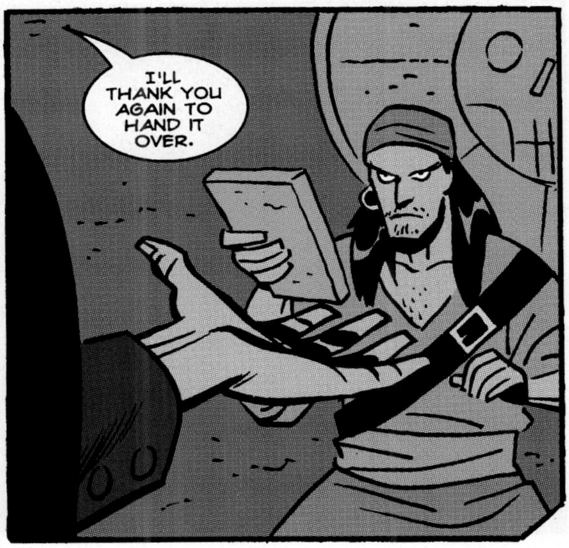
I'LL THANK YOU AGAIN TO HAND IT OVER.

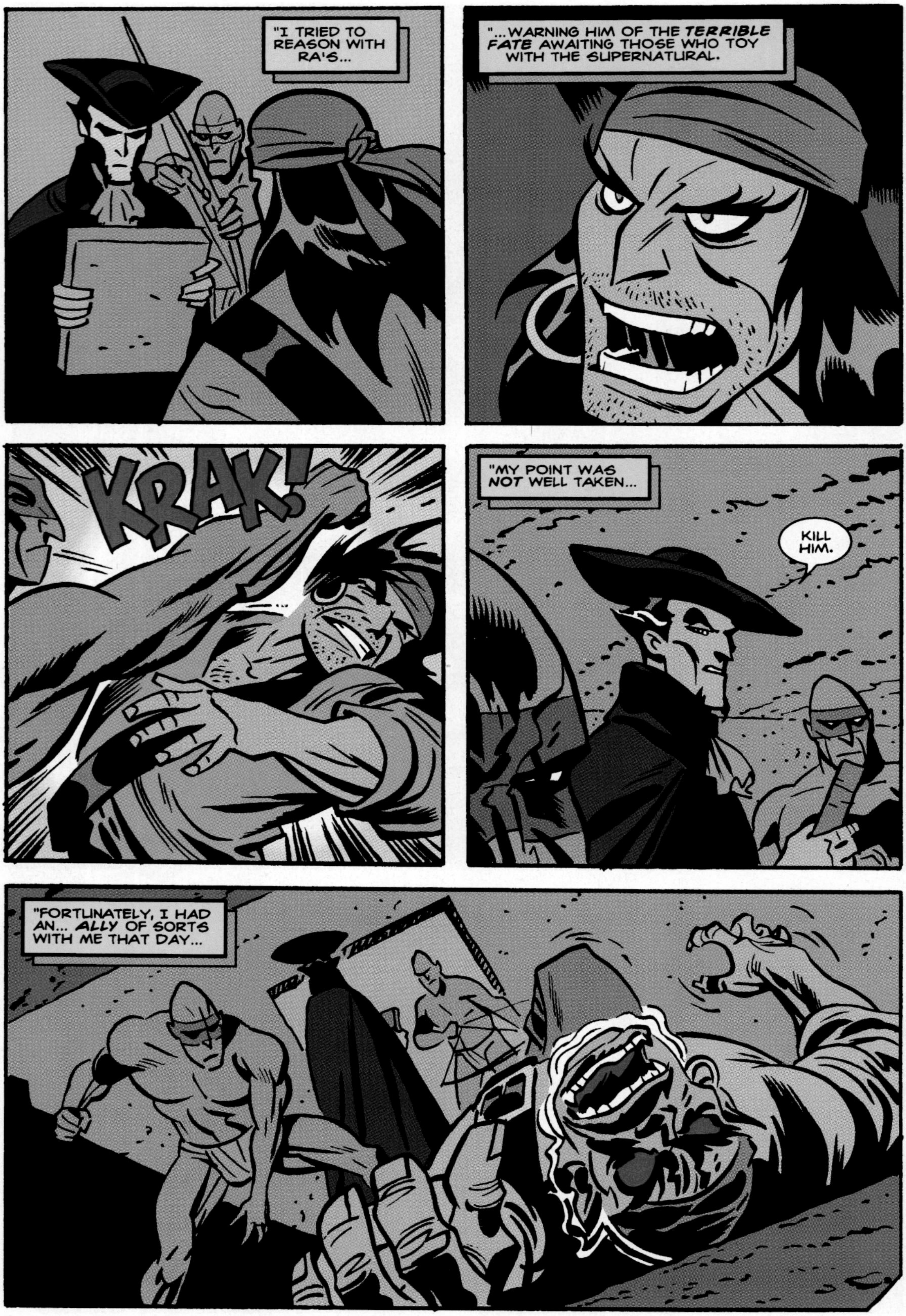
"I TRIED TO REASON WITH RA'S...
"...WARNING HIM OF THE *TERRIBLE FATE* AWAITING THOSE WHO TOY WITH THE SUPERNATURAL.
KRAK!
"MY POINT WAS *NOT* WELL TAKEN...
KILL HIM.
"FORTUNATELY, I HAD AN... *ALLY* OF SORTS WITH ME THAT DAY...

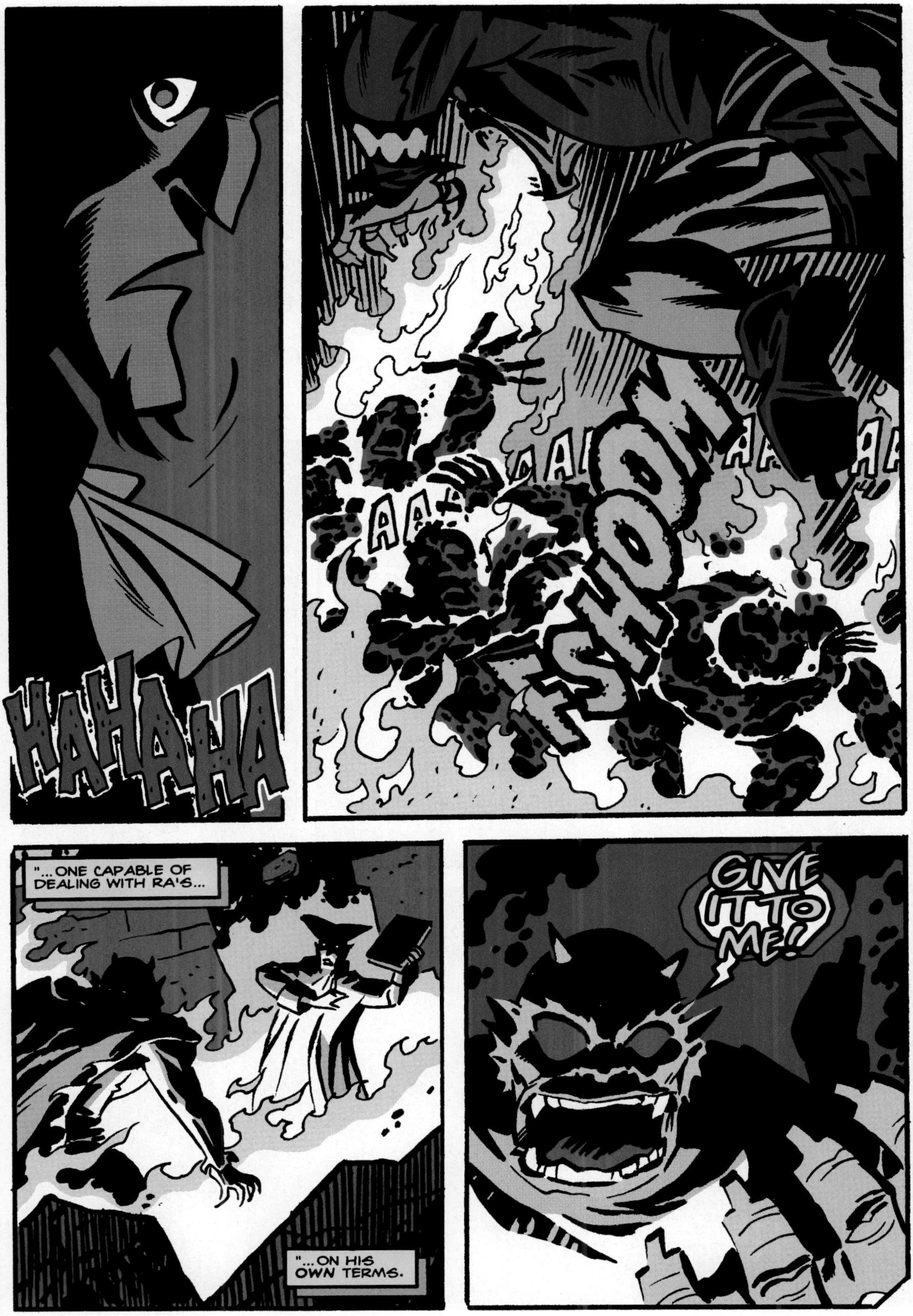
HAHAHA
FSHOOM!
"...ONE CAPABLE OF DEALING WITH RA'S...
"...ON HIS OWN TERMS.
GIVE IT TO ME!

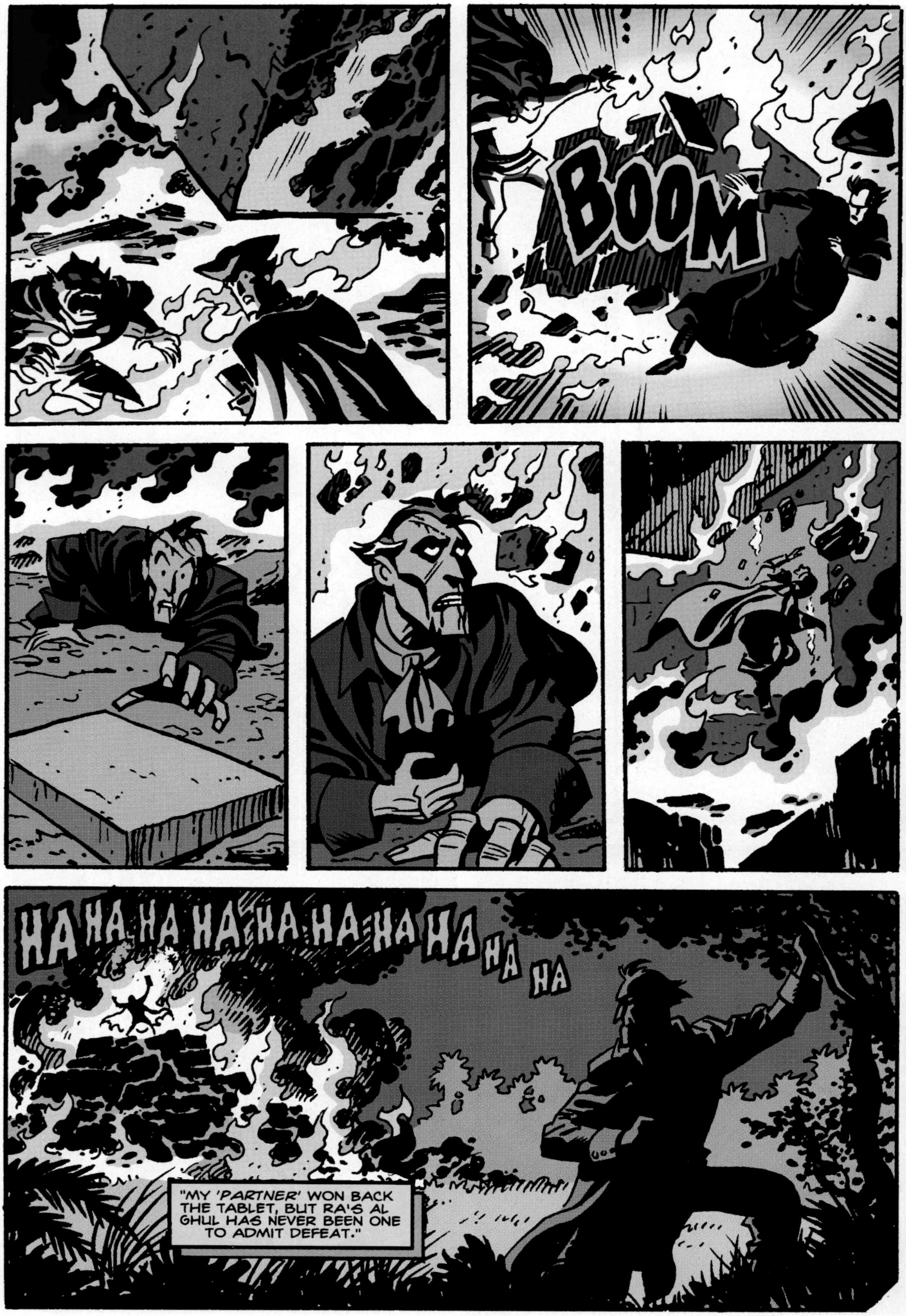
BOOM
HA HA HA HA HA HA HA HA HA HA HA
"MY 'PARTNER' WON BACK THE TABLET, BUT RA'S AL GHUL HAS NEVER BEEN ONE TO ADMIT DEFEAT."

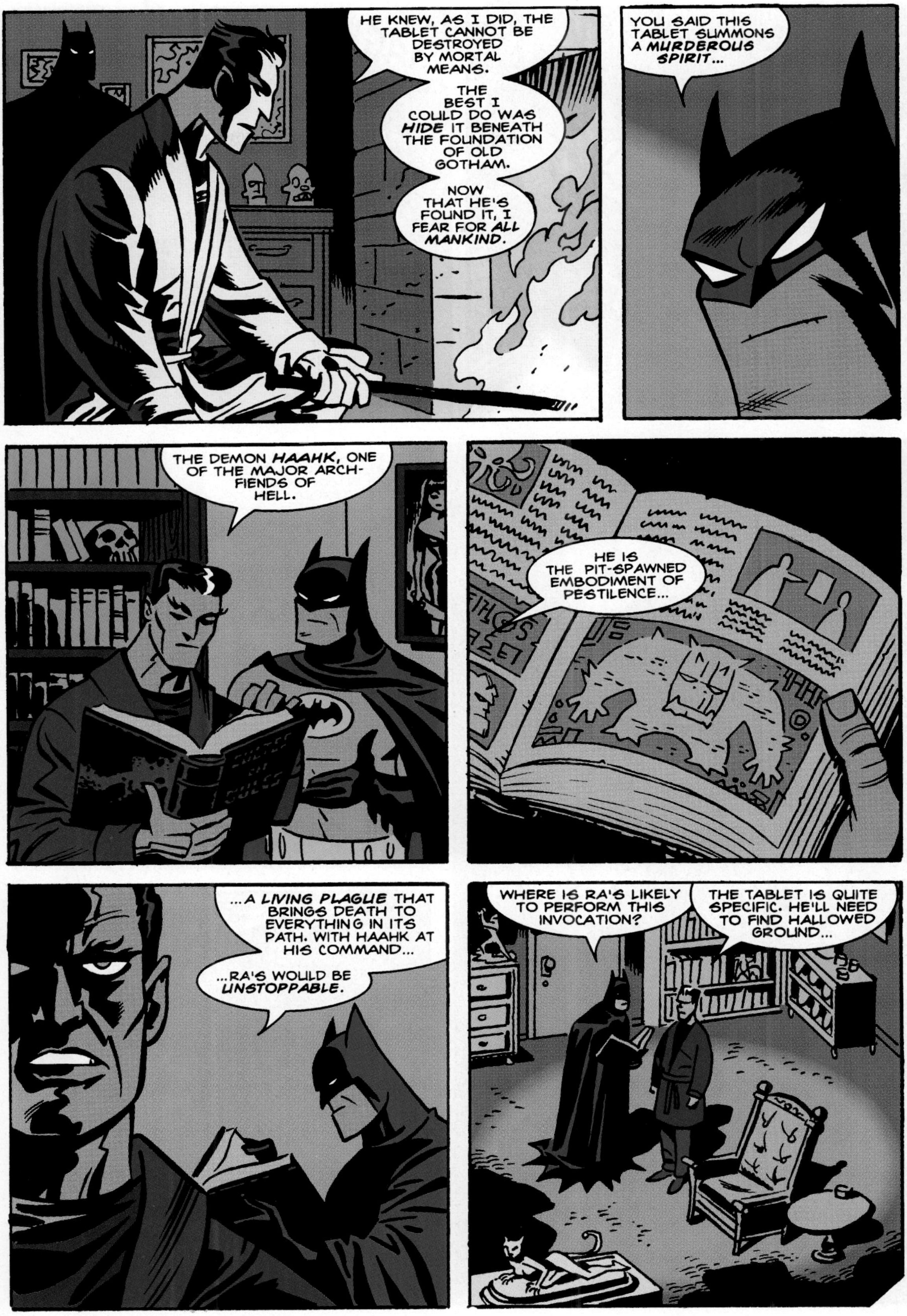
HE KNEW, AS I DID, THE TABLET CANNOT BE DESTROYED BY MORTAL MEANS.
THE BEST I COULD DO WAS HIDE IT BENEATH THE FOUNDATION OF OLD GOTHAM.
NOW THAT HE'S FOUND IT, I FEAR FOR ALL MANKIND.
YOU SAID THIS TABLET SUMMONS A MURDEROUS SPIRIT...
THE DEMON HAAHK, ONE OF THE MAJOR ARCH-FIENDS OF HELL.
HE IS THE PIT-SPAWNED EMBODIMENT OF PESTILENCE...
...A LIVING PLAGUE THAT BRINGS DEATH TO EVERYTHING IN ITS PATH. WITH HAAHK AT HIS COMMAND...
...RA'S WOULD BE UNSTOPPABLE.
WHERE IS RA'S LIKELY TO PERFORM THIS INVOCATION?
THE TABLET IS QUITE SPECIFIC. HE'LL NEED TO FIND HALLOWED GROUND...

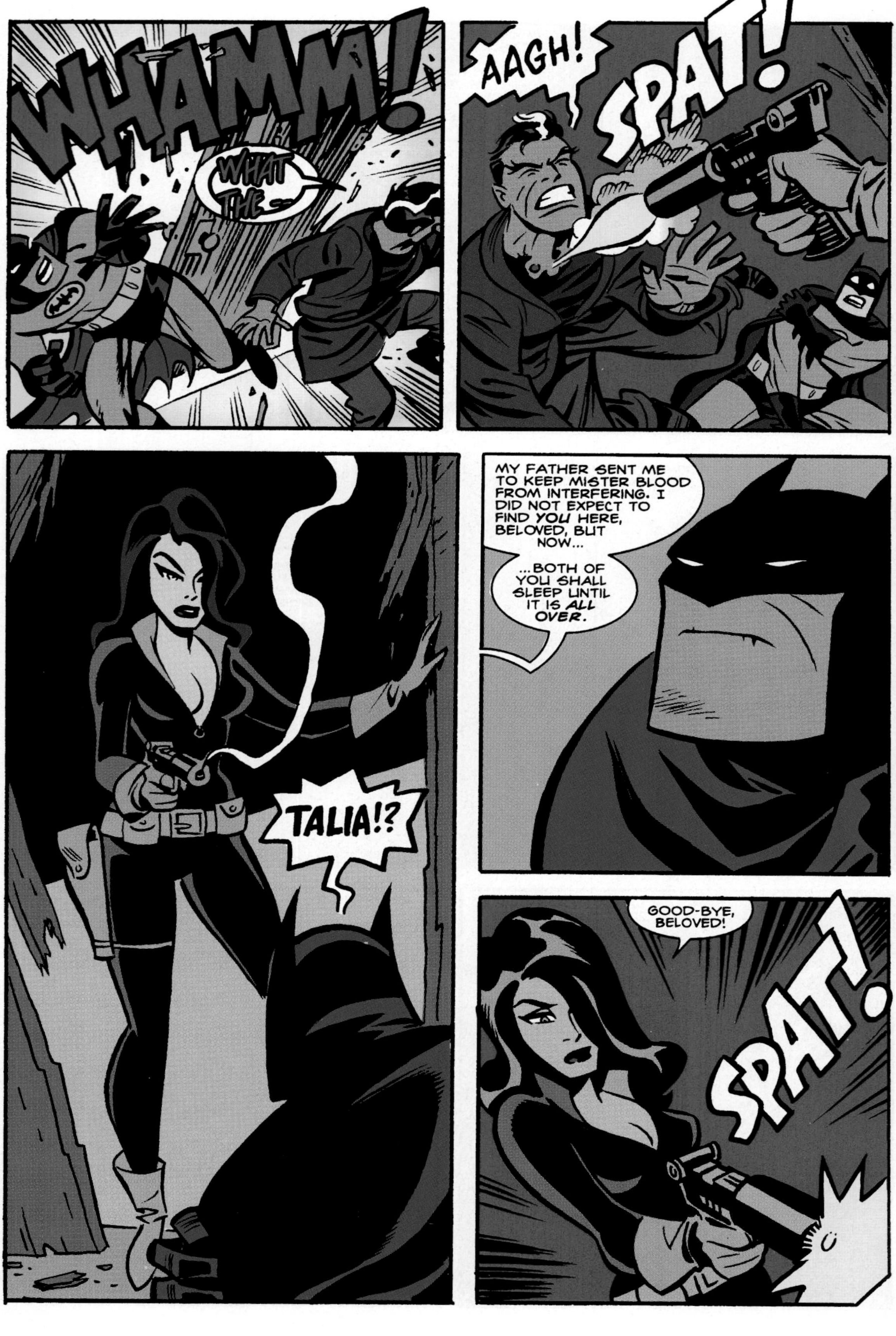
WHAMM!
WHAT THE--
AAGH!
SPAT!
TALIA!?
MY FATHER SENT ME TO KEEP MISTER BLOOD FROM INTERFERING. I DID NOT EXPECT TO FIND YOU HERE, BELOVED, BUT NOW...
...BOTH OF YOU SHALL SLEEP UNTIL IT IS ALL OVER.
GOOD-BYE, BELOVED!
SPAT!

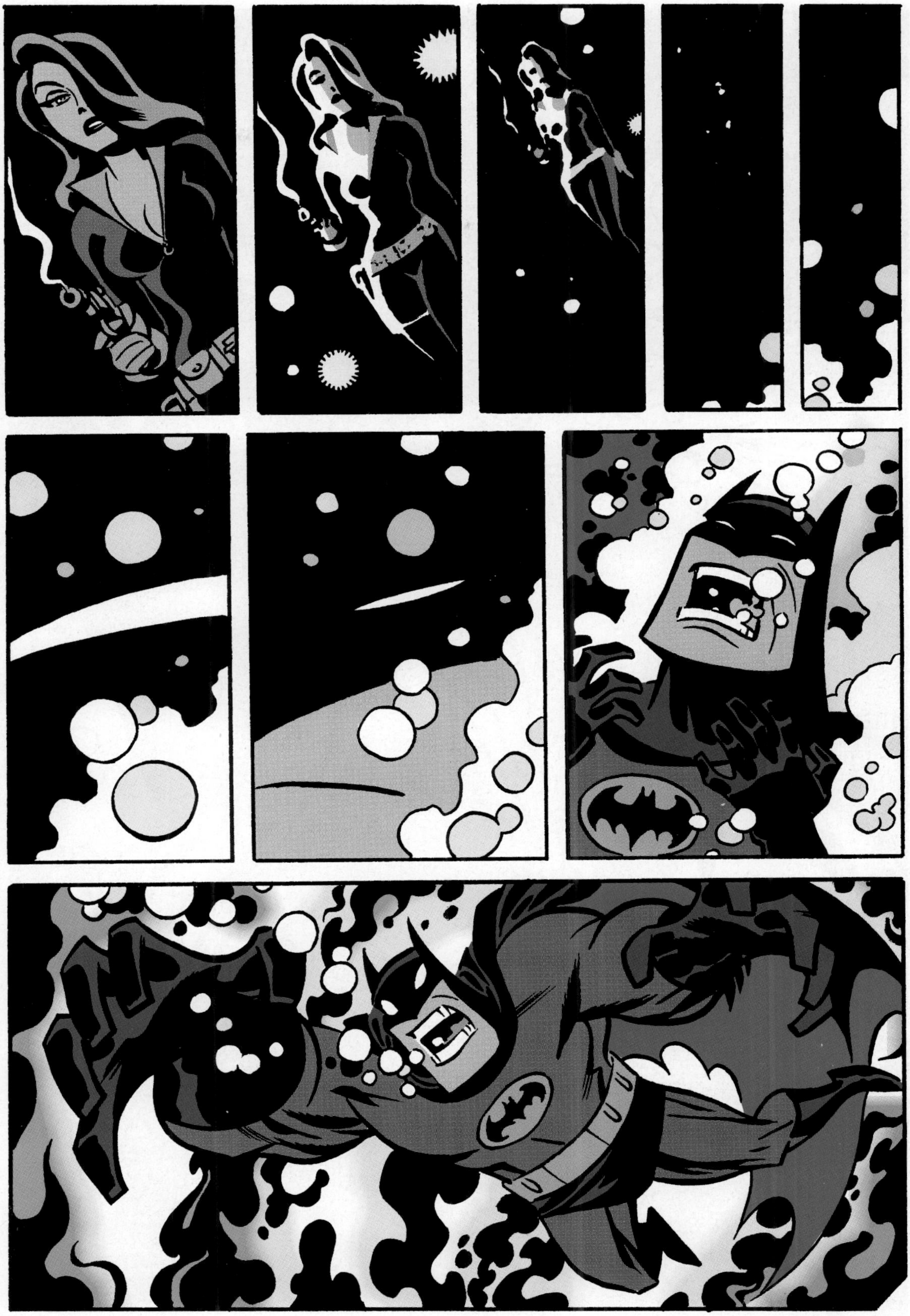

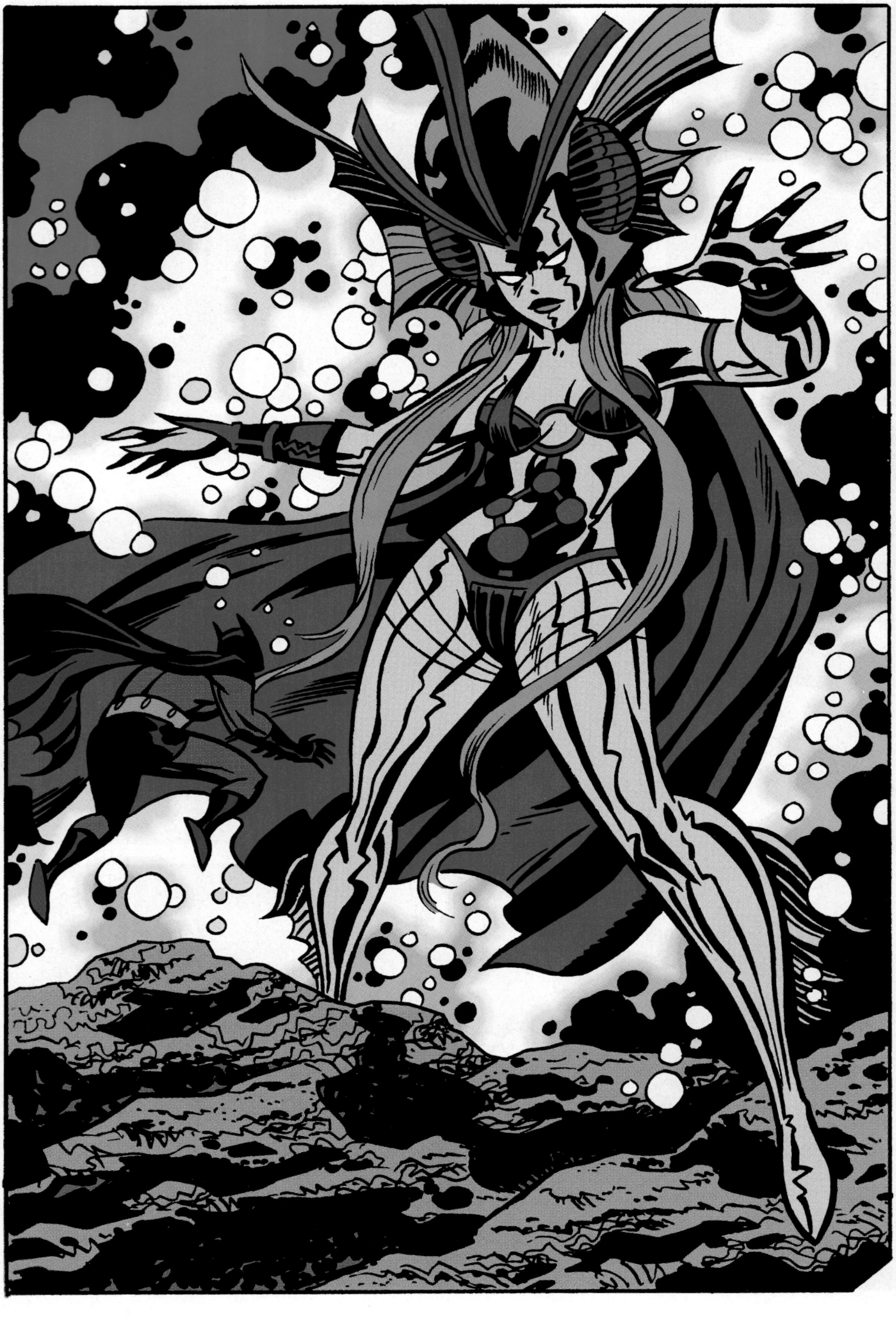

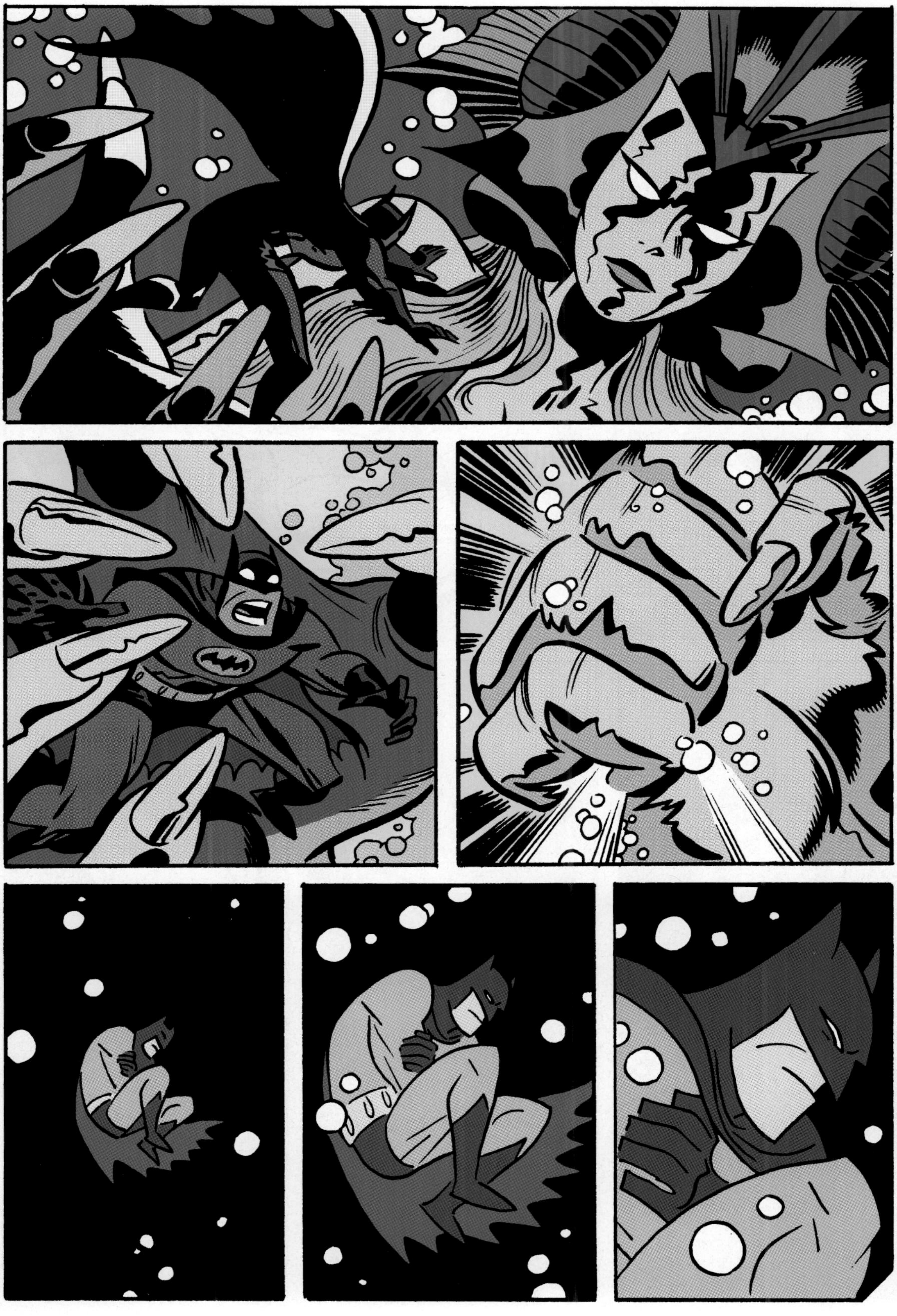

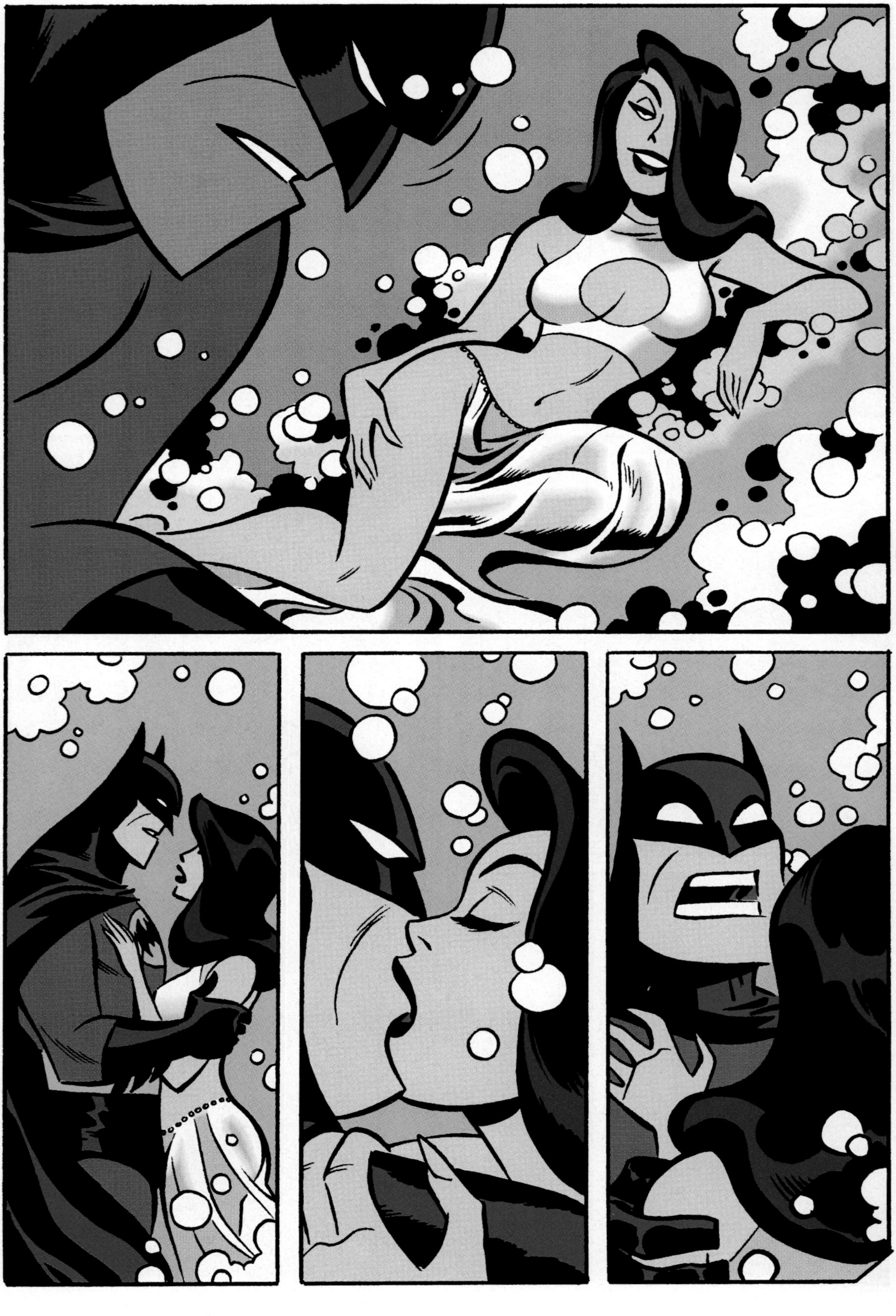

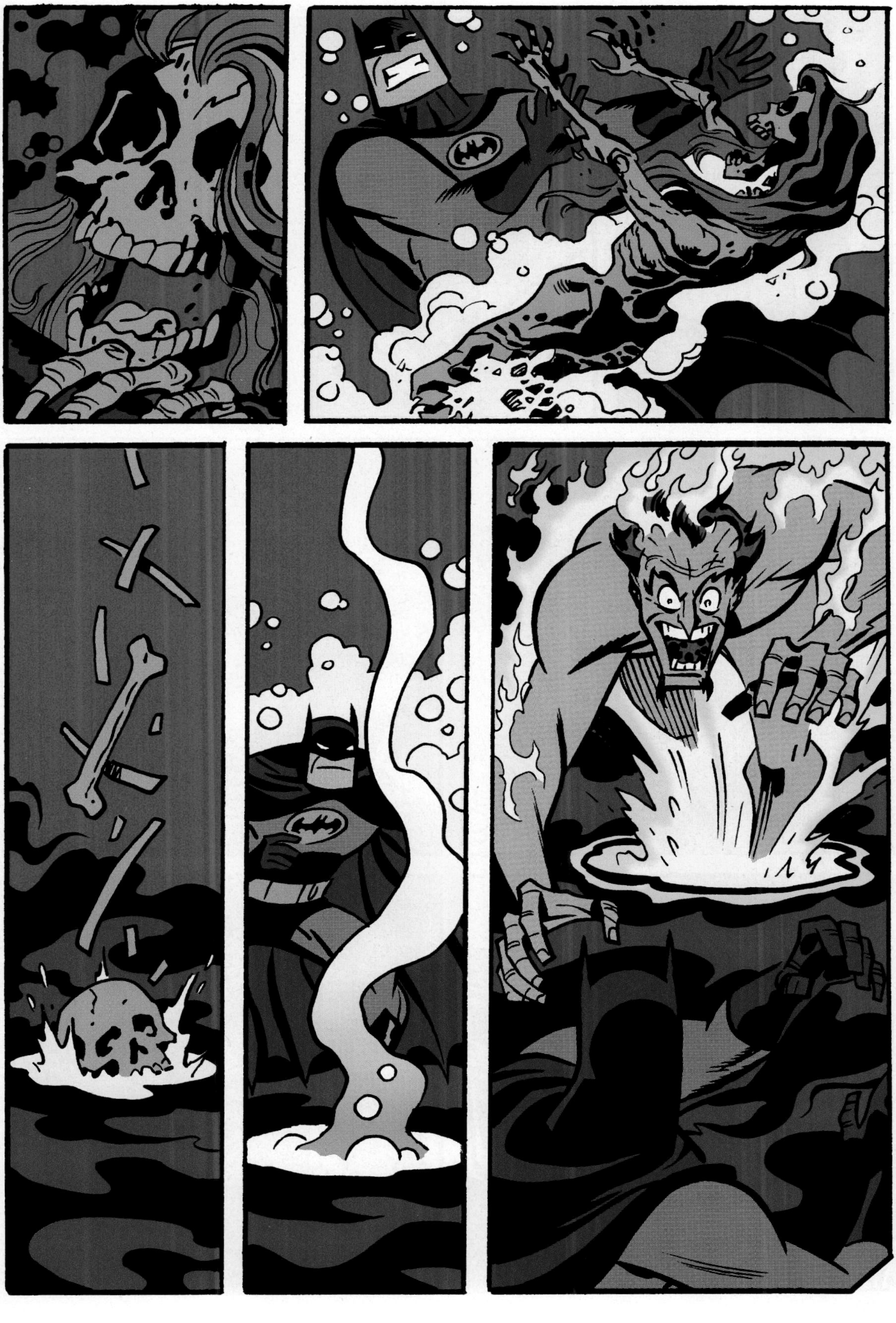

BONG BONG

BONG

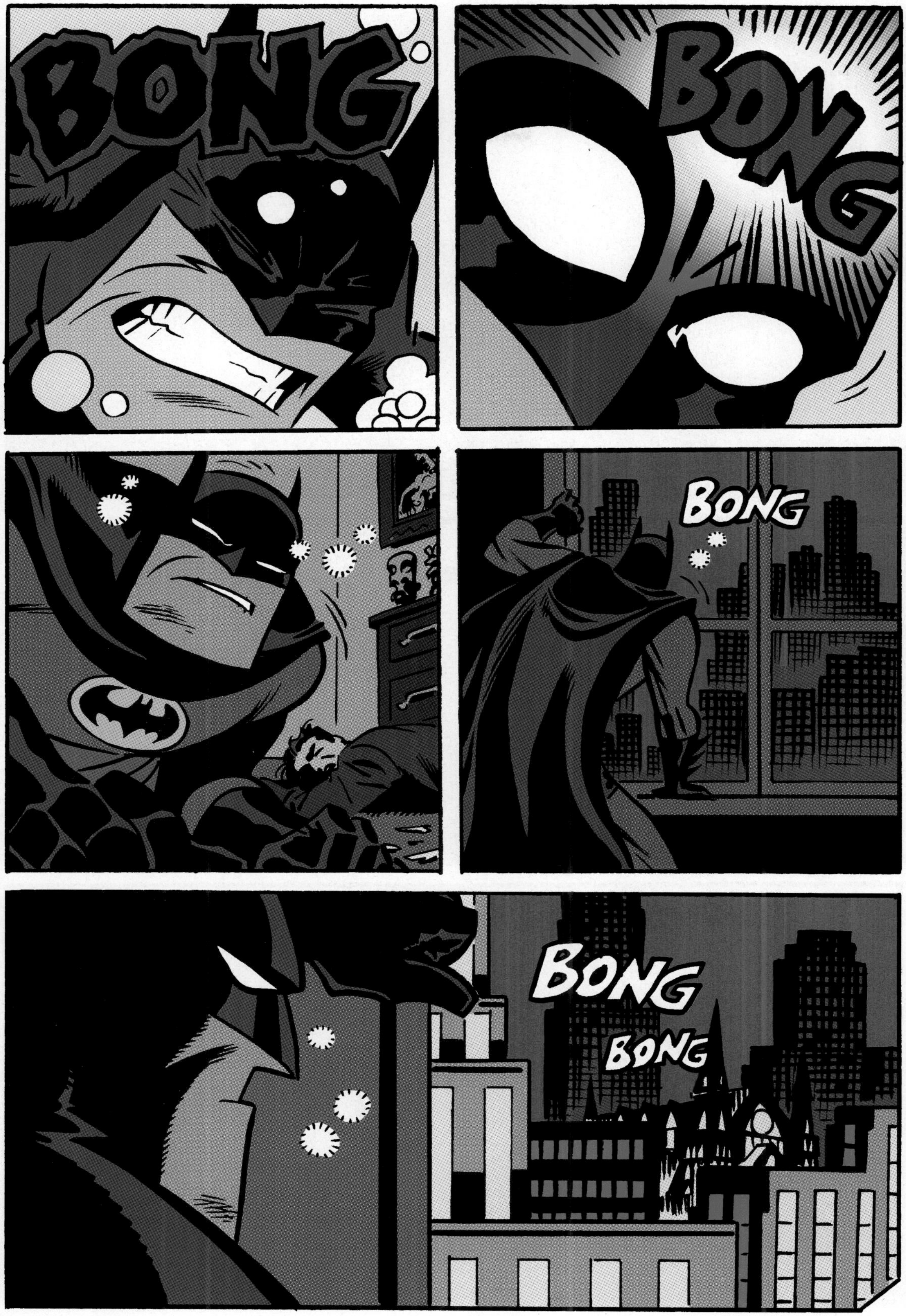
BONG
BONG
BONG
BONG
BONG

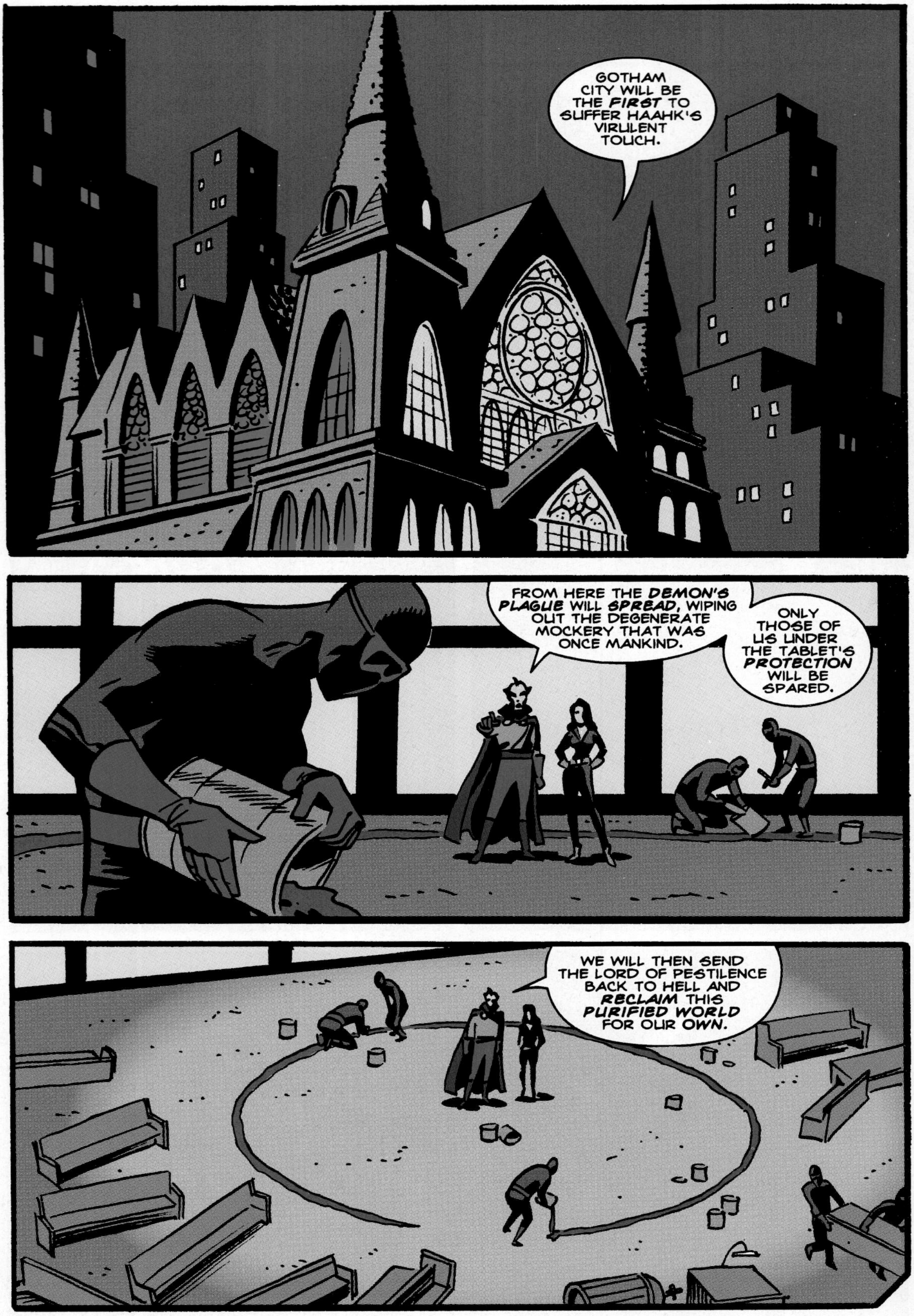

GOTHAM CITY WILL BE THE *FIRST* TO SUFFER HAAHK'S VIRULENT TOUCH.
FROM HERE THE *DEMON'S PLAGUE* WILL *SPREAD*, WIPING OUT THE DEGENERATE MOCKERY THAT WAS ONCE MANKIND.
ONLY THOSE OF US UNDER THE TABLET'S *PROTECTION* WILL BE SPARED.
WE WILL THEN SEND THE LORD OF PESTILENCE BACK TO HELL AND *RECLAIM* THIS *PURIFIED WORLD* FOR OUR **OWN**.

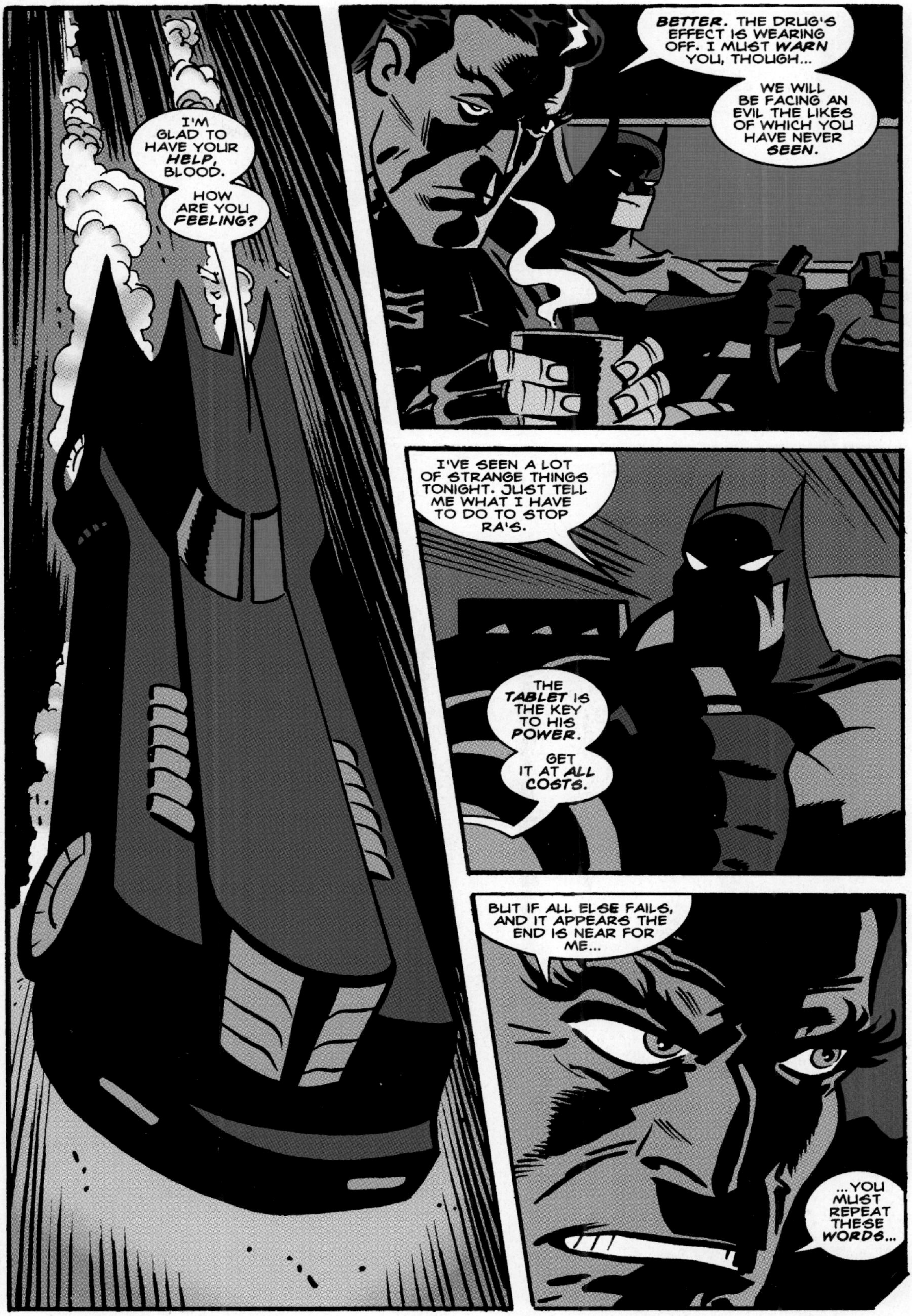
I'M GLAD TO HAVE YOUR HELP, BLOOD.
HOW ARE YOU FEELING?
BETTER. THE DRUG'S EFFECT IS WEARING OFF. I MUST WARN YOU, THOUGH...
WE WILL BE FACING AN EVIL THE LIKES OF WHICH YOU HAVE NEVER SEEN.
I'VE SEEN A LOT OF STRANGE THINGS TONIGHT. JUST TELL ME WHAT I HAVE TO DO TO STOP RA'S.
THE TABLET IS THE KEY TO HIS POWER.
GET IT AT ALL COSTS.
BUT IF ALL ELSE FAILS, AND IT APPEARS THE END IS NEAR FOR ME...
...YOU MUST REPEAT THESE WORDS...

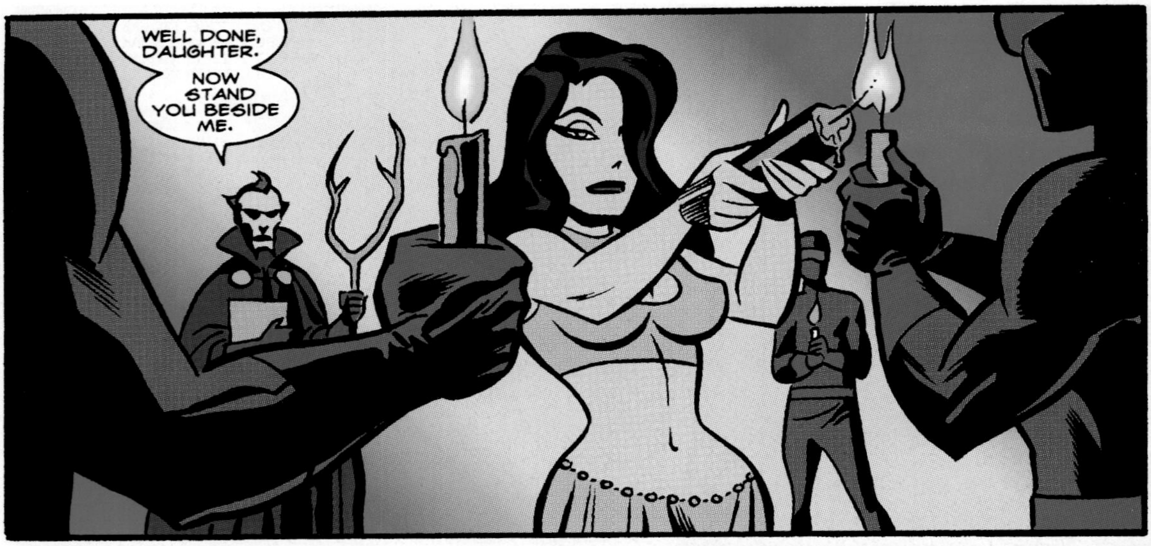
WELL DONE, DAUGHTER.
NOW STAND YOU BESIDE ME.

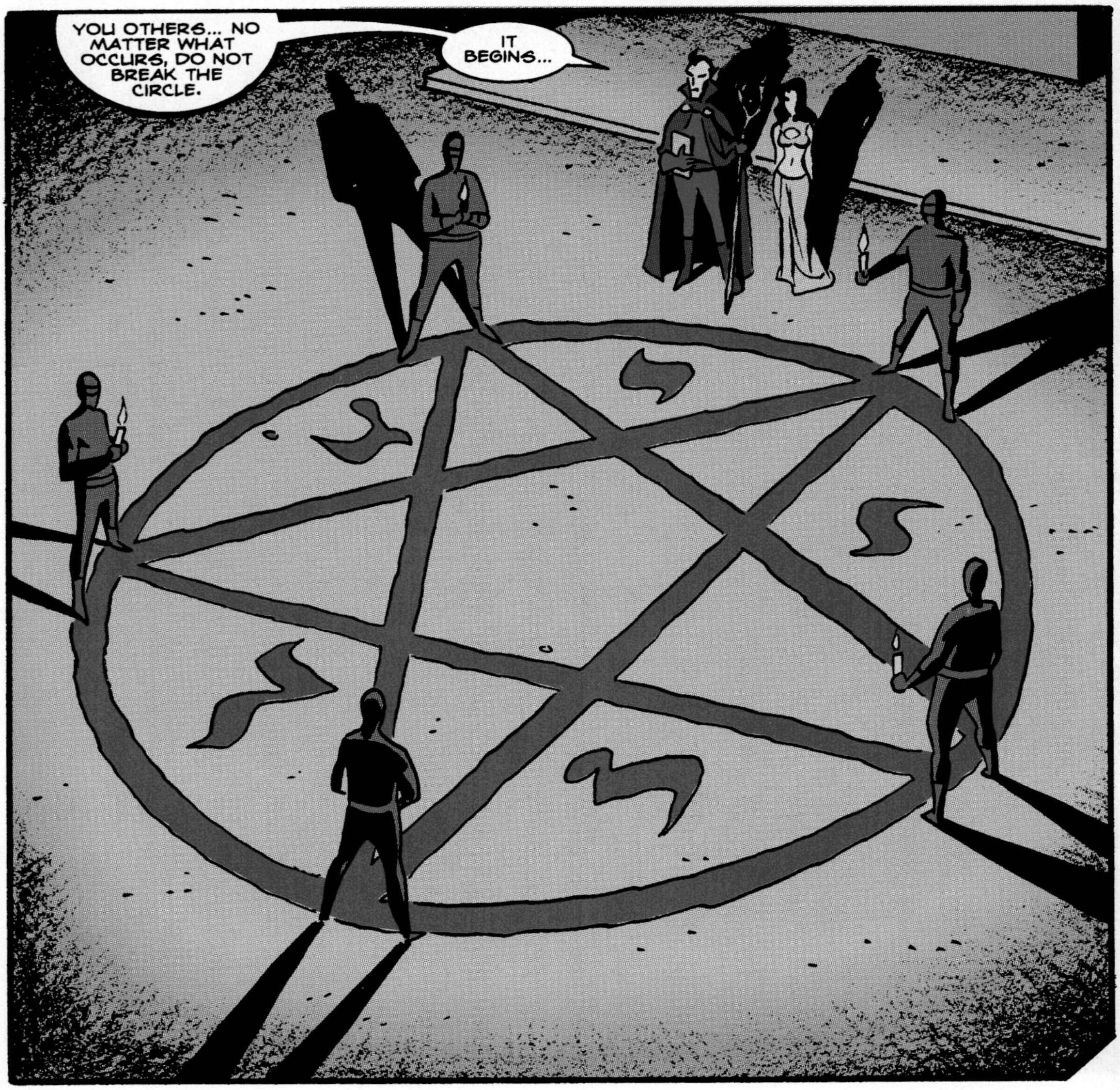
YOU OTHERS... NO MATTER WHAT OCCURS, DO NOT BREAK THE CIRCLE.
IT BEGINS...

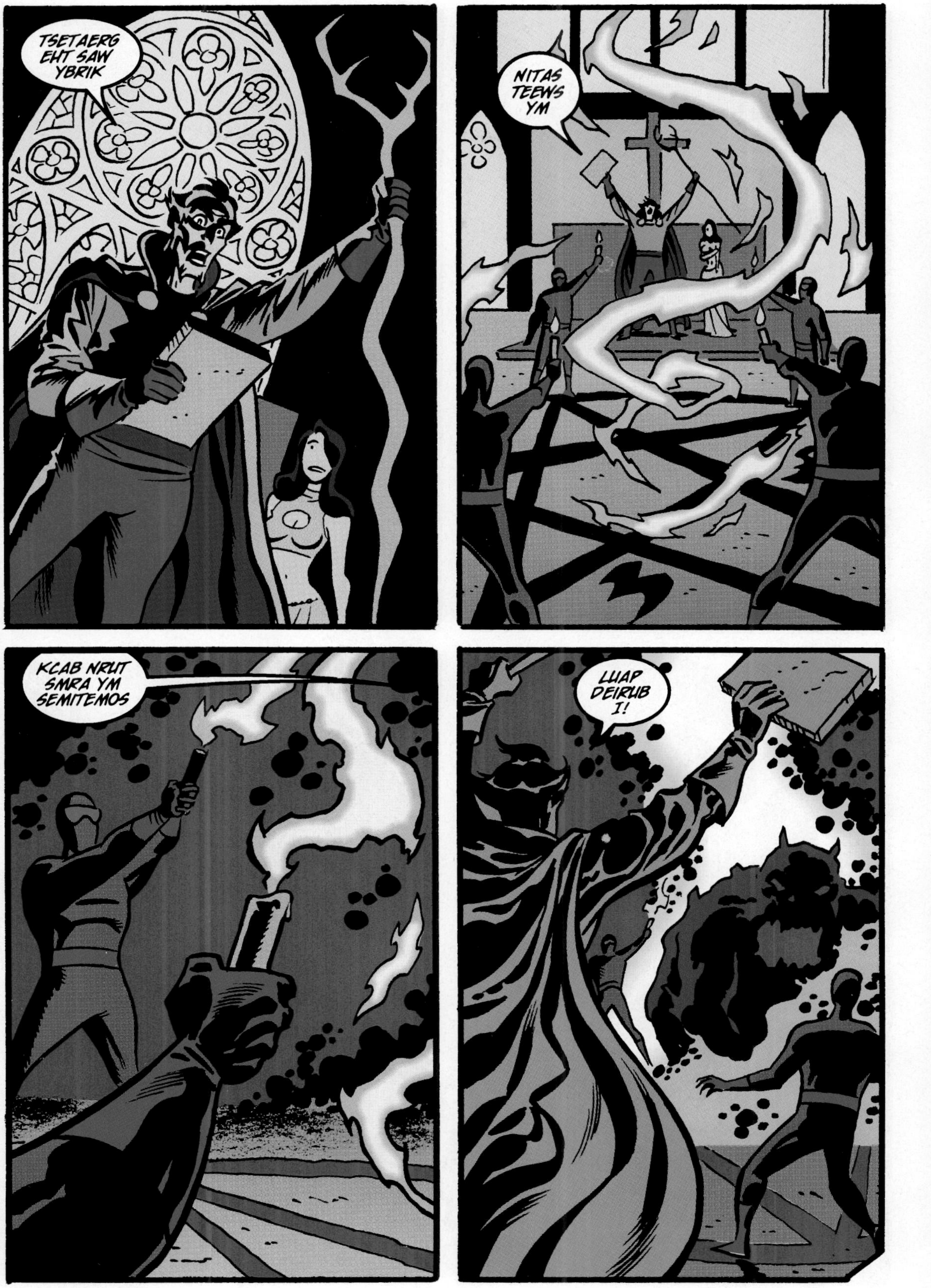
TSETAERG
EHT SAW
YBRIK
NITAS
TEEWS
YM
KCAB NRUT
SMRA YM
SEMITEMOS
LUAP
DEIRUB
I!

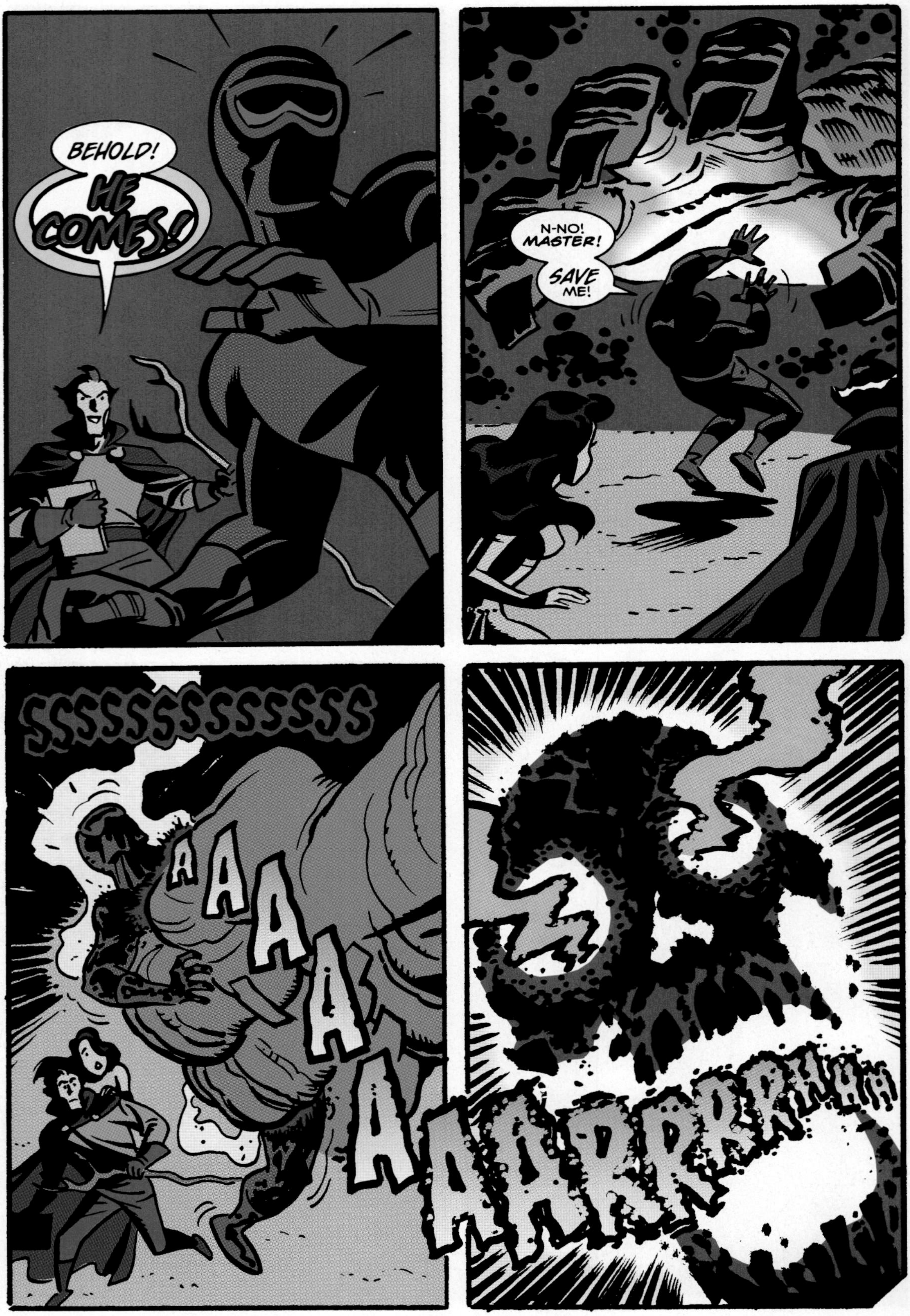
BEHOLD!
HE COMES!
N-NO! MASTER!
SAVE ME!
SSSSSSSSSSSSSS
AAAAAAA
AAARRRRHHH

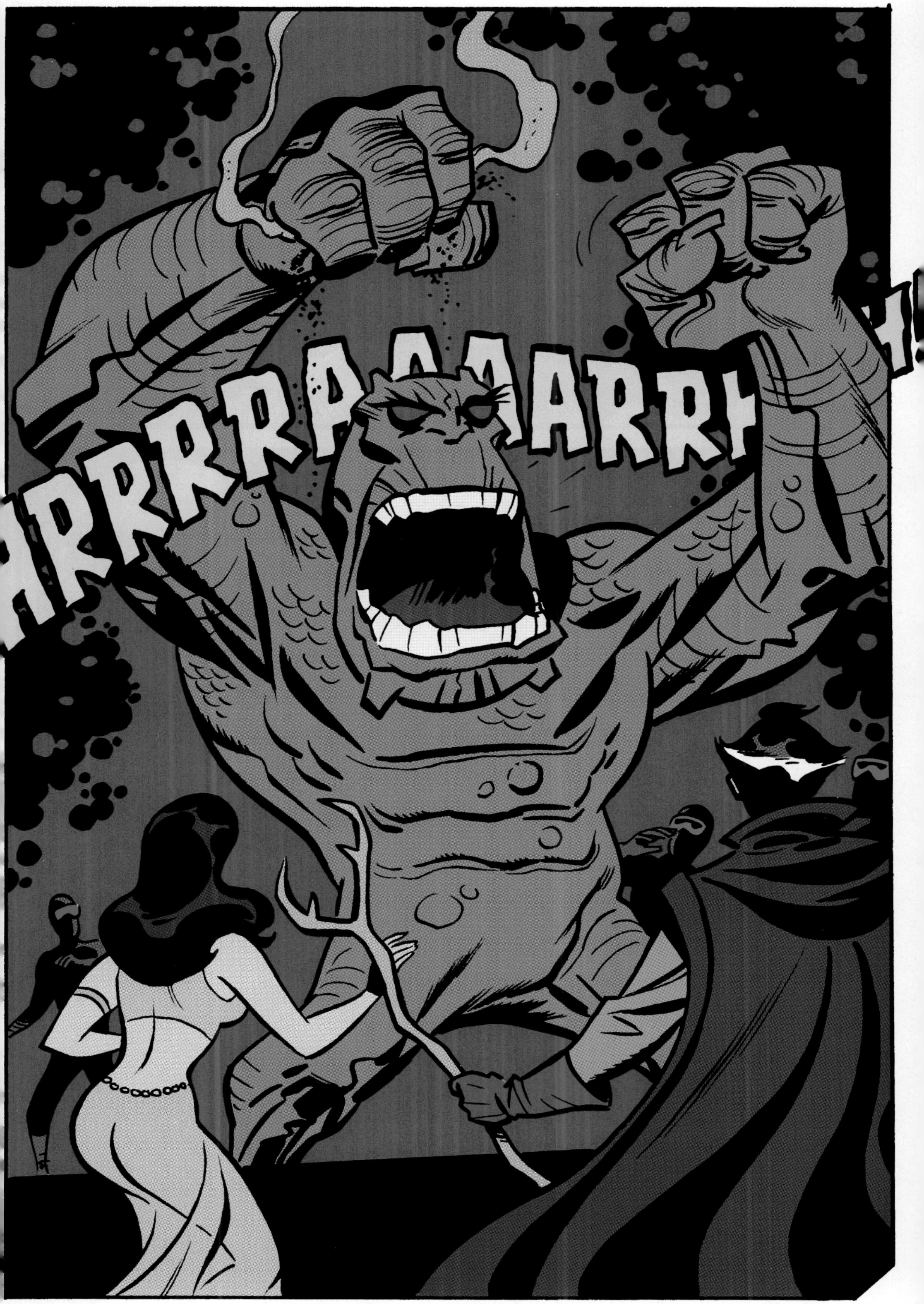
HRRRRAAAAARRRH!

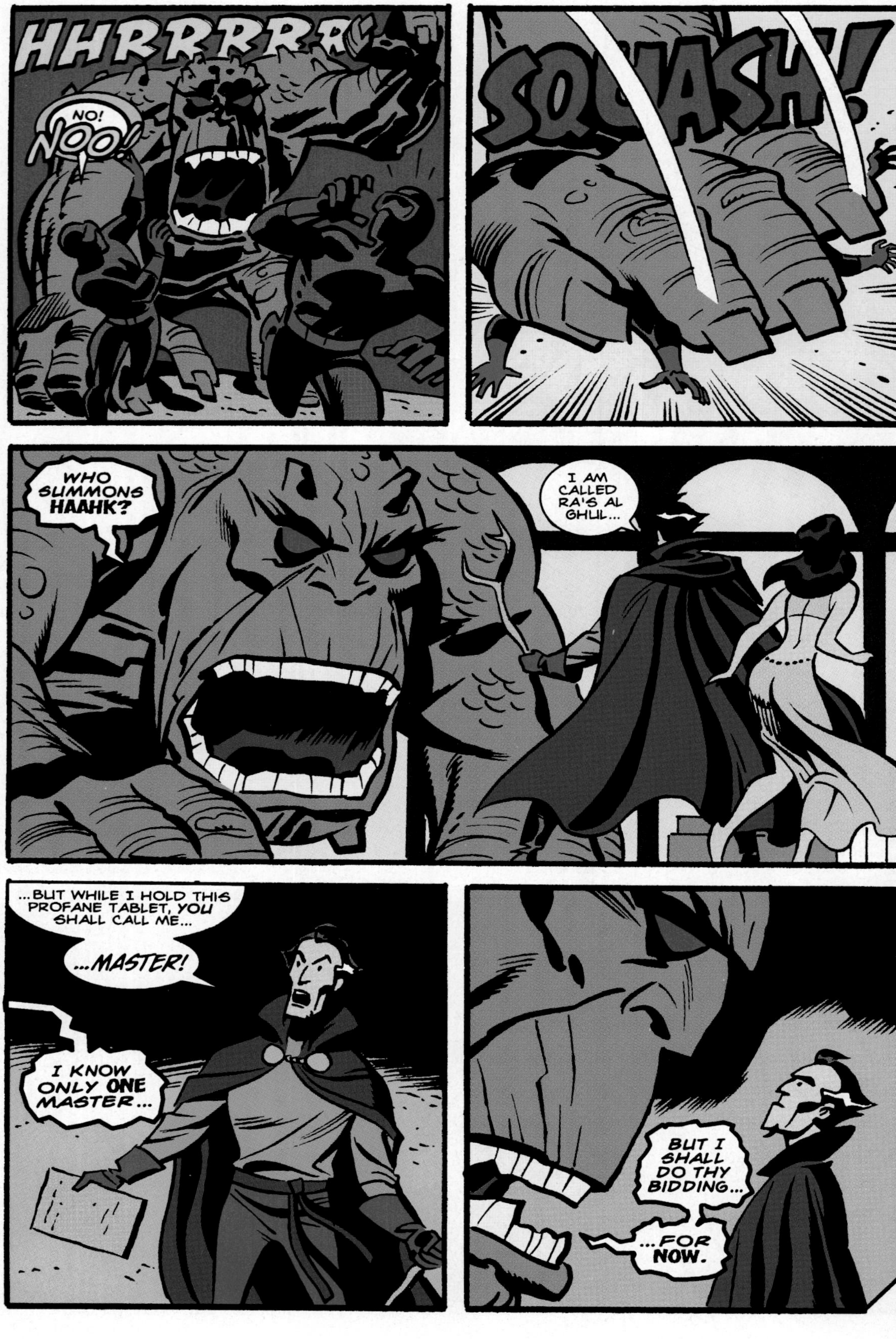
HHRRRRR
NO! NOO!
SQUASH!
WHO SUMMONS HAAHK?
I AM CALLED RA'S AL GHUL...
...BUT WHILE I HOLD THIS PROFANE TABLET, YOU SHALL CALL ME...
...MASTER!
I KNOW ONLY ONE MASTER...
BUT I SHALL DO THY BIDDING...
...FOR NOW.

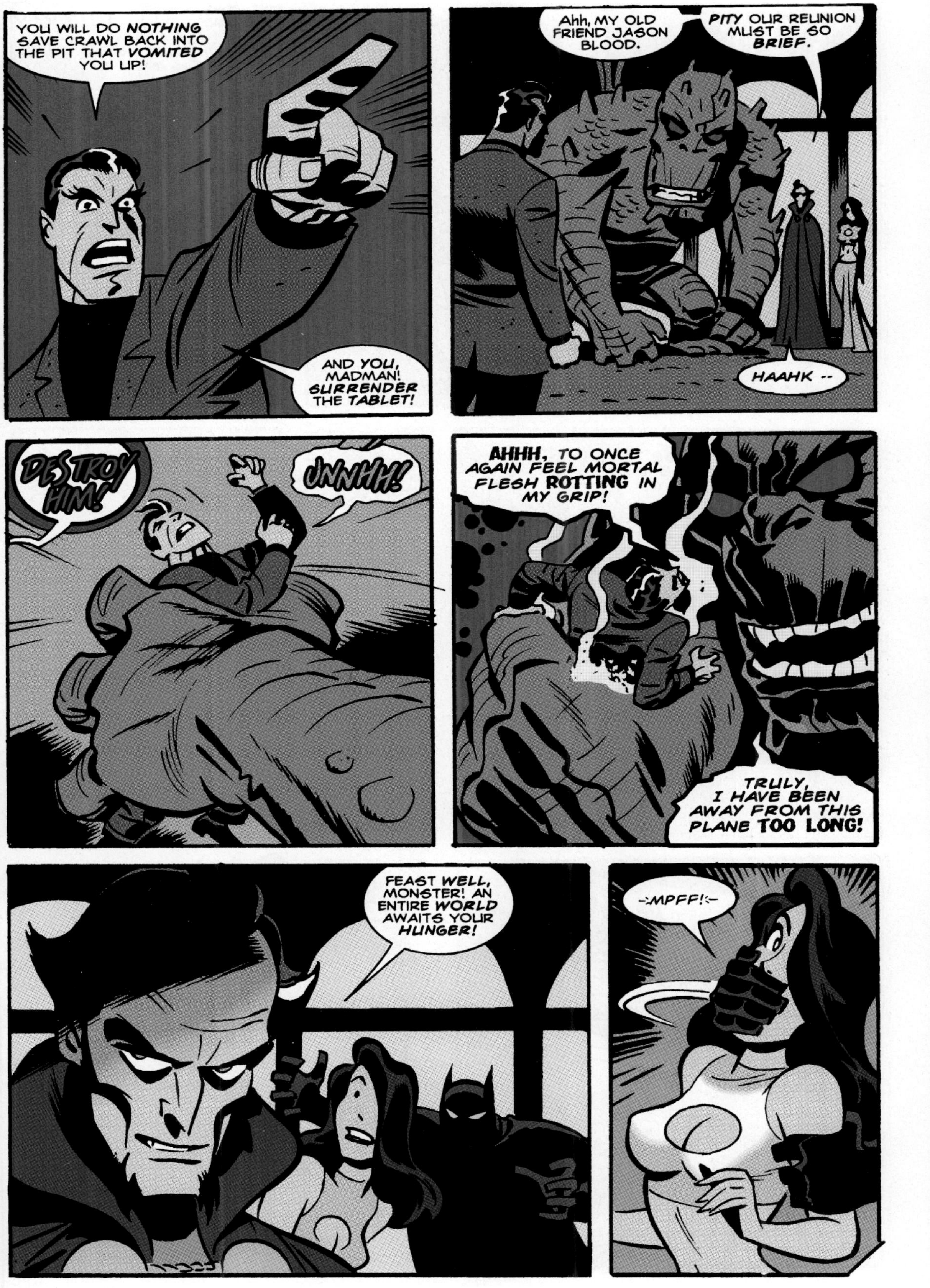
YOU WILL DO NOTHING SAVE CRAWL BACK INTO THE PIT THAT VOMITED YOU UP!
AND YOU, MADMAN! SURRENDER THE TABLET!
Ahh, MY OLD FRIEND JASON BLOOD.
PITY OUR REUNION MUST BE SO BRIEF.
HAAHK --
DESTROY HIM!
UNNHH!
AHHH, TO ONCE AGAIN FEEL MORTAL FLESH ROTTING IN MY GRIP!
TRULY, I HAVE BEEN AWAY FROM THIS PLANE TOO LONG!
FEAST WELL, MONSTER! AN ENTIRE WORLD AWAITS YOUR HUNGER!
-MPFF!-

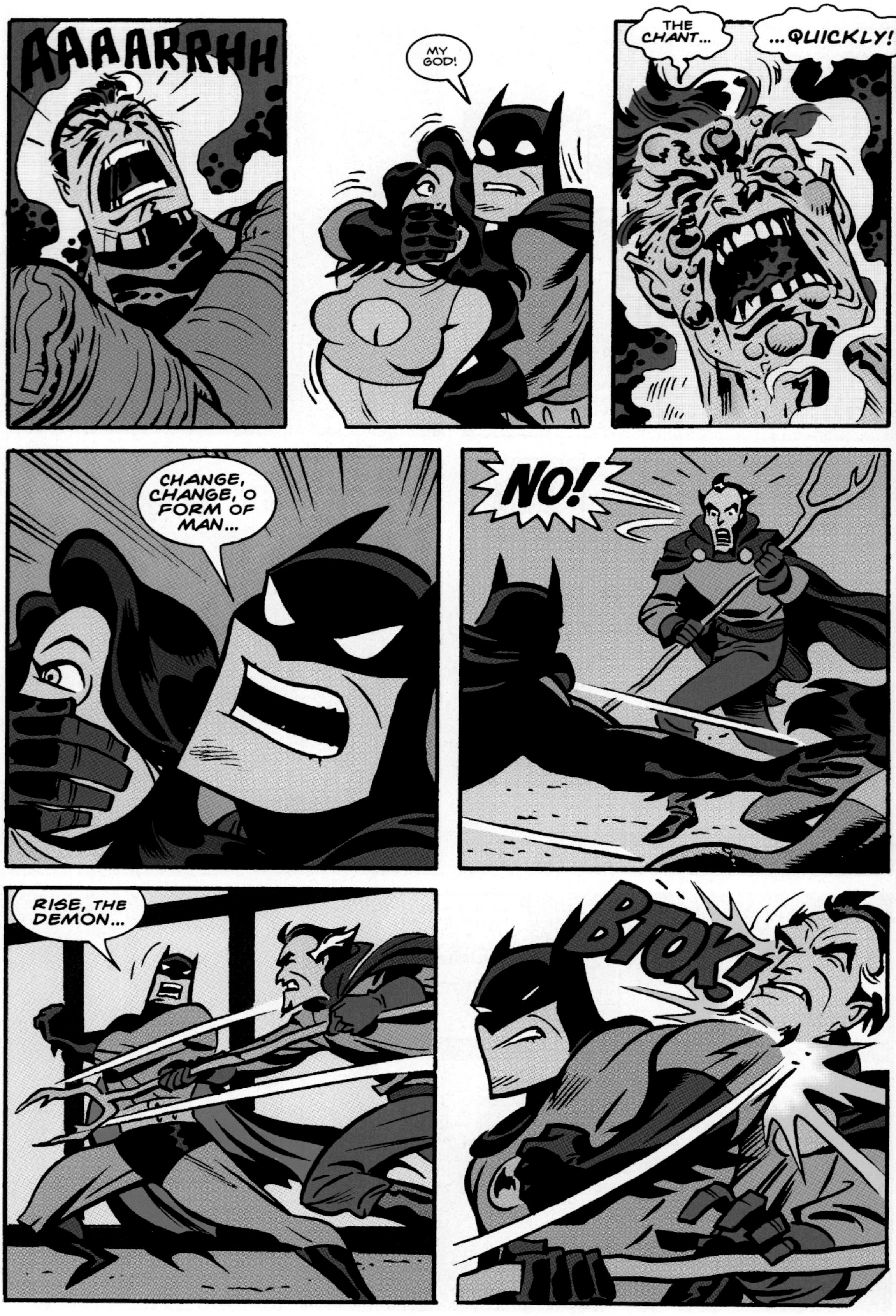
AAAARRRHH
MY GOD!
THE CHANT...
...QUICKLY!
CHANGE, CHANGE, O FORM OF MAN...
NO!
RISE, THE DEMON...
BTOK!

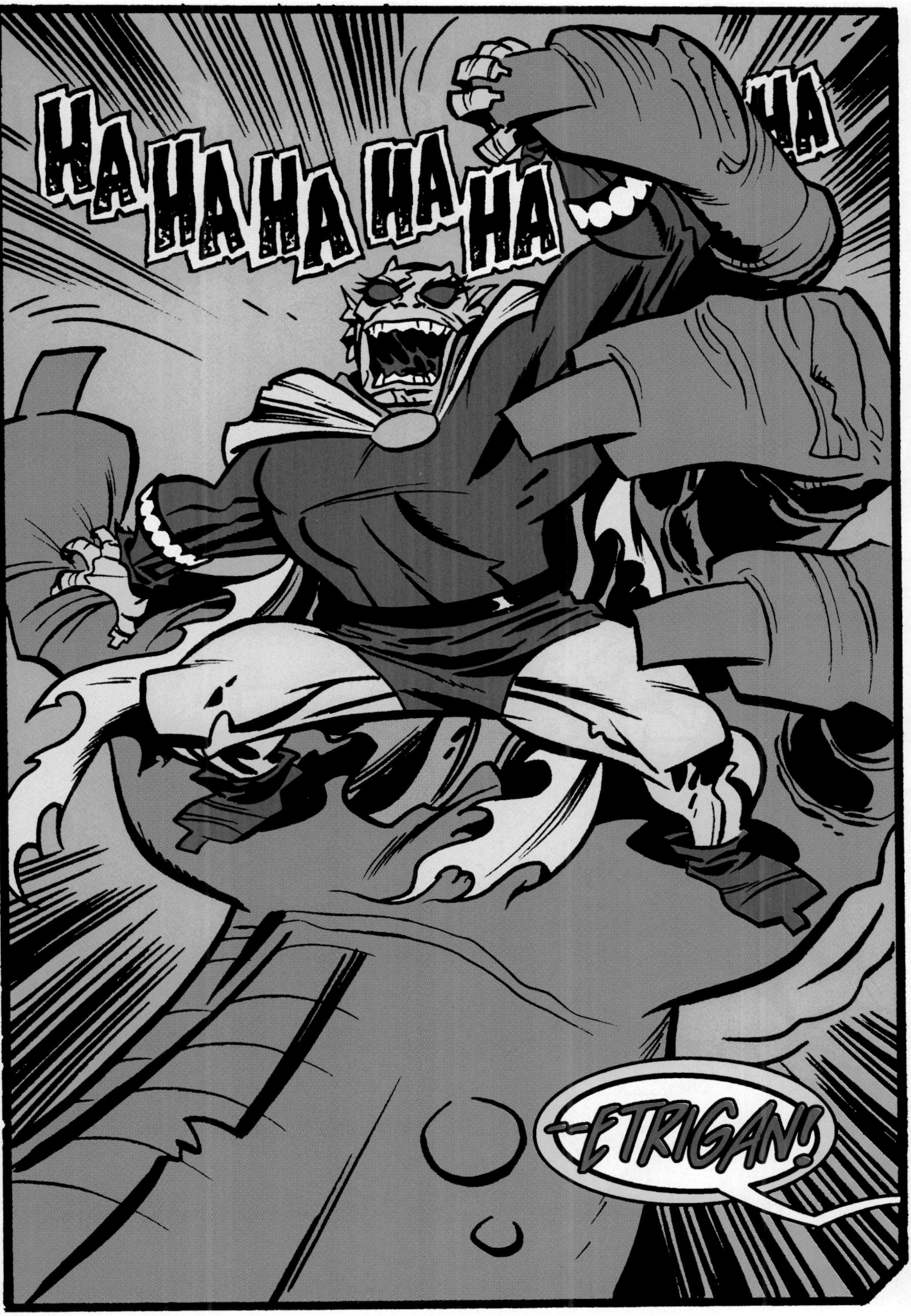
HA HA HA HA HA HA HA
--ETRIGAN!

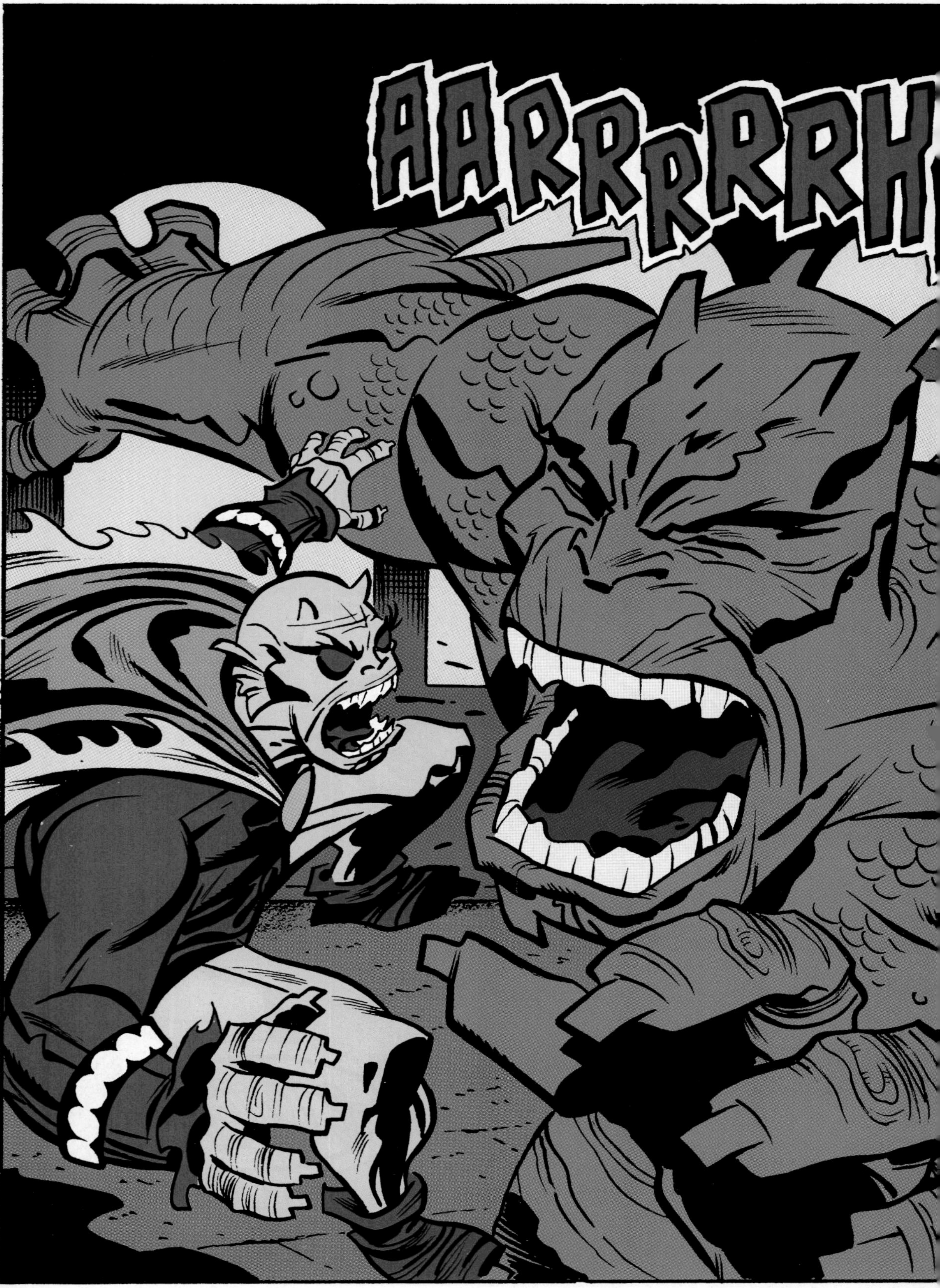
AARRRRRH

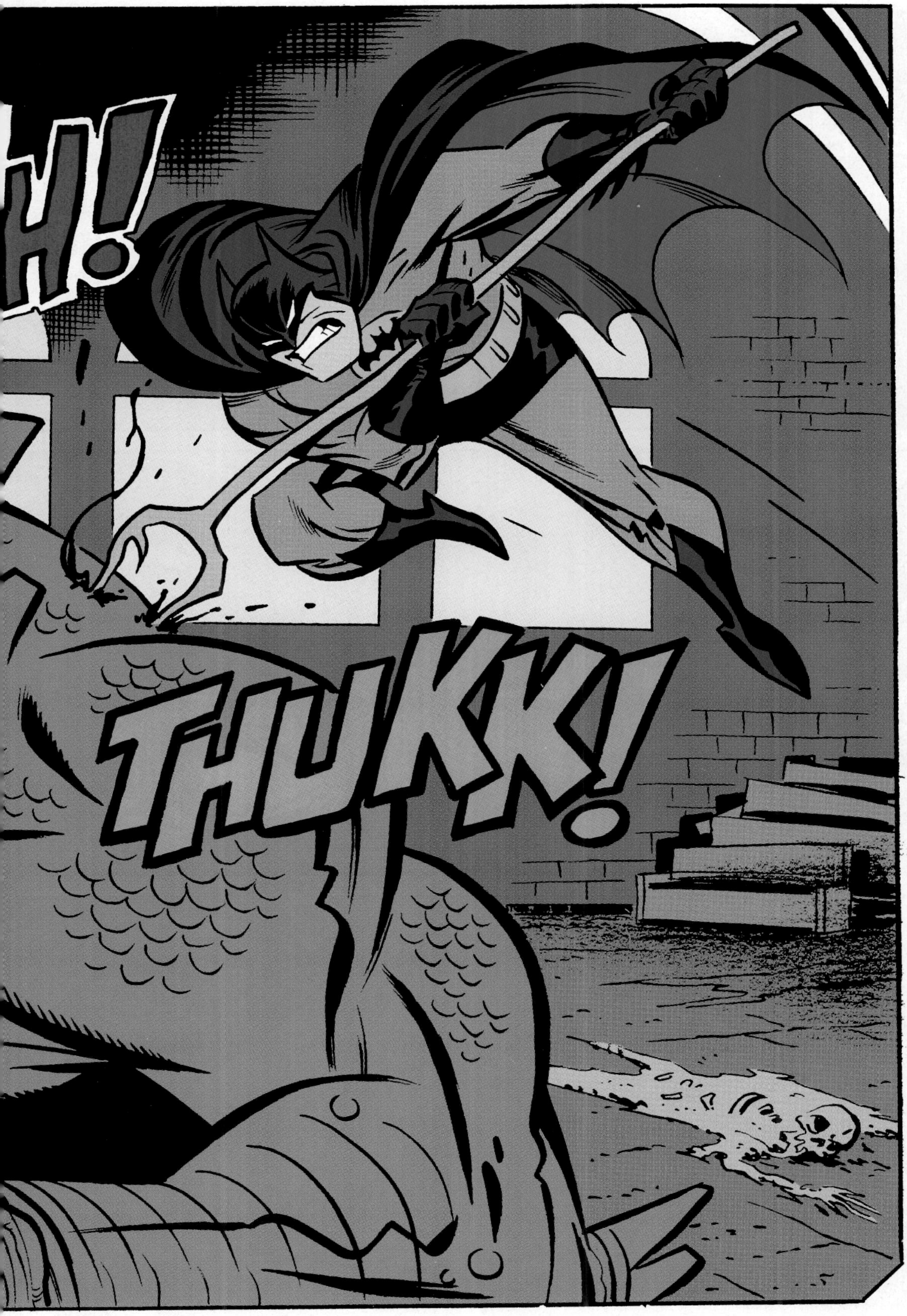

H!
THUKK!

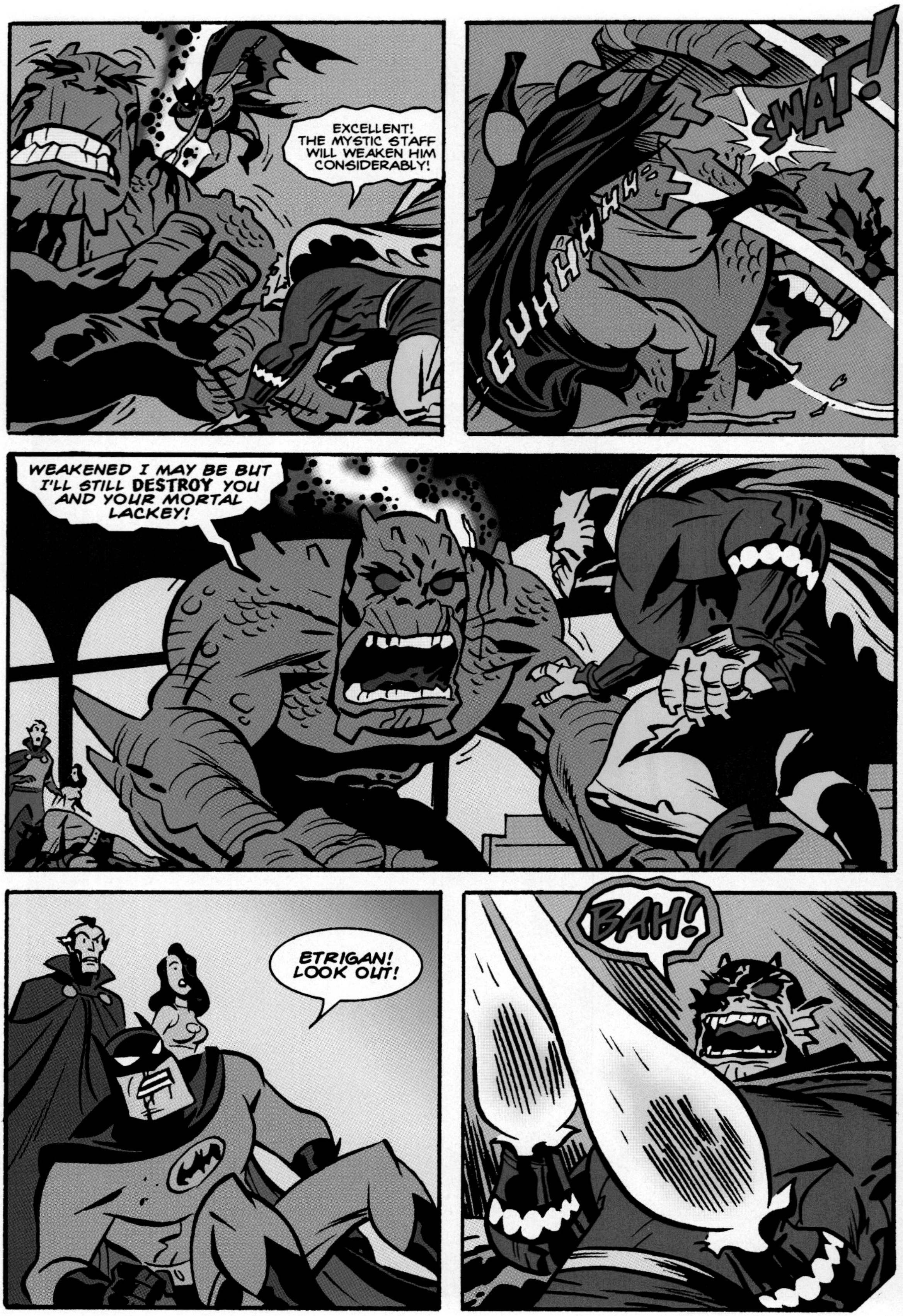
EXCELLENT! THE MYSTIC STAFF WILL WEAKEN HIM CONSIDERABLY!
SWAT!
GUHHHHHH
WEAKENED I MAY BE BUT I'LL STILL DESTROY YOU AND YOUR MORTAL LACKEY!
ETRIGAN! LOOK OUT!
BAH!

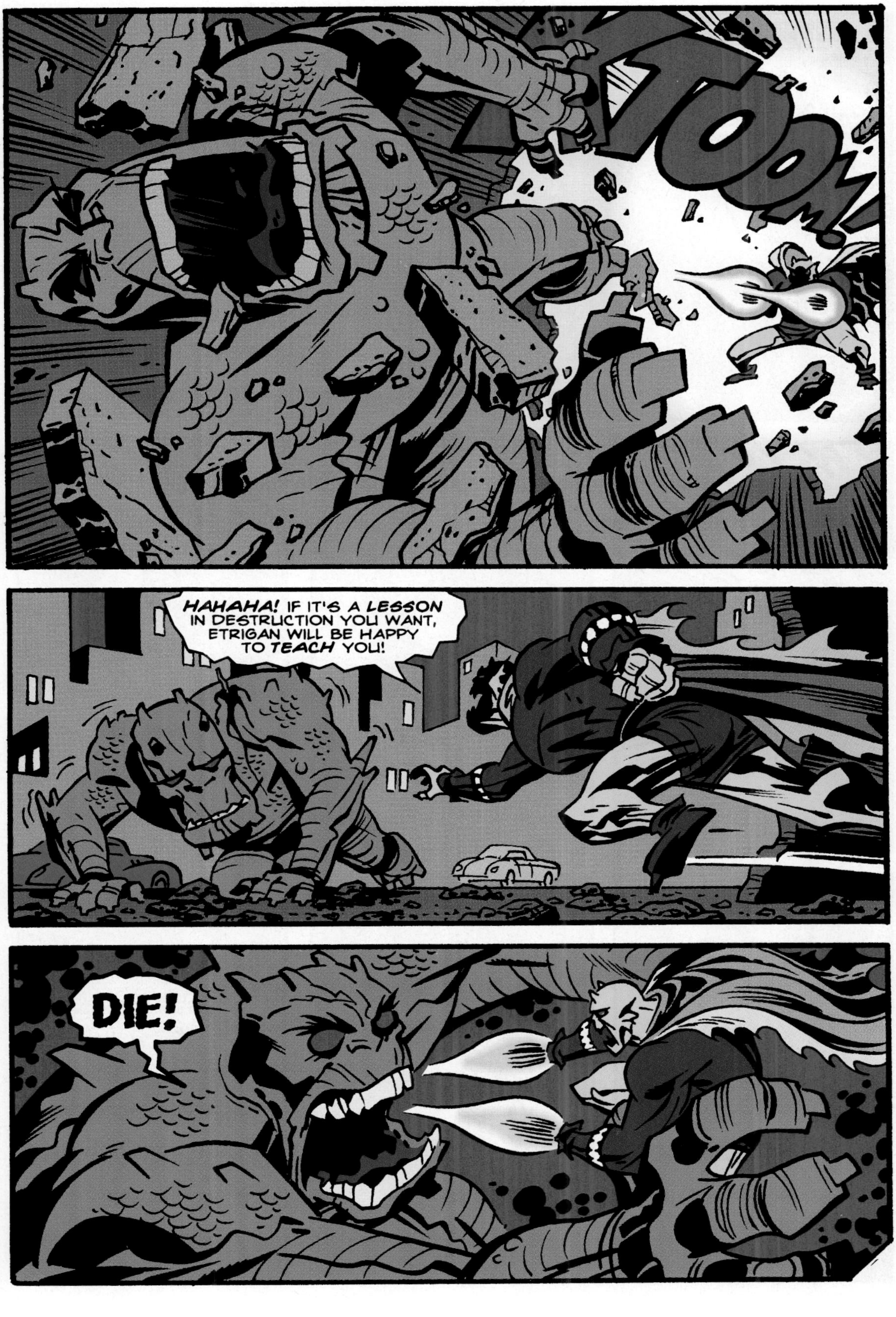
TOOOM!
HAHAHA! IF IT'S A LESSON IN DESTRUCTION YOU WANT, ETRIGAN WILL BE HAPPY TO TEACH YOU!
DIE!

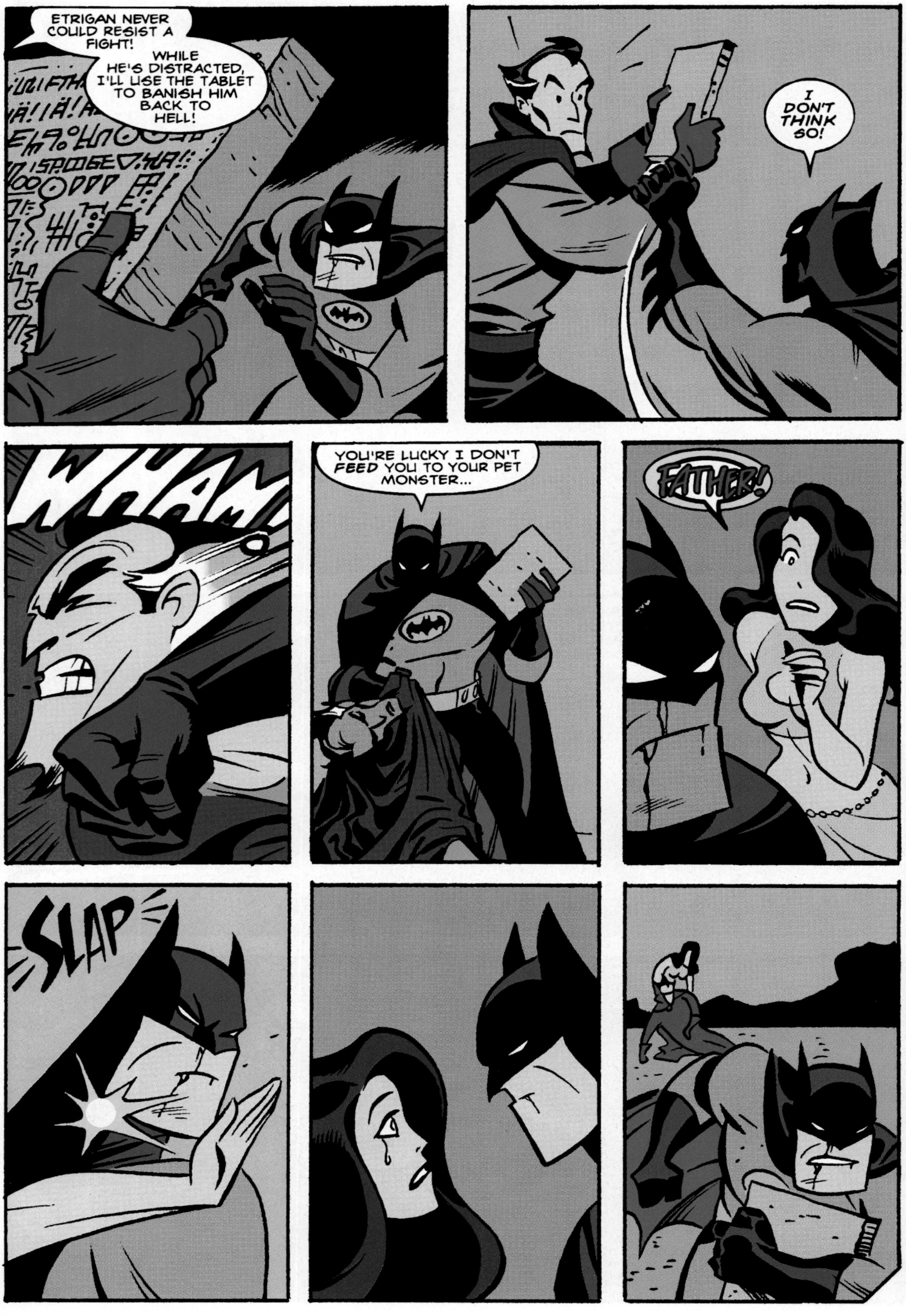
ETRIGAN NEVER COULD RESIST A FIGHT!
WHILE HE'S DISTRACTED, I'LL USE THE TABLET TO BANISH HIM BACK TO HELL!
I DON'T THINK SO!
WHAM
YOU'RE LUCKY I DON'T FEED YOU TO YOUR PET MONSTER...
FATHER!
SLAP

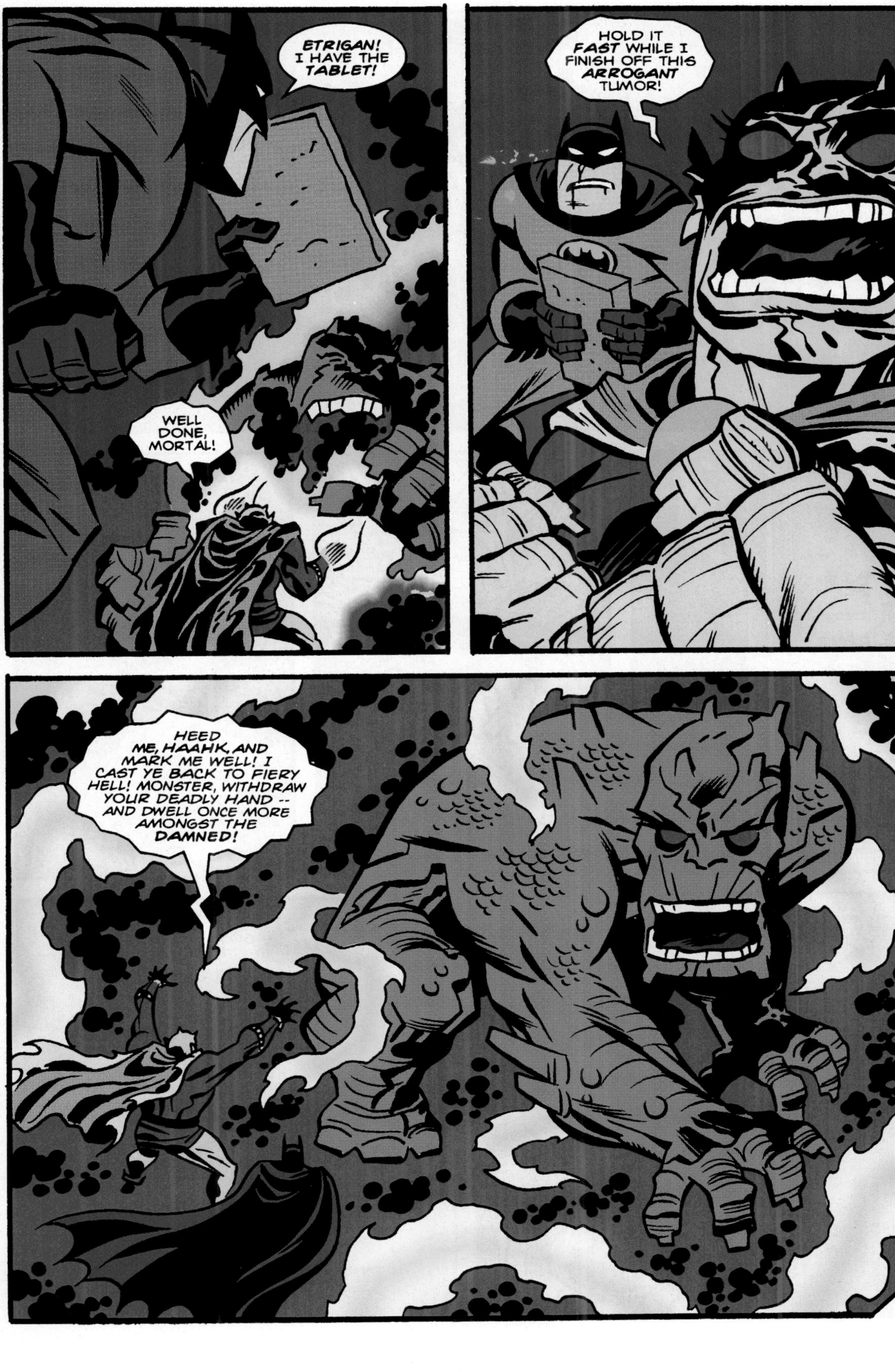

ETRIGAN! I HAVE THE TABLET!
WELL DONE, MORTAL!
HOLD IT FAST WHILE I FINISH OFF THIS ARROGANT TUMOR!
HEED ME, HAAHK, AND MARK ME WELL! I CAST YE BACK TO FIERY HELL! MONSTER, WITHDRAW YOUR DEADLY HAND -- AND DWELL ONCE MORE AMONGST THE DAMNED!

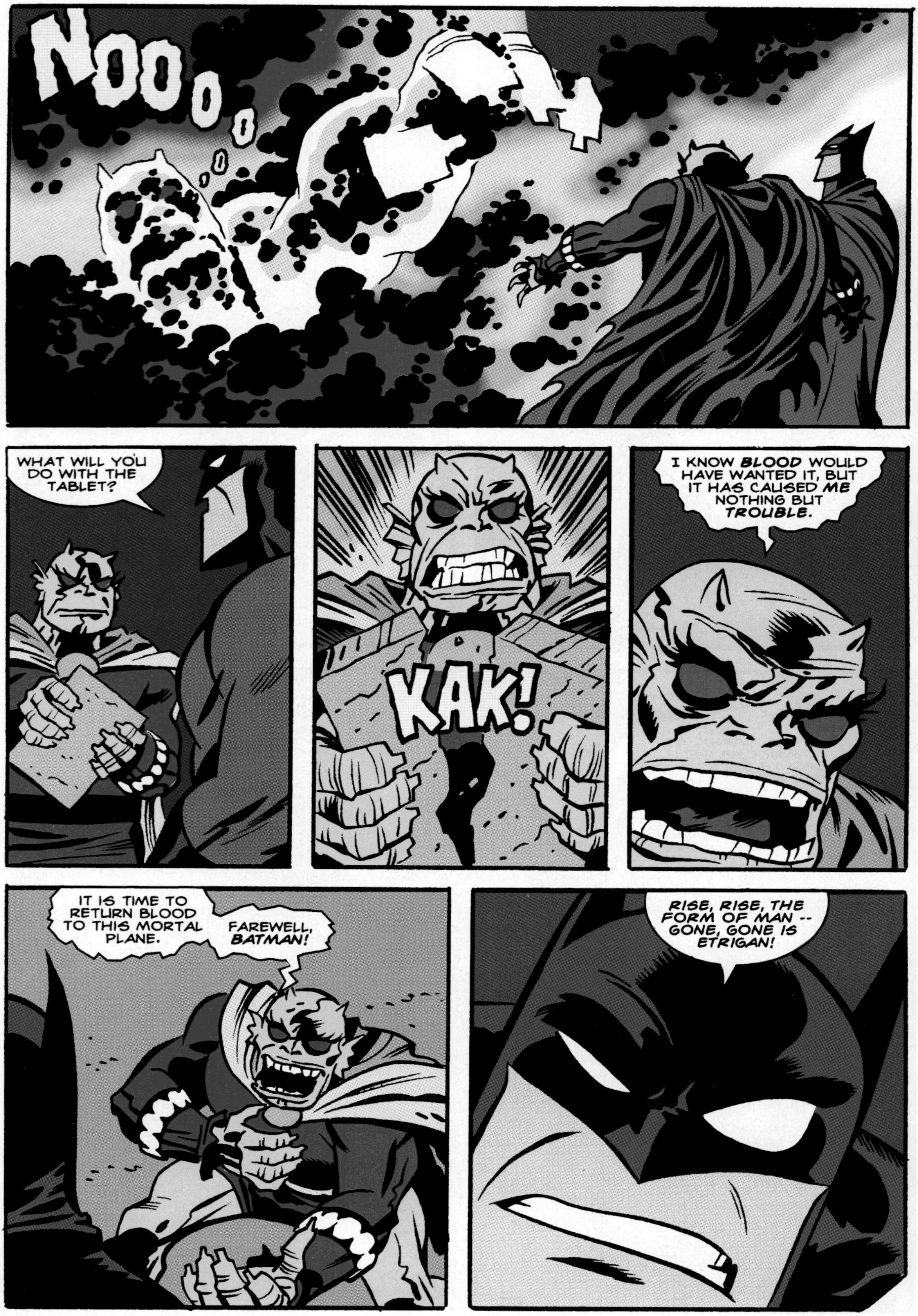
NOOOOO
WHAT WILL YOU DO WITH THE TABLET?
KAK!
I KNOW BLOOD WOULD HAVE WANTED IT, BUT IT HAS CAUSED ME NOTHING BUT TROUBLE.
IT IS TIME TO RETURN BLOOD TO THIS MORTAL PLANE.
FAREWELL, BATMAN!
RISE, RISE, THE FORM OF MAN -- GONE, GONE IS ETRIGAN!

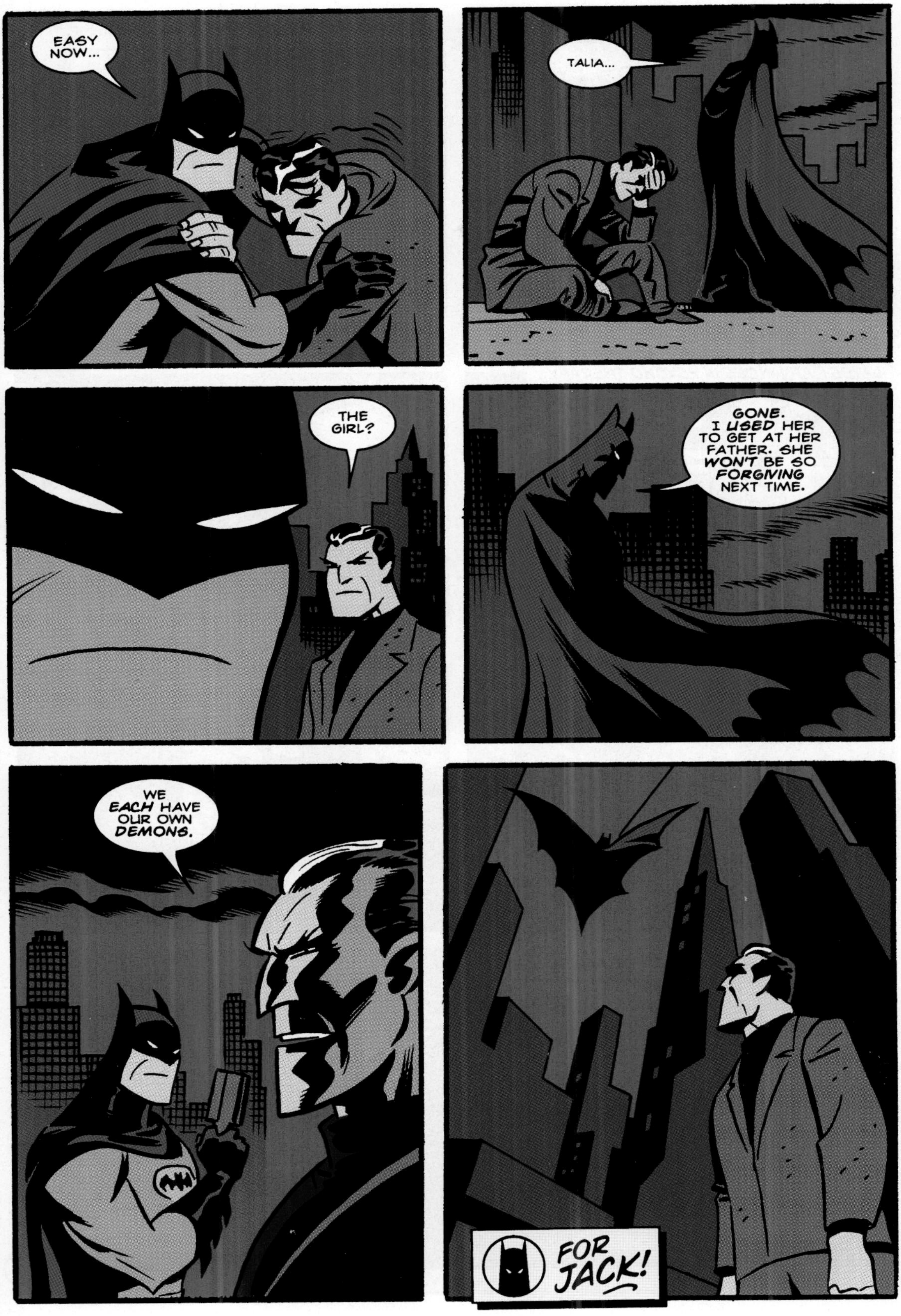
EASY NOW...
TALIA...
THE GIRL?
GONE. I USED HER TO GET AT HER FATHER. SHE WON'T BE SO FORGIVING NEXT TIME.
WE EACH HAVE OUR OWN DEMONS.
FOR JACK!

SHE WAS THE PRIDE OF GOTHAM CITY...

NEW HOPE

Dr. Marilyn Crane returns from triumphant trip to Geneva Medical Conference

AS BRILLIANT AS SHE WAS BEAUTIFUL...

HER INNOVATIVE, STATE-OF-THE-ART PLASTIC SURGERY TECHNIQUES, COMBINED WITH THE LATEST ADVANCES IN PSYCHO-THERAPY...

...ACCOMPLISHED WHAT BATMAN AND THE ENTIRE GOTHAM POLICE FORCE NEVER COULD--

--THE COMPLETE DESTRUCTION OF THE CRIMINAL MASTERMIND TWO-FACE.

IF I'D KNOWN THEN HOW IT WOULD ALL TURN OUT...

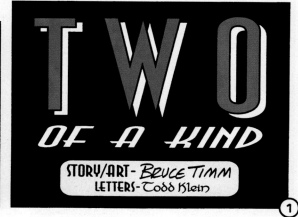

...I WOULD NEVER HAVE LET HER FALL IN LOVE WITH ME...

TWO
OF A KIND

STORY/ART- BRUCE TIMM
LETTERS- Todd Klein

①

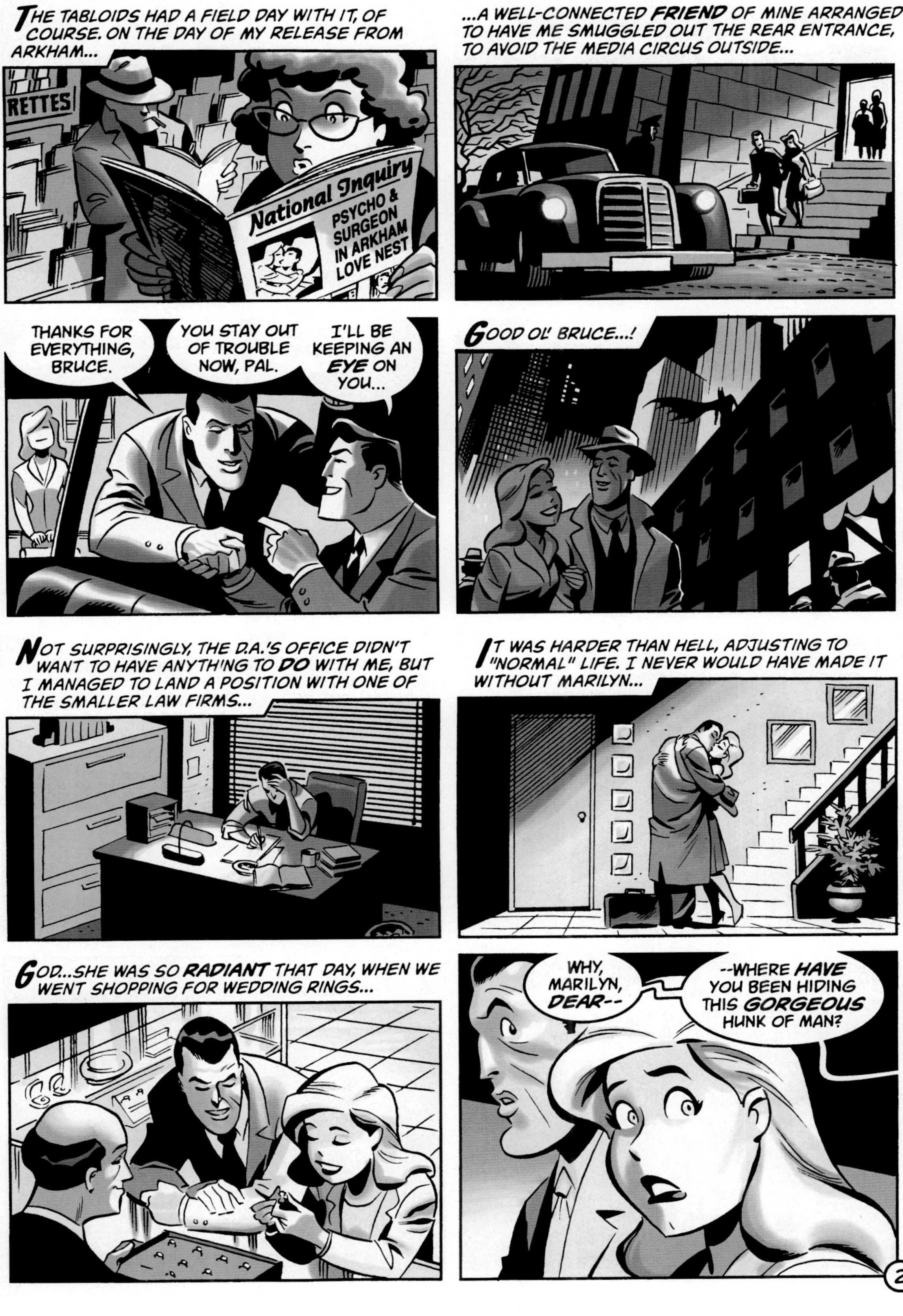
THE TABLOIDS HAD A FIELD DAY WITH IT, OF COURSE. ON THE DAY OF MY RELEASE FROM ARKHAM...
RETTES
National Inquiry
PSYCHO & SURGEON IN ARKHAM LOVE NEST
...A WELL-CONNECTED FRIEND OF MINE ARRANGED TO HAVE ME SMUGGLED OUT THE REAR ENTRANCE, TO AVOID THE MEDIA CIRCUS OUTSIDE...
THANKS FOR EVERYTHING, BRUCE.
YOU STAY OUT OF TROUBLE NOW, PAL.
I'LL BE KEEPING AN EYE ON YOU...
GOOD OL' BRUCE...!
NOT SURPRISINGLY, THE D.A.'S OFFICE DIDN'T WANT TO HAVE ANYTHING TO DO WITH ME, BUT I MANAGED TO LAND A POSITION WITH ONE OF THE SMALLER LAW FIRMS...
IT WAS HARDER THAN HELL, ADJUSTING TO "NORMAL" LIFE. I NEVER WOULD HAVE MADE IT WITHOUT MARILYN...
GOD...SHE WAS SO RADIANT THAT DAY, WHEN WE WENT SHOPPING FOR WEDDING RINGS...
WHY, MARILYN, DEAR--
--WHERE HAVE YOU BEEN HIDING THIS GORGEOUS HUNK OF MAN?
2

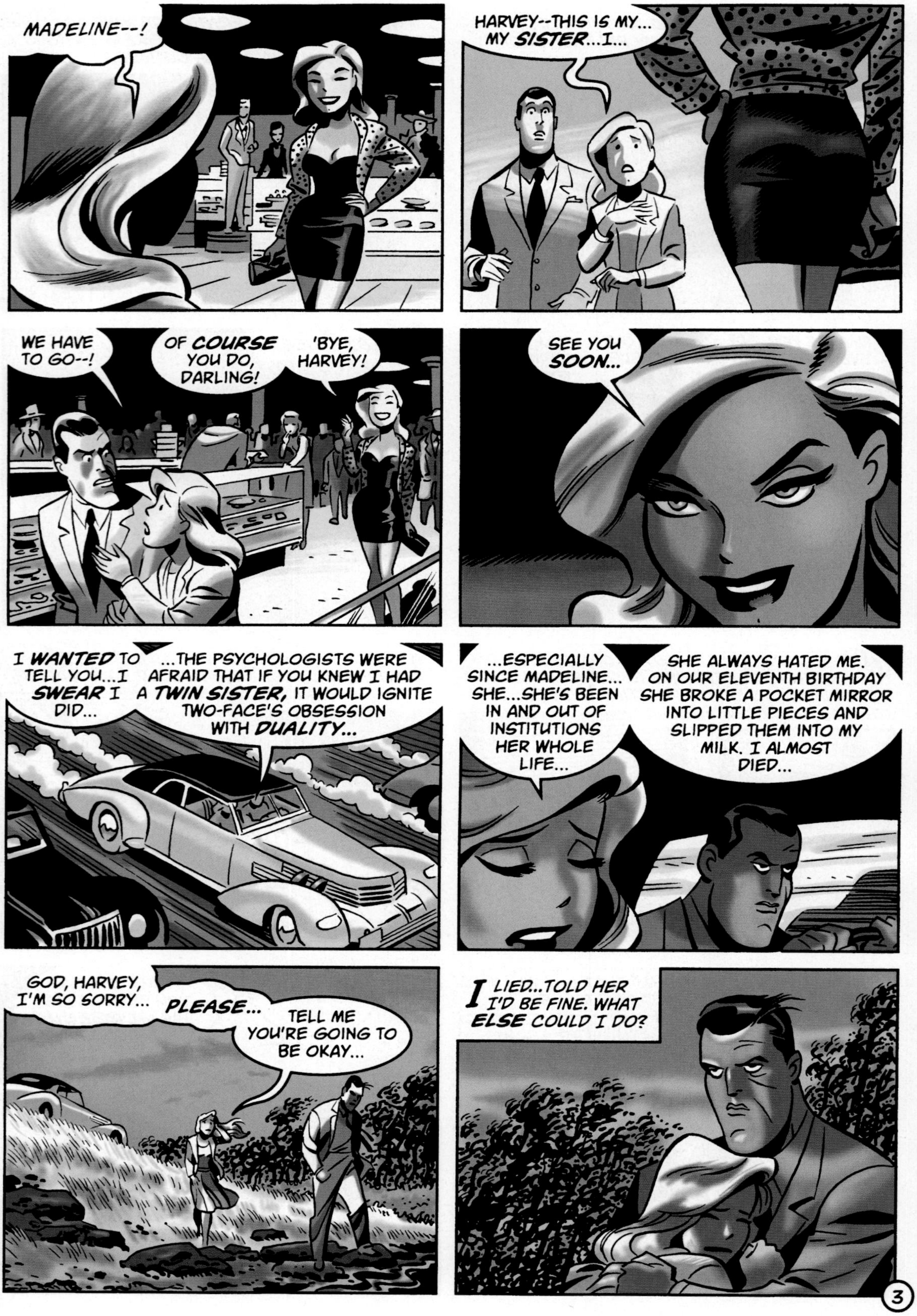
MADELINE--!
HARVEY--THIS IS MY... MY SISTER...I...
WE HAVE TO GO--!
OF COURSE YOU DO, DARLING!
'BYE, HARVEY!
SEE YOU SOON...
I WANTED TO TELL YOU...I SWEAR I DID...
...THE PSYCHOLOGISTS WERE AFRAID THAT IF YOU KNEW I HAD A TWIN SISTER, IT WOULD IGNITE TWO-FACE'S OBSESSION WITH DUALITY...
...ESPECIALLY SINCE MADELINE... SHE...SHE'S BEEN IN AND OUT OF INSTITUTIONS HER WHOLE LIFE...
SHE ALWAYS HATED ME. ON OUR ELEVENTH BIRTHDAY SHE BROKE A POCKET MIRROR INTO LITTLE PIECES AND SLIPPED THEM INTO MY MILK. I ALMOST DIED...
GOD, HARVEY, I'M SO SORRY...
PLEASE...
TELL ME YOU'RE GOING TO BE OKAY...
I LIED...TOLD HER I'D BE FINE. WHAT ELSE COULD I DO?
3

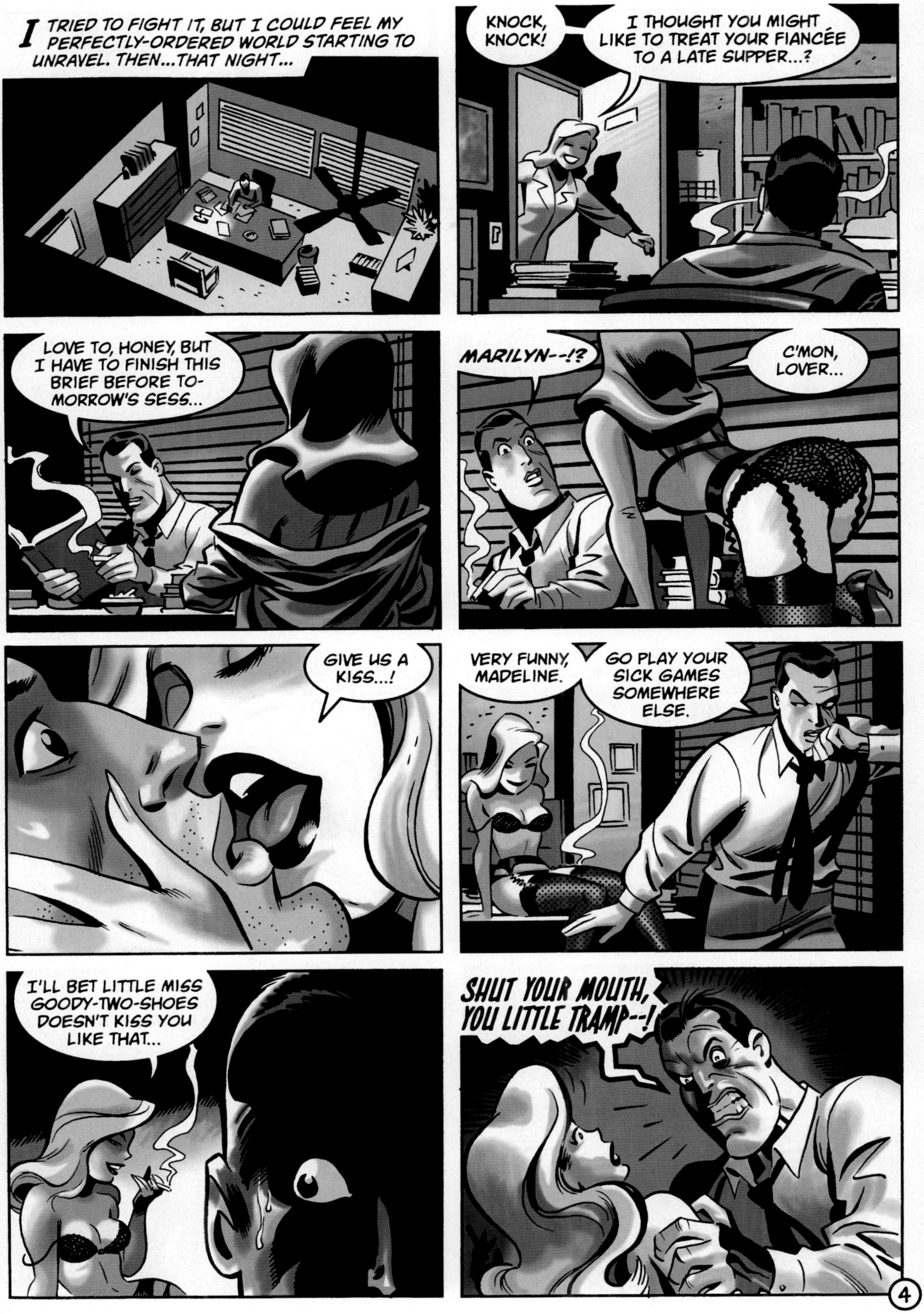

I TRIED TO FIGHT IT, BUT I COULD FEEL MY PERFECTLY-ORDERED WORLD STARTING TO UNRAVEL. THEN...THAT NIGHT...
KNOCK, KNOCK!
I THOUGHT YOU MIGHT LIKE TO TREAT YOUR FIANCÉE TO A LATE SUPPER...?
LOVE TO, HONEY, BUT I HAVE TO FINISH THIS BRIEF BEFORE TO-MORROW'S SESS...
MARILYN--!?
C'MON, LOVER...
GIVE US A KISS...!
VERY FUNNY, MADELINE.
GO PLAY YOUR SICK GAMES SOMEWHERE ELSE.
I'LL BET LITTLE MISS GOODY-TWO-SHOES DOESN'T KISS YOU LIKE THAT...
SHUT YOUR MOUTH, YOU LITTLE TRAMP--!
4

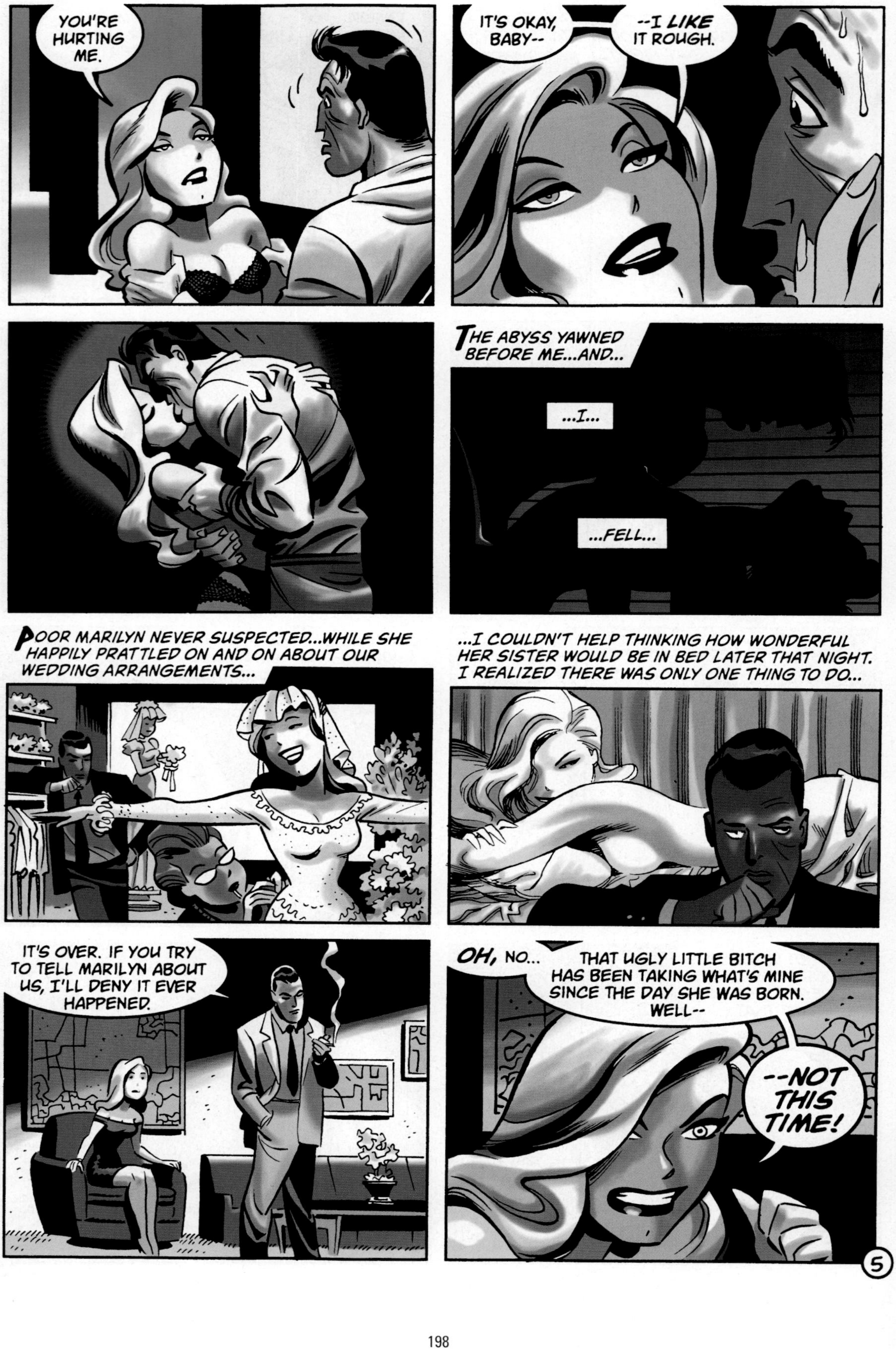
YOU'RE HURTING ME.
IT'S OKAY, BABY--
--I LIKE IT ROUGH.
THE ABYSS YAWNED BEFORE ME...AND...
...I...
...FELL...
POOR MARILYN NEVER SUSPECTED...WHILE SHE HAPPILY PRATTLED ON AND ON ABOUT OUR WEDDING ARRANGEMENTS...
...I COULDN'T HELP THINKING HOW WONDERFUL HER SISTER WOULD BE IN BED LATER THAT NIGHT. I REALIZED THERE WAS ONLY ONE THING TO DO...
IT'S OVER. IF YOU TRY TO TELL MARILYN ABOUT US, I'LL DENY IT EVER HAPPENED.
OH, NO...
THAT UGLY LITTLE BITCH HAS BEEN TAKING WHAT'S MINE SINCE THE DAY SHE WAS BORN. WELL--
--NOT THIS TIME!
5

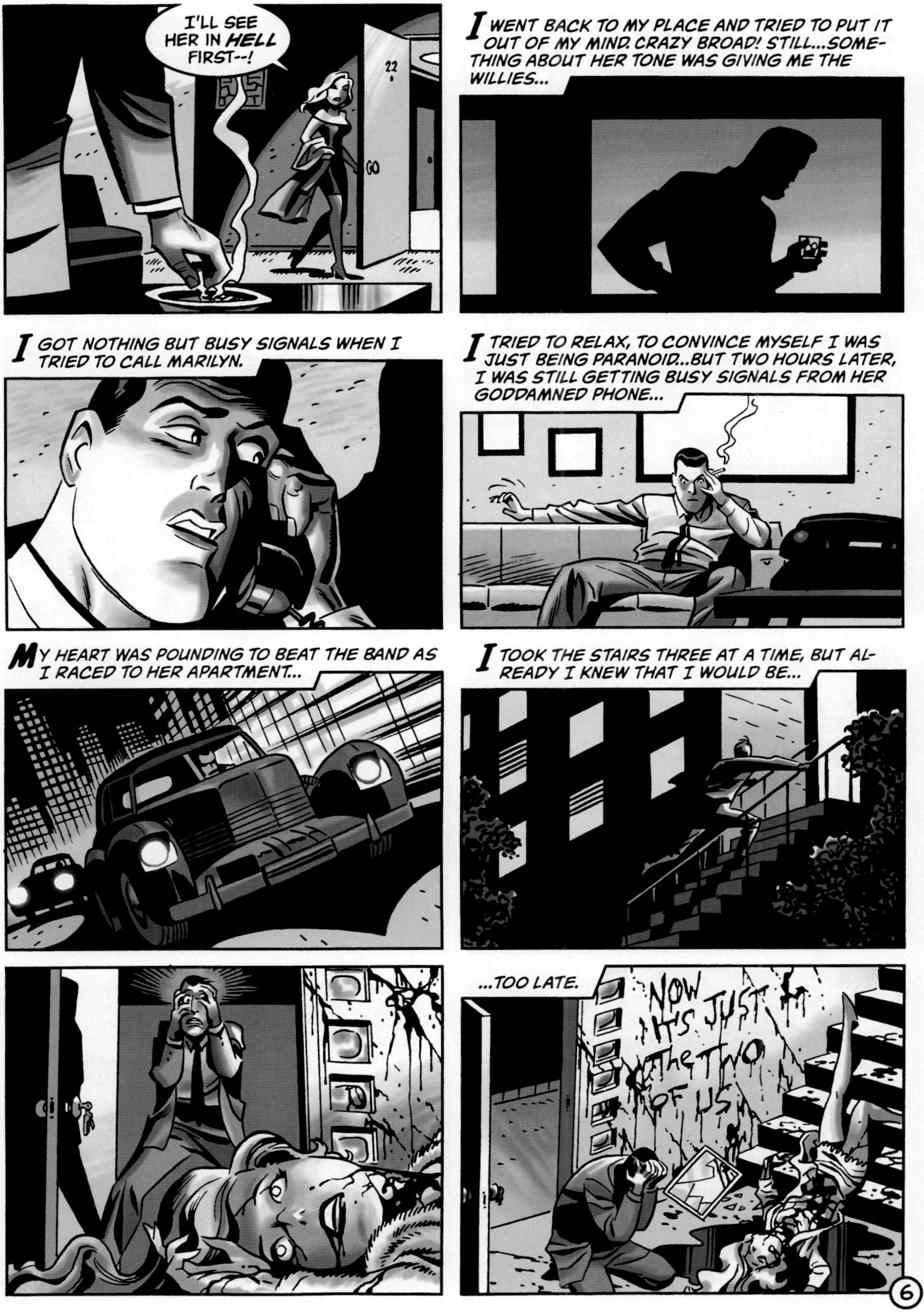
I'LL SEE HER IN HELL FIRST--!
22
GO
I WENT BACK TO MY PLACE AND TRIED TO PUT IT OUT OF MY MIND. CRAZY BROAD! STILL...SOMETHING ABOUT HER TONE WAS GIVING ME THE WILLIES...
I GOT NOTHING BUT BUSY SIGNALS WHEN I TRIED TO CALL MARILYN.
I TRIED TO RELAX, TO CONVINCE MYSELF I WAS JUST BEING PARANOID...BUT TWO HOURS LATER, I WAS STILL GETTING BUSY SIGNALS FROM HER GODDAMNED PHONE...
MY HEART WAS POUNDING TO BEAT THE BAND AS I RACED TO HER APARTMENT...
I TOOK THE STAIRS THREE AT A TIME, BUT ALREADY I KNEW THAT I WOULD BE...
...TOO LATE.
NOW IT'S JUST THE TWO OF US
6

*I STAGGERED ABOUT THE APARTMENT, MY MIND WHIRLING...EVERY FIBER OF MY BEING CRIED OUT FOR VENGEANCE...FOR **BLOOD**...*

*BUT...I WAS **CURED.** THAT'S RIGHT. THAT'S WHAT THEY SAID. CURED. **SANE.** HARVEY DENT WAS NO KILLER...*

FORTUNATELY...

*...I KNEW SOMEONE WHO **WAS**...*

AAAK RRHH

SOMEHOW, SHE FOUND ME.

I HAD TO DO IT, YOU KNOW.

SHE DIDN'T LOVE YOU. NOT THE **REAL** YOU.

SHE LOVED A PRETTIFIED, WATERED-DOWN VERSION OF YOU.

SHE COULD NEVER LOVE YOUR PASSION, YOUR RAGE, YOUR INNER FIRE...LIKE **I DO.**

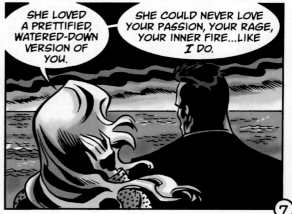

7

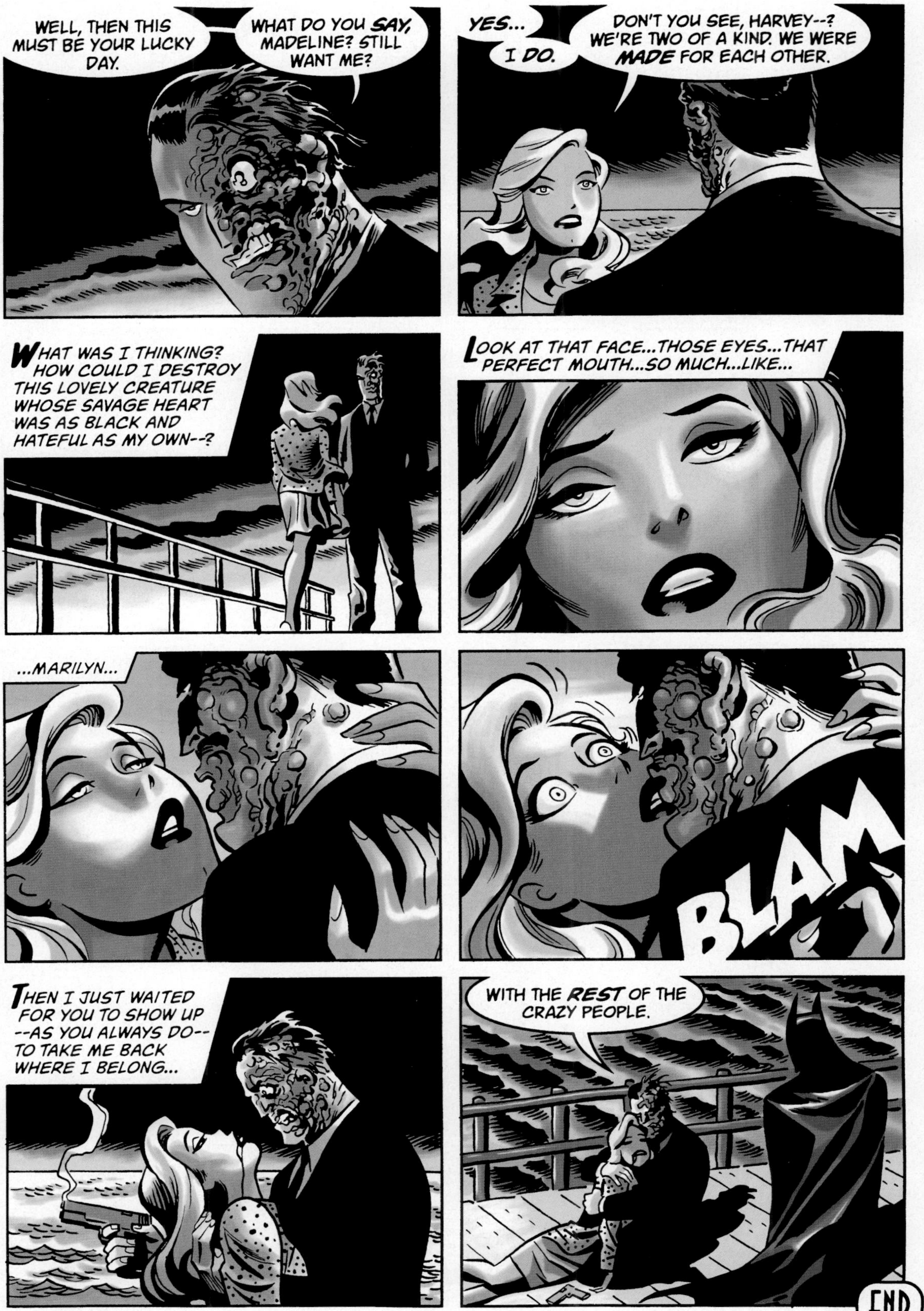
WELL, THEN THIS MUST BE YOUR LUCKY DAY.
WHAT DO YOU SAY, MADELINE? STILL WANT ME?
YES...
I DO.
DON'T YOU SEE, HARVEY--? WE'RE TWO OF A KIND. WE WERE MADE FOR EACH OTHER.
WHAT WAS I THINKING? HOW COULD I DESTROY THIS LOVELY CREATURE WHOSE SAVAGE HEART WAS AS BLACK AND HATEFUL AS MY OWN--?
LOOK AT THAT FACE...THOSE EYES...THAT PERFECT MOUTH...SO MUCH...LIKE...
...MARILYN...
BLAM
THEN I JUST WAITED FOR YOU TO SHOW UP --AS YOU ALWAYS DO-- TO TAKE ME BACK WHERE I BELONG...
WITH THE REST OF THE CRAZY PEOPLE.
END

AFTERWORD
By Bruce Timm

BATMAN ADVENTURES ANNUAL #1

"ROCKET GIRL"

Roxy was a deliberate attempt on our part to create another strong female antagonist for Batman, along the lines of Harley, but she never really took off (no pun intended). Oh well. I still think she's a fun character and the story's an amusing little trifle. She did end up in the animated series as well, in what is probably the most blatantly risqué episode we've ever done, "The Ultimate Thrill." You can thank Alan Burnett and Hilary Bader for that one.

"24 HOURS"

For me, the special thrill of that annual was getting the chance to ink the work of one of my idols, Dan DeCarlo. I was too intimidated to actually ink over his gorgeous pencils, and lightboxed 'em instead. When I met him a few years later, he graciously praised the job I'd done... you coulda knocked me over with a feather! Sadly, as most longtime Betty and Veronica fans know, Dan passed away in 2001. He was a great, underrated artist, and a sweet guy.

"CRUISE TO NIGHTMARE"

This story was originally done for Charlie Kochman's short-lived SUPERMAN & BATMAN MAGAZINE — hence the odd, squarish dimensions — but that book was cancelled before the story could be published. It eventually appeared as a backup in ADVENTURES IN THE DCU #3.

Not much else to say about this one except that my pal Mark Chiarello agreed to color it as a favor to me. It's probably the nicest coloring I've ever had on my work — just lovely, lovely stuff.

BATMAN ADVENTURES HOLIDAY SPECIAL

"JOLLY OLD ST. NICK"

When we originally plotted this story, Bullock and Montoya were supposed to be the main protagonists, but after Paul turned in his script, I decided I wanted to put Batgirl in it, too (I love to draw pretty girls, in case you didn't know). As I recall, Paul's reaction was "WHAT!!??!!" I explained how I thought we could do it and subsequently wrote most, if not all, of her dialogue myself directly on the boards. I think Paul was ultimately happy with the final result, but you'd have to ask him.

The "UNCUT" BARBARA CHANGING SEQUENCE (RUFF)

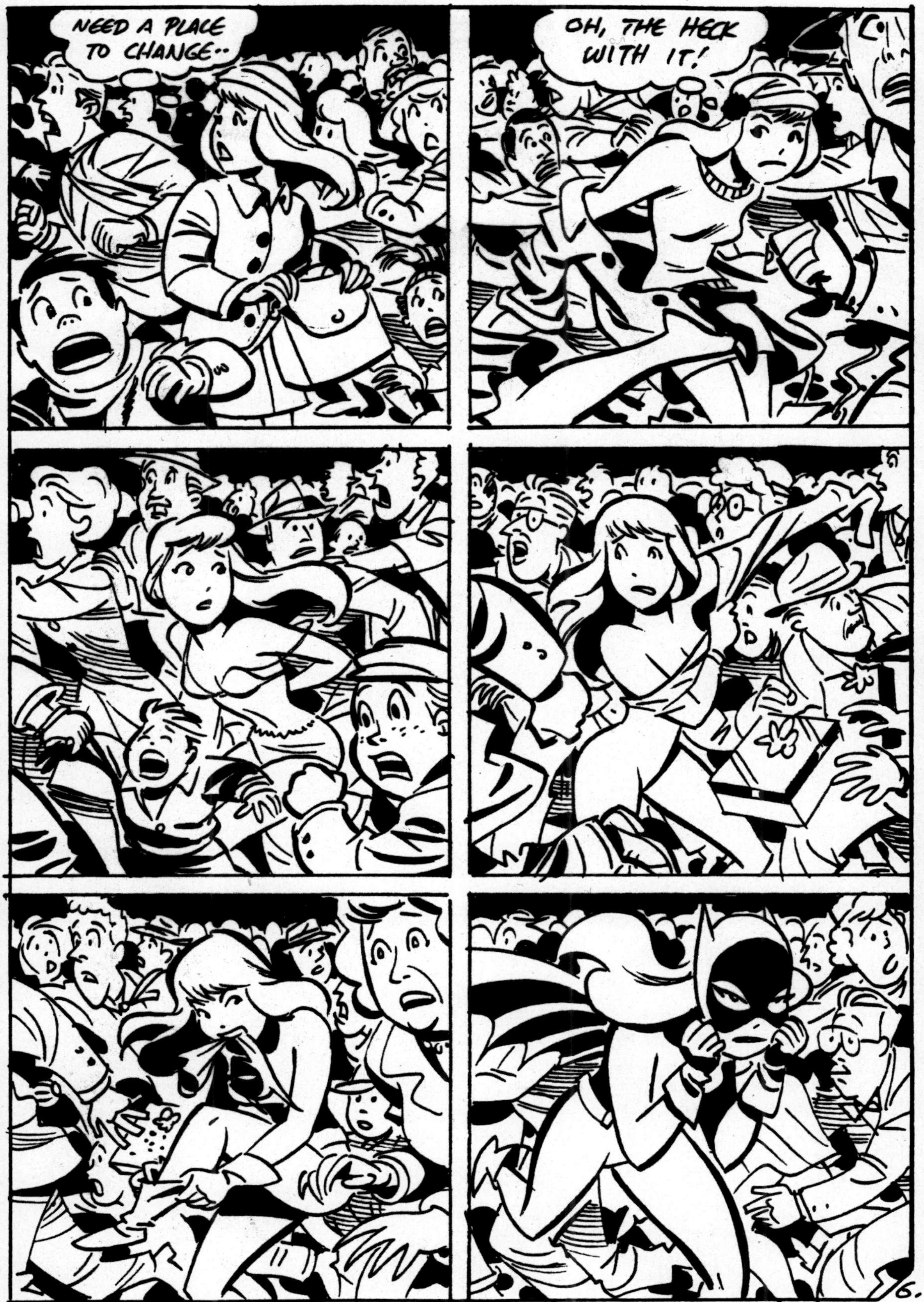
NEED A PLACE TO CHANGE..
OH, THE HECK WITH IT!

BiTL

Two "naughty bits" ended up on the cutting room floor: page 7 originally consisted of six panels of Barb changing into her Batgirl outfit right in the middle of the panicked crowd. Even after I explained that I'd lifted the gag from an old Supergirl story, DC said, "*No way!*"

The story originally ended with an off-color joke involving cold weather and Montoya's skimpy elf outfit. For the record, I like the "revised" versions of both pages better.

BATMAN ADVENTURES ANNUAL #2

FASTER, PUSSYFOOT, DRAW, DRAW!

After cutting his comics teeth on the Mr. Freeze story in BATMAN ADVENTURES HOLIDAY SPECIAL, Glen was itching to do a longer story... maybe another Annual? I think it was his idea to pit Jack Kirby's Etrigan against Ra's al Ghul. He, Paul, and I came up with some very rough story ideas, Paul mentioned it to Scott Peterson, and Scott said, "Sounds great!" Then we all got busy with our "day jobs" and forgot about it.

Months pass. Scott calls Paul: "So, how's the script coming along?" Paul says: "Uh... *what* script?" Scott says, "The script for the Annual that hits the stands *a month and a half from now!!!*" Yikes! We hadn't realized they'd already put it on the schedule!

We knew the only way to meet the deadline would be to bang it out "Marvel Style" — the three of us nailed down the plot details (over Mexican food this time), and Glen just started drawing. He was working out of his house at the time, so

he'd fax me his roughs, I'd make suggestions/changes, then fax 'em back to him — dang, it was taking too long! Eventually we got to the point where I'd just make the changes myself as I was inking. It was a little tricky — Glen's roughs with my inks definitely had a different look from my "all-solo" stuff, so, for consistency's sake, when I drew all-new panels I tried to make it look like there were Glen drawings underneath. It was "Me copying Glen copying Me... with Kirby on top!" Weird!

In an effort to save time, I inked the whole thing actual "printed size," instead of the usual 150%, which accounts for the juicy, extra-thick linework.

SLOW DOWN ALREADY!

In the middle of all this, I get a frantic phone call from Glen: "I'm only halfway through the story, and I'm all out of plot! We can't just have them all *fight* for the last 20 pages!" To slow the story down, we decided to throw in a 7-page hallucination/dream sequence, incorporating an obscure Kirby character from an old issue of DC's WEIRD MYSTERY TALES. Scott thought we were daft but signed off on it in the interest of getting the *fershlugginer* thing done. I pulled a few all-nighters to finish it up, Paul scripted it (using large chunks of dialogue that Glen had scribbled on his layouts), Glen colored it, we enlisted longtime Kirby Kollaborator Mike Royer to ink the cover, and two weeks later the whole wild mess appeared in the shops.

Forty-eight pages in three weeks, from start to finish. The end result is kind of fun, slap-dash warts and all. Make of it what you will.

BATGIRL ADVENTURES #1 cover by Bruce Timm

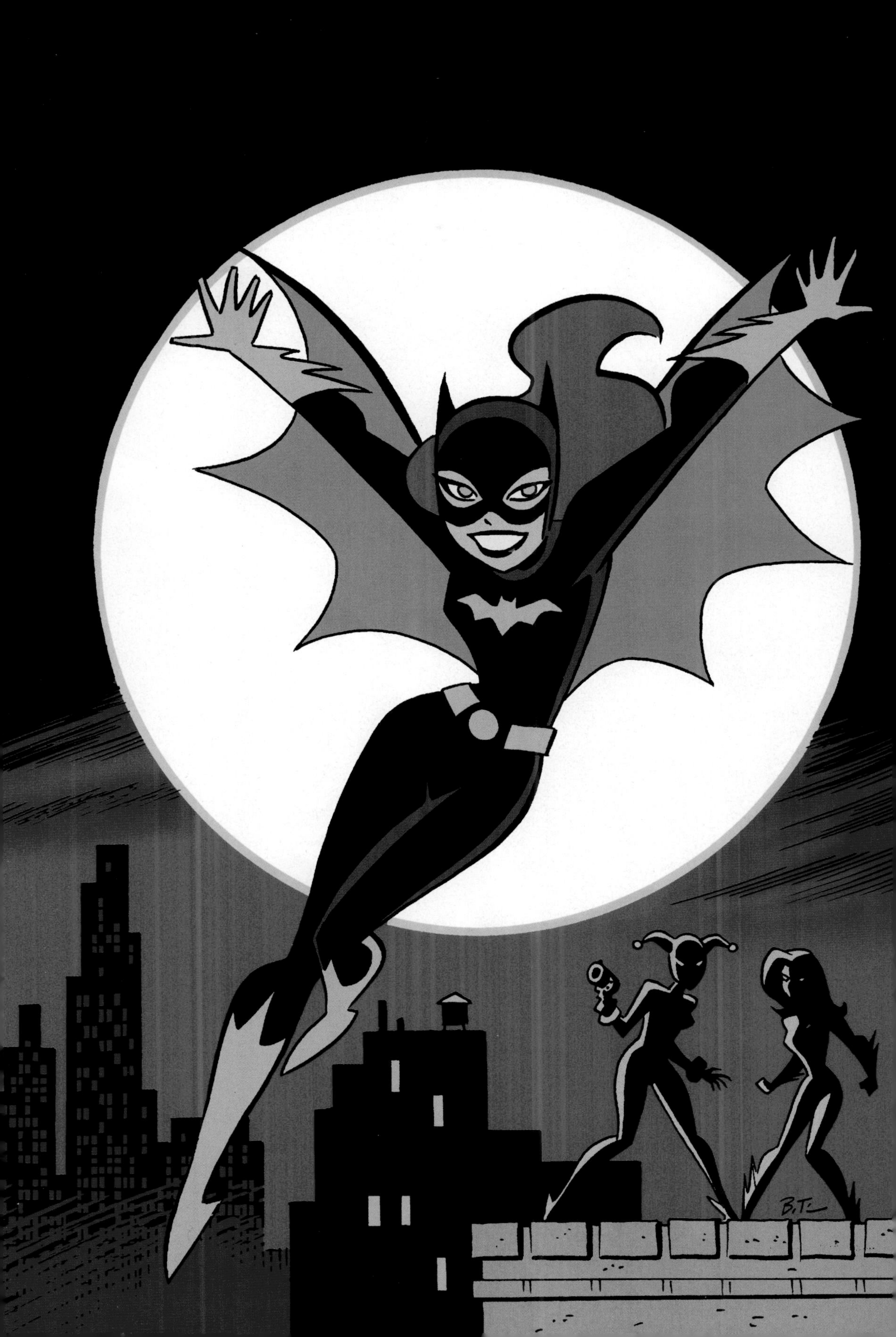

THE BATMAN ADVENTURES: DANGEROUS DAMES & DEMONS trade paperback cover by Bruce Timm

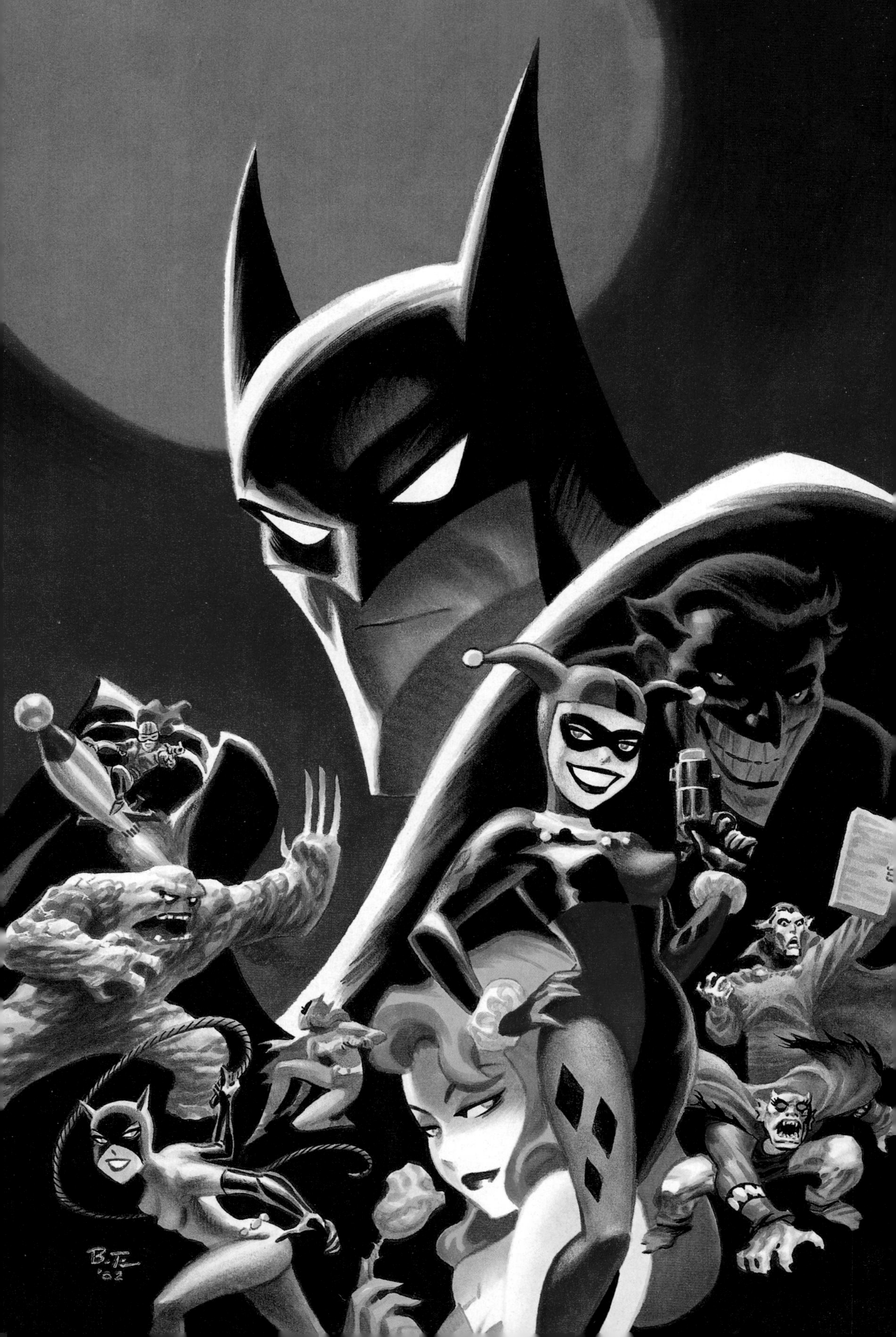

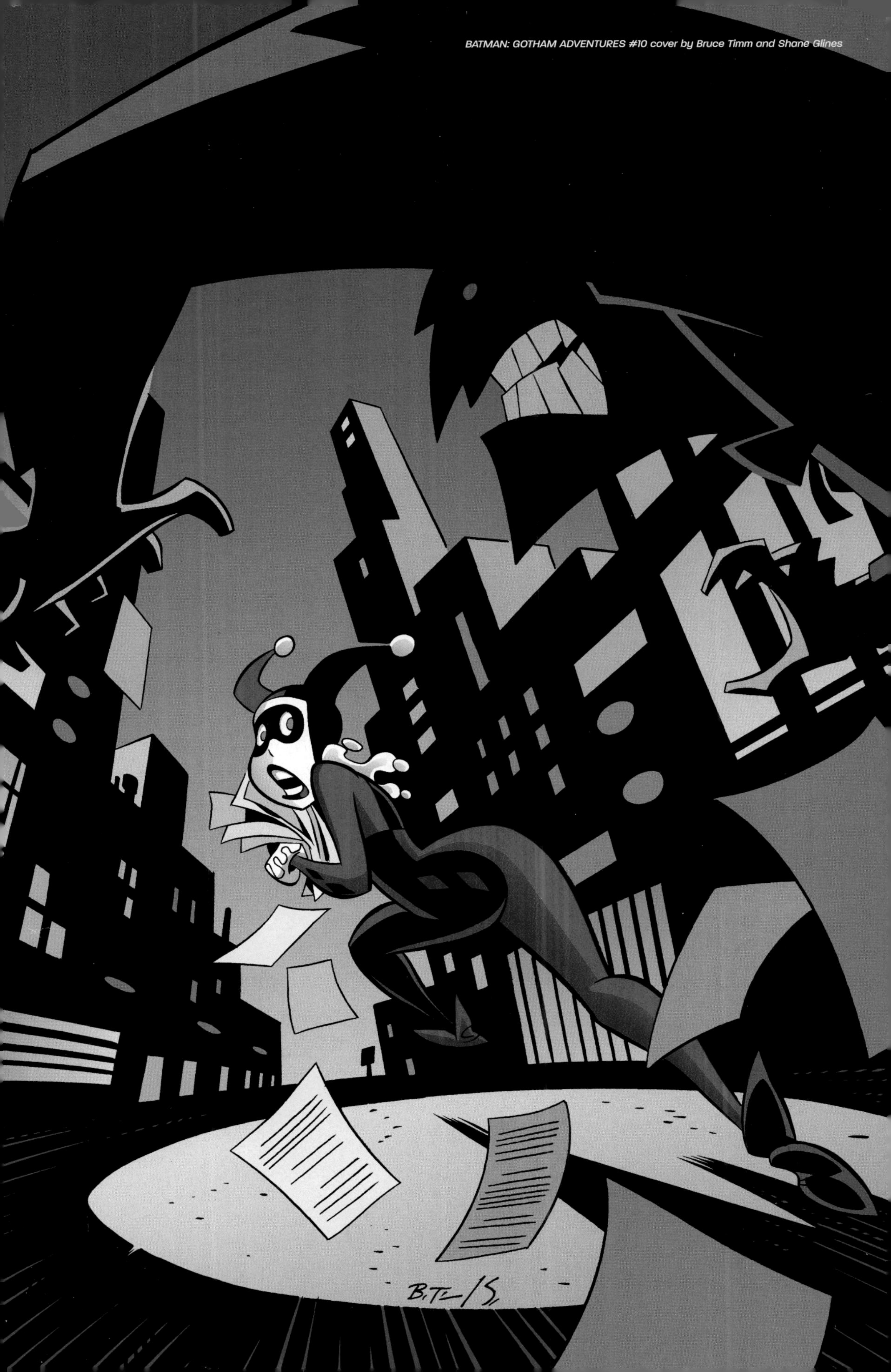

BATMAN: GOTHAM ADVENTURES #10 cover by Bruce Timm and Shane Glines

BATMAN ADVENTURES #3 cover by Bruce Timm

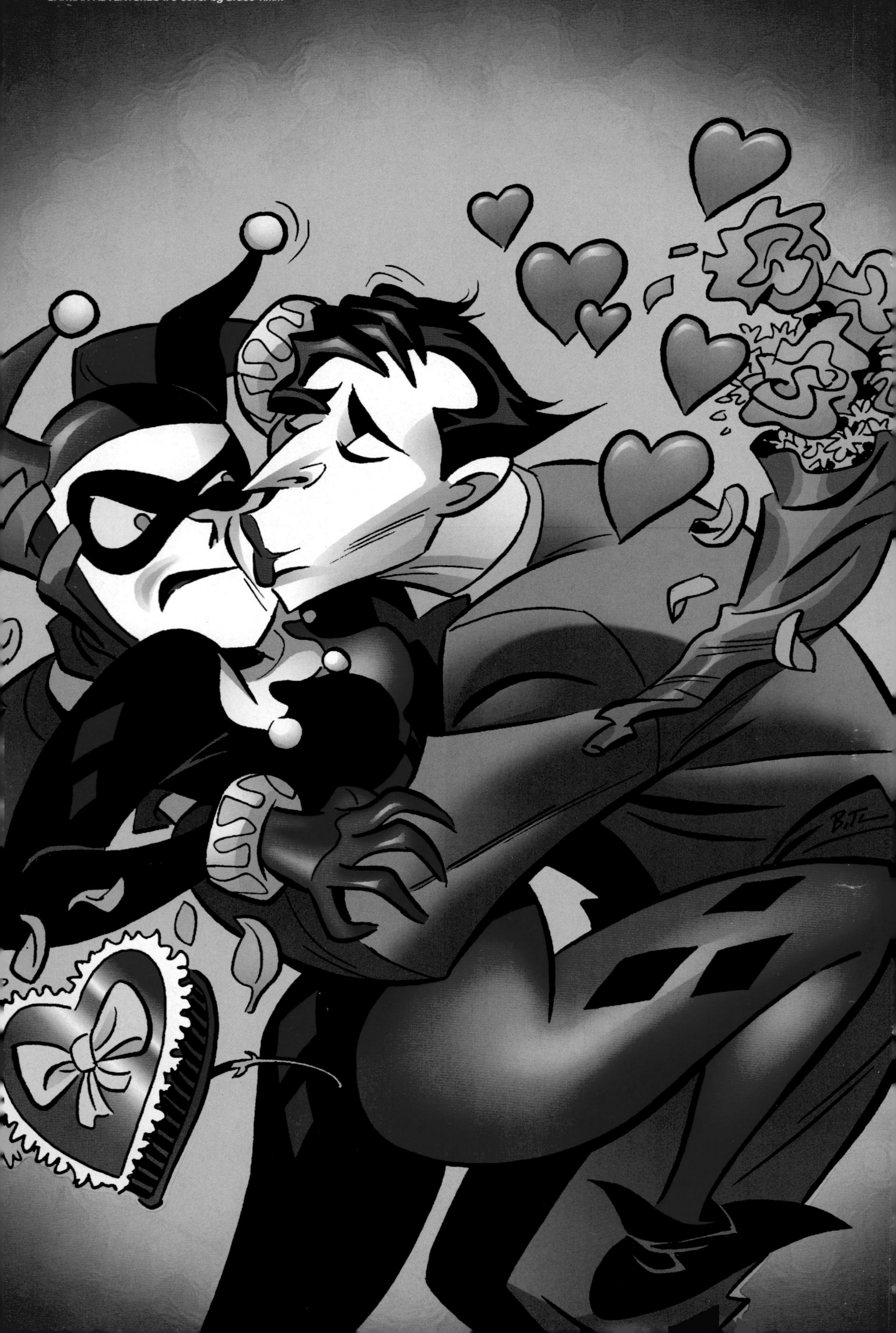